JACQUES DE LACRETELLE

An Intellectual Itinerary

CORMATIN
SAONE & LOIRE

Jacques de Lacretelle

An Intellectual Itinerary

DOUGLAS ALDEN

RUTGERS UNIVERSITY PRESS
NEW BRUNSWICK, NEW JERSEY
1958

Library of Congress Catalogue Number: 58:10826

The author acknowledges the following permissions to quote from the works of Jacques de Lacretelle: Librairie Gallimard, the principal publisher, for all works bearing this imprint listed in bibliography hereinafter; Editions Bernard Grasset for *La Vie inquiète de Jean Hermelin*; Librairie Ernest Flammarion for *Histoire de Paola Ferrani*; Editions Albin Michel, successor to Editions du Milieu du Monde, for *Le Pour et le Contre*; Librairie Arthème Fayard for *Le Voyage de Grèce* (originally entitled *Le Demi-Dieu, ou Le Voyage de Grèce*, published by Editions Bernard Grasset); and Brentano's for *Libérations*. He also acknowledges permission to quote from Aldous Huxley's *Point Counter Point*, published by Harper and Brothers, successor to Doubleday and Company. All translations, except a brief quotation from the *New Statesman and Nation*, were made by the author.

Made and printed in Great Britain by
William Clowes and Sons, Limited, London and Beccles

A mon collègue et ami

MAURICE COINDREAU

sans qui ce livre n'aurait peut-être pas existé

FOREWORD

I FIRST met Jacques de Lacretelle in January 1950. The scene was a baroque hotel room in the venerable Plaza, which is like a bit of Versailles transplanted to the southern perimeter of Central Park and allowed to grow somewhat uncharacteristically upward in the new American soil. In this setting, so much like his Paris apartment in the rue Vineuse, he must have felt at home. At any rate, he seemed thoroughly acclimated to the American metropolis, as though he had left it only a fortnight before. This was his third visit to New York, but one sensed that had it been only his first, he would have been as much at home. Obviously he was a man of the world, almost Anglo-Saxon in his attitudes, cordial and yet reserved, in short, someone who bore definitely the mark of a gentleman but not necessarily that of a man of letters. Perhaps I had a preconceived notion of what a man of letters should be; at least I did not expect someone so normal.

M. de Lacretelle was on his way to Haïti to represent the French Academy, accompanied by his young and much shorter wife (for a Frenchman he is abnormally tall), and a sword which added enormously to his luggage problems. I was chagrined to discover that he had increased these problems by bringing with him for my personal use a set of the 1920 periodical *L'Œil de bœuf* and an entire file of *Candide*, containing the first version of his *Retour de Silbermann*.

Although this first conversation, as we sat huddled in a corner of the hotel room to get out of the hubbub, was soon interrupted by the arrival of my fellow townsman, Robert Casadesus, I was able to resume it several months later in the rue Vineuse. During the summer of 1950 I was the guest of the Lacretelles at Paris and Cabourg while they catered most graciously to my insatiable appetite for unpublished manuscripts. I was back in Paris for a year in 1952 as I composed my first draft, so that I was able to knock on the Lacretelles' door whenever in doubt about a fact or an interpretation. And now, in late October 1957, as this book goes to press, I have been talking to Jacques de Lacretelle in Princeton, clearing up what I hope will prove to be the last remaining question marks in the margins of my manuscript.

Lacretelle is a distinctly French phenomenon. He is not Dostoevski, Hemingway or Joyce; nor is he Malraux, Camus or Sartre, who have tried to break with French novelistic tradition. He differs also from certain contemporaries like Gide, Mauriac and Bernanos, who have subordinated the art of the novel to a way of life. The basic French novelistic tradition puts the art of the novel before every other consideration and is a form of *art for art's sake*. The primary function of this kind of novel is to be a mirror of reality, undistorted by any metaphysics or personal prejudice. Flaubert brought this objective technique to perfection, and later Marcel Proust gave it greater depth, at the same time that he invented a discursive structural pattern which dealt a severe blow to the logical structure of the French novel.

If Proust marks the end of the French novel, as some critics have said, then Lacretelle came too late. Such a statement is too speculative to be worthy of serious consideration; only the literary historian a hundred years from now will know the truth. In the meantime, one can only point out that Lacretelle belongs to the great tradition of the French "psychological novel," as French critics call it—a tradition which has its origins in the French classical theater of the seventeenth century.

While emphasizing the classical principles of Lacretelle's art, I do not wish to imply that he is an anachronism in the twentieth century. No author who was as successful as Lacretelle between the two world wars could have been out of touch with his times. Perhaps the best way to define Lacretelle's novelistic manner—altering slightly a remark which Albert Thibaudet made in 1929—would be to say that it is Proust and Gide rewritten by Flaubert. These Proustian and Gidian themes are still so close to us that they will continue to appeal, for many years to come, to devotees of contemporary French literature.

In studying Lacretelle's work in the following pages I have sought to approach my subject in the same spirit of lucidity and analysis as one finds in his work. My purpose has been to understand rather than persuade. If I have succeeded in being persuasive at the same time, so much the better. Since understanding a novel also means to me understanding the circumstances in which the novel is written, I have begun with two exclusively biographical chapters and have kept a thread of biography running through the entire study. But biography must be considered only a kind of by-product or, rather, some of the raw material which goes into the finished product, the work of art.

DOUGLAS ALDEN

Princeton, New Jersey
October, 1957

ACKNOWLEDGMENTS

THIS book could never have been written in its present form without the cheerful and friendly collaboration of M. de Lacretelle himself. I hope that this tribute to his work will compensate in some small measure for all of the trouble to which I have put him these many years. I wish also to thank my colleague Professor Maurice Coindreau, for first introducing me to M. de Lacretelle and for all the encouragement and assistance which he has given me from the inception of this idea. The criticism of Professor Justin O'Brien and of Professor Marc Chadourne, who read the manuscript, has been exceedingly useful. Professor Ira Wade's moral support has helped me through one critical moment. My wife, as usual, and Professor George Jones have assisted me with the proofs.

I am also greatly beholden to the following individuals: for lending Lacretelle manuscripts in their possession—to Mme Faure-Dujarric, M. de Biéville-Noyant, M. Simonson, and M. de Vaux de Lancey; for lending a collection of Lacretelle clippings—to M. Borgeaud; and for authorizing the publication of letters—to Mme Mante-Proust, M. Guéritte, M. Martin du Gard, M. Paulhan, Mme Isabelle Rivière and Mme Lambert-Gide. Princeton University has been very generous in financing my initial summer in Paris, in granting me an additional year there under the "preceptor" system, in purchasing manuscripts (through the Friends of the Library) and in giving a substantial grant in aid of publication (through the Research Committee).

D. A.

CONTENTS

JACQUES DE LACRETELLE
An Intellectual Itinerary

I

CORMATIN

CORMATIN, Saône & Loire. Monsieur & Madame Amaury de Lacretelle have the honor to inform you of the birth of their son Jacques, 14 July 1888.

Above the inscription on the announcement is an engraving of a noble castle in the style of the French Renaissance with high roofs, ornate dormer windows and delicate turrets clinging to the principal *corps de logis.*

If the reader is now tempted to imagine a long, romantic line of ancestors in powdered wigs, in plumed hats and in shining helmets, let him scrutinize another family document of the same period. It shows the Lacretelle coat of arms: "Party azure and silver, dexter a palm gold, sinister a burin in bend sinister, point downwards, sable."[1] Two lions rear up in support on either side of the shield, and the crown of a count hovers above. But let us not be deceived. The artist has imagined the crown, for it is not mentioned in the original grant of arms. What is really significant is the burin, that is to say, the etcher's needle; these are not the arms of a man of war but rather of a man of the pen. A noble family of the pen—only the bourgeois nineteenth century could create such an anomaly.

Lest the reader now suspect that the castle itself was erected in typical bad taste by some contemporary of M. de Nucingen, we hasten to add that Cormatin is an authentic historic monument standing to this day on the fringe of a Burgundian village of the same name not far from Mâcon. For a small fee which goes into the pocket of the present *châtelain*, the tourist may still visit and admire—with certain reservations of his own in respect to the encumbering bric-à-brac—the sumptuous Hall of the Guards and other "state" apartments with their gilt-encrusted beams and elaborately ornamented panels in which the portraits of the lords of Cormatin alternate with mythological and bucolic paintings.

Or, with special permission, the tourist may view the castle in proper perspective from the cow pasture to the north, whence he sees a dwelling of harmonious proportions—in short, the scene depicted on the announcement of Jacques's birth.

One is not often born in a castle with impunity, and that is the reason for evoking Cormatin in beginning to study Jacques de Lacretelle's intellectual development. In his experience it represents a graceful way of life, a horse-and-buggy existence with enough servants to perform the menial tasks, tea in the afternoon on the terrace, dinner with the older members of the family discussing the latest literature or other intelligence from Paris. It might have represented much more. If the same family has been living in a castle for a few hundred years, the memories of a more aristocratic past may still be alive to give a certain haughtiness to the family manners. The impoverished but proud old noble living in his ruined castle is a favorite subject for novelists. This would be an entirely erroneous picture of Cormatin when the Lacretelles were there.

Although they had enough to be proud of for other reasons, the Lacretelles were really a bourgeois family who attached little importance to their recently acquired letters of nobility. At the time of Jacques's birth, Cormatin belonged to his grandfather, Henri de Lacretelle, but the latter was the first—and also the last—Lacretelle ever to own the place. The estate had come to him as his first wife's dowry, but her family, too, had been only transitory residents by European standards and were apparently not in any way related to the Du Blé family, who had built the castle about 1616 and two of whose members, bearing the title of Marquis d'Uxelles, had been marshals of France.*

Even as a small boy, Jacques did not live continuously at Cormatin; his father, Amaury de Lacretelle, was in the consular service and usually took his wife and children with him. Summer vacation always brought Jacques back to Cormatin until his eleventh year, when the castle had to be sold on the death of his grandfather. Henceforth Cormatin lived on as a nostalgic memory —not of the sword-bearing Marquis of Uxelles but of the old literary gentleman who had been his grandfather. Cormatin did not

* See the "Genealogical Notes" at the end of this volume for a more detailed discussion of this and similar points.

pass completely out of his memory, since he made it live again years later as the castle in his tetralogy, *Les Hauts Ponts*.

Although Jacques tended to look upon Cormatin as a symbol of family tradition, since it signified the only permanence in his itinerate way of life, the real Lacretelle tradition which so strongly influenced him was altogether different. The Lacretelle family tradition was built, not around an old castle and a piece of land, but rather, as their coat of arms indicates, around their skill in using their pens. One cannot fully understand Jacques de Lacretelle without considering the part which family tradition has played in his intellectual development. This family tradition becomes doubly significant when one realizes that it is the same as the current of liberalism which links the French Revolution with the Dreyfus Affair.

The Lacretelles had originally been a family of barristers—*sans particule*—from Lorraine.[2] A few years before the Revolution, two brothers, Pierre and Charles Lacretelle, came to Paris, worked with the Encyclopedists, played a prominent role as liberals in the Revolution until the terror took over, supported the Empire and received seats in the French Academy as their reward. Pierre, a lawyer, opposed the Restoration and, but for a humiliating appeal to the king, would have spent his final years in prison. Charles, a historian whom the Empire had made a professor at the Sorbonne to compensate him for suppressing his liberal newspaper, supported the Restoration and received various honors, including a *particule* which he rarely used. But he joined Chateaubriand in opposing Villèle's press gag law and welcomed the July Revolution, only to find himself rebuffed by Louis-Philippe, who could never forgive him for the treatment accorded Philippe-Egalité in Lacretelle's history of the Revolution. He spent his later years attacking the Jesuits, whom he saw as a threat to the intellectual freedom of the university. One of the most popular lecturers at the Sorbonne, a friend of Vigny, Hugo and Deschamps, he was "one of the last French conversationalists."[3] Charles Lacretelle was Jacques's great-grandfather.

Charles Lacretelle had moved to Mâcon after his retirement from the Sorbonne and had thus become a neighbor of his fellow Academician Alphonse de Lamartine, who was known by this time as an outstanding champion of French liberalism. Soon there were very close bonds between the two families. Charles's second son, Pierre, married Léontine de Pierreclau,[4] the daughter of Léon de Pierreclau, whom recent literary scholarship has revealed to have been Lamartine's own illegitimate son.[5] There is no evidence to indicate that the Lacretelles were aware of this subterranean ramification of the family tree. Charles's elder son, Henri, married Marguerite Verne, the heiress to Cormatin and a cousin of the Pierreclaus.

As a young man, Henri de Lacretelle dogged the poet's footsteps and proclaimed his ambition to become Lamartine or nothing. The great man contributed a poem to his young disciple's first volume of poetry *Les Cloches*,[6] and when republishing this piece in his own collected works, he introduced it with the remark that Henri de Lacretelle was already stammering verse in his cradle and "when the years have ripened him, he will bear healthy fruit of all savors; the name of Lacretelle will shine in him."[7] Outdated by at least two decades, Henri's Lamartinian novels and poems attracted little attention, and his name never shone far beyond the hills around Mâcon. Today his only claim to fame is as Lamartine's Boswell; his *Lamartine et ses amis* appeared in 1878 and was subsequently translated into English.

To the great annoyance of his father who had only harsh words for Ledru-Rollin and this newfangled thing called socialism but who left his son complete liberty of thought, Henri's sympathies turned toward the Left. Because his wife was pregnant (so he tells us in his biography of Lamartine), he missed the excitement in Paris in 'forty-eight but managed to head the local revolution at Mâcon, where he was a member of the provisional government. His loyalty to Lamartine and his consistent opposition to the Second Empire gained him a seat in the Chamber with the return of the Republic in 1871. As a Deputy, his first act, says a contemporary pamphlet, was to propose a law making primary education free, compulsory and secular.[8] Although the same pamphlet classifies Henri de Lacretelle as a member of the "Extreme Left," Albert Thibaudet—who grew up in Tournus—calls him the venerable Deputy from Mâcon who "made a specialty, in the Chamber, of defending the existence of God and immortality in the school curricula."[9] That the debonair Henri had difficulty persuading his more radical constituents we may gather from his editorializing in his book on Lamartine: "One does not have the right to feel oneself to belong to the people and to think of the Republic because, poor combatant of the pen that one is, one lives in the dwelling of a marshal of France."[10] It is ironical that the first *de* Lacretelle to dwell in a castle spent his time trying to live down his ill-starred nobility. Alphonse *de* Lamartine had had much the same trouble. Down to the very last detail, Henri de Lacretelle patterned his life on that of his mentor, living with the same disdain for earthly matters and, like him, leaving behind an estate loaded with debts.

Jacques de Lacretelle remembers him as a tall, thin, elegant man of eighty, inclined to be dreamy and decidedly impractical. If it is necessary to affix a hereditary responsibility, Henri de Lacretelle is the one in all the Lacretelle line most accountable for his grandson's artistic nature.

His son Amaury returned to the family tradition by taking a law degree at Paris, where he capitalized on his family's liberal connections and frequented the anticlerical milieux which were to provide the continuity from the Revolution of 1848 to the new outburst of liberalism at the time of the Dreyfus case. His particular friends were the Hugo clan, thanks to whom he met his future wife, Juliette Brouzet, a Protestant from the south of France.[11] Like Amaury, who had lost all trace of Catholicism in this liberal environment, Juliette had ceased to be a Protestant under the influence of her radical cousins, the Ménard-Dorians; the latter were friends of the Hugos and became even more closely allied with them when Pauline Ménard-Dorian married Georges Hugo, grandson of the poet. Amaury de Lacretelle and Juliette Brouzet were married in a civil ceremony at which Victor Hugo was a legal witness.[12] They raised their two children, Pierre and Jacques, outside all religious persuasion. Without giving undue importance to the terms, one may say that the Lacretelles, in their intellectual development, had now added some elements of Second Empire positivism to their original social romanticism.

This family heritage of nineteenth century liberalism in the broad sense left its imprint on Jacques de Lacretelle, first in his childhood excitement over the Dreyfus case and then in his ultimate return to realism. But this return to realism was a delayed reaction, for Jacques de Lacretelle grew up in a very different atmosphere: the age of symbolism.

2

"WHAT I LEAVE BEHIND HAS BEEN ONLY A GAME"

A LONG time ago," said Olivier, "when I was a child and was lunching with my grandparents, I looked at the flower stand in the middle of the table, and suddenly I said to myself: 'I must always remember this heliotrope blossom which is leaning toward me.' As for my grandparents, it is impossible for me to describe them to you because I was six when they disappeared. But I still see this blossom."[1]

Olivier is the central character of Lacretelle's novel *Le Pour et le Contre*. The heliotrope, here transposed into fiction, was once real, and it stood one day on the dinner table at Cormatin. If we attempt to reconstruct the life of Jacques de Lacretelle, we are more likely to encounter heliotropes than objective facts. His memory, like that of Marcel Proust who had such a profound influence on him, collects sensations rather than facts. He attaches so little importance to objective facts, that he has not accumulated around him those bits of paper, letters, diaries or even newspaper clippings, which would enable his biographer to establish accurately the main events of his life. Furthermore, he has not indulged in memoirs or confessions, as so many writers of his generation have done; but, interspersed among his fictional work or casual articles for the periodical press, there are numerous heliotropes, that is to say, personal impressions, reminiscences, even half-confessions in which he seems to reveal himself, without giving the reader the benefit of being able accurately to separate fact from fiction. These are the materials with which we shall have to work, plus a few miscellaneous documents which have accidentally survived among the author's unclassified papers.

In his earliest photograph, the future Academician wears the typical white dress and flowing curls of a child so unfortunate as to be born in the Victorian era. These curls, which also adorn the protagonist of his first novel, he was to wear reluctantly until the age of four. Because he was very ill during the first two years of his life, his mother showered affection on him and pampered him. As a result, he was a difficult child to bring up; a reference to the good-night kiss in his first novel suggests that it was as much a drama for him as it was for the narrator of *A la Recherche du temps perdu*. If the following message were not in the handwriting of the youthful Jacques himself, we might even suspect someone of plagiarism:

> Dear Mémé
>
> i have just gone to sleep you are coming home late but wake me i insist have the night light turned on i have no temperature now
>
> i adore you
>
> Viscount J. de L.

This childish blackmail was to continue until he was thirteen.[2]

The child's earliest memories are made of sensations: the colored flashes in his eyes as he rubs them when going to sleep;[3] the sound of fire engines at Salonica (the fire department was near his father's consulate); the murmur of his brother's voice saying a prayer on the other side of the screen in their bedchamber at Cormatin.[4] As he shares his time according to the season between the Middle East and his grandmothers, one at Cormatin and the other at Lunel in the Midi, he begins to take an interest in the contrasts between these three different worlds in which he lives.

When the Lacretelles moved to Alexandria, Jacques was already eight and in a mood to appreciate this cosmopolitan crossroads of the eastern Mediterranean. Some of his earliest memories are Proustian impressions which he was to recapture years later while watching red beetles climb a slope.[5] They reminded him of the animated vermilion uniforms which he once saw from his window performing military maneuvers on a neighboring hill. When news came of an insurrection in Crete, all Alexandria became excited, and the children pushed their lead soldiers about with bellicose abandon. Everything was exciting about living in this world of the *Arabian Nights* whose characters became real whenever the boy spoke to a pasha or heard the muezzin's call to prayer or passed before the door of a harem. For the future commentator of Gobineau and author of *Silbermann*, the sight of these Oriental crowds with their salient racial types was to be a significant experience. Not only was the East vividly represented, but racial specimens abounded from all the world's capitals. When his parents made a diplomatic or social call, the boy took his *goûter* with the younger representatives of the courts of London, Vienna or St. Petersburg and, by exchanging postage stamps and observing strange customs among his hosts, traveled over innumerable meridians while seated at the tea table.

Sheltered by private tutors from any unfortunate experiences in a hostile educational system and reassured by the affection of his parents, Jacques should have been a happy child, but he seems on the contrary to have been oftentimes a melancholy one. He remembers how he liked to "eat his tears," generally in seclusion but sometimes by making his mother recite Richepin's tear-jerking *Histoire de Ravageot*, about the boy who demands of his mother her eyes, her hair, her jewels and finally her heart, and, having taken everything, runs away so fast that he falls—whereupon the adoring mother asks: "Did you hurt yourself, my poor child?"[6] Undoubtedly Jacques's primary cause of maladjustment was his early sickliness. In reliving some of these experiences while composing his first novel, the author imagined other causes of maladjustment which seem to have no foundation in fact. The first episode, found only in the manuscript version of that first novel, deals with a French governess who is the first love of the semi-autobiographical narrator. The second episode, found only in the printed version of the novel, is concerned with the narrator's jealousy of his father. The author now denies that there is anything autobiographical in either episode.

In the life of the boy Jacques de Lacretelle, there was a governess (while he was at Salonica), but she made little or no impression on him. Because of a strong English linguistic tradition in the Lacretelle family, she was English. Imitating Lamartine, Henri de Lacretelle had always affected a knowledge of English, though he had never been to England, and even corresponded with his son Amaury in that language. At Alexandria, Jacques's governess was superseded by a French teacher who came to the house. Amaury always supervised very closely the education of his two sons.

As for Amaury, he was a good father who liked to play with his sons. He loved his wife, but this affection was no cause for conflict with his son Jacques—at least so the son now maintains. Some of the real nature of Amaury de Lacretelle appears to be present in this letter which his widow wrote much later to her son Jacques:

> I have not only begun but have made considerable progress in the calvary of reading the hundreds of letters that we exchanged, your father and I, either during our ten months of betrothal separated from each other, or after our marriage, for various reasons. It is all our life of great happiness which each day I burn, and in the evening I am in tears. I didn't have the courage to write to you. At first I didn't want to read everything over, and then I wanted to keep a few letters which mentioned you both in childhood—especially Pierre when I left your father at Varna and was in terror of never seeing him again; and I remained five months in Paris waiting incessantly for the return of Amaury, who was obliged to remain out there because of the disturbed political events in Bulgaria. At last it is coming to an end, and I am both happy and unhappy. It seems to me that it is also a little bit of my life which is going to end, and I envy those who have a firm belief in an eternal meeting place.[7]

Although Amaury de Lacretelle's influence on his son was not negative, it appears not to have been positive either, at least not positive enough to explain in any degree Jacques's later literary vocation. His mother writes in another letter:

> So often he told me (when he spoke of the futures of both of you) that he would like one of his sons to have some disposition for literature. Today his wish would be amply fulfilled. This continuity in the family line would have delighted him, for both of you are gifted. It is perhaps because he was not gifted in this type of intelligence that he was anxious for you to be. His diplomatic reports were superior in logic, penetration, clarity, but their style was dry even though the form was perfect. Imagina-

> tion was something that he did not know. He envied those who, like me, partook of its joys, and often he would say to me: "When we are both of us old you shall tell me the plots of some of the hundred thousand novels which you have devoured."[8]

Jacques likewise remembers his father as an understanding but somewhat distant person who in judging his son "perhaps confused contemplation and idleness."[9] Above all, says his son, he was insensitive to nature and did nothing to encourage those penchants which were to be the mainspring of the son's originality.

During the last year of his life, while consul at Florence, Amaury de Lacretelle was already in poor health as a result of having lived too long in the Middle Eastern climate. He died in 1898, only a month after his return to France. His death is the subject of a poignant passage in his son's first novel. Even more poignant is this unpublished letter:

> My dear Grandmother,
>
> I know how grieved you must be over the misfortune which has struck you, and that is why I am trying by this letter to console you. Mama told me that you insisted that I should write to you during the vacation, that is why I have done so. If you had seen him, you would certainly have found him extremely changed. The last days his cheeks and eyes were hollowed out because he had grown so thin; but in spite of that, we had him near us and that consoled us. He was very happy when I brought him the news that I had been 1st, 2d, 3d in application, 1st in dictation and 2d in French composition. We have looked for and kept all the letters which he had written to us, and I am sure that Mama would be very happy if you did the same.
>
> Good-by, dear Grandmother. I give you a great big hug. Your grandson who adores you,
>
> J. de Lacretelle.

Shortly thereafter, Henri de Lacretelle also died, and Cormatin was sold. This was the end of an era.

Mme Amaury de Lacretelle was left with the problem of bringing up her two sons. Although an intelligent and well-read woman, she did not have the dominant personality which was needed under the circumstances. One early photograph of her in profile shows a pensive and rather beautiful brunette with regular and delicate traits featuring a slightly acquiline nose, prominent eyebrows and a narrow forehead. In a later group picture, still antedating her husband's death, she appears as a young matron already threatened with a certain *embonpoint*, gentle, self-effacing, but also self-sufficient. Among her friends, in later life, she was noted for her moral qualities and her devotion to a charitable organization called "Le Vestiaire," over which she presided at the *Mairie* of the 16th Arrondissement.

It is very difficult to reconcile this notion of her character with the portrait which Mme Guéritte, Lacretelle's collaborator in translating Mary Webb, gives of her many years later: "She has irresistible eyes, and fascinating hands, the hands of a woman skillful in making other people, whom she has decided to lead by their noses, do what she wants. Looking at her, I had continually the impression of seeing you, with another face superimposed. At certain moments she has your look, your smile, an inflection of the voice which is yours and the same manner of hammering her words out. But it is not from her that you get your imagination; she has none. . . ."[10] There is no indication whatever that she was severe with her children, who remember her mainly for her gentleness. Subsequent events will show that she, like many parents, lacked a true insight into the nature of her son Jacques.

Contact with her legal-minded husband had early toned down her natural vibrancy, and she had quite forgotten the joys of nature as she had known them on the slopes of Mont-Aigoual in her own Midi.[11] In spite of this, her son inherited her sensitivity to nature. Mme de Lacretelle was an avid reader and undoubtedly communicated some of her enthusiasm to her sons—who soon read circles around her and pursued tangents which would not always have met with maternal approval, had they been known. It is rather by having literary friends than by any premeditated action on her part that she really contributed to the artistic apperceptions of Pierre and Jacques.

The case was similar in religious matters. Because of her indifference to her former Protestant beliefs, she did not attempt to influence her sons in matters of faith. In spite of any nostalgic religious feeling which she may have had in her old age, it is erroneous to identify her with the mother in the "Roman protestant" who surreptitiously goes to the Protestant *temple*. Whereas Pierre took an interest in both Calvinism and Catholicism, Jacques remained indifferent (and later, in his first novel, made considerable point of this indifference). The only time that he ever set foot inside a *temple* was in Italy when his mother took him to an Easter service.

Except for certain financial retrenchments, the death of Amaury de Lacretelle did not greatly alter his wife's mode of life. She moved from 88bis Avenue Kléber a few blocks away to 14 rue Cortambert and renewed her symbiotic relationship with her Ménard-Dorian cousins and the Hugo clan. She and her children were already in the habit of spending their vacations with them. One season, at Guernsey, they lived in Friend's House, to which memories of Juliette Drouet still clung.

A few days before his death, Amaury de Lacretelle had taken his son walking in the Bois de Boulogne. There the boy had espied a strange white flower whose beauty he admired. Having expressed his horticultural ignorance, he heard his father exclaim: "What! You've never seen any lilacs!"[12] He had a lot to learn.

In addition to being unfamiliar with lilacs, he had never experienced anything like a French *lycée* when his parents enrolled him at Janson-de-Sailly after the Easter vacation of 1898. The Institution Domangé at Florence, where he had had a taste of formal schooling, had been nothing like this. One readily imagines the irony or indifference of these Parisian scholars in the presence of this late arrival from the hanging gardens of Babylon. "Est-ce que tu es demi-pomme?"* asks the first one. "Non, merci," replies Jacques in his encyclopedic ignorance.[13] Jacques is not a Silbermann who suffers physical and moral torture, but he writhes inwardly at the crassness and vulgarity of his fellow students. He never becomes one of them. When school eventually ceases to be a shock to his nervous system, it continues to be a bore. With his father no longer there to applaud his grades, he grows indifferent to academic honors. For the time being he is a *mauvais élève*, but he is not in open revolt.

A few boyish letters which survive from this period are written during summer vacation by an affectionate son in daily communi-

* *Demi-pensionnaire.*

cation with his mother. They are dated Trouville 1899 or 1900 and relate mainly the earthy details of an everyday existence: the difficulty of cleaning a hat, because Mme Lockroy will not let him wear his cap; the need for patent leather shoes which were left behind; the inevitable rain which prevents sea bathing. One has the impression of a vigorous and healthy boy taking pleasure in donkey rides and in the obscene humor of his young companion Charles Daudet. In his imagination he is still playing soldier, this time with the Boers, who march about even in his dreams. But he is maturing, for he tells his mother that on the train he discussed politics with a gentleman who was an "enragé anti" (meaning, of course, anti-Dreyfusard). Another letter, ending with the usual affectionate greeting, is signed "Jacques de Lacretelle, in 31 years Governor of the Tonkin, in 51 years socialist deputy." Another concludes: "Jacques-Amaury Lacretelle. N.B. I have suppressed the particule, for I am a socialist-anarchist."

This was not his mother's doing but rather the inevitable result of frequenting the Hugo clan. Examining Jacques's boyhood letters, we discover a list of names which reads somewhat like the index of the *Journal* of the Goncourts—in which many of them occur, moreover, but at an earlier date. Most frequently mentioned is Mme Lockroy, the wife of the politician Edouard Lockroy; she had married Lockroy after the death of her first husband, Charles Hugo. From her first marriage she had two children, Georges and Jeanne Hugo. Georges had, of course, married Pauline Ménard-Dorian. Jeanne had been married to Léon Daudet, but, at the time of Jacques's Trouville letters, she had obtained a divorce and was married to Commandant Charcot, son of the famous doctor who was the first mentor of Freud. Jacques's boyhood companion, Charles Daudet, was the son of Jeanne Hugo. Other names slip casually into Jacques's letters, and every one proves to be somebody of note: "Catherine" is Catherine Vivier, daughter of the painter Alfred Stevens; Delna is an actress; Mme Jacquemaire is the daughter of Clemenceau; Raffaëlli is the well-known painter.

In this entire society, the most outstanding personality is Mme Paul Ménard-Dorian herself, and it is perhaps she more than anyone else who is responsible for the radical turn in Jacques's political beliefs. By this time, Mme Ménard-Dorian, whom the Goncourts had described a few years previously as one of the most beautiful women in Parisian society, had developed into a domineering character like Proust's Mme Verdurin. With Mme Verdurin's despotism, she ruled over a small literary salon in which a certain number of unsuccessful geniuses formed a timid and permanent nucleus. Whenever some *lâcheur*, an Elstir, a Vinteuil or a Morel, threatened to bolt, we can imagine the same dramas ensuing as in *Du Côté de chez Swann* and its sequels. Principal exhibits of this salon were Eugène Carrière, the painter, Reynaldo Hahn, the composer, and Alfred Cortot, the pianist. The recently published collection of Proust letters entitled *Lettres à Reynaldo Hahn* contains no allusion to Mme Ménard-Dorian, and there is, as yet, no documentary evidence of any connection between her and Proust; but there can be no doubt that Proust knew her, since he knew all her friends and relatives by marriage, the Daudets and the Hugos. There is no reason to question Jacques de Lacretelle's undocumented assertion that his "Aunt Ménard-Dorian" knew Proust well, and his contention that she is a model for Mme Verdurin seems altogether credible.[14]

A few more years were to elapse before Jacques met Proust himself, but at his "Aunt's" salon he did meet a number of avant-garde writers and several important political figures, such as Clemenceau and Colonel Picquart, who made the sensational revelations during the Dreyfus Affair. It is easy to understand how, in this atmosphere, the young Jacques became a Dreyfusard. If he had not been molded by this Dreyfusard environment, he probably would never have written *Silbermann*. One is tempted to add that he might never have written at all, since he also absorbed most of his literature and art from this same environment.

Years later, in a casual article, Jacques de Lacretelle was to describe what he calls the normal literary development of a French boy;[15] undoubtedly he was describing his own. Step one is the usual childhood literature of imagination plus Jules Verne and the fantastic. Then (step two), the fantastic must be coated with reality, and hence the historical novel is indicated: Dumas and Fenimore Cooper. Next (step three), this reality must be rendered even more plausible by relating it to everyday life: hence the need for Daudet's *Le Petit Chose* or *Jack* or for Dickens. Step four is the adolescent revolt: Chateaubriand, Musset, Vallès and ultimately Gide. Step five brings in lyricism: Hugo, Baudelaire and Vigny; and the final step is the objective novel: Balzac, Flaubert, Tolstoi, Stendhal, reinforced by the critical ideas of Sainte-Beuve, Taine and Renan. At the time of the Trouville letters, Jacques was only in step two, since his favorite reading was Dumas's *Le Chevalier d'Harmental*. At fifteen he was precociously in step five (lyricism), all from having had a thorough bath of symbolism in Mme Ménard-Dorian's drawing room.

To escape from the tedium of Janson-de-Sailly, he began to browse in his brother's company among the bookstalls of the Seine. The first discovery was a little novel of adolescence, *Petit-Cœur* by Jean Viollis—hardly great literature, to be sure, but a work which was eventually going to help in shaping Jacques's first novel. These precocious boys did not stop at adolescent novels but went on to buy the books of the avant-garde authors whom they had seen in the flesh at Aunt Ménard-Dorian's (Rodenbach, Marcel Schwob, Maeterlinck) or had heard discussed. Rodenbach's *Bruges-la-Morte*, found along the quays in a first edition, struck the first spark of literary enthusiasm, and a little later a thin volume by Rimbaud set off the conflagration. Weekly excursions to the theater, either with or without maternal accompaniment, widened Jacques's literary range by exposing him to Ibsen in the interpretations of Eleonora Duse or of Firmin Gémier and Suzanne Desprès. One week it might be Racine at the Comédie Française, but the next week it would be D'Annunzio at the Théâtre Antoine. Reluctantly, Mother even gave her consent to his attending Debussy's scandalous *Pelléas et Mélisande* at the Opéra Comique.

Once, having found a first edition of Henri de Régnier's *Esquisses vénitiennes*, he dared to take it to the poet himself for an autograph. Although he had to deal with menials and did not see the poet in person, the volume finally came back, after having been lost for two days, with eight more lines of verse which the novelist was to recite years later in the French Academy in eulogizing his predecessor.[16]

There was something very incompatible between this type of literature and the fossilized proceedings of Janson-de-Sailly. In *troisième*, however, the presence of André Bellessort in the professorial chair brightened the academic horizon for a time. "Belles," in spite of his whirling cane and epigrammatic classroom manner, had an inspired way of talking about literature, even if it was the classics, and often deviated from the prescribed program to read to his pupils Verlaine or Kipling. What a temptation to the boy to slip into his composition a phrase cribbed from Albert Samain or Stuart Merrill! Immediately, however, this Cerebus standing guard at the gates of the classics slapped him down. "A certain feeling for style, but be more simple and sober,"[17] he wrote. Bellessort's favorite method of teaching literary appreciation was to present a poem with certain rhymes and words suppressed and then require his class to deduce the original. Another device was to allow the pupil to choose his own poem to memorize, the theory being that he disclosed thereby his literary capacities and predilections. But there was an inevitable danger. Give a boy an inch and he will take a mile. Directed to learn a Hugo poem in honor of the centenary of the poet, Jacques showed his disrespect both for Aunt Pauline and for his professor by learning the shortest and most banal Hugo poem he could find. His punishment was to learn all of *Oceano Nox*.

Another bright spot that year at Janson was his acquaintance with a fellow pupil, Henri Franck, whose brilliance and originality made him a worthy companion. The boys shared ideas and went to each other's homes. Forty years later Jacques de Lacretelle was to describe him thus: "He was a Racinian Jew who, in spite of an unpleasing physical appearance, makes me think today of the young companions of Esther. Franck had then, in our schoolboy essays, a Gebhart sort of style, that is to say studded with intentional archaic expressions, which I sometimes criticized him for. I remember a certain *Mort de Roland* in which the refrain of *l'Empereur-à-la-barbe-fleurie*, recurring in each paragraph, had got on my nerves; and I told him so. He looked at me with his limpid eyes, without bothering to reply to me that my forest of Roncevaux, described according to the best processes of the worst symbolists, produced a pitiful effect. That is precisely what Bellessort told me."[18]

Everyone predicted a remarkable future for this precocious lad. Bellessort said years later, when speculating whether Franck was the original of Lacretelle's Silbermann, that in *deuxième* Franck had composed such a remarkable essay that few *agrégés* could have done better.[19] Franck finished the Ecole Normale Supérieure, became the devoted friend of Anna de Noailles and of Barrès, but succumbed to consumption at the age of twenty-four.[20] During his lingering illness he composed *La Danse devant l'arche*, a Biblical poem of epic sweep and Whitmanesque qualities which summarizes his aspirations and disappointments:

> Quand j'aurai trouvé Dieu, je reviendrai en France,
> J'espérais le saisir sous ton ciel, ô pays,
> Mais je dois abdiquer cette chère espérance,
> Puisqu'il te manque aussi.[21]

Against the background of Silbermann's tragedy, there is something distinctly moving about this forgotten poem.

The next year at Janson things went decidedly sour. Perhaps it was the inevitable result of adolescence coming on top of a basic maladjustment; perhaps it was the fault of the French educational system, which makes no allowance for sensitive natures. There seems also to have been yet another contributing factor—Lacretelle's surdity mentioned in a 1930 entry in Gide's *Journal* and noted at a slightly earlier date by Maurice Sachs in *The Decade of Illusion* (that is to say prior to 1928, judging from the subtitle of the book). There is no other text, not even a literary allusion, however, which would lead one to suspect that the problem began in adolescence. Yet, in answer to a definite inquiry on this point, Lacretelle has written: "I noticed, toward my fifteenth year, that my hearing was less good in one ear. The progress of this infirmity has been relatively slow, but, as always happens, it has reached the other ear. I was deeply saddened by it in my youth. But perhaps I have gained a certain force of concentration over myself, a certain taste for withdrawal which, in the last analysis, has helped me to write. Today I no longer think about it too often. At sixty-six I am not, as you know, isolated from the world. It is not dramatic; it could be worse."[22] If it was not dramatic and if it was not the primary cause for the boy's adolescent problems, this deafness goes a long way toward explaining the introspective qualities of Lacretelle's art, as Sachs was the first to note: "The deafness from which he suffers seems to separate him from any environment. He seemed deeply sunk in himself, as if his eyes saw only a world private and impenetrable, as if he heard in the surrounding stillness voices which spoke to his heart."[23]

One imagines the adolescent Jacques de Lacretelle drawing further and further into his shell and not yielding to the attempts of his mother and teachers to draw him out. In desperation, Mme de Lacretelle finally transferred her son to the Lycée Hoche at Versailles. Cancellations on his letters at this time prove that this was the spring of 1902 and that he was actually fourteen, rather than fifteen. At Versailles, the boy boarded with Pastor J.-H. Messine and his wife. It seems that his mother had no ulterior motive in selecting a Protestant environment and that the only factors which entered into the decision were convenience and suitability. Jacques closed his ears to the grace at the beginning of each meal and managed to absorb nothing Protestant. One can see the expression of this sophisticated Jansonian as he writes to his mother: "I am writing you directly on getting up from table, not wishing to profit by the useful colloquy of these 2 august ancients. Mediocre dinner, even quite bad. Cabbage soup. Fritters with nothing at all. Roast pork with potatoes. Pots of chocolate cream (inedible), etc."[24] In the same tone of superiority he continues: "*A frightful catastrophe.* I have had the misfortune to utter the name of Brouzet at table, and Mme Messine immediately discovered a relationship with you, claiming that the sister of her sister-in-law married a Brouzet. I greeted this news with a *sang-froid* of which I did not think myself capable." As for the Lycée Hoche, it is peopled by "stupid city-dwellers or peasants whose coarseness disgusts me."

Sophistication yields sometimes to complete distress when he writes, in another letter: "This life is frightful, everything is repugnant to me."[25] Whenever he does not escape to Paris on Thursday and Saturday, he bombards his mother with requests to come to see him. Like Jean Hermelin, one of his first fictional characters, he roams the streets of Versailles by night, agitated by lascivious thoughts and awkwardly resisting the calls of puberty. Literature is the only refuge, and every letter to his mother asks her to bring one more of his favorite books: Théodore de Banville, Lemerre edition; *Hortensias bleus* (by Robert de Montesquiou of Proustian fame); verse and prose of Mallarmé; *Les Fleurs du mal*; Rodenbach; *Le Parnasse de la jeune Belgique*. In all this agitation we still see the old Jacques breaking forth in his enthusiasm for politics, tennis and boating (during these years he was not a sedentary boy).

At last the pressure is off as the school year ends, and the happiness of escaping from it all is reflected in the joyous letters that summer from Guernsey, where, as usual, he is staying with Aunt Pauline. He has so well forgotten his own troubles that he becomes concerned over the outcome of his brother "Pierrot's" examination for the *baccalauréat.* As the vacation comes to an end the worries return. Will his mother please let him go back to Janson, and does she think he will get Bellessort? One stormy day he cries: "In any case take me out of Versailles; I have no desire to return to that beastly place."[26]

His mother did acquiesce to his going back to Janson. The second year of his return, in July, he failed the bachelor's examination and, in October, managed to fall ill before the re-examination. Beginning rhetoric over again, he was in such a state of depression that his mother had to withdraw him from school and take him to Saint-Jean-Cap-Ferrat near Hyères for the three winter months. In philosophy he had another bad year with a philosophy professor who dictated his course. Now he broke into open revolt and spent much of his time at the races, forging his mother's name on the *billets d'absence* in order to get back into school. At the races one day he met a junior master who had the same weakness for the pleasures of the turf. "What are you doing here?" said the master severely. But he added on a different note: "You are missing the steeplechase."[27] Another time Jacques arrived late at history class without a *billet de rentrée.* When the professor scolded him, he replied insolently that he could get a *billet de rentrée* any time. He spoke the truth, because, as every pupil in the class knew, he had an entire package of them, all duly "signed" by proper authority. The upshot of this affair was that he was suspended from school for a time. In July 1905 the reckoning came: a "double failure" at the *baccalauréat.* At home there was the expected drama, and Jacques was classified as the imbecile of the family. October was the last straw. Although he passed the written, he was eliminated in the oral. No greater disgrace could fall on a Frenchman in his social class.

Shortly thereafter, thanks to family influence, he entered the employ of the Banque Française pour le Commerce et l'Industrie. It took him eighteen months to convince his employers of his inaptitude for banking; they tried him out in every department of

3

the institution and then fired him. To the great despair of his mother, he refused to work any further for his living.

The next few years were intellectual and emotional doldrums for Jacques. He had lost all confidence in himself and doubted more than ever his ability to accomplish anything in the only field which interested him—literature. No longer could he turn to his mother for consolation and protection. He was getting too old for that, and, on her part, his mother could see no ability, literary or otherwise, in this prodigal son. Pierre was the only hope of the family, and he, at least, would have a brilliant career.

Escaping from himself, Jacques found a new remedy in travel, with its *dépaysement* and the incognito which it conferred on the traveler. In different worlds, one could be a different person, unassailed by doubts and uninhibited by family protocol. He had had his first taste of this new life during two happy weeks at Staines, England, when he was on holiday from the bank. After leaving the bank forever, he headed straight for England again and for a boarding house on Trumpington Street, Cambridge. Although it was spring vacation and there were few students about, he enjoyed going around hatless in the evening and being apprehended by the proctors. This is the closest he ever came to being a *Cantab*, but, since then, several hasty biographers have made him a bona fide member of the university, on the strength of an allusion in Abel Hermant's reply to Lacretelle's *Discours de réception*. During this brief sojourn at Cambridge, young Lacretelle did a lot of reading. For the first time he began to appreciate the depth of his own inner life and to wonder, as he reread with greater discernment *Le Rouge et le Noir* and *War and Peace*, whether there was any parcel of originality within him. The revolt and audacity of Julien Sorel, which contrasted so strongly with his own ineffectual grip on life, as well as the deflated style of Stendhal, which was a change from the obscurantism of his cherished symbolists, made a lasting impression on him.

In 1908, France had a new, if reluctant, engineer in the person of Private Jacques de Lacretelle, 5th Engineering Regiment, based at Satory near Versailles. Every morning at an uncivilized hour Private de Lacretelle was heaving sections of rail near the Pièce d'Eau des Suisses to build a hypothetical railway. In the evening he was bathing in his room at the Hôtel des Réservoirs, trying to get some of the filth out of his body and soul. At nine o'clock democratic army regulations forced him to return to barracks. Although there is no contemporary record of his state of mind at this period, Lacretelle outlined in 1920 for his never-to-be-finished "Roman protestant" the following episode which is probably autobiographical in parts:

> He leaves to do his military service in Versailles, in the Engineers, at a time when he is disposed to love humble people and to hate what is superior in society. And in the army he finds all the kindness which I found among the workers of the 5th Engineers. Altruism. Collectivism. No enviousness. Helpfulness. Taste for work. Equal sharing of anything hard. Hate for injustice.
>
> It is a revelation. A few figures. Dupuy (obscure), the big light-haired fellow who did not like unfair privileges and had a grudge against me on that account. The young Parisians (more intelligent, more uninhibited).
>
> Happy, healthy but hard life. He is not accustomed to work. Fatigue. Toil, rewarded by the intoxication of the mornings at the menagerie, of the races, of the labor.
>
> Winter. The conversations in the barracks. The contempt in which he holds the officers. (One, servile when he learns whose son X is.) To be a worker is the most noble career, for it is the only one which rests on individual merit and on nothing else.
>
> In the barracks, the celebration of the recruits. The midnight suppers with the violin. He wants to embrace them, to call them "my friends," to press them to his heart.
>
> He scarcely ever goes to see his family.
>
> The officers. One, just, his heart good probably but deformed, dried up by the requirements of his trade (same face as my lieutenant). The others, heartless, ambitious or uncaring (but no exaggerated portraits).

The above document may be suspect because it is both fictional and retrospective; and yet some parts have an authentic ring. The phrase "which I found among the workers of the 5th Engineers" shows that there must have been, on his part, some new efforts toward understanding others and that his army experience, disagreeable though it was, left no permanent scars on his soul, as the *lycée* had done. To take pleasure, however briefly, in the company of these humble peasants was only another way of expressing his indifference to polite society of the 16th Arrondissement. The experience was well designed to transform a symbolist poet (who had never written a serious line of poetry) into a novelist in the tradition of the French realists. In the spring, Lacretelle developed a cold with bronchitis complications and was dismissed as unfit for military service.

Twenty-one and nothing to do. Being no longer tied to his mother's apron strings, he traveled—Italy, England, Germany, Africa, even Hungary. In Paris he shunned society and spent his time at the Ballet Russe or at concerts—for he had discovered the pleasures of music. His misanthropy was depriving him of all literary contacts or inspiration; he no longer went to Mme Ménard-Dorian's receptions.

Meanwhile his brother Pierre was beginning his career as a literary journalist. In 1911 Pierre de Lacretelle published his first literary study, *Les Origines et la jeunesse de Lamartine*. Since then he has continued to follow this profession with success; he has published biographical studies on Hugo, Queen Hortense, Mme de Staël and Racine, and has been a regular collaborator on various literary periodicals.

Near the end of July 1914, while traveling in the north of Scotland, Jacques chanced to glance at a newspaper and noticed that a war was about to break out. He managed to get back to Paris just before it was declared. Because of his medical discharge, he was not subject to recall, and he therefore volunteered. His regiment, quartered at Fontainebleau, was entirely composed of *réformés* like himself or of Frenchmen who had been living abroad. In due course, Fontainebleau being threatened by the German advance, the regiment was evacuated to Marvéjols in the department of Lozère, far to the south. Volunteering with a group of thirteen or fifteen for front line duty, Jacques was assigned to the 46th Infantry Regiment at Clermont-en-Argonne. At that point trench warfare was still in its infancy. His unit was bombed but not attacked. After three weeks he again caught cold and was sent to a hospital at Chaumont. In December he was back in Paris.

Again there was nothing to do.

3

PROUST'S WAY

NOTHING to do but read. How many times, in the same predicament, Jacques had heard his parents say: "Don't remain idle. Get a book." Although no one admonished him now, he fell readily into the old groove. Retrospectively, he was later to date his literary awakening from the Cambridge sojourn and was to imply that his tastes had been classical from the outset. The evidence points to a slightly different conclusion. In the first manuscript of his first novel *La Vie inquiète de Jean Hermelin*, never published in that form, he mentions Huysmans's *A Rebours* and Wilde's *The Picture of Dorian Gray* as inspiration. He has remarked in conversation that his favorite reading during this wartime idleness was Dostoevski, and in many a printed interview he has pointed to Proust as a primary source of inspiration. On the basis of still extant first manuscripts, it will be evident that the strongest influence of all must be attributed to Marcel Proust.

Lacretelle had already begun reading *Du Côté de chez Swann* before departing for the front, and when he returned to his books, he immediately picked up Proust's novel again. It fascinated him. If Proust met with indifference and incomprehension on all sides when his novel appeared in late 1913, the attitude of the Ménard-Dorian clan was an exception to the rule. For years they had been counting on Proust's precociousness to produce something unusual. To Jacques de Lacretelle it seemed that everyone was talking about Proust, and he had only to open *Le Figaro*, *Excelsior*, or *L'Echo de Paris* to find eulogistic articles by Proust's friends, Lucien Daudet, Jean Cocteau and Jacques-Emile Blanche. Since he had not yet happened to meet Proust, probably because he himself had been avoiding society, he prevailed on his friend Henri Bardac to take him to see the eccentric writer in his cork-lined room. There is no record of the date of this meeting.

Years later, in *La Table ronde*, he described this visit: "This first meeting with Proust, how I remember it! Was it the dark oak furniture, the greens of the wallpaper, or he himself, pale, slightly bearded, with great leaden eyes which looked fixedly at the visitor—but, on my way out, I said to my companion, without knowing exactly why, that it had made me think of a Renaissance nightmare." And he continues: "This first conversation and most of those which followed between Proust and me were not always attuned. First because I was somewhat intimidated. Also because I came to see him as a questioner, and he received me rather as an informant."[1] Lacretelle had asserted that he knew some of the originals of the characters, whereupon Proust, having denied that there were any originals, began to ply him with questions about various individuals. Later, to oblige Lacretelle, Proust wrote on the flyleaf of a copy of his novel the famous dedication so often quoted in which he gives some rare information on the keys to his characters and episodes. "I repeat," he said, "the characters are entirely invented, and there is no key."[2] What had begun as polite conversation on Jacques's part had turned into a lesson on literary creation by which he was soon to profit.

Proust's example convinced Lacretelle momentarily that the only valid technique for a novelist is to reach inside himself for his subject. For a time he still doubted whether his inner life was rich enough to provide the framework for a novel, but finally he took pen in hand under the urging of his friend Jacques de Zogheb, member of an Egyptian family and a playwright.[3] Paul Brach encouraged him, and Reynaldo Hahn even consented to read the manuscript. There is no record of the date at which he began. After blackening paper for a time without seeming to get anywhere, he began to realize that something more is needed than reams of *papier écolier* and a scratchy pen. He would have to withdraw further into himself and concentrate all his strength on the creative act.

At this time he formed the habit, which he was to keep the rest of his life, of escaping to the anonymity of a provincial hotel room whenever there was serious work to be done. First he went to Moret near Fontainebleau, then to Hyères (where he learned of the armistice) and finally to Provins. There, in a nondescript room of the Boule d'Or, his beard grew longer, he read *Anna Karenina* and rediscovered, somewhat like Pascal stumbling onto the principles of Euclid, certain elementary rules of the novel. To use his own expression, he was nearing the end of the tunnel. One morning he got a shave and set out across the fields:

> For three days the sun had been shining again. Toward noon I stretched out in a field halfway up a hillock. On another slope a farmer was guiding his plow; occasionally I lost sight of him, but without ceasing to hear his voice and certain gratings of the plowshare; then, at regular intervals, the horns, the yoke, the muzzles of the oxen, finally the entire yoke and the man himself reappeared on the crest. I remained there a long time; I do not remember having had what one might call an idea, except that I thought of the passage in *Anna Karenina* wherein Levin joins the reapers. I looked at the sky, I watched the insects buzzing around the overheated clods of earth, and that was all. *I did nothing but feel.*[4]

Feeling was no longer the parasitical act of an obstinate day-dreamer but rather the fecundation of the creative process. Something now counted more than the mere act of feeling. It was the expression of the feeling in words.

In 1919, after what may have been as much as three years of labor, a manuscript was ready for publication, but its author soon found that, like Proust a few years before, he had a reputation for idleness to overcome. Aunt Ménard-Dorian promised to get Ferdinand Hérold to intercede with Alfred Vallette at the *Mercure de France*. After Vallette had summarily rejected the book, they pinned their hopes on the son of Calmann-Lévy. The result was still negative. With Fayard it was the same. Finally there came a *pneu* from Bernard Grasset. He agreed to publish but asked the author to share in advertising expenses to the extent of 1,500 francs since the book would not be a best seller. Decidedly Lacretelle was following in the footsteps of Proust, whom Grasset had published on even more unfavorable terms.

The book appeared on May 14, 1920, with the title *La Vie inquiète de Jean Hermelin*. In the Princeton University Library there is a manuscript of this novel which corresponds closely to the printed text but which bears the title "Les Cahiers de Jean

Hermelin." Beneath this is another title, crossed out, "La Vie de Jacques Lamiel," and throughout the manuscript the change from "Jacques Lamiel" to "Jean Hermelin" is everywhere visible. Today Lacretelle does not recall why "Les Cahiers" became "La Vie inquiète." It may have been because of too pointed a resemblance to Gide's *Les Cahiers d'André Walter*, of which Lacretelle had heard but which he had not read.

The very first manuscript of the novel is still in the author's possession and provides us with an unusual record both of the creative process and of the development of Lacretelle's talent as a writer. After awkward beginnings, the style gradually improves, and, at the same time, there is a shift from a subjective to an objective technique. A study of this first manuscript is a necessary prelude to an understanding of Lacretelle's art.

In the printed version the novel has two major divisions. The first, in the form of a first person narrative, relates the childhood and adolescence of the hero, Jean Hermelin; the second, in the form of a diary, records his brief military career in World War I. According to the author, there was no interval between the writing of the first and second parts, but the reader of the printed version cannot fail to sense a difference in technique when comparing the two parts. This difference is accentuated in the first manuscript. In analyzing these stylistic problems, we shall begin by concentrating on the first half of the first manuscript, which is considerably different from the final version.

Among Lacretelle's miscellaneous papers, there is a brief outline for an autobiographical narrative in which the main character, Jacques Pasquier, is misunderstood by his mother, fails in his *bac*, and finally awakens to a new life in England, where he has an affair with Flossie. This outline bears no tangible relation to the first manuscript, but it seems to be the earliest version of the story nevertheless.

The first manuscript is written, for convenience, in notebooks—just as the preface to the printed version states. The manuscript bears no title, and the hero has the name Jacques Lamiel. After giving a brief account of his childhood in France, Jacques leaves with his family for Damascus at the age of ten. There he conceives a passion for his governess Hélène. After his parents have wisely sent Hélène back to France, thoughts of suicide enter his mind.

Subsequently, Jacques returns with his family to France by way of Naples, and, at about the time of his father's death, he enters the hated *lycée* of Versailles. His teachers call him "Hamlet or the young invalid with the slow steps or Chatterton," and his fellow pupils soon give up trying to make friends, treating him "as a sort of bad comedian whose roles they know only by the hisses of the critics." At the *lycée* he makes one friend in the person of André Laumière (rebaptized Malo de Kerlon).

When Jacques meets Antoinette Laumière (later Antoinette de Kerlon), he "resolves" to fall in love with her, and finally, in the tower of Notre-Dame, he kisses her in the darkness as they climb the corkscrew staircase. Like a child who has broken his toy "because he is furious at not knowing how it works," he immediately proceeds to hate her and drops the Laumières altogether. Now his repressed sexuality nearly drives him to madness, and he roams the red-light district of Versailles at night, provoking and then repulsing the advances of the professionals and finally ending up by throwing stones at miauling cats—"for I was not unaware of the meaning of these passionate calls" (the cats are still in the final version, but, for greater subtlety, the explanation is not).

For reasons we are not told, his mother transfers him to a Paris *lycée*, which the author identifies as Janson in the final version of the text. There he meets again Eddie Valbert (later called Pierre Dollé), a minor character with whom he had previously discussed literature at Versailles. Eddie introduces him to a prospective mistress, Madeleine Chavrier (renamed Lucienne with no last name), he goes to her apartment and, as in the final version, pusillanimously rejects her advances. That puts him right back where he was, and again, for page after page, he wanders through the streets. The first half of the manuscript version ends inconclusively on this repetitious note.

The first few pages of the life of Jacques Lamiel record in word, if not in deed, an amazing verbal impotence. The author is groping for his stylistic tools as he writes: ". . . but I am incapable of expressing with objective precision the charm of an old low-ceilinged house and the grace of a park descending with swelling slopes toward a stream bordered with nut trees." Or again: "Doubtless I will fail likewise in describing the country where our habitation is located." A similar hesitancy in the use of language crops up frequently in the unwieldy similes of the carly pages, with their inevitable *tel, ainsi que* or *comme.* He needed to write more precisely and more imaginatively than this: "... it has become evident to me that this country, squeezed in between two rivers in the center of France, offers one of the most beautiful scenes that can strike the senses."

To anyone familiar with contemporary French literature, it is immediately apparent from the following passage what Lacretelle was trying to do:

> Thus I remember that one day, having gone into the garden after a day spent at reading things which had particularly inflamed my imagination, my glance came to rest on a little pavilion situated at the end of the park, at some distance, its walls entirely covered with ivy. Two dormer windows, of circular form, on the panes of which the setting sun reflected an orange-colored light, appeared in the midst of a mass of green. At that moment, I thought I perceived the bitter odor and the savor of a fruit. This strange illusion immobilized me, and after a few moments of obstinate searching, I noted that it was due to an unconscious rapprochement of two images; that the sight of the foliage, from which stuck out two orange balls, had brought on the mental representation of bushes in large boxes which, as soon as summer came, used to flank in a regular pattern the perron of our house, and had awakened thus sensations of taste and smell of which I was seeking the cause; I was dazzled by this discovery.
>
> It seemed to me that I got a glimpse of the mechanism of my thoughts. I had a vague notion, but at the most rudimentary level, of what I learned later about the association of ideas and the unconscious connection between them and our sensations.
>
> My glance did not leave this hovel, thanks to which new hypotheses had risen on the horizon of my mind. I was as though bending over the inside of a watch, and through the narrow opening of [blank], certain wheels were revealed. The revelation of these unsuspected workings left me speechless.*

* Ainsi, je me rappelle qu'un jour, étant sorti dans le jardin après une journée employée à des lectures qui m'avaient particulièrement enflammé, mon regard s'arrêta sur un petit pavillon situé au bout du parc, à quelque

This is obviously a conscious effort to duplicate Proust's famous passage about the madeleine and cup of tea, out of which surges—at least in theory—all of *A la Recherche du temps perdu*. Ten years later the autobiographical narrator of *Amour nuptial* was to tell how he shied away, in the very beginning, from a school of literature addicted to the "mental representation of things" and to the "rough transcription of the image," because he was incapable of expressing himself "without order or clarity." The foregoing passage from the manuscript of Lacretelle's first novel is proof enough that, on the contrary, Lacretelle did not originally turn his back on the "mental representation" school but that he tried his best to imitate it.

There are also many Proustian reminiscences, originally in the first manuscript, which have survived in the printed version. When Jacques Lamiel's mother, playing the piano, causes memories of childhood to surge through the boy's mind, we inevitably recognize an echo of Proust's sonata of Vinteuil. During an illness, Jacques (that is to say, Jean Hermelin) loses the "notion of time and being"[5] and gives birth to a "twin body which was my enemy"—all of which is recognizable Proustian terminology. Proustian also is the concept of the "reciprocal misunderstanding of beings"

---

distance, et dont les murs étaient entièrement recouverts par du lierre. Deux lucarnes, de forme circulaire, sur les vitres desquelles le soleil couchant reflétait une lumière orangée, apparaissaient au milieu de la masse de verdure. A ce moment, je crus percevoir l'odeur amère et la saveur d'un fruit. Cette illusion étrange m'immobilisa, et, lorsque après quelques instants d'une recherche opiniâtre, je constatai qu'elle était née d'un rapprochement inconscient de deux images; que la vue de la frondaison sombre, d'où jaillissaient deux boules orange, avait attiré la représentation des arbustes en caissons qui, dès la belle saison, flanquaient systématiquement le perron de notre demeure, et avait éveillé ainsi les sensations de goût et d'odorat dont je recherchais l'origine; je fus ébloui par cette découverte.

Il me sembla entrevoir le mécanisme de mes pensées. J'eus vaguement conscience, à l'état d'ébauche grossière, de ce que j'appris plus tard sur les associations d'idées et la correspondance inconsciente de celles-ci avec nos sensations.

Mon regard ne quittait pas cette masure grâce à quoi des hypothèses nouvelles s'étaient levées à l'horizon de mon esprit. J'étais comme penché sur l'intérieur d'une montre, et par l'étroite échancrure de [blanc], certains rouages étaient à nu. La révélation de ce travail insoupçonné me laissait interdit.

which will become basic to all Lacretelle characters. Against the background of *Un Amour de Swann*, we appreciate the full implications of Jacques's remark that he and Adrienne (the main female character in the second half of the novel) were "already strangers for each other," and we are not surprised to learn later that he had become altogether indifferent to her. In fact, if it were not for the early letter of the boy Jacques de Lacretelle to his mother (quoted in Chapter 2), one might well insist that the good-night kiss in the early pages of the novel is a direct reminiscence of the famous scene in Proust.

In writing the first half of the first manuscript, Lacretelle hoped somehow to approximate the miracle of Proust by transferring his emotions and the vague outlines of his life to paper without resort to the techniques of the traditional French novel. The only concession which he made to outmoded considerations of plot and character was to rearrange his life very slightly. Instead of returning from the eastern Mediterranean at ten, as had been the case in real life, he had his hero leave at that age. When his hero came back to France, he had him enter the *lycée* at Versailles rather than the one at Paris. All of the hero's emotions are Lacretelle's own emotions. Speaking of the physical appearance of his dying father, the narrator says: "But why insist on this decadence? It is my feelings that I want to define."

In the manuscript, Jacques Lamiel's childhood is a series of "feelings" which recur with the persistence of Proustian themes. Perhaps these themes are even too symmetrical to be truly Proustian, but their source is obvious. Like *Du Côté de chez Swann*, this novel begins with an overture, the initial theme of which is sleep, or rather the intermediary zone between sleep and waking when sensations are beyond the control of consciousness but leave their impression on the memory. The eccentric child prefers dreamland to reality and goes about peopling the woods with vegetable-like fauns and faun-like vegetables. All of this culminates in a vision of his inner workings set off by the sight of the little pavilion. In the final version, only the rudiments of this overture remain, since the key passage was sacrificed.

Thereafter each subdivision of the novel opens with a Proustian theme, focuses on some episode, and then fades away in another Proustian theme. The subdivision following the overture begins with the boy's "half-consciousness," as he dozes in his bunk aboard the boat taking him to the eastern Mediterranean; it ends with the boy's restless dreams at the time of his father's death. In describing the Middle East in this subdivision—"the ocre, the indigo and the brick color of certain clothes, the white of the burnooses and the feminine veils, dull or incandescent according to the time of the day"[6]—he is again concentrating on sensation, although the result seems to be more Loti than Proust.

The subdivision on the *lycée* resumes with Jacques's daydreams as his mind wanders from the lessons to a certain gas light burning in front of him. The high point is the scene in which, through a lowered window, he sees the indistinct form of Antoinette and loses all sense of reality. Although this vision scene has survived in the final version, it is bereft of much of its Proustian meaning, since it was originally intended to demonstrate the splitting of Antoinette's personality into two parts: the real (so-called) and the imaginary. At the end of this subdivision, after the kissing scene in the tower of Notre-Dame, the image of Antoinette fades away, obliterated, as in *Un Amour de Swann*, by forgetfulness. In characteristic fashion, the next subdivision again picks up the dream theme when the narrator, having fallen ill, once more loses his grip on reality. After a few minor episodes, this part tapers off into sensuous and sensual wanderings about Versailles. In the next subdivision, the opening theme is the musical passage inspired by the sonata of Vinteuil, and the tapering-off theme is more sensuous and sensual wanderings, this time with a change of locale to Paris.

Even in the second half of the manuscript—the plot of which will be mentioned presently—the Proustian rhythms continue, although they have vanished from the printed version. As Jacques Lamiel wanders about Paris in a trance brought on by acute sadness, the city is transformed before his eyes into lava and pink granite. Soon, however, the Proustian rhythms break down under the weight of a new realism in this part. To maintain the artistic continuity of the subconscious mental processes, the author occasionally interrupts this new realistic narrative with flash backs, faintly reminiscent of mnemonic passages in Proust. The sound of detonations on the battlefield calls forth extensive memories of the narrator's childhood in Passy. Finally the first manuscript dwindles away in a poetic meditation on human destiny and the meaning of the narrator's life. This conclusion is missing from the published version, which now ends in an action scene concluding with the narrator's death.

Thus a poetic armature was originally intended to sustain the novel. If any external realism or any action crept in, it was coincidental. Most of the characters were mere silhouettes. About the only information we have on Hélène, the governess, is that she had a peculiar way of pronouncing her sibilants[7] which had a bewitching effect on the boy. Exceptionally, we discover that Antoinette was "tall, slender; her face was thinned out by a mass of thick chestnut hair; her serious expression had a certain amenity." But one passage, later sacrificed for no apparent reason except that it was extraneous, stands out strikingly in the early pages as a lapse into traditional narrative style:

> I remember one day when a girl who was carrying baskets filled with lemons, came over toward us from a spring beside the road. She was barefoot and dressed in a tight smock of drab blue linen. The majestic nonchalance of her manners, the somewhat soft curve of her wax-like face and the indolence of her black eyes reminded one of the unforgettable grace of Biblical characters.
>
> Already my father was on his way toward her, and, having paid for a few fruits an unexpected price which brought a blush of pleasure onto the cheeks of the woman, he arranged her dark hair, disengaged an ear decorated with a silver ring, and caressed her neck, while murmuring in a playful tone some puerile words.
>
> The game amused me very much, but soon the unexpected spectacle in which my father revealed himself to me from a spontaneous and frivolous angle, quite different from the angle of exemplary austerity that he had everlastingly presented to me, opened up to my observation an unsuspected field.

In spite of his prejudice in favor of subjectivity, Lacretelle found himself inventing certain episodes to make his narrative more interesting. The entire story about his adolescent love for Antoinette was such an invention. When he came to write the second half of his novel, he imagined a series of episodes having little or no connection with his own biography, and these he narrated in the clear, objective manner of a traditional French novelist. Then he returned to the first half of his novel, and found it altogether wanting in precisely those principles which he had meanwhile come to consider essential to the art of the novel.

The first part of Lacretelle's novel was deficient in three respects, characters, plot and style. He had tended to write what came into his mind without objective controls. He had not sufficiently examined the reasons why the main character, Jacques Lamiel, acted as he did; and between the episodes of his novel he had failed to establish that subtle logic which shows the author to be the master of his creation and which distinguishes the French "psychological" novel from a novel of adventure.

Since the real nature of his autobiographical character had emerged only in the period of adolescence, it was imperative for Lacretelle to reduce the childhood episodes to a strict minimum, retaining only those episodes which helped to explain why Jacques Lamiel turned into a frustrated adolescent. By eliminating altogether the long passages on the Middle Eastern trip and sojourn, Lacretelle effected an immediate economy with one stroke of the scissors. Then he proceeded to change what was left.

One type of change can be seen in the minor details of plot. In the original version, things had tended to happen with no apparent reason, and on the rare occasions when things did happen, the events lacked vividness, so that they left little or no impression on the mind of the reader. Originally, there was no particular reason why Jacques was unhappy as a small child. In the new version, he acquired a limp and long curls, setting him off from other children, who now threw very precise stones at him. In another instance, the original version presented the narrator at Versailles as a Hamlet whose fellow pupils shunned him, whereas the final version, at this point, starts with the whimsical scene in which the narrator, trying to make friends with Legallard, only succeeds in losing his knife. In due course the erstwhile Hamlet must fight with the bully Roucaud. Then, instead of slipping in unobtrusively, as André Laumière had done, Malo de Kerlon comes vividly onto the stage as he offers his handkerchief to Roucaud's victim. If one looks back at Vallès's *L'Enfant* or Daudet's *Jack*, which were favorite novels of the young Jacques de Lacretelle, it is apparent that our author has rediscovered some of the vividness of this late nineteenth century realism. In fact, Lacretelle drew very heavily on another of these novels of childhood, Viollis's *Petit Cœur*, in creating a new and important episode to fill the vacuum left by the suppression of the Middle Eastern journey. In Viollis's story, Bernadette joins her young guests in mocking the late object of her affection; in Lacretelle's novel, exactly the same thing happens to the narrator in his first childhood affair with a new character, Odette.

The narrator's second love affair with Antoinette remains (in the manuscript Hélène, the governess, is his first love, and in the final version, Odette is his first). The author himself asserts that the Antoinette episode is not autobiographical, and there is little reason to doubt this statement, since, in the original version, the reader senses an immediate artificiality in the fact that the narrator behaves much like Stendhal's Julien Sorel in the willfulness of his love-making. The new version of this episode is infinitely more subtle. Instead of meditating on the "sexual initiation" of Antoinette and her friends, the narrator is now initially unaware of his attitude toward his friend's sister. Then, on a hot afternoon at the Laumière (Malo's) estate at Buc, the narrator, from the window of his room, catches sight of Antoinette in the garden, and suddenly he has a new sensorial experience:

> Suddenly, through the thin lattice of the window shade, I saw, born of my dream perhaps, a white form going and coming in the twilight. It was she.
>
> I could scarcely see her. However, thanks to the whiteness of her dress as it moved about, I could see her outlines more precisely when she bent over the flower baskets.
>
> Then she approached the house, climbed on the bench which was under my window and cut a few leaves from the Virginia creeper which mantled the wall. I could hear that she was there from the rustling of her dress and the quivering of the plant. Without her suspecting what I was doing, I went toward the window, holding my breath, my body amorously pressed against the wall. I perceived, so near that they might have touched me, the fingers which were breaking the stems with a sharp crackling sound; I smelled the recently renewed perfume

with which her arms were impregnated and in which mingled the unwelcome odor of the marigolds cut from the flowerbeds.

Rumblings of thunder rolled through the clouds. . . . A commotion in my brain had caused I know not what imperious sweetness to spread through me. . . . It seemed to me that I saw the universe from a new position. . . .

The foregoing passage, here considerably abbreviated in the last paragraph, comes only with slight alteration from the first manuscript. Originally, it was another "Proustian" sensation, but here it has a deeper psychological significance, since the narrator is just beginning to be conscious of his love for Antoinette. When he is fully conscious of his emotion, he will no longer be able to behave naturally with his friend André (that is to say, Malo), and he will alternately embrace Antoinette lustfully in secret and then repulse her, until the poor girl is completely bewildered by this inarticulate madman. At this point this pattern of flight from sex becomes firmly established as the dominant psychological pattern of the book.

Lacretelle expanded the next important episode in much the same manner. Madeleine Chavrier, the prospective mistress, had made only a brief and inconclusive appearance in the first manuscript. Renamed Lucienne in the final version, she assumed a more important role when she attempted to tame the luckless "Caponnet," as she called the narrator. In this part, the same retreat from sex continues.

In the chronology of the narrative, we now come to the second major division of the novel. It was the experience of writing this part which originally convinced Lacretelle of the inadequacy of his method up to that point. In these pages, there is, among other things, a long episode which is straightforward, linear narrative so concisely written that Lacretelle was able to retain it almost without alteration (it was to cover forty-five pages of printed text). This episode is the affair with Adrienne Rouvière (called Georgette Lerbier in the first manuscript) while the narrator is in training as a soldier. She is married but is temporarily without benefit of husband, since this is wartime. On this occasion the narrator makes valiant attempts to overcome his timidity, and if he fails in the end, it is only coincidence, because there is nothing wrong with his

4

technique. Although love apparently precedes awareness, the narrator soon wakes up to his role of "seducer"—"guessing the fortunate effect that they might produce, I no longer withheld my tears." With a flourish which might have been appropriate a hundred years earlier, he goes through the motions of throwing himself on his knees.

There is something definitely Stendhalian about this new lucidity, and there is also something distinctly Flaubertian about the manner in which the author has conceived this part of his novel. The walks along the canal, the secret meeting of the two lovers in the inn, the mutual sharing of moods and ambitions—all of that has the same flavor as *Madame Bovary*. As seducer, the narrator is either Lucien or Rodolphe, of course, but in other respects he is, strangely enough, Charles Bovary, since he goes about repeating the name of his beloved[8] and, to bolster up his flagging courage, selects check points along the road at which he determines to speak—and then, like Charles when he could not get up his nerve to speak to Farmer Rouault, remains silent when he has overtaken his marker.

At this point in the writing of his novel, Lacretelle developed a technique which, for want of a better word, one may call mood-analysis. Originally, in his more Proustian moments, the direct record of a sensation interested him most. Now, as he polished his style and tried to write more precisely, he used the mood as a method for analyzing the psychology of the character. The following passage, which was not in the first manuscript, is a good example of this technique brought to perfection:

> Adrienne was not saying a word. She was taking care to walk in step with me. I had laced my arm in hers, I caressed her hand; she let me do what I wanted, and I understood by her silence that she was entirely won over.
>
> I felt an immense pride in this victory. To love, to be loved, was the only aspiration in my life; I was finally reaching that point. I was stopping at this objective, not at all disappointed by the price I had paid, and like a conqueror who looks behind him at the obstacles overcome, I thought of my past—of the sentimental complications among which I had so long struggled, of my fearful prejudices, of my scruples. What blindness! What

time lost! Now I had to be audacious, to speak. I perceived today how easy it was; at the first attempt, I was succeeding in making the one I loved into a charming slave.

All these thoughts were coursing through my mind. I was trembling and serious, and it also seemed to me, vaguely, that I had somewhat aged.

We stopped still. I entreated her in a low voice: "Adrienne, look at me."

The next passage shows another degree of mood-analysis; this time the author is concentrating on a sensation, but he is analyzing it rather than recording it by some metaphorical device:

We remained thus, standing, enlaced: I had closed my eyes instinctively, but I wanted to *see* this minute, and so I opened them. The line of the bridge cutting the dark stream, a tree, other trees, and beyond, the black and indistinct roofs dominated by the sharp steeple, engraved into my ecstasy a clear background. Then I saw, in the center of things, like a cell which was creating the universe, the vague milky whiteness of Adrienne's face in which only the opposing arcs of the eyelids and eyebrows were outlined with distinctness.

It would not take much searching to find a similar passage in *Madame Bovary*. On several occasions, Flaubert records what Emma Bovary feels at moments when her mind is wandering or when it is in a semiparalyzed condition as a result of emotion (as when she runs from Rodolphe to the arsenic while fiery globes pass before her vision). In perfecting what was originally a Proustian manner of recording sensation, Lacretelle had unconsciously come back to Flaubert. Unquestionably, the pattern of Flaubert's style was in his mind. Lacretelle, himself, was not aware of any change of allegiance at this time, for he added to the text of his novel a remark telling how the narrator neglected the classical foundations of his studies. The narrator concludes: "I perceived only a dried up, infertile beauty and one that I consider today to be not subjective enough."

In the plot sequence, the affair with Adrienne is interrupted just at the point where it seems about to be crowned with success, because the narrator had previously volunteered for front line duty and has to leave. The rest of the plot is concerned with events at the front and is, in a sense, autobiographical, except that the episode dealing with the narrator's inoculation and his triumph over fear is imaginary. Like the pages devoted to Adrienne, these final pages are written in the manner of the traditional French novel. As in the Adrienne episode, dialogue and indirect discourse are frequent, and all notations are succinct and direct. Events succeed each other in a natural movement well calculated to retain the interest of the reader, and it is obvious that Lacretelle has now mastered the traditional technique of plot.

Since the narrator is killed in battle, the narrative comes to a somewhat abrupt end. This would lead one to inquire whether the novel, as a whole, really had a plot. If, by plot, we mean a long-range preparation so that the action at one point will seem logical in terms of what preceded—as when the narrator volunteers for front line duty long in advance so that there will be a plausible reason for his having to leave Adrienne—then there is no such plot running through the entire novel. On the other hand, the novel, as rewritten, does conform to the principles of a traditional French "psychological" novel which derives its unity of plot from the systematic development of the psychology of the principal character.

As he reread his first manuscript Lacretelle came to understand that he would not have a novel until he was able to imagine a coherent psychological pattern for his main character. In a novel so deeply introspective, so exclusively devoted to the one subject of the narrator's behavior in an actionless situation, there appeared to be no other solution. At least none occurred to this Frenchman brought up in a logical tradition. Instead of going deeper inside himself for further explanations, as Proust might have done, Lacretelle decided to stay on the surface and to become a traditional French psychological novelist who writes with logic rather than instinct. He appears to have asked himself a series of questions about the behavior of his central character and then to have supplied plausible explanations.

Why did Jean Hermelin's parents misunderstand him? The new answer was that the boy was jealous of his father whenever his mother called her husband "my beloved." The maladjustment became so intense that, as in the original version but for different reasons, the boy yearned to commit suicide. After his father's death he was overcome by a feeling of guilt. Why was he maladjusted in society? The new answer was that he was physically weak and an object of ridicule for the other children. Why was he obsessed with sex? Even though it might have been autobiographically true, it was too implausible that Jacques Lamiel first learned about sex by reading the books of the family library. The story of Odette came to replace the library. In her innocence, she taught him nothing, but by allowing him to kiss her, she released the psychological tension which the precocious boy was experiencing. With Antoinette, the situation was reversed. Although she too, in the new version, allowed him to kiss her, there was no release because he desired much more. From this new voluptuousness he fled in horror, imagining that it was identical with the revolting acts of his fellow *lycéens* who had previously disgusted him.

The resulting frustration explains the psychological pattern of the book. Lucienne almost overcomes his resistance until she maladroitly revives the disgusting *lycée* memories. With Adrienne, we are left in suspense, although the original version contains an unsubtle passage in which the narrator lyrically expresses his gratitude to "Georgette," who has liberated him. In order to achieve a logical conclusion in the development of his character, the author introduced in the final version the notion that the scene of the men bathing in the river is a final liberation. As now presented, it is the culmination of a back-to-nature and back-to-the-proletariat movement which is intended to give meaning to the life of Jean Hermelin. His death on the battlefield confers on his life a certain nobility which it would have lacked if he had not achieved some degree of serenity.

Despite the fact that this unraveling of a confused and inconclusive ending was a considerable improvement over the original, it is still difficult to understand how the mere act of bathing in a river could have such a profound psychological effect. The retrospective explanations which follow are unconvincing at this point in the narrative. For example, it seems almost dishonest to hold back until now the information that Antoinette had once disgusted the narrator by allowing him to come into her room while she was dressing. The curious fact is that although this little detail about Antoinette was an afterthought and was not in the original manuscript, a nudism theme ran in a Proustian manner through the original version of the novel, from a scene of unclothed native children in Damascus, to the locker room of a football field, and finally to a crude homosexual scene among the soldiers after the bathing episode. For the sake of propriety, this scene has become heterosexual in the final version.

Reynaldo Hahn's advice, contained in some notes which have been preserved, was to eliminate all homosexual elements from the novel.[9] He objected particularly to the narrator's ambivalent voluptuousness, heterosexual for Antoinette and homosexual for Malo, and counseled the suppression of the "vision" scene when the narrator observes Antoinette in the garden. The author's reply was to reinterpret the narrator's disturbed relationship with Malo as emotional upset because of his voluptuous feeling toward the sister. This transformation was very effective, but the systematic deletion of the homosexual theme throughout the book (only the homosexuality at the *lycée* remains, since it does not contaminate the narrator) should have been accompanied by a more careful preparation for the bathing scene if it was to be so important in the psychological development of the narrator.

All these efforts at artistic unity, though successful in the main, did not altogether eliminate certain other uneven spots. To relate the monotonous life of a maladjusted adolescent to whom nothing in particular happened, except at the very end, and who, instead of fighting back, always presented to the world an impassible mask, was a challenge which only a Proust or a Flaubert would have taken up; and perhaps only a Proust or a Flaubert could have recorded this dreadful monotony with artistic variety. Lacretelle's revisions went a long way toward achieving this variety, but still a certain monotonous uniformity remains in the behavior pattern of the narrator, particularly when he wanders about Paris after having done the same thing for innumerable pages at Versailles. The splitting of Antoinette Laumière into two characters, Odette and Antoinette de Kerlon, to whom the narrator reacts in an almost identical manner, was not a happy decision because the repetition is inescapable to the reader. Probably the greatest danger, as Reynaldo Hahn pointed out, was the over-use of mood-analysis technique in the early pages. Apparently the author did not agree, for the narrator, as a child, still displays a precocious lucidity.

On the positive side, the book had two definite qualities which commended it to a discriminating reader. It possessed a high degree of authenticity (to use a Gidian word which Lacretelle had not yet added to his vocabulary), that is, it seemed to be closely attached to the inner being of the author himself. As a result of the careful reworking in style and structure, it also had artistic qualities which would quickly give rise to Lacretelle's reputation as a stylist.

In retrospect, the novel seems to us today strangely Freudian in tone, and yet, at the time that it was written, Freud was unknown in France, except to a few specialists in clinical psychology. André Gide, whose work Lacretelle had been following assiduously in the *Nouvelle Revue Française* ever since its foundation in 1909,[10] had not yet made the shocking revelations for which he was subsequently to become notorious. To be sure, he had written *L'Immoraliste*, which Lacretelle had read, but it is hard to see any but a most tenuous connection between this moral treatise by the philosophical Gide and this passionate but objective novel by Lacretelle, who, although he does occasionally mention a feeling of guilt and a "notion of evil" on the part of the narrator, never once comments on the moral implications of his psychological problem. It is likewise difficult to see how this theme of sexuality could have come from Proust, the more "Freudian" parts of whose work had not yet appeared. The only literary source which Lacretelle suggests is Dostoevski, whom he mentioned in a brief journal in 1917.[11] In this journal he speaks of a Dostoevski-like character (to use his own expression) for a future novel which continues the behavior pattern of *La Vie inquiète de Jean Hermelin*. But, in the journal, Lacretelle does not allude to sexuality, and there is no reason to believe that this theme bears any relation to the work of the Russian novelist. There is manifestly no ground for denying that Lacretelle is, independently of anyone else, a precursor of "Freudianism" in the modern French novel.

By a curious coincidence, *La Vie inquiète de Jean Hermelin* appeared at about the same time as Louis Chadourne's *Inquiète adolescence* and André Obey's *L'Enfant inquiet*. With so common a word as *inquiet* there could be no question of plagiarism; obviously each author was putting into the words of his title a common anxiety. In due course, critics were to call this new *mal du siècle* the *inquiétude d'après-guerre*. Marcel Arland is credited with having launched the term in 1924. Lacretelle's novel also fitted into another literary category, the novel of adolescence, which, as Justin O'Brien has demonstrated in his *Novel of Adolescence in France*, was enjoying unprecedented popularity in 1920.

Although Lacretelle certainly could not have planned it that way, he quickly found himself riding the crest of a literary wave, and his little book was remarkably successful for a first attempt. With the exception of a petulant review by Fortunat Strowski,[12] who, at this time, objected to the vogue for anxiety in literature (later he was to make it the subject of a course at the Sorbonne), comments on Lacretelle's novel in the press were very favorable. Three reviews in particular stood out because of the names of the critics: Henri de Régnier in *Le Figaro*, Abel Hermant in *Le Gaulois* and Fernand Vandérem in *La Revue de Paris*.[13] It is noteworthy that these leading critics, as well as several of the minor critics, lauded what Régnier called Lacretelle's "rare maturity of style." Hermant even implied that Lacretelle's style was superior to Proust's because it was based on a choice.

Already we note a tendency on the part of critics to build up Lacretelle in opposition to Proust and to encourage him personally in a manner of writing which is gradually going to set him apart from his contemporaries. For the next few years, Lacretelle's success as a writer will be due to his ability to appeal to that enormous middle-of-the-road public which is classical because of the heavy weight of French tradition but which is nevertheless in search of new themes.

It was an encouraging beginning, and Lacretelle called personally on his three distinguished critics to thank them. This was the start of useful literary relationships and particularly of a friendship with Abel Hermant, to whom Lacretelle was subsequently to be greatly in debt.

Marcel Proust also wrote him a commendatory letter in which he praised the more lyrical passages: "Pieces like those which describe this childhood, the richness of the inner life of which so little is suspected around you, the first kiss, the frightful effort to pierce the barrier and the analysis of the scruples which dictate it, those are among other things the pages which surpass what, with all my predilection for your thought and form, I could expect of you."[14] A second letter followed in which Proust claimed to have persuaded Jacques Rivière to review the book personally in the *Nouvelle Revue Française.*

Subsequently, Rivière wrote to Proust in a letter of which Lacretelle had no knowledge: "Jacques de Lacretelle's book appeared to me to be full of remarkable qualities, and especially it was extremely attractive to me. I am going to see about finding someone to do a review of his book in the *N.R.F.*"[15] Written by Louis Martin-Chauffier rather than by Rivière, the review did appear in the May number; it was largely descriptive and ended with this flippant remark: "Let us console ourselves. Jean Hermelin is dead. Long live M. de Lacretelle!"[16]

Lacretelle was so emboldened by all this that he decided to become a candidate for the Prix Goncourt. Learning of his candidacy, Proust wrote him a long and involved letter in which he said (with his usual circumlocutions) that he was supporting him, although he really thought that the prize should go to Giraudoux—but that Giraudoux should not be a candidate unless he was to be chosen unanimously, because he had already suffered the ignominy of defeat several times, and it seemed unlikely that there would be unanimity. "The same day," continues Lacretelle in his account of the episode, "I received a new message of which I made little sense, except that Proust's kindness would be inefficacious."[17] A few hours later, a third letter arrived from the famous author, telling the truth this time: Léon Daudet, who had used his influence to get Proust the Goncourt prize the year before and on whom Proust was counting to do the same thing for Lacretelle, had written simply: "I find little Lacretelle's book to be idiotic." Probably Lacretelle was the victim of the old animosity between the Daudets and the Hugo-Ménard-Dorian clan because of Jeanne Hugo's divorce. At any rate, the prize went to another, now forgotten author.

4

HUGUENOTS AND HIPPOLYTUS

TO write a first novel was easy in 1920. One never lacked a subject because the aesthetic of the period encouraged cultivation of the ego, and the only problem remaining was form. For all practical purposes, the real hurdle was the second novel if one had already poured everything into the first.

In the fall of 1920, Lacretelle fled, according to a now well-established habit, to the greater tranquillity of Versailles and there started work on what was intended to be a major novel. For reasons which we shall presently discover, it never coalesced. In December he abandoned it momentarily to write a short story, *La Mort d'Hippolyte*. This story, when written, so closely corresponded to his artistic ideal that although he did not yet have a publisher for it, he pulled up stakes, sailed for Tunis and, with this fresh start, developed an episode of his abandoned novel into *Silbermann*, which was to be acclaimed almost unanimously as a masterpiece in 1922.

La Vie inquiète de Jean Hermelin had left him a prey to two opposing forces represented by Proust and Flaubert, but Lacretelle, himself, was unaware of any conflict. He felt definitely attuned to his times and was pleased to find himself thrust suddenly into the vanguard of contemporary literature as a result of the success of his first novel. Although he needs isolation to write, Lacretelle is not a sedentary person and has always possessed a strange faculty for being in two places at once. In the 1920's he somehow managed to write in seclusion and to be simultaneously in the center of the Paris literary world. It was a remarkable burst of energy on the part of a man already in his thirties who had hitherto been only a drone in society.

However, he never imagined himself in a boisterous role. He never led a literary group and never even tried to found a periodical, which is rare behavior for a French *littérateur*. Nevertheless, in early 1920, he had yielded to Paul Brach's persuasion and had joined the staff of *L'Œil de bœuf*, which "opens every month" at a respectable address on the Avenue Victor Hugo. Parading as eclectic, opposed to either "Da" or "Isme" (to quote the manifesto), this ephemeral review customarily watered down Jean Cocteau, Henry de Montherlant and Pierre Benoit with selections from their elders, Henri de Régnier and Abel Hermant. One day Lacretelle and his friends even obtained a poem entitled *La Fausse Morte* from a little known elder named Paul Valéry.[1] When asked to contribute to the May number some pre-publication pages of *La Vie inquiète de Jean Hermelin*, Lacretelle selected his most modern passage, the Proustian vision scene at the Kerlon's house, because he realized that this kind of writing would be welcomed in a publication whose columnists were in the habit of signing "Swann," "Verdurin" and "Saint-Loup."

In 1921, Lacretelle managed to step up considerably this minor literary activity. In addition to several book reviews and one long "chronicle" in *L'Œil de bœuf*, he contributed articles and book reviews to *L'Opinion* and *La Revue hebdomadaire*, and also began in *La Revue de la semaine* a regular column entitled "Among the Younger Generation," which continued until the demise of the periodical the following year.

Loyally and with encyclopedic information, he tried to welcome and interpret all of the attempts of his contemporaries, however radical, to be original. For him, Proust is an undisputed master, and, appropriately, he begins his column in *La Revue de la semaine* with a quotation from *Le Côté de Guermantes*. While urging tolerance on the part of his readers for the dadaists and cubists, he hastens to add: "Let no one be frightened! Literature will not remain cubist; nothing will survive of this extreme form, intelligible to a single person and barbarous to others." Among these convergent and divergent attempts to be original, there may be a "mind endowed with a powerful creative faculty as well as a feeling for perfection and, making use of these experiments, completing them, discarding what is bad and retaining what is good, he will be able to produce a work which, in spite of its new and strange workmanship, will soon be added to our literary tradition."

Frequently Lacretelle seems to be favorable to the poetic experiments of Claudel, Cocteau, Max Jacob, Fargue and the late Guillaume Apollinaire and to the prose of Giraudoux, Morand, Mac Orlan and other *fantaisistes* (although he does think Cocteau's "incessant mobility" goes too far and although he acknowledges Morand's ability only after *Ouvert la nuit*); but when he tells André Salmon somewhat pontifically that his book would be better if he read Flaubert and observed "the rules to which our literature of imagination has been subjected for half a century," we suspect that, in other cases, he has been camouflaging his personal reservations. It is possible that these fluctuations in attitude correspond to a real hesitation on his part regarding the direction which he wishes to take in his own literature, but it seems more likely that he had already determined on a middle course: not newness at any cost but rather artistic perfection coupled with a profound understanding of human nature.

He had always known that one group, to which not every nondescript scrivener was admitted, incarnated these principles. In 1920 he had received the following letter (dated November 2d):

> Sir:
>
> I read in its time with great interest *La Vie inquiète de Jean Hermelin*, and I had even requested one of my colleagues to write a note on this work for the *Nouvelle Revue Française*. Unfortunately, it was a little long, and I have so little space at my disposal that I was unable to find the means of including it.
>
> I should not like you to interpret this silence as proof of indifference toward your effort. My friend Marcel Proust tells me you will perhaps write a few critical notes on novels and works of psychology, and I wish to assure you that, if you are as well disposed to do this as he assumes, I should, for my part, be very happy to read the essays of this type which you might send me. I am persuaded that they would fit very well into the *Nouvelle Revue Française*.

The letter was signed with the magic name of Jacques Rivière (he did, of course, find space for the critical note at a later date). Now that the correspondence between Rivière and Proust has appeared, it is interesting to read the letter from Proust which probably provoked the letter above (Philip Kolb, the specialist on Proust's correspondence, conjectures that it dates from the end of November, but it would seem rather to date from the beginning of that month):

> Dear Jacques,
>
> I do not know if you remember having told me and having written to me how likeable you found Lacretelle to be (through his book). Now I am unaware whether that signified (I don't have your letter at hand) that you would be glad to see him collaborate in the Review. If that was in your thoughts (and without wishing at all to force your hand), since I believe (this between you and me) that Jacques de Lacretelle is having right now some moral and literary setbacks, I believe that if on receipt of my letter you wrote immediately to him to propose doing some notes in the Review, it would give him a lift. Perhaps he will not be able to, for he is very friendly with a well-known writer, almost an Academician, who will doubtless make arrangements for him to write wherever he wishes. But as Lacretelle, I believe, has a very noble nature and is very serious and hard-working, perhaps he will prefer the *N.R.F.* In any case the moral *tonus* of your proposal would be efficacious only if it was immediate. He is very intelligent. His address is 11 bis rue des Réservoirs, Versailles.[2]

Probably the setbacks existed more in the imagination of Proust and had to do with his failure to support Lacretelle for the Prix Goncourt. The well-known writer mentioned was undoubtedly Abel Hermant.

Now Lacretelle had the opportunity of drawing further away from unpredictable companions like Jean Cocteau and to steer a middle course among the moderns. He wrote the notes, beginning with one in August 1921, became a frequent visitor at the *N.R.F.* offices in the rue Madame and occasionally went to Rivière's studio apartment near the Lion de Belfort. In these informal gatherings Lacretelle's belief in the high seriousness of art was strengthened. This was not art for art's sake, art detached from life, but rather art as it springs from the very fibers of the individual. Rivière, by his example and searching conversation, continually spurred his interlocutors to greater efforts. As Lacretelle was to write at the time of Rivière's death, ". . . he questioned others much less to derive personal profit from them as we generally do, than to help them to derive profit. To be sure, he did not lack curiosity; he desired to know other beings, but he particularly wanted them to know themselves. That explains this strange mixture of kindly interest and detachment which one reads sometimes in his eyes."[3]

These new associations produced no revolution in Lacretelle, for the *N.R.F.* had long played a preponderant role in his intellectual development. The immediate result is to be seen in his style when one compares the contributions to the *Nouvelle Revue Française* with those to other periodicals. The latter are more discursive. By exacting a maximum effort in a minimum space, the *N.R.F.* taught Lacretelle the value of words. *Silbermann*, bearing the imprint of the N.R.F. publishing house, was to show the effect of this lesson.

If Lacretelle could solve his aesthetic problems on a critical plane by a compromise between modernism and more staid classical principles, the solution was not so easy in the practical task of composing a novel. The road to *Silbermann* in 1920 was to be tortuous indeed. Since the novel which he began at Versailles that year never was to have a name, we shall adopt the phrase which he has used for it in conversation and call it "Le Roman protestant" (in the only printed reference to it, found in the *Journal de Colère*, he calls it "a novel on a Protestant family"[4]). The hero was to be an adolescent torn between a Catholic and a Protestant heredity. The subject was timely since it combined the theme of adolescence with the theme of Protestantism, which had long borne the trade mark of the high pontiff of the *N.R.F.* group—in other words, of André Gide himself. For that matter, Gide's latest novel on the subject, *La Symphonie pastorale*, had just appeared in the *Nouvelle Revue Française*.

An initial misconception vitiated the entire plan for the "Roman protestant." As though he had learned nothing about his own analytical propensities, Lacretelle started his novel like a snowball which rolls along without a destination, picking up extraneous bits as it goes. He was still relying on some sort of Proustian intuition to supply him with the substance of his novel—which had no more plot at the outset than the original "Vie de Jacques Lamiel."

The first document on the new novel is an outline which has little connection with the subsequent manuscript. It follows the sensorial experiences of the hero through a series of impressionistic scenes, beginning with evening prayer (at Cormatin, says the note). By contrast with the general lack of direction, two episodes stand out in the author's mind: The first has to do with a Protestant friend who commits suicide and the second with a Jewish boy, Georges Silberfraun, who is persecuted at the Lycée Lakanal. We shall presently see the fates of these two episodes. As for the rest of the story, it fritters away inconclusively. At twenty the nameless hero takes a mistress, who converts him to socialism. In revolt against society, he becomes jealous of his successful brother and critical of his mother, who frequently compromises her principles for mundane reasons. The only other developed episode is the hero's military training at Versailles. The outline breaks off with the hero in a Versailles hospital after he has been injured while carrying a rail.

The manuscript version of the novel begins quite differently with a Walter Scottian concern for local color. The clouds settle over the Cévennes; in a picturesque mountain inn two episodic characters, one of them a white-haired patriarch, are conveniently discussing the religious wars for which the region was once famous. Then we learn about the hot-headed old Protestant Brousson, whose daughter married a wealthy Catholic manufacturer and who has just died in solitude. This is the excuse to bring the daughter, Juliette Durtal, onto the scene. Proceeding next to the daughter's son, we discover that Michel Durtal is a slightly less restive Jean Hermelin, assailed like him with a double notion of good and evil, represented allegorically from time to time. At the *lycée*—Carnot this time—he discovers that his timid and maladjusted friend Blanchod is a Protestant, and presently an aunt informs him that his own mother was born a Protestant.

When he makes a trip to the Cévennes with his mother and his brother Georges, this Protestant region fascinates him. While in the Cévennes, he receives a letter from Blanchod composed of lyrical descriptions of the Swiss mountains and religious exhortations. Back in Paris once more, he decides to become a Protestant, and Blanchod's mother sends him to a pastor named Winfrid.[5] Finally, in great emotion, he goes to his own mother, who persuades him that to keep peace in the family he must not openly espouse Protestantism. During this time Blanchod has been corresponding with the daughter of the Swiss pastor who was in charge of his summer camp. The correspondence is discovered and judged to be "guilty" for reasons unspecified, and this causes Blanchod's family to withdraw him from the *lycée* and send him to live as a virtual prisoner in a pastor's family at Versailles. Indignant at this treatment of his friend by fanatical Protestants, Michel abjures his new religion. At about this point, the manuscript dwindles away into another outline in which Michel becomes a *raté*, has many mistresses and, finally going mad, kills his mother by striking her forehead with a wrench. In some mysterious manner his Protestantism "has been the misfortune of his life."

Although the manuscript of the "Roman protestant" was a decided improvement over the first outline, Lacretelle, in the presence of his second novel, was having difficulty in breaking away from the pattern of his first one. What this novel still lacked was some unifying, dramatic idea, something more dynamic than this vague religious antinomy in the character of Michel Durtal. In his search for an "authentic" element, he had tried to pry loose from his own character a second Protestant personality. This was impossible because no such personality ever existed. Even the place name Saint-Sauveur des Pourcils, where his mother's family estate had been in the Cévennes, and the family name Brousson (obviously standing for Brouzet, since a Lacretelle family tradition makes Dr. Brouzet an adversary of Pasteur, just as old Brousson is in the novel) had no evocative value inasmuch as Lacretelle had never been to the Cévennes and had never known his grandfather. In reality, like an early romantic, he had concocted most of his local color with guide books. Likewise the feeble efforts to draw on his own biography—by calling the mother Juliette or by referring to his own exile in Versailles—lead nowhere. Things do not come to life, and, in consequence, the novel lacks movement, even in the episodes dealing with Blanchod, whose story was to be related so dramatically a few years later in *Le Christ aux bras étroits*.

The stronger elements of the novel, which were destined to

survive as *Silbermann* and as *Le Christ aux bras étroits*, have a literary rather than an autobiographical origin. In the first outline of the "Roman protestant," there occurs this statement: "The Protestant friend will now be fatherless. His mother will be like Merminod's, having raised her children with a horror for love and the flesh." Merminod is the principal character of a novel by Abel Hermant, *Le Disciple aimé*, rewritten in 1894 after having appeared nine years earlier under another title. It is the story of a Swiss Protestant boy, Merminod, who conceives an insane passion for a younger schoolmate, George Moore. He tyrannizes George with his affection, breaks up the boy's adolescent love affair, tries to force him to become a Protestant and finally urges him to run away from home. It is at first a monotonous story but becomes suddenly dramatic when George finally summons up enough courage to call his parents to his aid. Merminod, after an illness, pursues George to his family's house at Cannes, does not find him there because he has been sent to Paris, and again falls ill. The Moores care for him until his mother, that incredible monster of ingratitude and Protestant bigotry, arrives on the scene. The crowning touch comes when she and her son drive away, the son having just cut his mother a bouquet of the Moores' flowers as a final gesture of defiance. In his 1894 preface, Hermant claimed that it was a true story.

In the "Roman protestant," Mme Merminod becomes Mme Blanchod, the bigoted Protestant, domineering, fanatical, unpleasant in the extreme. Blanchod is not despotic like Merminod, but the relationship of master and disciple is maintained between him and Durtal.

The episode of Georges Silberfraun does not occur in the manuscript. According to the author's account, he interrupted his writing at the point where Silberfraun should have come in because he realized that, for the first time, he had an original subject for a novel. For reasons which we shall discover in the next chapter, it is impossible to determine accurately where the author stopped writing in 1920 and where he resumed for a short time in 1922, before discarding the manuscript definitively.

"Silberfraun," of course, became *Silbermann*. It is at first difficult to understand how a closely knit masterpiece like *Silbermann* could have come from an inchoate mass like the "Roman protestant," in spite of the subject matter and character relationships. The key to the stylistic transition is elsewhere and, more exactly, in the short story *La Mort d'Hippolyte*, the first manuscript of which is dated "Versailles, December 1920." The story appeared in the *Revue hebdomadaire* for April 15, 1922, reappeared in a limited edition under the N.R.F. imprint in 1923, was revised and republished in the *Nouvelles littéraires* in 1925 and in a limited edition by Eos in 1926, which text serves for the collection *L'Ame cachée*, issued in 1928. The Versailles manuscript,[6] which varies only slightly from the first printed text, reveals a painstaking attention to style. If the story flows with a natural limpidity worthy of the best stylists of the French tradition, it is because this simplicity is the studied result of an enormous labor. No exotic words, no tortured syntax, arrest the attention of the reader, who therefore remains unconcerned about problems of style as such. A study of the various manuscripts and printed text reveals that from the beginning the author is the absolute master of his subject. Only one noticeable change occurs and that only in the 1926 version, in which the composer Carle Vignet (the name may be a vague reminiscence of the name Carle Vernet, an artist mentioned in Anatole France's *Le Petit Pierre*) emerges as an ex-trapeze artist—an added touch which was far from indispensable. *La Mort d'Hippolyte* is the first example of Lacretelle's mature style.

The title of the story is practically a neoclassical manifesto in itself. To return to the Greeks is not necessarily an act of classical austerity, as certain modern dramatists seeking a modern myth in a classical palliative have amply demonstrated; but to return to the seventeenth century *Phèdre* in a serious frame of mind is quite another matter. Even a certain temerity is needed to treat a subject which every French school child, who has had to memorize the tirades of Racine's play, is likely to consider hackneyed.

The subject of *La Mort d'Hippolyte* is the Greek myth in modern dress. Whereas Racine did not greatly change the basic lines of the original story, Lacretelle made some important alterations. In the Greek myth Hippolytus does not return the incestuous love of his stepmother Phaedra, and she, in revenge, arouses the anger of her husband Theseus by accusing her stepson of her own crime. Theseus calls upon the gods for aid, and

Neptune sends a monster who destroys the innocent son. In Lacretelle's story, André Vignet is Hippolytus, and Charlotte Vignet is Phaedra, but with the essential difference that their love is apparently reciprocal. Carle Vignet, whether justly or not, suspects his son and wife and, like Theseus, is the cause of his son's death.

As in the case of so many of Lacretelle's later works, *La Mort d'Hippolyte* is the dramatization of an abstract psychological principle. Later on he will suggest the possibilities of such dramatization in an essay on "The Novels of La Rochefoucauld."[7] However, the basic psychological principle of *La Mort d'Hippolyte* is not the incestuous love of the stepmother, as in the Greek fable, but rather an entirely new subject which had matured in Lacretelle's mind as he meditated on the meaning of his own art. In 1917 he had noted in his intermittent and short-lived diary, after seeing Cocteau's cubist ballet *Parade*: "We must try to move about in time and not vegetate in the small portion of ourselves which is sensitive. There are perhaps in the idea of the 'futurist' party, truths which will appear evident in a hundred years and will then be surpassed."[8] In 1921, apropos of Marinetti's *tactilisme*, Massine's version of *Le Sacre du printemps* and a revival of Cocteau's *Parade*, he said again in *L'Œil de bœuf*: "And the writer who describes in 1920 the functioning of the most modern machines, who makes use of the most recent inventions, will not please anyone a century later, because of the futurist side of his work. He will appear on the contrary singularly out of date beside someone who has analyzed the movements of the human soul or sung the light of day or of the moon." But a little later on, his hesitancy revives: "It would therefore seem that in the uncertainty in which we find ourselves regarding the destiny of things, one's duty is to welcome all attempts."[9]

It is this problem of the validity of modern art which Lacretelle has dramatized in *La Mort d'Hippolyte*. Both Carle and André Vignet are musicians, the father representing a traditional point of view in clash with the modern point of view of the son. Like Lacretelle himself, André has misgivings about modern art: "It was clear that André had a taste for the discoveries of modern musicians and made use of them, but one felt that he was bending over them and was not among them. Assuredly, he had understood that there is no invention in art which does not soon degenerate into a stereotype, that the breaking of a convention often becomes an even more enslaving convention; and although he was curious about new things, he did not wish to get involved in a blind alley." At this juncture Lacretelle has identified himself with André and seems to be urging only the mildest compromise with modern art. But, in reality, this is a gratuitous aside as far as the story is concerned, for it is André's modernism superimposed on the Racinian pattern which will precipitate the tragedy. André has not solved the problem, nor does this theorizing provide Lacretelle with any solution within the limits of his story. In the story, the tragedy will still come about because Carle Vignet resents his son's modern point of view at the same time that he suspects him of having an affair with Charlotte.

Outside the limits of the plot itself, we are entitled to see Lacretelle's answer to this artistic problem. In selecting a classical myth as the vehicle for a contemporary drama and in seeking to relate the subtleties of a modern soul with all the clarity of a classical French style, he has obviously indicated that his choice has been made and that it is a compromise between the two artistic forms. Through his personal point of view he has rejuvenated an ancient subject, but naturally that is only a first step, because one does not write fiction with ideas alone.

Therefore, let us not force the issue by suggesting that *La Mort d'Hippolyte* is an abstraction. Lacretelle is first of all a writer of fiction, and the measure of his strength is his ability to infuse life into his characters through the free exercise of his imagination. In achieving this he still accepts the N.R.F. principle that art must be a *témoignage*—a personal testimony—in order better to establish the illusion of reality so vital to fiction. This is slightly different from the Proustian belief that art should be a transposition of reality, and in this change of heart we sense a shift of allegiance from Proust to Gide. Like Gide, he harks back to the eighteenth century in his fictional conventions and leans heavily on a narrator to create the illusion that all is true.

From this point of view *La Mort d'Hippolyte* resembles Gide's *Isabelle* or Prévost's *Manon Lescaut* in that the author purportedly intervenes as *rapporteur* but not as narrator. For the narrator to report reliably anything as intricate as the psychological relationships in such a novel he cannot be a passive observer but must have some stake in the action. That is why Lacretelle has his narrator dodge around a pillar to avoid meeting Carle Vignet and his wife, while the *rapporteur*, his curiosity aroused, views the scene dispassionately and reports objectively on the physical appearance and actions of the characters. The process is almost three-dimensional and anticipates the more elaborate techniques of Gide's *Les Faux-Monnayeurs*. Even though the narrator never successfully intervenes to change the course of the action, he would like to, and in harboring the thought of seducing Charlotte Vignet, he produces the most revealing physical reaction on her part:

> André was playing a *Nocturne* of Chopin. Suddenly I saw a shiver cross the nape of Charlotte's neck. She turned three-quarter-wise, and slowly moving her pupils toward the corner of her eyes, she looked at me. It was only a flash, but I surprised in her a bold, burning and keen thought. Then she turned her head aside, lowering her glance. I felt myself blush. I had the impression that this glance had stripped me naked.

The illusion of reality is increased by a process of perception in depth rather than by omniscient analysis as in the traditional novel of the nineteenth century. Such preoccupations anticipate still another aspect of *Les Faux-Monnayeurs*, which, of course, is only a systematic presentation of aesthetic themes already sketched in Gide's previous work. Both André and Charlotte appear to be infinitely complex because there is no limit to the substrata of their characters. Carle Vignet we can fit into a formula: a father doubly jealous of his son—jealous because his second wife seems to vibrate in unison with this son of his first marriage and jealous because he has been surpassed as a composer by the younger generation incarnated in his own son. André and Charlotte will not fit completely into a formula because their characters are exposed gradually and never completely. We can see that André has extraordinary emotional depth and cannot accept the crudities of life. His inner life is a well from which surges beautiful music and emotions so elevated that he can no longer live when the edifice of paternal affection crumbles:

Je tâche à n'être pas adroit
Et ne cède qu'une âme morte.

Charlotte is transfigured in his presence. We surmise from the shiver along the nape of her neck what she might have been but for this transfiguration, and we are free to assume whatever we wish about the purity of her relations with her stepson. By making the reader a free agent in the presence of this artistically suggested reality, Lacretelle remains a modern despite his classical style and subject and, incidentally, achieves one of the finest artistic triumphs of his career.

If a character is to be understood only to the extent that the narrator observes his actions, the importance of the visual imagination is obvious; this usually implies contour and photographic accuracy. In Lacretelle's case this visual faculty remains essentially Proustian, since his visual impressions always seem to be sifted through the memory. The result is not vividness but rather a dreamy quality which nevertheless adds up to a subtle and logical impression of the character. Allegiance to Proust (reviewing the short story in the *Nouvelle Revue Française*, André Maurois[10] also thought he saw a Proustian influence) is still visible in this passage:

> But often the visual memory penetrates better than any other faculty into the physiognomy of those whom we shall never see again. Now that he is situated on an unreal plane, his face—which I had contemplated with no more reflection than one gives the face of a comrade—has taken on meaning. I see his pressing manner of observing living beings and inanimate objects, the subtle flashes of his glance hidden behind lowered eyelids. I see his lips which half open with an imperceptible ungluing or which fold back as though on a bitter taste; and these different masks, rough-outlined and fugitive, revealed to me joy, determination, suffering, in short a passion of which I had not suspected the burning flame.

An illusion of depth is created in André's case, and even more so in Charlotte's, by successive retouches, not one of which may really be considered definitive. Charlotte expands and, at rare moments, opens like an exotic flower, each time dazzling the narrator in a new way—she of whom the narrator first said: "Why she hasn't got a thing!" She is all the more mysterious because she never seems to speak (two inconsequential remarks are quoted, but the reader may well fail to note them). Lacretelle appears to believe that dialogue detracts from the subtlety of a character. Perhaps that is why Carle Vignet seems, by contrast, to be so lacking in depth, for his unsubtle remarks are recorded with stenographic precision.

In describing his settings, Lacretelle is far removed from the photographic techniques of Balzac, because everything seems to be sifted through memory. How different in technique is the following passage, which might have been inspired by Balzac's *Le Père Goriot*:

> But now that I think I have discovered what lies beneath this face, I see very well what artifices she used to seduce. Charlotte Vignet had a veritable genius for arranging around her whatever showed her up best. It is claimed that the surest and most delicate way to impregnate oneself with a perfume is not to pour it on but to disperse it in the air. Charlotte Vignet did this. It was around her that the charm emanated. Everything in the setting which I have described to you—simple and made to give confidence to masculine taste—served for a perfect presentation of this modest form and this naked face. The chairs were of a style and size which permitted a nonchalant pose without the firm outlines of the body being lost in them; the luster of the materials was prudent; the light was low, uniform, stopped on the surface of the skin and left the eyes in a carbonized shadow, but often a keen ray, come from one knew not where, projected its fire on her golden hair.
>
> And Charlotte Vignet governed surely, with an air of true innocence, this world which was her accomplice.

Gone is the impressionistic writing which characterized *La Vie inquiète de Jean Hermelin*. If the illusion is maintained that the reader is perceiving things through the nervous system of the narrator, it is obviously only an artistic convention which is as artificial as the convention of having a *rapporteur* and a narrator.

La Mort d'Hippolyte not only is written with a delicacy of touch and feeling, but it moves forward to its tragic ending with a simplicity which seems to belie all that Lacretelle learned, in writing his first novel, about the necessity for a plot. Although the death of André Vignet may not fit into the definition of heroic tragedy, there is a unity of tone throughout the story which confers a dramatic nobility on the denouement. The plot structure is not the least factor in this harmonious effect. It is so natural and the movement so inexorable that one would never suspect, at first glance, that the plot is really a tour de force and is measured quite visibly by the spaces in the printed text into a five-act tragedy with an epilogue. In Act I the characters of André and Charlotte are exposed, and in Act II the focus is on Carle Vignet. In Act III the psychological conflict deepens, and only a spark is needed for the explosion. Act IV produces the spark (André's evasion of the draft), and Act V is the explosion. The story ends with an epilogue after André's death.

Thus *La Mort d'Hippolyte* was above all a lesson in artistic harmony. It is this harmony, transferred to *Silbermann*, which supplies the continuity from the short story to the novel and explains the extraordinary difference between this new novel and the aborted "Roman protestant," in spite of the subject matter relationships.

5

SILBERMANN

NO sooner was *La Mort d'Hippolyte* finished than Lacretelle set to work transforming Silberfraun into Silbermann. Returning from Tunis, he continued to write at Maisons-Laffitte and then at Montfort-l'Amaury at the house of Jacques de Zogheb.[1] In a letter dated May 29, 1922, Rivière acknowledged receipt of the manuscript of *Silbermann* and discussed arrangements for publication in his review. A second letter came from Rivière, dated June 6th:

Dear Sir:

I have submitted your manuscript to Gide. I do not think I can describe his impression any better than he does himself. He writes me:

"I think Lacretelle's book is swell.* I have read it almost in one breath, and I am finishing it at this very moment. It is excellent; it has been a long time since I have seen anything published which has caused me a joy so complete. It is excellent through and through and from the beginning to the end. I have read it with super-tense attention (he made me miss my métro stop) without discovering a spot, a loose thread, a relaxing of interest, emotion or thought—not one incorrect use of language, which remains always what it should be, fluid, perfectly adapted, very expressive and never too much."

Perhaps it won't be impossible to persuade him to write the preface you wanted. I have done what I could, but you ask him frankly. He is well disposed toward you.

I continue to be very much concerned about the arrangement to give to my next number and don't yet know whether I can begin publication of *Silbermann*. I shall keep you informed.

* "Je suis très épaté par le livre de Lacretelle."

Although Gide invited Lacretelle to the dress rehearsal of *Saül*, gave him an autographed copy of the play and served him a martini (Gide, somewhat ignorant in such matters, expressed surprise that it was not sweet), the preface was never written. In the meantime, publication of *Silbermann* had begun in the August number of the *Nouvelle Revue Française*, Lacretelle having received 1,000 francs for his manuscript.[2] Gallimard had the volume out in time for the annual competition for literary prizes in the fall.

It is indeed regrettable that Gide never wrote the preface to this work so obviously inspired by him. His endorsement of the literary techniques and especially of the classical chastity of the style is implicit in his letter, but was his opinion the same on the moral issues? Perhaps he had not read the last page when he penned his enthusiastic letter.

Lacretelle has said in informal conversations that the character of Silbermann (or rather Silberfraun) appeared to him vividly at the outset. It is partly this involuntary vividness which accounts for the classical unity of the story. One can see from the following description of the Silberfraun episode in the first outline of the "Roman protestant" that Lacretelle already possessed all the elements of his story:

> (Frank-*********).* Georges Silberfraun. A little Jew, quite the type. Rather ugly, but extraordinary black eyes. Extraordinary also his intellectual precocity, his impatience to live. At the *lycée*, always in advance of what is being taught to him. Prodigious taste for things intellectual. Abnormal comprehension. Which make him despise his family (his father a big antique dealer).
>
> Description of their home—very XVIth Arrondissement.
>
> Desire of Silber. to be French. His ambition: "You understand, to be called Silber. and to be someone like Taine." His admiration for French Genius. What Pascal says of the Jews.
>
> At the *lycée*, a cabal against him. The scandalous affair of the faked furniture. The episode of the bench which collapses. (He is persecuted like ***********.)

* Asterisks have been substituted for real names in the manuscript.

Disagreement between X and his family apropos of S. "I had asked you not to receive that boy here," X's mother will say one day, after having been scarcely polite to S. at her home.

At the *lycée* the brother is mixed up in the cabal. X reproaches him. "Why did you act that way? You knew he was my friend."

The brother has a quick mind which, unable to get to the bottom of things, understands only what is necessary, makes work easy and insures success. "Those are my friends." And he points out in the Gerson ranks Xaville de . . . and Gaston . . . (hyphenated) who were looking at the scene and whose pretty girl-like faces possess a cruel gracefulness.

Then the revolt of S. against injustice. Pride at being a Jew. The Jews are dirty? And he cites the example of the town house of the Ganays, where his father has been and where there is no bathroom. The Jews are thieves? And he relates the scene between his father and a Morny who is a crook. Pride. He gets excited. He looks like a sheep. Instinctively he rediscovers the characteristic signs of his race. He is very adept at acting out the intonations. Assimilation of the gestures. Something like a puppet. His voice hoarse.

He is obliged to leave the *lycée* because they persecute him so much. And a few months later he leaves to make money. "Fundamentally father was right. Only money gives power." He has given up all his ambitions.

With only minor variations this is the story of *Silbermann*. The only noteworthy change is the disappearance of the brother from the final version. As a result of having written *La Mort d'Hippolyte*, Lacretelle was now the master of his style; he had perfected the literary tool which he needed to write the book that was to prove to be his masterpiece.

Silbermann possesses the same classical unity of conception as the Racinian short story which preceded it. It begins with an exposition of character; then comes the persecution of Silbermann, in other words the exposition of the situation which, despite the minor peripeties and the climactic recital of Hugo's *Dieu*, will lead nowhere without the introduction of a new factor; then this new factor turns out to be the alleged crime of Silbermann *père*; as a result there ensues a drama on several planes which reaches its climax in the long, dramatic soliloquy of Silbermann on the eve of his departure; and then the epilogue follows. As far as Silbermann is concerned, the movement is predominantly Racinian.

The concepts of classical tragedy are also to be seen in the subsidiary plot in which the narrator becomes involved, but this time the tragedian is Corneille rather than Racine. The narrator says: "I compared the situation in which I found myself to one of these conflicts brought on by a horrible fatality, which form the subject of tragedies." In having to choose between Silbermann and his own family, the narrator is obviously caught on the horns of a typical Cornelian dilemma. Although often likened, with reason, to *La Princesse de Clèves*, *Adolphe* and *Dominique* because of the simplicity of movement, economy of words and focus on the psychological drama, *Silbermann* really derives its classical qualities from seventeenth century tragedy.

Undoubtedly Gide was pleased to note that the novel was constructed as a *témoignage* related from the point of view of the narrator. This likewise is a direct carry-over from *La Mort d'Hippolyte*, which we have already called Gidian for this very reason. A remark in a self-interview at this time in *Les Nouvelles littéraires* shows that Lacretelle was giving thought to the theoretical aspects of the problem, for he says: "The *I* allows reticence, suspicion, confession, thanks to which the faces are exposed to a less crude light. Now, in this short work where three social environments . . . are contrasted with each other, it was necessary to make very minute shadings in the characters and to develop the plot with that sort of intimate understanding which only a *témoignage* can give to the narrative."[3] Although Charlotte Vignet is subtle and elusive, whereas Silbermann is often grotesquely caricatural, they have one thing in common: Aesthetically, they are seen through the eyes of the narrator, who, only glimpsing their personalities, sees now one aspect, now another. At times Silbermann is a Semitic lizard, at others he is an inspiring literary genius; at times he displeases because of his calculated servility, at other moments he is a specimen of suffering humanity; just after he has suffered martyrdom at the hands of his fellow pupils, he mocks the nurse who is helping him. The narrator will never quite know whether he is perfidious or noble. Being both, he is perhaps all the more human.

There is, however, a predominantly un-Gidian tendency in Lacretelle's manner of viewing the character—a tendency which presages, no doubt, a later development in his literary method. It consists of wishing to imprison the character in the formula of the precocious Jew, favored over the Gentiles because of the emphasis on memory in French secondary education, but lacking in true originality. Evidently this is as much a postulate for the character as the yellow skin, thick lips and protruding cheek bones. The formula also includes a notion of character evolution which is more exactly a change of attitude rather than a basic alteration in the precocious Jew pattern. Silbermann has hope in the beginning but is defeated in the end; his bitterness increases as his hope fades. This evolution could be plotted geometrically with the top of the curve corresponding to Silbermann's climactic recital of the poem *Dieu*; although he is physically defeated, this is a moral triumph for Silbermann, and yet it is also the beginning of his moral collapse. But in spite of all this, Silbermann escapes one last time from the formula and achieves the sublime in his final soliloquy. How remote he then is from the sniveling apple-polisher whom the teachers grew to detest! Occasionally one glimpses in the character of Silbermann a deep sensitivity born of wearing always an open wound. Probably no scene in the novel is more vivid and yet more subtle than this:

> Silbermann, having taken off his hat, had approached her [the narrator's mother], his hand courteously outstretched.
>
> Hardly turning towards him, she ejaculated at him without pity: "You ought to understand, sir, that circumstances have made impossible any further association between you and my son."
>
> This insult brought immediately to the face of Silbermann an expression of hate which, mingling with his first attitude, gave him a bizarre and ambiguous mask. Cut short in his bow but still bent over, his body appeared ready to spring into the air. His hand, drawn back, concealed itself in an evasive gesture. And I felt inside this being, long oppressed, a boiling so violent that, suddenly comparing his somewhat Asiatic face and his

equivocal attitude with I know not what fictional image, I had the thought that I was going to see this hand reappear, brandishing over my mother a long curved blade.

He hesitated a moment, smirked towards me a smile which revealed his clenched jaws, and turned his back on us.

Is hate going to save him from suffering? Having seen him suffer before, we can only believe that he will suffer again. Where is the real Silbermann? Is he the precocious Jew intent on outwitting the hated Gentiles, or is he an idealist who exclaims: "To be a Jew and a Frenchman, how fecund this alliance could be!" The author purposely leaves a question mark when during the visit of Silbermann to the narrator's house, he holds up a typically Gidian mirror to the character and bids us look at him through the eyes of the narrator's parents; or when he leaves us in doubt as to the real culpability of Silbermann *père* and his son's possible moral complicity. Thus there is a Gidian ambivalence in the character, who seems to resist the author's tendency to encase him in a formula. We shall see what happens to him when the author returns to his subject a few years later.

For greater credibility, as in *La Mort d'Hippolyte*, the narrator participates in the action, and it is this participation which gives such unusual depth to the novel. Silbermann himself, in spite of the nuances which we have just distinguished, is predominantly a "type" character. Not only would the nuances disappear altogether if he were not perceived through the sensibility of the narrator, but the entire novel would lack those human qualities and that illusion of veracity which are due to the echoes of Silbermann's drama in the soul of the narrator. The narrator is really much more alive than Silbermann, partly because he is subjective and partly because he participates in an autonomous plot with a psychological conflict which, although stemming from his associations with Silbermann, is of quite a different nature. In one sense, he is encased in a formula almost as restricting as it was for Silbermann. He is a Protestant—the very mention of such a word making him a type character in French literature. And like Silbermann, he evolves within the limits of the formula from puritanical altruism to a mild form of debonair cynicism. But in another sense, he is freer than Silbermann because he overflows the pages of the novel.

Aesthetically, that is the great originality of *Silbermann.* The author has created a narrator who deceives us into believing that he might be in a large measure autobiographical. Without question it was from having written the "Roman protestant" that Lacretelle was able to imagine the character of the narrator in depth. To appreciate to what extent *Silbermann* is an objective artistic achievement, we have only to examine the proportion of imagination to reality in the composition of the work.

Lacretelle has insisted several times that he never witnessed any such overt persecution of a pupil during his *lycée* experience. What happened to Silbermann is entirely fictional, although there is no doubt that the vividness of the novel is the result of the author's childhood contacts with the Dreyfus Affair. Of course, there is also a certain transference from *La Vie inquiète de Jean Hermelin*[4] which provides an advance rehearsal of the persecution scene, stemming, as it does, from the self-instigated ostracism of the author himself in his *lycée* days. When it comes to a model for Silbermann, that is another matter. In his commentary on *Silbermann*, in the *Revue juive* three years after the novel had been published, Lacretelle denied that there was any model whatever.[5] However, in a review of *Silbermann* in 1922, Benjamin Crémieux had been quick to point out similarities between Silbermann and Henri Franck, although he did not speculate why the similarities should exist.[6] In 1930, reminiscing on the world of Silbermann, André Bellessort wondered whether Lacretelle had known Franck at Janson.[7] In re-examining *Silbermann* in a lecture in 1952, Lacretelle admitted:

> But I nevertheless borrowed from Henri Frank [*sic*] his astonishing intellectual precociousness and his ambition. I even took from him a sentence extracted from his correspondence (which was published later at the N.R.F.) in which he exclaims: "To be a Frenchman, a Jew and a professor, one can dream of nothing finer."
>
> Nor is he a certain other fellow pupil—I will not mention his name because he is still alive and furnished me with one of his mannerisms—but it is nevertheless he who came again before

my eyes when I described the physical appearance of Silbermann in class. Motionless, his chin protruding, his lip hanging, his Adam's apple sticking out, he resembled these little lizards which the sun drives out of a wall and which come, with a restless beating of the neck, to survey the human race.[8]

The outline for *Silbermann* contains, in addition to the name "Frank," not one but two real models for Silbermann. Silbermann is obviously a composite character who has his roots in the author's own experience, not only at Janson, where Jews were numerous but also, a few years before that, at Alexandria, where the Oriental Jewish types made such a vivid impression on his memory.

Naturally Janson-de-Sailly is the *lycée* described in the brief introductory paragraph, for the geographical references leave little doubt as to the relative location of the institution. Saint-Xavier, called Saint-François-de-Sales in the manuscript of the "Roman protestant," is identified in the first outline of the latter as "Gerson," which is a real institution located in the rue de la Pompe. Without naming this "religious boarding school," Bellessort remarks that, in reality, the *externes* from this institution did not stay long enough in the *lycée* to mingle with the other pupils.[9] The meeting of the French bishops at the Château de la Muette is a reminiscence of a historical event which Lacretelle witnessed as a boy. Real also is the statue of La Fontaine. Aiguesbelles, transformed poetically into a childhood paradise, is inspired by the *mas* of Fourques near Lunel, where Mme Ménard-Dorian lived. Even Silbermann's recitation of *Dieu*, it will be recalled, has its origin in Bellessort's habit of letting his pupils recite poems of their own choice. But all this adds up to very little reality in the total fiction.

It is striking that in this new novel Lacretelle preferred a combination of reality and imagination to documentation from secondary sources. Perhaps it is for this reason that his Jewish family receives only summary treatment which borders on the arbitrary. Silbermann *père* is represented as a slovenly merchant straight from the ghetto in spite of his luxurious surroundings. Mme Silbermann, on the contrary, is entirely occidentalized and might even be termed attractive but for her false gestures.

Although both these types are quite plausible, the result is a singularly disunited Jewish household—which leads the narrator to make the curious observation that "these three beings seemed to be united less by family ties than by those of association, or, if one wishes, by the laws of the same tribe." This last is but an insignificant concession to the principle of local color. Lacretelle purposely did not reread the Jewish literature which he had previously encountered at odd times: Jean-Richard Bloch's *Le Tacot*[10] and his *Et Cie*, Henry Bernstein's *Israël* and Jean and Jérôme Tharaud's *L'Ombre de la croix*. In fact, he was somewhat apprehensive that critics might see a resemblance between his novel and Benjamin Crémieux's *Le Premier de la classe*, which appeared when his own book was still in manuscript. Curiously enough, he also seems to have forgotten that his great-great-uncle, Pierre Lacretelle, originally gained his reputation as a liberal by publishing in 1777 his *Plaidoyer pour deux juifs de Metz*.[11]

The one literary source which Lacretelle has acknowledged in print is Gobineau. In the original version of his commentary on *Silbermann*, he said: "When later my memory showed me again those faces [of adolescents] and the scenes of those times, I thought I saw, aided no doubt by the study of Gobineau and his thought, some marionettes held by strings between coarse hands which grouped them or knocked them together. So the day when the intention came to me to sketch in fictional form a conflict of races, it is quite naturally among those innocent and docile actors that I went to get my characters." Lacretelle had joined the small group of Gobineau enthusiasts during the war, largely as a result of his bibliomania, had written two short notices on him in the *Œil de bœuf* and was subsequently to publish various articles brought together in 1926 as *Quatre Etudes sur Gobineau*. This vogue for Gobineau, culminating in the recent designation (in 1952) of *Les Pléiades* as one of the thirteen best French novels of the nineteenth century—a decision in which Lacretelle had no small part—was a homage to the narrative gifts of this forgotten author and had little to do with the overwhelming *Essai sur l'inégalité des races humaines*, which has not been republished in France since the second edition in 1884. If Gobineau contributed anything to *Silbermann*, it was only some vague notion of race. There is no part of the *Essai* which might have served for the racial vignettes in Lacretelle's novel, nor is Gobineau's fetish of the superiority of the so-called Aryan race present except by implication in the superior attitude which all Gentiles, whether Aryan or not, assume toward the Chosen People. In fact, one may even read a veiled condemnation of Gobineau's Aryan theories in the character of the bully Montclar, who is supposed to be a throwback to the brutal days of chivalry. *Silbermann* could have been written without reference to a line of the pan-Germanic Count. If Silbermann himself has literary ancestors, it is more likely Balzac's Nucingen, Shakespeare's Shylock or—better still—Marcel Proust's Bloch, whom Lacretelle mentions in his commentary.

The real origin of *Silbermann* is not Gobineau but rather, as we already know, the "Roman protestant," with Abel Hermant's *Disciple aimé* as its primary literary source. In the original plan for Lacretelle's unfinished novel, the account of Michel Durtal's adolescence was to consist of two complementary episodes: that of the Protestant Blanchod and that of the Jew Silberfraun, both representing misunderstood minorities in France. In *Silbermann*, the author has merged the two aspects of the "Roman protestant." As for Abel Hermant's novel, *Le Disciple aimé*, there is little of it left in *Silbermann*; however, one may trace the narrator's notion of a mission back to Merminod, and one may also attribute to Mme Merminod some of the unpleasantness in the character of the narrator's mother.

As a further indication of the objectivity of *Silbermann*, let us now examine the narrator, who parades for aesthetic reasons as a subjective character. In the narrator's scholastic inaptitude and in the mother's habit of choosing the right friends for her son and of constantly planning his career, we are entitled to see autobiographical elements. But that is all. Logically we should expect the narrator to be a continuation of Jean Hermelin, particularly since Michel Durtal owed much to his predecessor. Such is not the case. The autobiographical Jean Hermelin survives only in an occasional lyricism engendered by meditation in the presence of nature. Hermelin is a psychopathic egotist riddled with "Freudian" complexes. His purity is the result of social and sexual inhibitions rather than of any profound moral quality. On the other hand, the narrator of *Silbermann* has apparently never thought of sex, and he is revolted by his father's accusation that his attachment for his Jewish friend is abnormal. Like Hermelin, the narrator is introverted, but the drama of his adolescence has little relationship to his sociability. He could have remained the friend of the normally adjusted Robin if he had so chosen. Naturally it is the religious exaltation which is central to his character at this period of his adolescence, and in this respect he is remote from Hermelin, who was, on the contrary, incapable of any religious sentiment.

It is particularly fortunate that Lacretelle was able to cast aside the guide-book Protestantism of the "Roman protestant" and to construct by purely imaginative processes a distinctly Protestant ambiance. In order to offset the caricatural qualities of Silbermann as well as to render the subjective approach more plausible, greater subtlety was needed in portraying the narrator. It is the very complexity of the Protestant situation which makes the narrator real. Although he has certain ingrained Protestant attitudes, it is imagination (note that in his literary predilections the other adolescent, Silbermann, is also an inveterate romantic) rather than heredity which explains the exaggerated puritanism of the narrator. His parents have likewise inherited some Protestant rigidity but have become absorbed by bourgeois ambitions. The son reluctantly decides that they are hypocrites and then, in a prodigal son act—ironically reversed—forgives them for being human. Because there is so much human frailty in these Protestants, their Protestant attitudes do not strike the reader as being stereotyped. The reader has this feeling only with regard to the grandparents, who remain very much in the background. By showing three different generations of Protestants, each with a different attitude, the author has avoided the danger of over-simplification.

Gide must have been pleased with Lacretelle's tendency to tempt the reader's intellect with the gravest moral issues and to leave him to think out the solutions for himself. The most masterful scene in the book is the narrator's intercession with his father in behalf of Silbermann *père*. Up to that point he had felt morally secure in his mission:

"It is he [Silbermann] who told me the truth, but it is my conscience, Father, my conscience which has brought me to you."

"You use your words without discernment, my child. Your conscience should have, on the contrary, forbidden you to perform an act which could result in a miscarriage of justice. I have not yet examined the charges against the father of your friend. I intend to remember nothing of what you have just told me, and I could not possibly prejudice the decision which I shall make."

The narrator may well exclaim that "these irreproachable virtues favored inhuman decisions and unworthy thoughts." Our own confidence in his mission is sorely shaken. In the same spirit of righteous indignation, he condemns his mother, who is trying to protect her son and her own selfish interests from this "eloquent Jew," as she calls him. Then, by a final shift of dialectics, we find the narrator hoping fervently that Silbermann *père* will be judged guilty, since it will be the sign that his father has heeded his conscience and has not yielded to political influence. One may rightfully ask: What becomes of the glorious mission in all this? The moral issues have been turned inside out with truly Gidian versatility.

Gide has said that one does not write good books with good sentiments. On this basis, maybe, he would completely endorse *Silbermann*, for certainly right did not triumph in the end. However, Gide would prefer to leave the moral issues turned inside out and would deplore any dogmatic intervention on the author's part. On this score, Lacretelle naturally disagrees with him, for his chief concern is the reality of his characters. As his novel reaches the end he yields to a natural desire to circumscribe their personalities in a definitive manner. Thus a surviving rough draft shows that he originally wrote a lengthy scene in which the narrator eavesdrops on a candid discussion between his mother and father. In the final version, although reduced to two short paragraphs, the scene has been preserved and is followed by the remark: "However, the change in their physiognomies had not been so rapid that I did not discover in the features of my mother an expression mixed with cupidity and insistence, and in the look of my father, a sort of vacillation." The author's meaning is inescapable. Whether Silbermann *père* is guilty or not (we may still have some slight doubt on that score), it is certain that the narrator's parents are conscious hypocrites. Their subsequent guilty reactions only confirm this judgment, and we are no longer free to accuse them of blindness to themselves, as we are in the case of the protagonist in *La Symphonie pastorale*. We are supposed to see only the final evolution of the character when the narrator concludes: "I had understood that the application of a lofty moral code is impossible for any of us." On the contrary, with the background of *La Porte étroite*, we cannot help interpreting this as an ultimate moral judgment in which the author clearly intervenes. This somewhat cynical conclusion marks the triumph of the novelist over the moralist, or rather it is the novelist reappearing in his true colors after falsely parading as a moralist. Gide would certainly have avoided so irrevocable a commitment.

The dogmatism of the end has its equivalent on an æsthetic plane in many early passages of the novel, such as the lengthy character analysis of the mother, and a similar self-portrait of the narrator two pages later. By this process the author confers a certain rigidity on his character which is quite intentional. Unquestionably, the literary technique which interests him the most is the analysis of character. In spite of frequent concessions to Gidian techniques, he is not satisfied to take occasional glimpses at his characters but must see them globally in their past and future as well as in their present.

This does not mean necessarily that the characters are static because, as we noted in the cases of both Silbermann and the narrator, they evolve within the limits of the initial definition. The manuscript of the "Roman protestant" contains a curious fragment which bears no relation to the story except that it is headed "Geneviève," which is the name of the mistress of Michel Durtal. The fragment begins with this reflection:

> The authors of novels in which psychological analysis holds the largest place follow a rule which is probably the worst sort of convention: the unity of character. They present human nature as lifeless matter, unchanging, incapable of any change in its constitution, and they study it in the course of the ages,

according to certain accidental relationships and certain external modifications. Is this method correct? Isn't a person capable of fundamental transformations due not only to change of environment or of vital conditions but also to an internal evolution, for example, the death of certain elements of the personality which were in us and made us act?

Among Lacretelle's papers there is another miscellaneous manuscript which repeats the same theoretical considerations and then relates a story to illustrate them: Jeanne imagines that she has a lover, even attempts to drown herself; but subsequently she is cured and has a happy marriage. The existence of these fragments shows that at the time of *Silbermann*, Lacretelle was resisting a natural tendency to make his characters too clear and logical. Although clear and logical on the whole, *Silbermann* manages to remain subtle, probably as a result of these theoretical considerations.

All of the minor techniques with which Lacretelle had successfully experimented to improve *La Vie inquiète de Jean Hermelin* have now come into play. He has learned the value of a vivid comparison—Silbermann struggling beneath a heap of boys "like the segment of a worm wiggling under someone's heel"; or of a striking anecdote to silhouette an attitude—the narrator's involuntary revulsion at Silbermann's facile manner of discussing the great men of French literature because it reminds him of the cook's remark about the uncouth Spanish peddler and his handling of beautiful fruit. At the same time, Lacretelle has not lost that special technique, coming from Proust, which we have called mood-analysis. In fact, answering the Varillon-Rambaud poll on contemporary literary tastes in 1922, he openly acknowledged Proust as his inspiration, adding: "I have always been drawn in literature by the study of emotion rather than the description of the act itself."[12] Like Jean Hermelin, the narrator of *Silbermann* daydreams after a religious service:

I liked to walk alone in the Bois, and, still moved by the grave droning of the organ, I liked to give myself up, in this state of spiritual intoxication, to completely animal-like activity: to run, to jump over bushes, to breathe the odor of the earth and the leaves, to let myself be touched by the living emanations of nature. Then, having raised by chance my eyes toward the sky, I would stop, not calmed but as though struck by love. The sight of a cloud sailing in the blue had awakened simultaneously my heart and my imagination. Quivering, I aspired to a sentiment more sweet, of more noble quality, and I dreamed of the adventures in which it would involve me.

Memory likewise plays its accustomed Proustian role, particularly in bringing back recollections of Aiguesbelles. In the now lost first manuscript, says the author, there was much more lyrical analysis, particularly a long passage in which the narrator imagines that he runs away.[13] The carefully trimmed passages which remain still give an emotional depth to the narrator which contributes more than any other thing to bringing him to life. This is true from the very first pages in which the maroon of the newly painted doors and windows of the *lycée* transports the narrator to the jujubes in the garden at Aiguesbelles at the same time that he looks forward eagerly to his meeting with Philippe Robin. Thus he lives simultaneously in the past, the present and the future, and the novel acquires in these masterful pages a truly Proustian emotional depth.

With *Silbermann*, Lacretelle emerged from the experimental stage, having learned the technique of the novel. Not that there is one technique of the novel or that Lacretelle, once he had discovered the magic formula, was to be able to repeat it indefinitely in future works: but for the first time, and with a precociousness which amazed many of his contemporaries, he had arrived at that balance of imagination and artistry which is necessary to make a work of fiction a lasting work of art.

Naturally, Lacretelle was a candidate for the Prix Goncourt; however, it went to Henri Béraud for *Le Martyre de l'obèse*. André Billy reported at the time that a member of the Goncourt Academy would not vote for Lacretelle's book because it was "another story about secondary school life."[14] Evidently the critics were becoming surfeited with novels of adolescence. Nevertheless, Lacretelle did get the consolation prize, the Prix Fémina, defeating Roger Martin du Gard, whose *Les Thibault* was in the competition. When the jury met, presided over by Mme Alphonse

Daudet, "never was unanimity more sudden and more complete," wrote Abel Hermant in *Le Temps*.[15] Critics and public openly expressed their preference for the Prix Fémina over the Prix Goncourt.[16] In the paean of praise which burst forth in the daily and periodical press, the word "masterpiece" was frequently heard.

Among the critics who praised *Silbermann* were André Chaumeix, Fernand Vandérem, René Gillouin, Henri de Régnier, François Le Grix, Franc-Nohain, André Billy and André Thérive.[17] Jean de Pierrefeu, who was continually berating Proust at this time (as the recently published Proust-Rivière correspondence reminds us), seized upon Lacretelle as the answer to a critic's prayer that modern aesthetic discoveries might be expressed in a style more in keeping with "true French genius, the sense of moderation, the art of composing and the art of choice."[18]

By invoking, however indirectly, the ghost of the Dreyfus case and, at the same time, by writing so clearly under the aegis of Gide that several critics remarked on the resemblance, Lacretelle laid himself open to attack from the conservative press. As was to be expected, the *Action française* was hurt at being portrayed as the *Tradition française*, and attacks also came from the *Revue des lectures* and from the *Revue universelle* (the latter article, a penetrating one, by Henri Massis, condemned the nefarious influence of Proust and Gide on a writer of talent).[19]

In still another quarter, the Jewish one, additional protests could be expected, but they were not forthcoming. In the *Univers israélite*, Rabbi Libert, writing under the pseudonym of "Alsaticus," called Lacretelle's novel a "masterpiece" and declared: "If the author is anti-Semitic, he is likewise anti-Catholic, anti-Protestant, anti-university and antiparliamentary. . . . His book is acrid, but it is beautiful."[20] At this time, Benjamin Crémieux wrote Lacretelle a letter in which he spoke of the enthusiasm of his Jewish friends, particularly of André Spire who later got Lacretelle to contribute the commentary on *Silbermann* to the *Revue juive*.

If there was never any opposition to *Silbermann* in print from Jewish critics, either in 1922 or later, one senses a certain hostility now and then, nevertheless. Crémieux's letter to Lacretelle, in which he was very conciliatory, was actually written in reply to another letter from Lacretelle, asking what Crémieux had meant when he said in the *Nouvelles littéraires* that *Silbermann* was badly written.[21] In the years to come, Crémieux never wrote a truly favorable review of Lacretelle's books and ultimately excluded him from the pantheon of his *Inquiétude et reconstruction*, although the novelist was a most likely candidate for a seat therein. Could Crémieux have objected to finding his own family name attached to a minor character in *Silbermann*?

But many Jewish readers did not see the novel as anti-Semitic at all. The author received a number of fan letters from Jewish readers. One says that he likes the book but hopes that Lacretelle will rewrite the end. Another offers the information that he was at Janson but was not persecuted. But another writes: "Your book has greatly interested an Israelite, an alumnus of Janson, who was a witness to the events which you relate in so precise, so original and so impartial a manner. . . ." And a Jewish woman says: "Blessed is he who stirs up in a Jewish soul the aspirations of the children of Zion." Perhaps the most touching tribute is the anecdote which Lacretelle relates in his first commentary on *Silbermann* about the young Russian Jew (Lacretelle later identified him in a conversation as Jacques Schiffrin, the friend of Gide, subsequently a publisher in New York), who wanted to translate the novel: "Like him [Silbermann], I wanted to do great things, especially to write—and, then, all was to no avail. Like him, I left my country, and today I have nothing, whereas you, the Christian, have written this book."[22]

6

THE BEARDED LADY

There was once a time, not so far in the past, when Marcel Proust used to say to me sometimes in a plaintive and mocking voice: "You are not nice to me, you never speak to me about M. de Lacretelle." This reproach irritated me. I was well aware of the clairvoyance and perspicacity of Proust, but I could not make out what directed his interest and curiosity toward a fellow whose personality seemed to me to be charming but recessive. "What do you want me to tell you?" I answered. "He was no doubt at Enghien this afternoon, and tomorrow, Sunday, you will certainly find him at Longchamp. He scarcely mingles with his fellow men except on the field of sport. The rest of the time he dreams. By going to see him one has the impression that one disturbs him in his inactivity, that one troubles him in his idleness."[1]

Thus Henri Bardac reminisces in 1925 about the author of *La Bonifas*. There is no doubt that since that unspecified time in the past, Lacretelle had inwardly undergone a change; for the man who sat down to write *La Bonifas* in 1923 with confidence and a sure command of his artistic tools was not the same person who stumbled through the first awkward pages of "La Vie de Jacques Lamiel." Outwardly, his friends may have noticed little difference. Horse-racing was still—and ever has remained—a compelling passion with him; and in social gatherings he continued to prefer a back seat.

Invited in 1923 to one of Paul Desjardin's humanistic conferences at Pontigny for a "decade" on the subject, "Is there in each literature a treasure inaccessible to foreigners?", he let Gide, Du Bos, Schlumberger, Maurois, Heinrich Mann, Chestov, Lytton Strachey and some thirty other illustrious guests of the

Gothic abbey settle this forensic problem without his intervention. Being a public figure, even at the age of thirty-five, was an ordeal for Jean Hermelin. Nevertheless, in a drawing room during an informal conversation, this scion of one of the XVIth Arrondissement's best families was more at ease, and he was to be seen often at the literary gatherings of Mme Marie-Louise Bousquet or Mme Serge André, where he saw frequently Régnier, Boylesve, Benda, Vaudoyer and the Tharauds. At the more boisterous Bœuf-sur-le-Toit, at which Proust made an occasional appearance (but, as it so happened, never when Lacretelle was present), he met with Cocteau, Auric, Poulenc, Tzara, Marie Laurencin, Picabia, and especially Radiguet, with whom he had much in common. When Mrs. Florence Keep of Paris and Washington founded the Prix du Nouveau Monde, he joined the jury composed of Cocteau, Giraudoux, Morand, Valery Larbaud, Max Jacob and Bernard Faÿ.

Tall, handsome and distinguished, he was an ornament in anyone's drawing room. With his bachelor's apartment on the ground floor of number 13 Avenue d'Eylau, he was becoming quite a man about town. The temptation is to identify him immediately with his later character Olivier Le Maistre, who makes his first appearance in *Le Pour et le Contre* in a piquant bathtub scene. "A true classicist is a romantic who has dominated himself,"[2] André Maurois was to write of him a few years later. After 1925, in a series of minor works, he compensated for the constraint of *La Bonifas* by some semispurious revelations which suggest that in his personal life the process of domination may not have been so complete. There is reason to believe—as we shall again note later—that he was still living intensely and with some of the "violence" of which Maurois speaks in the same article.

During this time he was going about his writing with the same intensity and with a discipline which was a contrast to his enthusiasm for horse-racing. No sooner was *Silbermann* in Rivière's hands than he returned with obstinacy to the "Roman protestant." Persuaded that his ersatz local color needed something on the order of a hypodermic, he went directly in the summer of 1922 to Saint-Agrève-en-Ardèche in the heart of the Cévennes to find the inspiration which he lacked. There is no evidence to prove whether he now proceeded to rewrite parts of his novel or whether he merely resumed where he had left off. Except for the outline mentioned previously, the surviving manuscript does not progress more than a few pages beyond the Blanchod episode, after which, in the original plan, Silbermann would have come on the scene. This seems to be approximately the spot where he stopped in 1920, having decided to make the projected Silbermann episode into a separate novel. All that can be said for certain is that when André Gide came to visit him in his mountain hide-out, Lacretelle read to him the scene of Michel's revelation to his mother. In an exchange of courtesies, Gide read to his host the opening pages of *Les Faux-Monnayeurs*. Gide's remarks on the younger author's work were noncommittal. Evidently it was not altogether to his liking.

Gide's sojourn at Saint-Agrève lasted only twenty-four hours, and part of this time was taken up by a visit to his uncle, Charles Gide, the economist, who lived in the vicinity. Lacretelle accompanied him on this visit. Not knowing where his uncle lived, Gide inquired of the local pastor, who was quite nonplused when he learned the name of his notorious caller. Gide was unconcerned over the coldness of this reception.

When Gide left, he took with him a slice of his younger friend's enthusiasm.[3] Lacretelle continued to work, however, until it was time to return to Paris for the launching of *Silbermann*. Then, in December 1922, he again took his manuscript out and reluctantly decided not to continue.

The reasons for dropping the "Roman protestant" were not exclusively artistic. Probably the disenchantment was due in part to Vandérem's remark in the *Revue de France* that he hoped Lacretelle would give up childhood memories and rise to the level "of still more accomplished works which will count."[4] Henri Bidou echoed this idea a few months later in the *Revue de Paris*.[5] Only a criticism like this was needed to convince Lacretelle that he would run the risk of being irrevocably stereotyped as a specialist in adolescence and Protestantism if he persisted in writing the "Roman protestant." Henri Massis, in the *Revue universelle*, only added fuel to the fire by his concluding statement: "Too many evil geniuses prowl around this precocious talent. Will he be able to drive them away?"[6] That was definitely a challenge to be original.

To conjure away the evil geniuses and to prove that he had in him the stuff of a great novelist, Lacretelle turned to a new and radically different subject which he had been mulling over for some time. In January 1923 he was hard at work on his new novel at Bormes in the south of France; he finished it at Beauvais in 1924, and it was published the following year under the title of *La Bonifas*. Before the novel had progressed very far in 1923, he had interrupted it to write a short story, *La Belle Journée*, which appeared in *Les Œuvres libres* in September 1923, reappeared in an illustrated edition in 1925, and made a final appearance in *L'Ame cachée* in 1928. It is this short story which must first engage our attention.

The plot of the story is so banal that it cannot be summarized without a superfluity of detail. Suffice it to say that Riquet visits his grandparents and discloses by his actions that he is really a problem child. The grandparents, though apprehensive, hope for the best until, spying on him from behind a lilac bush, they see that, instead of playing, he is stealing money from his grandmother's pocketbook.

La Belle Journée is a masterpiece of realistic writing, a perfectly balanced narrative which leads to the abrupt "surprise" ending so characteristic of Maupassant. There is no resort to the convention of a narrator to authenticate the narrative. The illusion of depth is not created, as it was in the preceding, Gidian works, by omission, by suggestion or by allowing reality to overflow the limits of the narrative; depth is achieved simply by the accuracy of the realistic observation.

Realistic writing requires a certain photographic vividness, which, though it tends to restrict the subtlety of the character, at least challenges the ingenuity of the artist to convey the individualizing traits of his character in a few deft strokes. The principal protagonists of *La Belle Journée*, the grandfather and the grandmother, are not encumbered with an elaborate biography but are reduced to two essential attitudes: their jealousy of each other in their affection for their grandson Riquet and their fretful anticipation of Riquet's arrival. For the first time Lacretelle relies heavily on dialogue to build up his characters:

She replaced the goblet with a glass. There was a silence.

"What!" exclaimed the grandfather, "you have put a cushion on his chair! Why it is useless; he is bigger than you, my sweet."

"All right, dear, let me do things my way."

"I repeat that a boy does not like all these attentions which humble his pride."

He had replied with a gentle obstinacy, raising both hands up symmetrically according to his favorite gesture.

In spite of their obvious affection for each other, resulting from a lifetime of living together, they will continue to exasperate each other with these quips until the grandmother has the good judgment to stop the football game between her overjealous husband and Riquet by resorting to trickery. Certainly they have reason to be upset, for Riquet is so obviously a problem child. Oddly enough, Riquet does not present so great a challenge to the artist, since the key to his character will be disclosed only in the last line; it is sufficient to observe from time to time his nonchalant attitude, his indifference and an occasional hostile wrinkle on his face to surmise that his soul may be perverted. The character of Riquet is more a problem of plot than of characterization. In order not to detract from the dramatic effectiveness of the last line, the author allows the reader to retain some hope that Riquet may not be a monster after all. He must be human from time to time; he must show an occasional interest in his toys and must show sincere enthusiasm for his acting, however horrified his grandparents may be; but when he transfers the same enthusiasm to the bloody story of the bandits, our attention is again directed without our knowledge to the impending denouement.

La Belle Journée shows great versatility in a completely realistic medium. No character, not even the cook, comes onto the scene without an accompanying physical description. When the protagonists go into the garden, the setting is described as though it were a stage. But these are accessories compared with the stringent application of the realistic aesthetic to the structure of the entire story. Aesthetically speaking, the reader must remain outside the characters, since he is obliged to deduce their nature from their conversation, physical appearance or gestures as all this is recorded by what one might call the "sound camera" of the omniscient author. Close adherence to the realistic convention may well result in a "modern" illusion of depth. Thus we only begin to see the drama which is going on inside the grandparents. As the omniscient observer, the reader knows that Riquet is an unpleasant character, but he never receives any direct assurance that the grandparents themselves perceive these warning signs. He can only deduce it himself from this passage: "He sighed, took his wife's arm again, looked at the sky, shaking his head sadly. 'We were hoping for a good day . . . ,' he said. She answered only by a pressure of her arm, which also admitted a disappointment. . . ."

This allusion to the weather summarizes a lifetime of disappointment and foreshadows the denouement which comes, not as a tragic disillusionment, but as a heart-rending confirmation that all their fears were justified. This so-called "surprise" ending really surprises no one, because, as in the case of *La Bonifas*, the characters are in the clutches of an inexorable and omnipresent fate.

To say that the author was intentionally imitating Maupassant or was conducting a kind of pilot experiment in realism is to lose sight of the originality of the story. It is not the neatness of the finish which counts but rather the subtlety of the psychological analysis and the delicate and imperceptible progression from the banality of everyday life to the complexity of a human drama. Rather than a return to Maupassant on Lacretelle's part, this short story registers his desire to be different, to break away from the first person narrative and thus to remove the obstacle of the author's personality from the reader's range of vision. In this story the author is no longer an individual; he has achieved that anonymity as an abstract creative force which Maupassant, in his preface to *Pierre et Jean*, demanded of all true realists and which is generally vouchsafed only the creators in the plastic arts.

This desire for renewal extends to subject matter as well as to form. On the surface the theme appears to be only the familiar one of childhood; in reality, the author is now attempting systematically to lean over the human soul with the detachment of a psychiatrist in search of those mysterious indications deep in the subconscious which are the key to personality and behavior. This systematic approach to the problem is very distinct from the lyrical attitude which predominated in *Le Vie inquiète de Jean*

Hermelin. It would not be exaggerated to speak of a Freudian influence on Lacretelle at this time. To be sure, he declared in his 1946 preface that he was "almost unaware of Freud" in 1923.[7] But in early 1924, writing for a special number of the Belgian periodical *Le Disque vert* devoted to Freud, he expressed a definite interest in Freud and queried: "Is not the art of the novelist to be ignorant of nothing in physiology but not to show it?"[8] In the same article he also mentioned his admiration for certain "Freudian" authors in France, particularly the playwright Lenormand.

His method of not showing the Freudian influence in his work was to adopt the rational techniques of realism and, contrary to the usual technique among "Freudian" authors, to avoid any suggestion that the human mind is something occult, unfathomable or supremely poetic in its irrationality. Under the veneer of realism there are definite Freudian preoccupations in Lacretelle's work. Riquet leads to La Bonifas; and La Bonifas, though Lacretelle does his best to make her human, grows up in the same intellectual climate as Aïescha, Thérèse Desqueyroux, Adrienne Mesurat or any of those psychological monsters who abound in the novel and drama of the between-the-wars period.

The genesis of *La Bonifas* must remain partly a matter of conjecture, for the three manuscripts, to which Lacretelle once referred in an interview,[9] now seem to have vanished. However, he has said himself, in the 1946 preface to the novel, that Maupassant was the point of departure:

> I first conceived this work in the form of a short story: The tale of a woman whose fellow citizens suddenly raise her to the clouds for the good qualities inherent in the defects which caused her to be dishonored up until then. If one wishes, the sudden change of fortune of Boule de Suif, but in reverse order. And of this aspect there remain in the novel certain threads of caricature and certain intentional arrangements made by an author laughing up his sleeve.

Lacretelle never revoked his initial decision to build the narrative around this typical Maupassant antithesis of La Bonifas, the social outcast who becomes a national heroine. But this antithesis ceases to be the main point of the story, or at least the second half of the antithesis becomes so extraneous to the main idea of the novel that one almost regrets that this final part was ever written.

The author's real concern is to analyze the character of Marie Bonifas, the homely old maid whom the provincial town of Vermont has ostracized. In order to achieve a total understanding of her character, the author starts with her childhood. A physically unattractive child from the very beginning, Marie is the daughter of a silent and indifferent old army officer living alone in a great town house. The one ray of happiness in the child's life is the new maid Reine, on whom she fastens all her affections. Reine's suicide, as the result of her affair with old Commandant Bonifas, is the great tragedy of Marie's life. Very possessive, she really craves the exclusive affection of one person and repulses everyone else. For a long time she directs her attentions to Geneviève, a fellow pupil at boarding school, but then she loses her when Geneviève leaves school and marries.

At the death of her father, Marie takes over the house in Vermont, and, being wealthy and of marriageable age, she has a few suitors—whom she repulses. Still seeking a replacement for Reine and Geneviève, she settles her affections on a poor girl, Claire Allandier, whom she makes her companion. When Marie drives away Claire's suitor, the fragile girl withers away and dies. Marie's conduct, both with Claire's rejected suitor and with Claire herself, has so antagonized the town of Vermont that she has become a monster in the eyes of the inhabitants. She nearly succumbs to their persecution but somehow manages to hold out.

Time passes. All is forgotten, and Marie becomes just an unsociable old maid. The story would logically end here if it were not for the antithesis which makes Marie Bonifas into the local heroine when she organizes the town's resistance to its German Occupiers during World War I.

Of course, Marie Bonifas is not Maupassant's Boule de Suif—although she might have been Boule de Suif's daughter. Nini Aile-de-Pie, that mysterious mother whom Marie was never to know but whose notoriety extended to every garrison city of the French Empire, could very well be the corpulent charmer from Rouen. Physically, Marie Bonifas is someone very different, probably a composite picture of many masculine-looking females whom Lacretelle had encountered. Behind her personality lurks the literary figure of Mlle Cormon, the heroine of Balzac's *La Vieille Fille*, which Lacretelle read with enthusiasm during the war years. To her predecessor Marie owes her *embonpoint*, her mental simplicity which she eventually outgrows, and also her running controversy with the town on the subject of her marriage. Perhaps also the strange physical attraction which Dr. Jacqueline, one of the suitors, feels toward Marie is equivalent in Balzac to Anathase's mad behavior in respect to the Old Maid.

That Marie's life should be dominated by problems arising from an abnormal sexual nature was, as a matter of historical record, the great originality of the novel in the 1920's. Although Lesbians had appeared before in Balzac and Zola, Lacretelle was a precursor in this revival of the subject in the twenties. With justification he pointed out in the 1946 preface that his novel was written before Pierre Benoit's *Mademoiselle de la Ferté* and Edouard Bourdet's *La Prisonnière* and when Proust's Albertine was only beginning to take form.

Lacretelle's review of Eugène Le Roy's *Mademoiselle de la Ralphie* for the *Nouvelle Revue Française* in 1921 shows that, at that date, he was already preoccupied with a subject somewhat analogous to that of *La Bonifas*. As he points out in passing, Valérie de la Ralphie is a retake of Mathilde de la Mole, and he might have gone on to mention a dozen other similarities with *Le Rouge et le Noir*. In his judgment what is important is that Le Roy modernized his subject by making Valérie a nymphomaniac, whose fate is rendered all the more tragic by her artistocratic haughtiness. Lacretelle's final comment reads like an announcement of the use to which he will put a similar subject in *La Bonifas*: "Very few novelists, taking feminine sensuality as a subject, have dared to study it in isolation. This boldness alone would be sufficient to give a positive originality to Eugène Le Roy's posthumous book."[10] With the increasing emphasis on homosexuality in the literature of this period, it was perhaps inevitable that Lacretelle should replace a nymphomaniac with a Lesbian. Doubtless there would be no exaggeration in calling Marie Bonifas a Mlle de Charlus.

It is a far cry from Mlle de Charlus to Emma Bovary; nevertheless, Flaubert's heroine does intrude her personality into the discussion, for she also revolted against provincial society and sought in vain an elusive happiness. It is futile, however, to follow the parallel any further.

Prior to *La Bonifas* there is no proof that Lacretelle had a distinct theory of the novel. However, in the early stages of *La Bonifas* he wrote in reviewing a Cocteau novel: "... we must feel constantly in our invented characters a sort of fatalism; they must yield to it, and each time they are on the scene we must think of their complete history in spite of ourselves and in spite of the author."[11] This is precisely the notion which is present when Marie Bonifas keeps insisting to herself that she is still the same person whatever other people may think of her. Once aware of the psychological forces at work in the character, the reader is conscious also of an inexorable tragic force which the author defined in his 1946 preface as "physiological fatalism." In all likelihood, although the review of the Cocteau novel does not antedate the beginnings of *La Bonifas*, Lacretelle's theory did precede his novel, since the latter is so carefully constructed to illustrate it.

While such a theory has its roots in modern "Freudian" psychology, it is expressed with a certain dogmatism and in terminology appropriate to the most classical aesthetic. In drawing ever closer to the classics, Lacretelle feels more capable of giving to his literature that classical perfection toward which he believes contemporary art should strive without sacrificing its originality.

The fragmentary notes for *La Bonifas* which have survived shed little light on the genesis of the novel. Some materials of this sort, among them a portrait of a bearded lady, have vanished with the lost manuscripts. Two surviving fragments show that Lacretelle was reading and thinking about Thomas Hardy's *The Mayor of Casterbridge* and Balzac's *Eugénie Grandet.* In describing Marie as she nurses the ailing Claire, he planned to make use of a "beautiful passage on the vision of a nurse and on the appearance which things take on when seen at night, and in the silence, by the eyes of those who remain vigilant." Likewise he noted, apropos of Balzac's novel: "This manner of cutting into solitary reflection with a sentence uttered aloud seems to me to be very successful." However, there is nothing like either one of these passages in the finished novel.

Other notes show that Lacretelle was still thinking about Proust.

There is one which explains that the asthmatic Miret, a minor character, is to become "unkind like Proust." Another note calls for a never-written Proustian episode: "The odor of mint at Fontaine Riante, one day during a walk, causes all the scene with Reine to pass before Marie's eyes." Elsewhere we discover Lacretelle thinking in terms of a subconscious when he plans a "portrait of Marie in a drawing room" in which he will show beneath her awkward gestures "the child who yielded awkwardly to the curtsy taught by the Mlles Deshousseaux, and the big girl lying on her stomach on the roof of the white house." For this portrait the original is a certain "Maggie" about whom we have no information (there was also a Maggie in the very first outline of *La Vie inquiète de Jean Hermelin*).

In the finished novel there is no subconscious. Rather, as the fragmentary notes show, Lacretelle was so close in his thinking to the writers of the nineteenth century that he turned back to Balzac's favorite source, Lavater's huge quartos on phrenology. He even made one of his minor characters, Duchastel, a phrenologist. Though ridiculed today as a pseudo-scientist, Lavater was in reality a moralist and a writer of no small merit, and Lacretelle derived an intellectual pleasure from reading him. One passage on vice and virtue struck him because of its similarity to the quotation from La Rochefoucauld which serves as an epigraph to *La Bonifas*—"Vices enter into the composition of virtues as poisons enter into the composition of remedies." Lacretelle even planned to write a passage comparing Marie's profile to Lavater's "queen of the bees,"[12] but it is not in the final text.

Other fragmentary notes show an attention to detail: reminders to get information on the advance signs of apoplexy, the external manifestations of asthma, the form of the cross of the Legion of Honor. Lacretelle is certainly going about his task in the spirit of a true realist.

His failure to write the projected passage on the odor of mint at Fontaine Riante is another indication of his intentional rupture with Proustian and Gidian aesthetic considerations. For an author who was once so Proustian, it is striking that he abandons almost completely his mood-analysis technique. Here, however, is an exception, a passage from the early pages of the novel which shows a momentary connection between Jean Hermelin and Marie Bonifas:

> And often, then, the child fell into a sort of numbness. It seemed to her that an extraordinary gentleness, emanating from Reine and spread through the air, was taking her strength from her. Vague sounds would come humming in her ear; a shiver would undulate over her skin; for a rather long moment she would become incapable of moving and would be only half aware of the scene which surrounded her. In her childish language she called this *melting*. This sensation was pleasant to her, and she willingly let herself go to it, but she had never spoken of it to Reine.

Random musing like this is rare in the novel. When Lacretelle penetrates into Marie's character, it is generally in a moment of great emotional stress after a succession of dramatic events. In these scenes there is a tragic pathos which is altogether different from the restless and aimless musings of Jean Hermelin.

Similarly, there is no Gidian ambivalence in the characters, with the two possible exceptions of Reine and Claire, who have some of that depth due to suggestion and omission which is present in Lacretelle's earlier works. It is more true of Reine than of Claire. Vivacious, affectionate, imaginative and intelligent though only a country girl, Reine is altogether human because we see her through the love which she instills in the ugly and neglected child. Her tragic end only heightens the poetic quality of her nature. The author seems to realize fully what he has done to her when he refuses to disclose whether her death is suicide or accident. A surviving variant suggests that it was an accident since, in this version, Reine falls from a chair while Marie is spying through the keyhole; but all indications in the novel point to suicide. Claire, on the other hand, takes on consistency as the novel progresses and as the sound camera reveals gradually her petulance, her self-centeredness and finally her cruelty to Marie. In the unfolding of her character, there is a certain modern ambivalence which, we are told eventually, is due to a latent viciousness caused by her humble origins. By a gradual change of the realistic focus, we cease to see her through Marie's eyes and penetrate omnisciently with the author into her personality, her motivations and even her thoughts as she revolts against Marie's domination.

Although the prevailing aesthetic in the novel is realism, there are no lengthy descriptive scenes as in a Balzacian novel; for contact with the Gidian point of view had taught Lacretelle the need for stylistic economy. The setting is always artistically present but reduced to a strict, almost conventional, minimum. Because of the role which the fictitious town of Vermont must play in the novel, the reader is somewhat aware of its shape, the fact that it has a main square surrounded by old buildings, that it has ramparts, a few towers, an old belfry with jack-o'-the-clocks serving as a town hall, a high church steeple and a few other oddments; but the reader would be hard put to it to draw a map of the town or even to describe the Bonifas house. As the novel progresses the author seems almost maliciously to invent new towers and landmarks which he forgot to mention in his initial panorama. Vague though it may be, Vermont is a composite of many real towns. The author is thinking of Compiègne when he mentions the jack-o'-the-clocks; of Provins when he mentions the ramparts, the dominating tower and the encircling watercourse; and of Beauvais when he makes an analogy between La Bonifas and the legendary heroine Jeanne Hachette, who—so he says in the novel—was reputed to have had "rather licentious habits before her ardor was put into the service of the besieged city." A town of Champagne artificially transplanted to the plains of Picardy, Vermont is anywhere and everywhere—wherever there is a conflict between the narrow provincial point of view and the aspirations of an individual.

With people it was another matter. In his resolve to give fullest attention to psychological realism, Lacretelle was this time not content to sketch summarily. Mindful of his own experiences and of the somewhat overwhelming precedent of all the realists who had gone before him, he sought to make vivid even an episodic character like the silver-tongued Midi doctor, who is introduced by the characteristic physical portrait before he presides over Claire's last moments. Sometimes the physical portrait is delicately subtle, as in the description of Claire Allandier's skin and pale pinched face. On other occasions, as in this description of Commandant Bonifas, the physical portrait is carved out with typically Balzacian attention to one striking physical detail: "In fact, with his straight shoulders and his strong legs, his body retained something like the shape of the armor and still gave an idea of vigor. His close-cropped hair was white but thick. His hands did not tremble; one of them, however, bore on the thumb a rather ugly mark: a nail cut through the middle and which made one think of a cloven hoof because of its thick yellow horn."

The salient detail of the cloven hoof has its equivalent in Marie's double lips or in the hereditary tuft of white hair which she acquires later. Similar simplification occurs in the psychological portraits of some minor characters: Mme Destrées is inseparable from her poetry; Duchastel's every act is dictated by his phrenological interests; Miret is all asthma and bequeaths the same malady to the son who succeeds him.

However, to achieve the stature of a Père Goriot, a great realistic portrait must be drawn again and again, even though each sketch may be vividly self-sufficient. Such a technique animates the portrait of an old Commandant Bonifas, in his viciousness a reincarnation of Baron Hulot from Balzac's *Cousine Bette*. His personality is reflected first through the curiosity of the provincial town, then through the snubbing to which he subjects chance acquaintances. Presently the reader joins the omniscient author to penetrate into the dreary interior of his home as he eats his meals in silence, finding it unnecessary to give orders to the servant, who has long since learned to anticipate his every whim. But this is only the beginning. By successive portraits he must expand into the passive but revolting character who is at the root of all his daughter's psychological problems. Because there is more spontaneous artistry in the shaping of this character, the Commandant finally makes a stronger visual impression on the reader than Marie, who suffers somewhat from an oversystematic presentation of her physical traits at the various periods of her life.

The type of realism so far described differs little from that which gave *La Belle Journée* its artistic unity. In *La Bonifas*, however, the sound-camera technique is restricted to the secondary characters. Marie's psyche is assembled by a process of systematic analysis always expressed from the point of view of the omniscient author. From the very first pages Lacretelle's new theory of the novel becomes operative. "A novelist who wishes to paint a character and does not take him in the egg has always seemed to me to omit the primary task," he says in one of his frequent interventions. Without ever shifting focus (as Flaubert does in turning from Charles Bovary to Emma after their marriage), he scrutinizes relentlessly every act of Marie Bonifas from the egg to the grave in order to leave nothing in her character subject to chance. On the accuracy of the analysis and on the author's ability to imagine dramatic situations to support the analysis depends the illusion of reality.

In creating Marie Bonifas, the author has said that he had "almost to sketch a sexual theory."[13] With all his omniscient interventions, he never formulates this theory, and consequently it gains in subtlety what it lacks in precision. The big question is whether or not Marie is a Lesbian and whether, for that matter, there is, psychologically speaking, a Lesbian type. To this there is no answer since the term "Lesbian" is never mentioned in the novel. By occasional touches the author does suggest that there may be in Marie's nature certain sexual dispositions. As a child, she scratches her breast to make herself more interesting to her "shepherdess" at the boarding school, and throughout the novel, breasts have some subtle significance until—like the bathing scene in *La Vie inquiète de Jean Hermelin*—there is a vague sort of liberation when the Italian woman asks Marie, who has become the local divinity, to examine her infected breast. Similarly, kissing runs through the novel as a sort of sexual leitmotiv, culminating in the final kiss from Claire when she lies dying. Except for these secondary manifestations, Marie seems rather to be completely asexual as she discovers herself when, after having provoked the advances of Rose, the corset-maker, she is incapable of responding to them.

If there is a sexual theory in the novel, it is entirely subordinate to a behavioristic theory of the emotions. Perhaps the author really means his statement to be taken negatively: that the so-called abnormalities of Marie are not sexual at all but are emotional behavior coming about from purely environmental forces. As a child, Marie's oversized head, protuberant forehead (Lavater again), double lips and badly combed hair do not explain her silence, her timidity and her amorphousness; for a child in the proper environment can be oblivious to such handicaps. On the other hand, when she sits silently moving her thick lips or runs in the garden uttering animal-like cries, we are given to understand that this is the result both of the neglect and of the example of her indifferent parent and his silent maid.

When Reine automatically showers on the neglected child all the affection which a normal child would expect but which this one had never known, the result is a strong emotional fixation arousing fierce jealousy reactions in the child if her emotional desire is thwarted. Since Reine is physically attractive to men, it is particularly the male of the species with a special glint in his eye who runs athwart the child's emotions. First her father, then the soldiers of the local garrison and finally her father again in the episodes preceding Reine's death cause her to hate the "dog" race, as she comes symbolically to imagine it. Like the cat who has been attacked by a dog, she will spend her life fighting back. However, it is a futile struggle, since in destroying Reine the male of the species has already won the battle.

Marie will go through life seeking, but never finding, a replacement for Reine, because her unquenchable thirst for affection requires complete domination and possession, the same tactics which served from time to time to embitter her relations with Reine. A second time she loses her prey to the hated other sex when Geneviève, her shepherdess, leaves the convent to marry. A third time, by superhuman efforts, she saves Claire for herself only to destroy her through moral suffocation. During the final stages of the struggle, society arrays itself on the side of the male, branding Marie as a Lesbian. She even succumbs momentarily to the force of suggestion and summons Rose. When she repulses the corset-maker, the character portrait is complete. There is no doubt that the conflict with the parent in early childhood explains all the so-called abnormalities.

The character is the result of an unending analysis which is the substance of the novel. The simplest examples of the analytical process are found in those passages which accelerate and condense time to bridge the gap from one event to another. It is noteworthy that even here action assists analysis:

> But in spite of all her afflictions, this independence was too well in accord with Marie's character for her anxiety to last,

Soon the satisfaction of making decisions and of running things healed her wound. She became promptly the mistress of the household. Immediately after the death of her father, she dismissed Jeanne and definitively engaged as a servant the honest and punctual woman who had been serving as a nurse. Now Marie bustles around everywhere, inspects the attic, the wine cellar, the linen closets, makes an inventory of everything.

The primary function of analysis is not to produce psychological generalizations but to create the illusion that the reader is entering inside the character so as to share his emotions. Since there is practically no gratuitous musing, every analysis registers an attitude to a specific event which has its importance in the total structure. In the following passage there is a vestige of mood-analysis, but here also we have really a specific attitude toward a specific event:

> However, as Mme Destrées spoke, Marie felt herself fascinated. The bland voice of the Muse of Vermont, the elongated movements of her hands which were white and beautiful, her eyes especially, big eyes with heavy black pupils over which the eyelids fluttered sadly, captivated Marie's attention. She felt in the nape of her neck a cottony softness. As Mme Destrées had paused, she tried to speak but could not.

More frequently the analysis records the moment when, in response to a definite situation, the emotion crystallizes into a significant attitude:

> Marie, as she listened to her, felt something inside her rise up against the opinion of the foreigner. She had never felt up until now this particular susceptibility, but so acutely did this last remark wound a certain fiber in her that she could not prevent herself from giving a start. She proudly looked the tall blonde girl up and down, and, flattered still by the respect which the gendarmes had shown her, she was on the point of cutting her short by declaring: "My father is a commandant."

One could continue to enumerate other ways of penetrating into the character: by interior monologue, for example. Rarely does dialogue serve this purpose, however, for it seems to be reserved for incidental conversation as part of the atmosphere of a "scene" (in a theatrical sense). Such is the case in the dramatic scene with the suitor Chenevis wherein the drama is in the attitudes of the characters and hardly in what they say.

Action never supersedes character analysis; rather, the entire purpose of action is to produce an emotional situation in which the character will react more violently and thereby disclose himself more fully. During action the author never relaxes for a moment his analysis of the inner struggle. When Chenevis comes to get Claire back, we see this process in motion:

> . . . It was he.
>
> For a minute Marie Bonifas was bewildered. . . . He was going to throw himself on Claire and carry her off. She thought for a moment of escaping into her bedroom with her and of barricading herself there. Suddenly, with the gesture of someone who accepts battle, she ordered him to be shown in.
>
> The visitor, who had no doubt thought that he would find Claire Allandier in the kitchen, showed signs of hesitation when he found himself on the threshold of the living room, in the presence of two women. He made a deep bow and then came forward awkwardly on the slippery floor. Marie Bonifas, standing in the middle of the room, held out her hand to him with no apparent emotion and invited him to sit down.
>
> He was a fellow whose average height, large regular bones and low forehead indicated peasant origins; but one could see from a certain assurance, a certain hardness, in his physiognomy that he had mingled with city people.
>
> After having found a few words of excuse, he looked at Claire, saying: "I have come to see you, Claire. So your health is not good?"
>
> [Instead of Claire, it is Marie who answers, and the conversation becomes apparently trivial.]
>
> Marie let him talk. A curious expression showed on her face: scorn, irony, an air of victory. The anxiety which she had felt when first affronting this man had disappeared. . . .
>
> [The conversation continues with further trivialities. Then Marie puts an end to the interview.]

"Visits always tire sick people a little. In the interest of her health, it is better for her not to receive, you understand."

Chenevis felt that he was being driven away—driven away in a definitive manner. He stopped abruptly. His eyelids blinked. He suddenly thought that he had done nothing that he had decided to do in coming; he had not even been able to talk to Claire. "That other one has made fun of me, she has played with me like a mouse," he said to himself, raising his head and looking at Marie. At this idea a sudden fury seized him. The muscles of his jaws began to tremble; his lower lip stuck out. He turned around toward Marie Bonifas, looked her straight in the face, and holding her in his gaze as though in a steel vice, he said in a brutal and hollow-sounding manner: "So it's true what they say?"

To appreciate more fully how the dramatic action is all internal, although dependent on external events for consistency and emotional depth, one has only to examine the chapter wherein Marie is a hunted beast going mad in her barricaded house. The only thing which saves her is her will power and the chance of escaping into the fields at night.

To say, as Lacretelle did in his 1946 preface, that the life of Marie Bonifas is essentially a tragedy is slightly misleading. Through the first two *parts* (as the three major divisions of the novel are called) the action moves forward with a dramatic tension and artistic harmony worthy of the greatest tragic fiction. But then the antithesis intervenes, the apotheosis of Marie Bonifas. At this point the author finally planned to replace tragic intensity with irony, thus maintaining a unity of tone. Like so many other novels, this one grew of its own momentum in a different direction from the one which its creator had foreseen, so that irony was unseemly in the midst of this objectivity. Unfortunately for the artistic unity of the novel, the pendulum swings too far in the opposite direction; in avoiding irony, the author falls into what seems almost to be sentimentality and, in a general amnesty, forgives society for its mistreatment of his heroine. No longer are there any wicked people, but all become good in their admiration for Marie's noble leadership during the German Occupation. In failing to say how stupid an infatuated public can be, the author seems to show the same lack of discrimination as Marie herself, who soon warms up to the new character which society has created for her. There is no lack of action. Marie goes on a solitary embassy to save the city from destruction by the advancing Germans and later engages in a battle to the death with a German soldier who tries to rape her. But the action is episodic since there is no longer any psychological conflict; Marie accepts her heroic personality and makes the best of it. Only when her life has nearly run its course does she realize that it is still unfulfilled, and she weeps at the graduation ceremony in her old school: "And Marie Bonifas, having no doubt discerned the thoughts of these young beings at the sight of a fat lady in tears, suddenly understood what separated her from these virgins to whom she had thought herself to be similar." Thus the novel concludes on a tragic note, but only after we have lost sight of the tragedy.

One might say—to borrow Lacretelle's phrase from the 1946 preface—that the defects of the novel are inherent in its good qualities. Up to the end of part two, it is a superb novel of analysis. Then, after a masterful and delightfully humorous account of Marie's indifference to the war which the males of the species are waging against each other, there comes the unexpected letter from Mme Destrées inviting her to join a local committee of mutual assistance. "At the end of the first session, Marie Bonifas seemed to preside over the meeting," the author asserts without comment. It seems as though he has surmounted this important psychological hurdle with too much alacrity, even though the entire chapter on the Cité Blanche was written with this brusque transition in mind. (The Cité Blanche is a Swiss boarding school which Marie attends in her late teens; for a brief period she becomes the chief organizer of the work projects at the school.) To accumulate in this third part other examples of Marie's leadership without the penetrating analysis to which the first two parts of the novel have accustomed us serves only to overtax our credulity.

The style of the novel is remarkable for its sobriety; there is no flashy writing, not even an occasional image. At the same time there are unusual structural qualities which set this novel apart and remind one of the master of structure, Flaubert. The narrative is divided into three almost equal parts: childhood and adolescence;

womanhood; maturity and old age. The first two parts have five chapters each, the last part only four. Each chapter is a semi-autonomous unit focused on a single dramatic action; it begins with a slow, analytical introduction and, in ending, gradually tapers off as the action vanishes into a contemplative attitude of the character which also denotes a passing of time.

The second chapter will serve as an example. It begins with generalities about Marie's attitude towards her father, becomes more precise as she perceives the glint in her father's and in the soldiers' eyes, and then moves forward to a dramatic action when the child begins to sense some mystery in the household; the climax is Reine's death and the curse of the woman in black; then the chapter tapers off, perhaps a little more abruptly than usual, as "cringing with fear, she [Marie] crossed her little arms on her chest, as if to protect her flesh from this unspeakable encounter."

Among the first ten chapters, only one, the fourth, fails to have a dramatic impact, simply because the action on which it focuses, the visit to the cottage of the wife-beater, is of a rather trivial nature; but the structure remains the same. On the other hand, in the third part, chapter twelve is the only one which comes even to a dilatory focus. That is doubtless one reason why the third part lacks the dynamic movement of the first two parts. As a whole, the novel comes to a focus at the end of the second part when Marie repulses Rose and resolves to resist the moral disintegration which the persecution of the townspeople is forcing upon her. In this sense, all of the third part is a tapering off for the entire novel and need not have the dramatic qualities of the first two parts.

The same process of ending in a delicate flourish of the pen extends to the paragraphs as well. It is a stylistic habit which has gradually grown on the author since *La Mort d'Hippolyte*; examples of it abound in *Silbermann*. One has only to compare the quotation from *La Mort d'Hippolyte* recorded on page 59 with the following extract from *La Bonifas* to see that the method of tapering off is the same:

> Claire Allandier had delicate and deceptive features. At first glance she presented the appearance of the most verdant youth. A way of tipping her head, a skin covered with an impalpable

bloom, small and pale lips, the thin bridge of her nose, the veins which showed through at her temples, gave her, so it seemed at first, a face hardly formed, a true child's face. But, in the long run, this coloring and these lips appeared too pale, these nostrils strangely pinched; the blue of the veins, piercing through a diaphanous tissue and deprived of the sap of life, stood out like the rare color of a poison; and all the prettiness of this face ended up by inspiring one with a sort of anxiety mingled with pity.

Opening *Madame Bovary* at random, one takes only a moment to find a similar passage:

In country style, she offered him something to drink. He refused, she insisted, and finally he agreed, laughing, to take a glass of cordial with her. So she went and got a bottle of curaçao from the cupboard, took down two little glasses, filled one of them to the brim, scarcely poured anything in the other and, after having clinked glasses, put it to her mouth. As it was almost empty, she leaned back to drink; and, her head back, her lips puckered out, her neck stretched, she laughed because she felt nothing while the end of her tongue, passing between her delicate teeth, licked with little strokes the bottom of the glass.

Now let us observe the same procedure on a larger scale. Here is the conclusion of Chapter II of *La Bonifas*:

The first impressions which the memory retains, our most distant recollections, are always associated with some vision of fire, of light, of a glimmering ray. Later when Marie Bonifas, relegated to the solitude of the accursed, reflecting on her fate and examining her own feelings, retraced in her mind the course of her life, she finally saw the incarnadine wood of Fontaine Riante and, in the radiant redness of the evening, the picture of Reine stretched on a meadow at the foot of a blooming peach tree, her bosom uncovered.

Compare this with the tapering-off paragraph of Chapter VIII, first part, in *Madame Bovary*:

> The memory of this ball gave Emma something to do. Every time Wednesday came around, she said to herself on waking: "Ah! a week ago—a fortnight ago—three weeks ago, I was there!" And, little by little, physiognomies blended in her memory; she forgot the tune of the quadrilles; she no longer saw so clearly the liveries and the suites of rooms; a few details departed, but the longing remained.

The two passages, though dissimilar in subject, bear a striking but unconscious similarity of theme and internal rhythm. There is no doubt that the best way to describe the style of *La Bonifas* is to call it Flaubertian; between the two authors there is an unusual affinity of minds.

Although he may not have been consciously aware of returning for inspiration to any specific author in the tradition of the French novel, Lacretelle certainly knew that the form of his novel was archaic. Otherwise, inspired perhaps by Gobineau about whom he was continuing to write at this time, he would not have exaggerated the archaic qualities by frequently admonishing the gentle reader to heed his future plans and judge his intentions. "The reader will judge later whether or not Marie Bonifas's conduct was determined by the noble sentiment which we have just seen dawning in her," he says. Such intervention, though frequent, could be excused on the ground of literary playfulness, even in the scabrous scene between Marie and Rose wherein the author appeals directly to the reader to decide whether this is a "brusque awakening of decency" or a "sudden intuition which has reversed the order of things." But when he causes his main character to reflect on the literary significance of his book, a certain artificiality is inescapable, for Marie is the last person on earth qualified to have literary opinions:

> Marie Bonifas had become interested in reading certain novels which set forth at length a woman's life. But none, so to speak, had satisfied her. The authors of these novels told this story as if, having to study a stone, they related that a kick had sent the

stone into a ravine, that the water had dragged it along, then that it had lodged in a hollow until the moment when another circumstance had transported it elsewhere, and so forth. From time to time, a glance at the stone, a remark on the color and the form that it had taken, but, in the last analysis, the novel retraced much more the road traversed than the history of the stone itself. And Marie, who distinguished no stages in her past, who had the feeling that all the romanticism in her life had been formed and was continuing to be formed around a nucleus which no external influence violated, would have liked to know better the nature of the stone itself.

To want to know more about the nature of the stone brings the novel right back to the twentieth century, but to insist dogmatically, as Marie continues to do through the rest of the book, that the stone never changes makes the novel subservient to a psychological theory which has not been proved and which probably never can be. Does Marie remain permanent in the last half of the novel as her hate for the male of the species subsides and as she accepts the role of national heroine which an adulating society foists upon her? The point is debatable even on the basis of the evidence within the novel itself. The fact of the matter is that the novel is a faithful image of life, and one does not regret the theory so much as one does the dogmatic insistence on it.

Lacretelle thought—and continues to think—that *La Bonifas* was his greatest novel. It was therefore disappointing to him that the critics were not as unstinting in their praise of it as they had been of *Silbermann*. If he had read only Jean de Pierrefeu, his loudest supporter at this time, he would have been persuaded that *La Bonifas* was one of the greatest literary events of the twentieth century.[14] Henri Bidou, Albert Thibaudet, Pierre Lœwel, Jacques Patin, Gérard d'Houville, Henri Martineau, Louis Martin-Chauffier and Albéric Cahuet still used very complimentary language, but Henri de Régnier, André Chaumeix, Jean Le Meur and Franc-Nohain were more reserved.[15] Fernand Vandérem urged the author to suppress the third part of the novel altogether, and René Gillouin, André Thérive, André Beaunier and John Charpentier registered strong objections to the psychological theories.[16] Edmond Jaloux and André Billy even went so far as to say that Lacretelle lacked the "quiver" necessary to a great novelist.[17] The criticism of Paul Souday, Alfred Colling, Robert Kemp, Louis Laloy, Maurice Martin du Gard, Raymond Escholier, René Lalou and Jean Remon was even more devastating.[18] Nevertheless, the multiplicity of these articles, their prominence and their respectful tone attest to the literary eminence of Lacretelle at this time. Even in adverse criticism, he was treated as one of the leading authors of his day.

7

ERMENONVILLE

IN a short story which Lacretelle was to publish in three different forms in 1926 and 1927, there appears a character named Damville:

> Although he is more than thirty, he still passes for a young author in the literary world. He has published two novels, of which the least that one can say is that they are written with a concern for style. For that reason he has been honored with a benevolent attitude from his elders, who were in fear of becoming out of date. At the same time, certain psychological investigations, which correspond to the taste of the day, have brought him nearer to the younger generation.
>
> . . . His physiognomy has not displeased people, for they have taken his nonchalance to be a penchant for dreaming and a certain retiring manner to be a modest mien. Furthermore, there is something secret in his sentimental life. Such is this Damville who tries to escape from curious women.[1]

One would be interested in knowing what Damville intends to write next, but he seems not to be too sure himself as he describes vaguely his plan for a "history of the amorous sentiment through the ages." Reading between the lines, one has the feeling that Damville is less concerned with his next major work than he is with his relations with himself, on one hand, and with curious women, on the other.

Whether or not Damville and Lacretelle are one and the same person, the fact remains that after 1925 the predominant note in Lacretelle's work is a new and, at times, undisciplined lyricism which contrasts remarkably with the chastened restraint of *La Bonifas*. Is it a momentary intellectual relaxation which developed for a time into a habit, or is it a search for a new literary form intermediate between the essay and fiction? Undoubtedly, it is a little of both.

The change is partly the result of what one might call an author's market. As an author who had arrived, Lacretelle continually received solicitations from publishers, generally minor ones, for the privilege of printing any kind of text in a limited edition, since it went without saying that any major work would automatically be snatched up by Gallimard or some other leading publisher. Of course, even Gallimard did not disdain collector's items, since it was he who published *La Mort d'Hippolyte* with a lithograph by Marie Laurencin in 1923, *Silbermann* with illustrations by J.-E. Laboureur in 1925, and *La Bonifas* with lithographs by Yvonne Préveraud in 1929. *La Belle Journée* appeared with etchings by Charles Laborde under the imprint "Au sans pareil" in 1925; Emile-Paul brought out *La Vie inquiète de Jean Hermelin* with engravings by Pierre Falké in 1926; and the same year D. Galanis illustrated a new edition of *La Mort d'Hippolyte* for Eos. To the minor publishers went small collections of articles: *Quatre Etudes sur Gobineau* and *Trébuchet*, both published by La Lampe d'Aladin at Liège in 1926; *Aperçus*, Marcelle Lesage, 1927; and *Etudes*, Librairie Picart, 1928.

Between *La Bonifas* and *Les Hauts Ponts*, only one Lacretelle text, *Amour nuptial*, was to appear directly in a popular edition without acquiring first the imprint of a minor publisher in a limited edition; and, what is more significant, it was the solicitations of minor publishers which were the pretext for some of the more original texts of this period. Such was the case for the very first text to appear after *La Bonifas*.

In late 1924 or early 1925, Emile Chamontin, publishing under the imprint "Le Livre," asked Lacretelle to write a preface for a limited edition of Rousseau's *Rêveries du promeneur solitaire*. Because Rousseau had been a favorite with him back in Janson days, he consented, and in February 1925, with *La Bonifas* completed and in the hands of the publisher, he betook himself to the icy solitude of Rousseau's Ermenonville with two volumes of the eighteenth century philosopher in his luggage. For anyone else, it would have been heroic treatment, but this was precisely the kind of escape which Lacretelle needed to find a new inspiration.

The result was *Dix Jours à Ermenonville*, which first appeared in the *Nouvelle Revue Française* for May 1925, was republished separately by Chamontin in 1926 and finally reappeared with Rousseau's text the same year. This highly original essay was not to remain buried, however, since it came out once more in 1927 as a substantial part of the collection *Aparté*, which has found a definitive place in Lacretelle's work.

One can imagine Lacretelle, in the cold of Ermenonville, sitting in an uncomfortable chair before an uneven table such as one finds in country hotels, as the fire crackles on the hearth. He has reread not only his text but also the *Dialogues* and parts of the *Confessions*. He lays pen to paper and begins to write in his most polished *N.R.F.* style:

> I have often wondered what we would think of Rousseau if we knew only his *Rêveries du promeneur solitaire*. Sensations so pure, a tone so perfectly resigned, above all an absence of declamation (which makes these pages without equal in his work). Everything contributes to presenting to us a man who is gentle, without pride, adapted to his misfortunes.

This tone is sustained for little more than two pages, after which comes this lyrical outburst: "Ah! How I love these souls and their confessions! How clear their movements are to me! How easily I accompany them in their rise and fall!" Despite momentary lapses into *N.R.F.* style as the author begins a new "promenade," the tenor of the entire essay is subjective, the personality of Rousseau merging with that of Lacretelle for what they have in common. Because Lacretelle himself has difficulty meeting his fellow man face to face and can commune with him only in his imagination, he understands Rousseau's misanthropy:

> It is because he has loved you too much, oh! mortals, that he flees you. He believes you to be naturally good; incessantly he caresses you in his dreams. Be sincere with yourselves, and you will understand why, when someone went up to the fourth floor of the rue Plâtrière to make the acquaintance of the friend of the human species and asked for Rousseau, a mistrustful face appeared at the door grating, while a rude voice answered: "He isn't here."

Yet, as a silent man but as one who is capable of maintaining an impeccable social front because of his upbringing, Lacretelle cannot condone Rousseau's rationalized defense of lying to keep face in a social gathering:

> Thus, Jean-Jacques, you lied (I am not talking about the serious business of Marion and the pink and silver ribbon)—you lied and you admit it when, having to sustain a conversation, the slowness of your ideas and the aridity of your conversation forced you to have recourse to fictions to have something to say.... You shouldn't have, Jean-Jacques, first of all because it is evil—and then, did you not know the inner beauty of silence? To let the sounds and the agitation of the world impress themselves on your brain; to keep the retort for oneself; to feel that the seed has fallen to the depth of the furrow, that it is already germinating and that later it will fructify; to listen to the harmonious rustling and to listen to one's silence—and instead of that, you put to your lips the water whistle of the talker.

Only in social comportment does Lacretelle feel superior to Rousseau. On all other points, he finds in himself the same weaknesses. He, too, might have given his children to a foundling home, since (and he relates the story), having decided to provide for the education of his native boy guide during a sojourn in Tunisia, he subsequently abandoned him to his viciousness.[2] He, too, failed to do a noble deed (and again he relates the story) when he might have saved a woman from drowning in the Seine.

Lacretelle's essay is a moral treatise as revealing of the strength and failings of human nature as the *Rêveries du promeneur solitaire* themselves. In these moral judgments, we see the classicist emerging once more. But Lacretelle displays also a praiseworthy desire to emulate Rousseau and to correct himself through self-examination and frankness. Behind all this are the same influences which once caused him to write *La Vie inquiète de Jean Hermelin*: a combination of Gide, Proust, and, of course, Rousseau himself, who was required reading for a *lycée* pupil. His novel was coated with fiction; now, with Rousseau as a pretext, he has written the most revealing autobiographical text. The tone of the essay is such that there is no reason to question its authenticity in this respect.

The story of the drowning woman comes directly from Lacretelle's 1917 diary. There is no reason to doubt the confessional nature of the following passage referring to Lacretelle's youth: "Having read everything which had been forbidden me, I no longer read anything; I was mad about gambling, and the pleasures of the flesh were too easy for me and appeared to me to be too insignificant for me to be tempted to indulge in them with delicacy."

This personal re-examination seems also to have stimulated an aesthetic re-examination. The following statement appears to be a complete negation of the author's aesthetic stand in *La Bonifas*: ". . . a narrative in the first person gives a character of authenticity superior to any other form." Dating his aesthetic program from his seventeenth year (which may be a slight overstatement), he goes on to express himself in the most Gidian terms: "And I imagined that if each one of us made a confession, if one could assemble these documents, study them, compare them, draw general conclusions from them, not only would one unmask false vices and false virtues and discover a means to useful reforms, but, by ourselves, we would tend more freely toward wisdom and holiness."

Undoubtedly there are ways to reconcile this point of view with the objectivity of *La Bonifas*, and the author himself would be the first to object to this compartmentalization of his work into "subjective" and "objective"; but the fact remains that *Dix Jours à Ermenonville* starts the aesthetic pendulum swinging in the opposite direction and puts him on the road to the first version of *Le Retour de Silbermann*. It is significant that in an interview with Frédéric Lefèvre[3] at this time he defends introspective literature and that in his essay on Rousseau he singles out with predilection the most Proustian passage in the *Rêveries*, the one in which the philosopher describes minutely his sensations as he recovers his senses after his accident at Clignancourt. All this presages a return to a semi-Proustian style in his next novel.

The essay on Rousseau is a most revealing document on the creative process as it functions in Lacretelle's case. In the account of his sojourn at Cambridge, we witness his first attempts to formulate sensations in words. As he dwells from time to time on other moral islands in Provence or at Provins (like Rousseau on the Island of Saint-Pierre in the Lake of Bienne) we learn to appreciate the importance of solitude and passive reverie in the early stages of artistic stimulation. And thus we can understand that no matter how objective a given novel of his may seem to be, it springs from his inner meditations and rarely from the direct observation of life. In a sense, it may be said that, whatever the form, Lacretelle approaches the creative problem in a completely Proustian frame of mind and that, therefore, he retains the indelible mark of his literary generation.

At one point, somewhat apologetically, Lacretelle records in one of his "promenades" the fragments for a fictitious "Diary of Claude Anet." Obviously the novelist was getting the better of the essayist, for in thinking over Rousseau's life, he could not refrain from dramatizing the perplexing triangular relationship between Rousseau, Anet and Mme de Warens. In thinking back from these passages to the essay as a whole, it is clear that *Dix Jours à Ermenonville* is successful, not so much for the qualities which make it a good essay on a moral subject, as for those novelistic gifts which enable the author to make his point by animating characters and unfolding scenes in a manner which leaves a lasting impression on the mind of the reader. The pages on the Arab boy and on the drowning woman, for example, are written not by an essayist but by a novelist.

Quite unintentionally, as he let his mind wander instead of channeling it in the limits of a formal essay, Lacretelle was led to break down the barriers between the essay and fiction and to merge the two genres. So successful was the result that he kept coming back to this kind of writing in the period from 1925 to 1930. Henceforth the borderline between reality and fiction is so ill-defined in what we may call these "reveries" that it is no longer possible to tell, in pages written with apparently the same frankness as in *Dix Jours à Ermenonville*, whether the episode being related is true or imaginary. After having confessed with disarming frankness, the author henceforth takes a malicious pleasure in jumbling the cards, leaving the reader perplexed and amused but never certain that he has the author under his thumb. Just as he once raised Gidian moral issues in *Silbermann* and then withdrew behind a smoke screen of objectivity, so he preaches Gidian self-evalution for a brief moment and then confuses the issue in his subsequent writings by allowing the novelist to usurp the place of the penitent. Even though he refused to condone this kind of "lying" in Rousseau, we are not justified in raising cries of indignation; rather, on aesthetic grounds, we must applaud this return to his basic function as a novelist.

Dix Jours à Ermenonville was a work of the utmost seriousness. *Mélanges sur l'amour et les livres*, written in much the same style but in a supercilious vein, had the effect of undermining permanently the didactic purpose of the "reverie" as a genre. Originally the introduction to Gallimard's catalogue for March 1925, this brief phantasy was also published separately by Gallimard, made an unexpected reappearance in an unauthorized private edition in The Hague, was reprinted in *Trébuchet* in 1926, and, minus three inconsequential pages and with the title of "L'Amour des livres," came to a final rest in *Les Aveux étudiés* in 1934.

Future biographers of Lacretelle may find some significant allusions in this piece. With the limited biographical knowledge we now have, it is impossible to distinguish between reality and fiction. When the author tells us how, as an adolescent, he collected rare editions of Rodenbach, Samain and Rimbaud, we recognize authentic biographical elements, but we happen to know that the encounter with the uncle among the bookstalls along the Seine is imaginary. Because of its fanciful form, we are inclined to doubt altogether the story of how he dreamed that the servant owned a copy of Loti's *Aziyadé* and when he went to ask her, found her in a compromising situation. What is one therefore to think of the story that he sold all his books at sixteen to "bear presents to other blondes whose hair easily became undone?" Obviously imagined for the sake of the subject is the account of how he put his prospective mistresses to the acid test by inviting them to come to his apartment to look at his dedicated copy of *Du Côté de chez Swann*:

> And if she acquiesces indolently, I foresee that once my desire has been satisfied, no durable attachment can remain between us. But if, on the contrary, I feel in her some curiosity, a still groping taste which I shall be able to strengthen, then I foresee immediately the possibility of a long liaison, of trips which I had long been planning in my imagination, of infinite gifts; I foresee the sacrifice of my independence. . . .

Whether or not there is a grain of autobiography in the anecdote, it is important to note that Lacretelle is building up a literary double of himself: a man who is a sensual intellectual, somewhat disabused, curious about women but also the victim of their curiosity. In the writings of this period, he will parade as Damville or as Jacques Legrand; many years later he will reappear as Le Maistre in *Le Pour et le Contre*. As an anonymous narrator, he continues to crop up, and we shall encounter him again as the central character of the first version of *Le Retour de Silbermann*.

With Rousseau disposed of and with *La Bonifas* safely through the press, Lacretelle left at Easter (1925) for Spain. The literary result of this trip was to be, in due course, *Lettres espagnoles*, but at least six months seem to have elapsed before Lacretelle actively began this new work. Naturally it was entirely incompatible with his working habits to write while changing trains or even to describe things while he was seeing them. In the fall, at the suggestion of the composer Georges Auric, he found a new hide-out, a boardinghouse at Bellevue to which he repaired frequently in the next few years.

Again the solicitations of a minor publisher were to interrupt the natural chain of events. At Bellevue, apparently in October if we may trust the indications in *Aparté*, he began his contribution to *Les Sept Péchés capitaux*, an omnibus volume to be published by Simon Kra; other contributors were Giraudoux, Morand, Mac Orlan, Salmon, Jacob and Kessel. The essay *Colère*, which Lacretelle composed during the next three months, lacks the spontaneity of *Dix Jours à Ermenonville*, but, artistically, it is much more unified. Far more interesting than the essay is the *Journal de Colère*, which appeared for the first time in *Colère suivi d'un Journal* under the imprint "Le Bon Plaisir" at The Hague in 1926. Subsequently, *Colère* and the *Journal* joined *Dix Jours à Ermenonville* to make the volume *Aparté*.

The *Journal de Colère* poses a problem in literary relationships since it resembles Gide's *Journal des Faux-Monnayeurs*—which is dedicated to "my friend Jacques de Lacretelle and to those whom the problems of our craft may interest." It is not a simple matter to say who influenced whom. Examination of the *achevé d'imprimer* of the two volumes shows that Lacretelle's work was in print in September 1926, one month before Gide's. There is no doubt that the *Journal de Colère* was at least an indirect result of conversations with Gide, though when these conversations took place it is impossible now to ascertain. They may even go back to Gide's visit to Saint-Agrève in 1922.

Both Gide's and Lacretelle's journals are intended to record the state of mind and activities of an author during the creative process. One, however, is writing a major work; the other, a minor essay. One is so absorbed by the major work that what he has time to say about the creative process seems disappointingly incomplete; the other is so absorbed by the journal that he fills it with general observations which far surpass in scope and significance the minor essay which is the pretext for them.

Without question, contrary to the rules of the game, Lacretelle was adding to and amending the journal months after *Colère* was finished—if we accept December, given in *Aparté*, as the authentic terminal date. The proof of this is in the manuscript. This manuscript, which seems to be in a large measure a clear copy of a previous document, records a discussion of the "gratuitous act" in which Maritain, Groethuysen, Arland, André and François Berge, Betz, Martin-Chauffier and Lacretelle participated. Subsequently, the manuscript mentions a letter from André Berge, dated March 21, 1926, continuing the discussion; Lacretelle replies and transcribes his reply in the journal. Although all this material disappears from the final version of the journal, it is possible to say that pages 118 and 121 of the *Aparté* text, which do not figure in the manuscript, were composed even later than March 21st.

At least two examples of grafting also occur in the *Journal de Colère*. One is the account of the murder of the Arab worker (*Aparté*, pages 84 to 90), which is transplanted without change from the 1917 diary. The other is the discussion of Bremond's theory of pure poetry (*Aparté*, pages 109 to 116), which appeared in precisely the same words in the *Revue hebdomadaire* for January 9, 1926. Because of the cohesion of this article, it was most certainly written for the periodical and not for the journal; but the date of publication makes it certain that it was composed while the original journal was still in progress.

Aesthetically, the *Journal des Faux-Monnayeurs* is a mirror held up to the novel, which, in turn, through Edouard's journal as well as various other techniques, is a series of concentric mirrors. Not only does the *Journal de Colère* bear the same relationship to *Colère*, but *Colère* is likewise a mirror turned on itself, since it relates the meditations and incidental activities of an author who is composing an essay on anger. In other words, *Colère* is a kind of journal, not written at random, however, but organized with artistry according to an outline which the *Journal de Colère* subsequently discusses in some detail. If the *Journal de Colère* did not lay bare so thoroughly the fictional origins of the essay, one would assume—at least that is the artistic implication—that *Colère* is based on fact. Since *Colère* is really fiction, must we assume that the *Journal de Colère* is entirely fact? In the light of Lacretelle's other writings at this period, a certain amount of skepticism seems justified.

Without doubt, the subject of "anger" appealed to Lacretelle because of its humanistic significance. It was not by affectation but rather through a desire to go directly back to classical sources that he read carefully Seneca's *De Ira* and then, in *Colère*, made on his own account a rough classification of types of anger ranging from a lovers' quarrel to Biblical wrath. On the humanistic level, he appears first to conclude that justifiable anger is an "admirable marriage of reason and will," whereupon he demolishes his theory on the fictional level by the story of the runaway horse. First the driver dominates the spirited beast with foolhardy bravado and appears to be the master. When the narrator passes the spot hours later, he learns that horse and driver subsequently came to grief, the driver having lost momentary control. To avoid pedantry, as he says at the same time in the *Journal de Colère*, the author submerges the abstract discussion in an over-all fictional pattern in which the narrator finds himself the unconscious victim of precisely the kind of lovers' quarrel of which he had been so contemptuous. The meaning of the fictional denouement is obvious, but the reader emerges from the story with the feeling that he has not read a humanistic essay but merely an agreeable fiction in which the author is only attempting to say, in the most bantering way, "I told you so."

Characteristically, the narrator occupies the center of the stage. He is again the disabused intellectual, who this time has a married mistress with a small boy who plays an important part in the plot. There is a certain lack of passion in the narrator's approach to life which makes any so-called passion on his part seem superficial and almost insincere. That is undoubtedly why his quarrel with his mistress leaves the reader singularly unmoved.

Turning now to the *Journal de Colère*, we meet the same personage again. He tells us what other people think of him: "It goes without saying that I was classified straight off among the *cerebrals* who, in love, never respond to a physical impulse or a spontaneous movement." His current mistress is Anne; his quarrels with her will serve as the inspiration for the final scene in *Colère*. At one point, since the *Journal* is supposed to be a bona fide diary, the narrator receives fortuitously a letter from a former mistress, "H*." He not only quotes the letter but narrates candidly in his best fictional style his last meeting with her when he still loved her, whereas she was firm in her intention to leave him for another man.

Before rejecting this so-called biographical episode as fiction, let us read the last lines of the *Journal de Colère*: ". . . I think that a good means is to write from time to time little stories about oneself and to publish them as though they were fiction. Thus one will acquire the habit of transcribing things seen and feelings experienced. The little imaginary fellows will walk about naturally in the mind with the living ones." To this let us compare the passage from Stendhal which is quoted somewhat earlier in the essay: "How can one depict passions if one does not know them? And how can one find time to acquire talent if one feels them palpitate in one's heart?" The implication of all this seems to be that these affairs are as real as they are fictional and that one would be wrong to classify them arbitrarily in either category.

Except for these occasional semifictional digressions, the *Journal de Colère* is a series of reflections on art and life, and the art of fiction in particular. For the discriminating reader, this is its principal interest. Thus we discover that the author is well aware of the principal innovation in *Colère*, the importance of dialogue:

> When I began to write, I avoided dialogue, which appeared to me to be vulgar if it was realistic, false and literary if it tried to avoid being vulgar. I scarcely used talking except to indicate precisely, by certain peculiarities of language, the *degree of quality* in a character, his origin or his education. . . . Today I

believe that the effect of a psychological revelation is dulled if the latter comes from an explanation and not from a scene. And then, how amusing it is to compose dialogue, to be simultaneously several characters, to get up and sit down, to make gestures for both sides, to incorporate oneself rapidly into several beings! The important thing is never to write a speech but to remain in contact with the flesh and blood part of the character.

This is a radical change of heart since *La Bonifas*, and one which will not have its full effect until *Le Pour et le Contre*. Remembering that he once disagreed with Radiguet on the importance of describing characters, he goes on to say that, for him, characters do not come to life until thoroughly described; but he adds: "The real artistry consists of describing incidentally in the course of scenes, by gestures and not by means of an artificially applied portrait." This again is a major break with the technique of *La Bonifas*. Once more he reaffirms his stand in *Dix Jours à Ermenonville* that the novel must be closely related to the life of the author, and this leads him to define the novel as "the art of inventing with the help of memory." From time to time, he gives us insights into his method of writing: when he tells how the sight of a building falling victim to wreckers, or of personal objects spread out at an auction, inspires him to reconstruct the lives of unknown individuals; or when he tells us that the denouement and the plot of a novel always occur to him simultaneously and that he is incapable of altering the denouement.

One thing leading to another, he discusses his unfinished "Roman protestant," which he says he abandoned because it was too long for a one-character novel ("What about *La Bonifas*?" one asks). Although one would not suspect it in examining the manuscript, the character of Michel Durtal was to have been complex indeed: "One would have discovered successively in his acts, but not in connection with any religious practices, different principles belonging to the Hussites, the Anabaptists, the Puritans and the Swedenborgians. The dominant trait of this character was revolt, protest, against the family first, against the established order next. In short, it was the novel of heresy." It is not clear how the novelist proposed to accomplish this incredible study of heredity; since he did not know himself, perhaps that is one of the reasons why the novel failed.

Two command performances and a personal diversion—surprisingly enough, all this adds up to *Aparté*, the most significant of Lacretelle's nonfictional work.

Next he proceeded to write up his trip to Spain, and immediately the subject grew in this "reverie" form intermediate between fiction and the essay. Reminded of another title with an honorable past in literary history, he called his work *Lettres espagnoles*. The surviving manuscript is dated "Angers, June 1926," which is a slightly misleading date since two parts had already appeared in print: "Histoire cynique" in the *Revue de Paris* for May 15th, and "Lettres espagnoles (fragments)" in the *Nouvelle Revue Française* for October. The complete text, minus the introductory selection in the *Revue de Paris* in which Damville appears and including some hitherto unpublished material, was assembled first in a limited edition with the imprint "Le Livre" in 1926 and then reappeared in an ordinary Gallimard edition in 1927. According to Lacretelle there were no significant alterations in the original text; the two articles were merely selections from the original, and the introductory passages in the *Revue de Paris* were padding which had no relation to the original version.

To complicate further these bibliographical details, Lacretelle published *Mort de la jalousie* at Liège the same year in a limited edition. This unsewed volume was a facsimile of a handwritten manuscript which Lacretelle must have prepared especially for this purpose, and the text was the same as "Histoire cynique," including the introductory passages.

The *Lettres espagnoles* were purportedly written by "Jacques Legrand," which is an invitation to ignore the author's remark that he would laugh in the face of anyone who said that he and Legrand were the same person. Jacques is in love, but his love is unrequited: "Sometimes, during my nocturnal walks, it happens that I revolt; I decide to make you give in or to see you no more. At the same time (Is it to defy you?), I strike my cane against the tree trunks. Then brusquely I stop, seized with fright. Suppose you had heard me, suppose you were to take me literally! Didn't you once do so? Then I stammer all kinds of silly things and sweet things to show you that it was only a joke. . . ."

This is the same cane with which the author of *Dix Jours à Ermenonville* fished the body of the drowned woman out of the Seine, the same one with which the narrator of *Colère* punctuated his reflections on anger, and the same one which prevented the author of the *Journal de Colère* from being mistaken for a policeman in disguise. The person who wields this cane will never be Romeo or Don Juan; his emotions will always have an intellectual quality, just as his attitude will never be Platonic. The *Lettres espagnoles* are addressed not to a Juliet but to an ex-mistress who did not like to be touched in her *faux-du-corps*. Since there is no plot, no action, only a vague adieu in the last letter, one wonders why the *Lettres espagnoles* had to be addressed to a mistress. Doubtless it was partly because of the desire to be informal, unpedantic, and partly because he wanted to suggest artistically some of the sensuality of Spain. Perhaps the principal shortcoming of *Lettres espagnoles* is to have suggested the sensuality of Spain by writing to an ex-mistress in Paris while brandishing a cane. Mérimée had a better idea when he created Carmen. But Lacretelle, when he went to Spain, was neither Mérimée nor even a romantic; he was a Parisian intellectual interested only in the quintessence of a civilization, in its art and particularly its painting, since he was not a student of its literature.

Lettres espagnoles is the record of an artistic experience in Spain; it tells us nothing about contemporary Spaniards, except for the isolated remark about a passer-by and a woman behind a grilled window gazing mutely at each other, and it overlooks even the picturesqueness of the country. At first the traveller is even bored by what he is supposed to admire: a bull fight, the Escorial, the "monstrous" six-headed cathedral of Toledo, even the Alhambra. In an epistle to the followers of Barrès, he cries: "Be suspicious of the pilgrimages inspired by your master." To be sure, he discovers eventually a few quaint spots like Ronda, but the true Spain for him is really the Prado. He appreciates the crowds of Madrid only when he sees them depicted in a painting by Goya. He becomes enthusiastic about the detail of a head in El Greco's "Crucifixion," which makes him imagine the painting which El Greco might have created if he had chosen as his subject the ecstasy of Pascal. An El Greco portrait reminds him of Proust, and Goya's "Maja desnuda" takes him back to his mistress. Naturally, the whole book is a series of digressions in keeping with the "reverie" genre to which it belongs.

One of the longest digressions is the story entitled "Histoire cynique," which seems to have no connection whatever with a travel book on Spain unless, perchance, the reader remembers that Mme de La Fayette's *Zaïde*, which inspired it, is situated in that country. Jacques Legrand's story, in a Parisian setting, is an elaboration of Adolphe's statement: "I am jealous of a dead man, and that is what drives me to despair."[4] Damville had said in the introduction to the *Revue de Paris* version: "My opinion is that jealousy and love are one and the same thing."

"Histoire cynique" is a story with a psychological thesis. Anna and François are medical students. When he becomes jealous of her past affairs, Anna, in exasperation, is unfaithful to him. This is the modern equivalent of taking the veil, which is the solution which Mme de La Fayette finds for her subplot. Eventually Anna leaves François, whereupon he makes a clinical study of his case and institutes a cure which consists of belittling her lovers in his imagination. When Anna returns to him once more, he becomes as indifferent to her as to her lovers; like the dog who lost a vital organ in an experiment, his love died when jealousy was amputated.

"Histoire cynique" is straight narrative, almost skeletal in form and lacking those subtle artistic devices characteristic of the best Lacretelle short stories. It is the first example of the simplified, rapid narration which will characterize the Italian stories of *Histoire de Paola Ferrani*. At the same time, with its modern preoccupation with abnormal psychology (it is interesting to note how amazingly modern Mme de La Fayette's treatment of the subject was), it provides a certain continuity between *La Bonifas* and the later short stories, *Le Cachemire écarlate* and *Le Christ aux bras étroits*.

Lacretelle composed another brief "reverie" in 1927. It came out first in the *Nouvelle Revue Française* for July, then reappeared three months later in a limited edition combining it with *Dix Jours à Ermenonville* under the general title *Rêveries romantiques*, published by Stendhal et Cie. "Le Rêveur parisien" found a permanent spot in Lacretelle's work in *Les Aveux étudiés* (1934). This long meditation continues the inspiration of *Dix Jours à Ermenonville* and the *Journal de Colère*; it is closely related to the latter, having been composed, according to the information on the manuscript, at Bellevue from April 12 to April 25, 1926.

In "Le Rêveur parisien," Lacretelle is seeking further insight into the creative process. He (that is to say, the narrator) is on his way to Italy by car, in company with his current mistress. The beauty of the Alps leaves him uninspired until an accidental stop in a village tavern brings him in contact with people and sets the machinery of his imagination in motion. He never talks to his models but observes them surreptitiously; then his imagination does the rest. Incapable of reconstructing the life of the Alpine peasant girl whom he is observing, he transports her back to Paris in his imagination and wonders how he, as a novelist, would complete her amorous education.

By a rather brusque transition, the "Parisian dreamer" is back in Paris, following Parisians around and imagining their life stories. The reality of these characters will only upset him; if he accidentally engages in conversation with one of them, he will have the same feeling of annoyance as a dramatic author "when he hears actors act out his play." Most of the time he absorbs atmosphere: lovers in the Luxembourg, workers near the Place d'Italie, Englishmen drinking tea near the rue des Pyramides. Sometimes he proposes *pensums* for himself, as when he observes Protestants coming out of the "temple" in the rue Madame: "Complementary question: Why is the male Protestant generally straight, reserved, morose, saturnine in a word, whereas the female is straight also, but more open, more generous and often kindly disposed toward a gentle sort of gaiety? He has a somber plumage; she, light-colored. One would say that the same teachings which keep him in prison have liberated her."

Only occasionally does action interfere with the wanderings of the "Parisian dreamer." Once he provokes it by pursuing an old "decorated" gentleman who has pocketed a child's ball; the narrator follows him about like a bad conscience until the old man, in desperation, throws the ball onto the sidewalk. Another time he overhears a prostitute unmask a false detective who is really an introvert asserting his personality.

Thus the "Rêveur parisien" rambles, going from introspection to fiction without any clear transition. Already, however, the Rousseauistic inspiration is fading because Lacretelle seems less and less inclined to record his intimate personality on paper. In a strict sense, "Le Rêveur parisien" is the last of the true "reveries." One time more Lacretelle will return to this mixture of essay and fiction when writing the Italian stories of *Histoire de Paola Ferrani*, but the intimate Ermenonville touch will be lacking.

8

STENDHAL'S WAY

THE road from Ermenonville leads to Naples. And the road away from Naples, with many detours back to Paris to attend to business, leads to Athens. A subjective aesthetic prevails at Ermenonville and an objective one at Athens. In Italy, where Lacretelle walks in the footsteps of Stendhal, there is a middle ground between the two aesthetic extremes.

Lacretelle's sojourn at Ermenonville opened up the possibility of a profound renewal in his manner of writing, and yet he made no major effort to outdo previous achievements in the years immediately following. Looking back over the years 1925 to 1927, we see that they are characterized by a dispersal of effort. Traveling explained many interruptions during this period: Spain in 1925, Italy in the summer of 1926 and Greece in 1927. To reconstruct an exact log of these travels is impossible. For example, "Le Rêveur parisien" mentions still another trip to northern Italy, evidently in the spring of 1926.

Near the end of 1927 Lacretelle acquired more sedentary habits when he purchased, with the profits from *Silbermann*, a small house and garden which Jacques de Zogheb called to his attention. Situated at 78 rue de Paris in the picturesque town of Montfort-l'Amaury, not far to the west of Paris, it is a charming little old house (in 1957 Lacretelle still owns it) lined up with the narrow main street, squeezed up against many other little houses, and divided on the inside into innumerable rooms which seem altogether too small for the owner's Nordic proportions. The ceremony of the extinction of the candle at the auction sale when Lacretelle purchased the house made such an impression on his memory that, a few years later, he introduced a similar scene into *Les Hauts Ponts* when his heroine buys back the family château. Number 78 rue de Paris was hardly a château, but at least it was soon furnished with heirlooms from Cormatin, including the 1830 Gothic bed in which Jacques himself was born. Amid these symbols of permanence, Jacques de Lacretelle was to do a large part of his writing until the outbreak of World War II.

According to the author's oral account, he began a new novel entitled *Le Retour de Silbermann* immediately after finishing *Lettres espagnoles*; that makes the date approximately July 1926. If he had made an all-out effort at this time, this new novel would have been the major work resulting from the new inspiration of Ermenonville. Actually *Le Retour de Silbermann* (not to be confused with the novel now bearing that name) was to take three years in the writing and was to prove so unsatisfactory that the author had to make some radical changes in it before publishing it in book form. This novel will be the subject of the next chapter.

The first version of *Le Retour de Silbermann* registers an evolution away from the Ermenonville inspiration during the period in which it was being written. The same evolution is visible in the secondary works of the period. In fact, two short stories, *Le Christ aux bras étroits* and *Le Cachemire écarlate*, show the same qualities of artistry and the same desire for classical perfection found in *La Mort d'Hippolyte* and *La Belle Journée,* with which they were joined in 1928 to form *L'Ame cachée*. It is almost as though Ermenonville represented, for Lacretelle, a feint in the wrong direction; when he makes a real effort, as he did in writing these two stories, he becomes essentially classical in his technique.

It is impossible to determine exactly when the two stories were written or even which was written first. In an interview with André Rousseaux published on April 7, 1927, Lacretelle is quoted as saying that *Le Cachemire écarlate* is finished, but not *Le Christ aux bras étroits*.[1] Since the second of these stories appeared in the *Revue de Paris* on April 15th, one is tempted to conclude that the interviewer confused the two stories. From the point of view of publication dates, *Le Cachemire écarlate* came second, since it appeared in *Les Annales politiques et littéraires* for June 1st and June 15th. Both stories reappeared in limited editions the same year. All of this, including the reworking of *La Mort d'Hippolyte* in 1925, was aimed at making a volume of short stories comparable in stature to a major work.

The earliest mention of the idea for *Le Christ aux bras étroits* is contained in the *Journal de Colère*. Speaking of his abandoned "Roman protestant," Lacretelle states that he may take up the theme of Protestantism again someday "to relate the drama of a child, a drama which will appear inexplicable on the surface." Also it is evident that while writing "Le Rêveur parisien," Lacretelle was actively thinking about Protestantism as a literary theme and may even have been writing the short story.

With minor modifications, *Le Christ aux bras étroits* is the story of the Protestant boy Blanchod as originally related in the manuscript of the "Roman protestant." As the story unfolds the spotlight is on Blanchod, who retains his original name, and not on Michel Durtal, who has regressed to the rank of a colorless narrator known only as "D***." The subject is no longer the antagonism of Catholic and Protestant heredities but the inexplicable drama of the Protestant boy. It is evident from the following passage that the subject was already in being in the unfinished novel, for Blanchod says in the manuscript:

> "I recognize that I am worth nothing, that I have no energy for doing good, but I am without strength against evil. In my feelings for Nancy, there were many shameful things. Often I am horrified with myself."
>
> He stopped, then said with a ferocious explosion: "But is it my fault if I am like this? I did not ask to come into the world. It is my parents who made me what I am."

Amazingly, however, most of the dramatic elements of *Le Christ aux bras étroits* are missing from the original version. There is nothing about the nocturnal visits of Nancy, the pastor's daughter, to Blanchod's room or any indication as to what was "shameful" in Blanchod's mind. All we know, from the long lyrical letter about La Spes, the Protestant youth organization with which originally Blanchod went into the Swiss mountains (the letter survived without alteration in the short story),[2] is that, like Michel Durtal himself and like Jean Hermelin before him, Blanchod is tormented by vague notions of good and evil. In the unfinished novel, Blanchod's mother withdraws him from the *lycée* because she has intercepted some "guilty" letters, whereas in the short story it is Nancy's confession to her brother which precipitates the crisis. Because we never learn what was in those letters, the novel purposely creates the impression that Mme Blanchod judges her son by some superhuman standard and acts without real motivation, as a result of which Michel Durtal is revolted by Protestant morality and changes his mind about becoming a Protestant; in the short story, there is the same intolerant rigidity on the mother's part, but the motivation is unmistakably clear. The worst treatment which Blanchod gets in the novel is to have to live with a pastor at Versailles, after which we lose sight of him; in the short story, he commits suicide, a denouement foreseen, strangely enough, in the first outline for the "Roman protestant," which also provided for a posthumous letter of confession.

In its definitive form, Blanchod's character is conceived on two levels. Like his mother, he is a Protestant stereotype reacting to ordinary situations with a puritanical inflexibility; but at the same time, he is a strangely tormented character whose subconscious life seems infinitely complex and anything but a stereotype. In the following vivid passage, which brings Blanchod onto the stage, we see the pattern of the Protestant stereotype (the narrator is speaking): "I offered, with a gesture, to pass my rough draft to him. But he refused, and with such signs of indignation that I felt embarrassed. At the beating of the drum, he got up, walked straight to the teacher's desk and placed on it a blank paper." This passage was transplanted without alteration from the novel to the short story. In the novel, the character was conceived entirely on this level, and there was no attempt to suggest by conscious artistic processes that there was more to the character than one saw on the surface.

Yet Blanchod had possibilities already inherent in the original conception of the character. Even though the manuscript of the "Roman protestant" had been discarded with apparent finality, Blanchod continued to live on in Lacretelle's imagination and engendered the even more mysterious character of Nancy, who had been only a name in the novel. We never know exactly what subconscious symbolism there is in Nancy's choice of red objects, on which she forced her sweetheart to gaze simultaneously with her when in the presence of others; or in this scene:

> One night the girl entered his room and, without saying anything else, ordered him to comb her hair. "She was kneeling," Blanchod told me, "and said in a low pleading voice: 'Comb my hair, comb my hair.' I obeyed, but I was so upset that I trembled. The comb fell from my hands, and when I picked it up, I happened to touch her feet which were bare. They were cold. I wanted to take them in my hands and warm them; but she stood up as though I had wounded her, and ran away."

Much later, flaunting his literary knowledge, D*** tells Blanchod that he may find the explanation of Nancy's character in Chateaubriand's *René*, but we are not certain whether he claims to see some subtle relation between the hair-combing and taking the veil or whether he is guessing at incestuous relations between Nancy and her brother.

Interpreted by D***, Blanchod himself is an enigmatic and complex character: "It is to him, I mean to certain of his confidential secrets, that I owe my first knowledge of the obscure parts of human beings. For a long time I have been unable to lean over a well and to glimpse the walls, the graminaceae, the sheet of water, without thinking of some veiled confessions which escaped from Blanchod." And he goes on to tell the story of the "God of the flies," whom Blanchod wanted to invoke to punish Perd-en-répond, a fellow pupil, for tormenting the insects. If he had seen D***'s representation of the god in the form of a great ink spot, he might have been seized with superstitious fear: "He was very fearful or, in any case, gave that impression. Do you ever get waked up with a start in the first stages of sleep by a falling sensation? You know, the whole body jumps. Well, one often saw Blanchod agitated by involuntary movements which resembled these jumps."

It is because our insight into Blanchod's character is projected downward into the well of the subconscious that we now appreciate fully his mental and physical anxiety as the day of scholastic reckoning comes. Ultimately his suicide, which is announced abruptly and without comment, seems entirely plausible because of this insight. Externally, he remains the same as in the "Roman protestant," since he wears the same tight-fitting grey suit and the same floating cloak which always makes him look as though he were "fighting incessantly against something." Inwardly, he has acquired something new: a subconscious.

If we now turn to the mother, we discover a simple example of how the author grafted a subconscious onto a stereotyped Protestant. First the stereotyped portrait has been transferred from the novel to the short story, the texts being identical:

> I recognized the woman whom I had perceived through the glass of the parlor. She wore, just as on that day, a black dress of simple material cut without elegance. However, a little garnet brooch glittered on her chest between the flaps of her collar. She nodded her head slightly toward me and held out her hand. Blanchod ran toward her.
>
> "Did you enjoy yourself, mother?" he asked.
>
> Mme Blanchod shrugged her shoulders slightly.
>
> "I do not *enjoy* myself, my child," she answered, insisting on the word which had shocked her.

One little instinctive act has to be added to give her the subconscious which will bring her in line with the other characters:

> I myself was very ill at ease, for his mother, while speaking to me, did not cease examining my hands as if they were dirty or as if I had stolen something.

Without question, there are new forces at work in Lacretelle's writings which make it difficult momentarily to recognize the author of *La Bonifas*. In fact, this goes even deeper than the reassessment of aesthetic principles which began in *Dix Jours à Ermenonville*. More than likely, the clue lies in Lacretelle's literary interests, which do not always coincide with what he is doing himself in the novel. To begin with, there was of course Proust, whom Lacretelle forsook in the early stages of "La Vie de Jacques Lamiel." At one point during the war, his favorite reading was Dostoevski's *The Idiot*, which might have some remote connection with *La Bonifas*, although no two novels could be aesthetically more different. In the *Journal de Colère*, the author mentions twice in detail a new admiration, Emily Brontë's *Wuthering Heights*, which he translated years later as *Haute Plainte*. In all likelihood

Blanchod and Nancy would never have come to life again in Lacretelle's imagination if he had not been haunted by Heathcliff and Catherine Linton.

It is not impossible also that in reading in *Les Faux-Monnayeurs* the Saas-Fé episode wherein, against the background of the Swiss mountains, there is a similar boy and girl relationship charged with abnormal psychology, he may have been reminded of a similar episode in his own unfinished novel. There is little likelihood of direct influence, however, since Blanchod's letter about La Spes, in the manuscript, precedes the episode which Lacretelle read to Gide and therefore must have already been written before Lacretelle knew anything about Gide's work.

Although in *Dix Jours à Ermenonville* Lacretelle seemed to announce an imminent return to the first person narrative, and this was promptly confirmed in a series of minor works, it remained to be seen whether he would persevere in this approach when he returned to pure fiction. *Le Christ aux bras étroits* revives the two-narrator technique of *La Mort d'Hippolyte*, but with one essential difference: The first narrator, the author, is not an aesthetic device but a distinct personality whom we have already encountered and that most recently since, though unnamed, he cannot be mistaken for anyone but our friend Damville. Only Damville would burden us with this story of how he cut his thumb by breaking a plate at an empty place just because, with his novelist's imagination, he could not avoid conjuring up a morose guest whose presence in the empty place dampened his enjoyment of the evening. For some reason, to which we are really indifferent, Damville has a strange curiosity about Protestants and, like the author of "Le Rêveur parisien," enjoys watching them come out of their "temple" across the street. Because he insists on his friend telling the story, he will never get to the antique dealer's to buy the "Christ aux bras étroits"—a Christ with his arms stretched over his head rather than in the form of a cross (today the author is uncertain whether he ever saw or heard of such a figure). This nonchalant intervention of the first narrator was not originally an artistic device, since it is really a mode of writing which Lacretelle had developed in moments of intellectual relaxation; but it has the very definite effect of breaking down the studied pattern so characteristic of Lacretelle's polished fiction up to this point. As a result, the story has a staccato rhythm which makes the reader feel that this time the author has subordinated art to reality.

The second narrator, called "D***" standing for "Durtal," is a fictional character who, if one wishes, symbolizes the impotent artist bogged down in reality. His aesthetic function in the story is to serve during his adolescence as an emotional sounding board for Blanchod, in other words to play a role similar to that of the narrator of *Silbermann*, with the difference that D*** does not live through any psychological drama himself. However, D***'s presence in the story may be attributed as much to accident as to design since he is really an atrophied survival from the "Roman protestant."

The short story bears a further relationship to Lacretelle's minor writing of this period. We have seen how, in "Histoire cynique" (*Mort de la jalousie*), he subordinated artistic considerations to the demonstration of a thesis. When D*** asserts that "Protestant atavism can assume a thousand disguises," we sense the initial presence of a thesis in the conceptual process. If this story really demonstrates a thesis, we are forced to conclude that Blanchod committed suicide because he was a Protestant. Such an arbitrary statement, on second thought, singularly restricts the psychological problem. Silbermann's psychological case was cut and dried: He was persecuted, suffered and disappeared from the scene because he was a Jew. Blanchod is beaten by Perd-en-répond, not because he is a Protestant, but because, physically and morally, he is a ready victim. He fails in school, not because he is a Protestant, but because he is convinced of his intellectual incapacity (there is no proof that he is unintelligent, however). Nothing that happens to him is the direct result of the fact that he is a Protestant, and yet all his maladjustment is undoubtedly due to his mother. And what is she but a Protestant? That brings us right around the vicious circle to the thesis. We see that the character of Blanchod is a subtle psychological structure which is successful because the implications far exceed the definition. *Le Christ aux bras étroits* stands out in Lacretelle's major work because of its apparent lack of artistry; in reality, never was Lacretelle's artistry more subtle and more accomplished.

Whereas *Le Christ aux bras étroits* tends to avoid the systematic character analysis which is typical of Lacretelle's major work, *Le*

Cachemire écarlate builds up the principal character with absolute precision. The only way in which this second story is related to the Ermenonville inspiration is in the use of a narrator; in other respects it is as objective as any Lacretelle work and is proof that whenever Lacretelle takes time to write with care, he comes quite naturally back to systematic character analysis.

Although *Le Cachemire écarlate* was written at the request of Pierre Brisson who had asked Lacretelle for a contribution to the rejuvenated *Annales*, it was not a command performance like many of the shorter pieces of this period. Brisson served only as the catalyst for an idea which Lacretelle was already mulling over. Because of an enthusiastic digression on Greece, it seems probable that the story was written in the period following Easter 1927, which was the date of Lacretelle's first trip to Greece. On its title page for June 1, 1927, the *Annales* classified the story as a "novel" and announced that it was publishing "the end." This was entirely misleading information, since *Le Cachemire écarlate* was never anything but the short story as we know it today.

In the interview with André Rousseaux, Lacretelle was quoted as saying about his story: "Under this title which reminds one a little too much of Barbey d'Aurevilly, there is the story of a sister of Thérèse Desqueyroux. I have no scruples in claiming this family relationship since Mauriac has told me that his heroine was a sister of La Bonifas." Except that she is a murderess who poisons a sick member of her family, Lacretelle's heroine, Rose-Marie, has nothing in common with Thérèse Desqueyroux. She is an instinctive creature who never analyzes her crime, and furthermore she is not really the central character of the story, although she might seem to be because she is the owner of the scarlet Cashmere shawl. The character which Lacretelle carefully builds up from childhood is that of Antoine Ancelin, the young medical scientist who, at a provincial festival at Villiers-le-Noble (a fictitious town allegedly near Versailles but resembling Provins), meets this small-town girl so unlike himself and marries her. She is so absorbed by her passion for her husband that she will not even have children for fear that he will transfer his affection to them. When her husband insists that she go back to Villiers to care for her aged and ailing mother, she actually poisons her mother in order to be able to return to Paris and her husband. Because of his medical knowledge, Antoine quickly pieces together her crime and then covers up for her. He gives up his scientific career and goes to live the rest of his life with her in a remote spot in the Cévennes.

Inasmuch as *Le Cachemire écarlate* ties in immediately with the declaration in favor of the first person narrative noted in *Dix Jours à Ermenonville*, one is tempted to consider it a step forward rather than a step backward. On closer examination, it is the links with the pre-Ermenonville period, rather than with the later period, which appear stronger. The difference is quite visible in the personality of the narrator. The author has returned to the same inspiration which once furnished the narrator of *Silbermann* and has almost completely parted company with Damville, whose profligacy is only remotely apparent in the allusions to the numerous affairs of the narrator as he grows up, and whose digressions on aesthetic theory are noticeably absent. Since the story is related in a natural chronological order beginning with the childhood of the narrator, the adolescent personality of the narrator overshadows his later evolution. This revival—on an aesthetic but not on a moral plane—of the narrator of *Silbermann* must be an indirect result of writing *Le Retour de Silbermann* at this time. As in *La Mort d'Hippolyte* and *Le Christ aux bras étroits*, there are really two narrators, since Antoine Ancelin, the central character, relates the denouement. Both narrators are carefully integrated into the story, and there is none of the casual intervention of the narrators which characterizes *Le Christ aux bras étroits*.

The reader of the story may choose to disagree with the statement that Antoine Ancelin is the central character, for it is the wife who holds the main levers of the action and who arouses the reader's curiosity and sympathy. On second thought, it will be seen that wherever the reader's interest may lie, Antoine is both structurally and aesthetically the real focus. In the initial conception of the character there is a certain rigidity which reminds one of the techniques of *La Bonifas* and the psychological thesis of "Histoire cynique." The point of departure of *Le Cachemire écarlate* is an abstract psychological problem: What happens when an intellectual with a puritan conscience marries an instinctive creature? In a sense, it is a reversal of the roles of the first version of *Le Retour de Silbermann*, wherein the wife stands for intellectual and moral integrity while the husband, although a so-called intellectual, yields to instinct. The initial rigidity of conception continues straight on down through the structure of Antoine's character. He is presented with the same methodical precision as Marie Bonifas, beginning even with the problem of heredity as set forth in the portrait of the Jansenist father. There is soon no element of this character which we do not understand perfectly: his intellectual capacities, his unimpeachable integrity bordering on self-righteousness, his attractive physical appearance and finally his idealism, which explains his idyllic love affair with the girl in the scarlet shawl.

This rigidity in the character provides a surprising contrast with the more subtle techniques of *Le Christ aux bras étroits*. However, the reader is likely to emerge from the story with the desire to judge Antoine for having ruined his life and that of his wife. If Antoine were an abstraction, a mere psychological edifice, the reader would not have an affective attitude toward him. Unbeknownst to the reader, there has been a cumulative effect, as always happens in the most thoroughly drawn psychological portraits in Lacretelle's work; and when Antoine begins to relate the tragedy of his life, he comes to life in an essentially unsympathetic light, although he is obviously pained, crushed and even bewildered by the strange fate which has overtaken him.

Because of the shift of emphasis from Antoine to Rose-Marie during the long narration of the crime, the reader may readily overlook the fact that the narration itself is the last stone in an elaborate psychological edifice concerned with Antoine rather than Rose-Marie. When he says, "I had finally perceived, I repeat, something logical and even natural in the act which she had committed," and when he decides, "I had to remain faithful to the memory of this love," he seems at first to have substituted himself for the author and to be speaking with the latter's omniscience. If this is truly the author speaking, then this portrait of Rose-Marie is only a neat psychological package much less subtle than the portrait of Antoine himself. In reality, while picking Rose-Marie apart and while imposing a certain Cartesian logic on her psychological mechanism, Antoine has only continued to reveal himself, just as he revealed himself in his tyrannical puritanism and his incomprehension. Of this we can be more sure if we examine the character of Rose-Marie.

In the beginning, Rose-Marie is encased in a narrow formula for which the narrator himself is responsible, for he says: "In spite of the narrowness of her mind, one could not have called her stupid. She spoke of herself and of her feelings with great penetration. And sometimes, notably when it had to do with her love, she made real and often poetic discoveries inside I know not what little compartment of her brain. Then, as the conversation shifted and went from the particular to the general, she lost all inspiration and no longer said anything, like certain flowers which close up when they no longer feel heat." It should be noted, however, that the narrator does not speak with the same dogmatism as Antoine; his point of view is wholly external, and in generalizing, he is only reporting the synthesis of his observations.

It is Antoine who says, substituting himself for the Divinity: "Instinct alone has developed in her. She lacks certain moral notions, and it is my duty to inculcate them in her." In his dogmatic ignorance, Antoine will never realize his own responsibility in his wife's crime, and his only qualms of conscience will be for having circumvented the law, which, but for his quick thinking, would have claimed the right to punish. From his impregnable moral viewpoint, Antoine has concluded omnisciently that his wife is irresponsible and even incapable of remorse. In his opinion, she is a creature of instinct; hence, he completely ignores the long psychological preparation for her act. He was blind to what was going on and even unaware of the significant fact that she brought from Paris the poison with which she murdered her mother. The narrator senses that there is something wrong with Antoine's interpretation when he remarks: "I had had the feeling, as I listened to him, that he was only repeating a confession long meditated and even often repeated inside him, as though to justify himself before an imaginary audience." And to Antoine himself, he says: "Do you really believe that she never thought again of the deed she committed? Can we even conceive of her remorse?" Antoine's last remark is that he cannot decide whether her revulsion for workmen covered with sulphate is remorse or physical reaction.

Thus Rose-Marie regains that ambivalence which her husband's dogmatism had denied her throughout most of the story, and some of the previous information about her appears in a new light. As she escapes from the formula we are left with but one central character, Antoine himself, who in the last analysis has revealed himself—as any good character should—through his deeds. However, it is undeniable that in spite of this more subtle conclusion, the total impression of the story is that the author has momentarily recaptured much of the inspiration of *La Bonifas*.

It is remarkable that at the height of a predominantly subjective period in Lacretelle's writing, this short story should have those structural qualities which distinguished *La Mort d'Hippolyte*, *Silbermann* and *La Bonifas*. The story is so carefully planned and executed that no element of the plot is left to chance. It grows naturally and smoothly from apparent trivialities which already contain in themselves all the ingredients of the drama. As in the classical Maupassant story, the factor of surprise is carefully prepared and held in reserve. We know that something tragic has happened long before we have any precise notion of the tragedy. Curiosity is aroused in ascending stages as one element of surprise leads to another, from the farmer covered with sulphate to Rose-Marie's admission, "I tried to go," when her husband asks her why she did not get the doctor. Likewise, in the harmonious blending of setting and character, there is a careful striving for artistic depth which is lacking in most of the fictional writing of this period in Lacretelle's career. For once, during this period, there is complete orchestration instead of a simple melody. *Le Cachemire écarlate* is truly an exception.

In the volume *Histoire de Paola Ferrani*, on the other hand, the author returns to simple melodies collected in the framework of a travel book. Although the inspiration dates from his Italian trip of 1926, the chapters seem not to have been composed until shortly previous to their fragmented publication in *Candide*, *Les Annales*, *La Nouvelle Revue Française* and *La Revue européenne* during the first quarter of 1928.[3] After an artificial separation of fiction and travel in the limited editions entitled *Album napolitain* and *Quatre Nouvelles italiennes*, the completed volume appeared during the spring of 1929 under the imprint of Flammarion.

Announced in the preface as an intentional blending of fiction and reality, *Histoire de Paola Ferrani* is manifestly an attempt to perfect the "reverie" genre. Yet we are a long way from the confidences of Ermenonville. There has been a distinct change in tone, a switch from the confessional to the impersonal. On the brink of

Vesuvius, Lacretelle rejects Chateaubriand's bombast on the same subject and prefers Stendhal's remark (in *Rome, Naples et Florence*): "Yesterday I went up to Vesuvius; it is the most tiring thing I have experienced in my life. The so-called hermit is often a thief, whether converted or not: a good platitude written in his book and signed Bigot de Préameneu."[4] Like any of Stendhal's works taken at random, *Histoire de Paola Ferrani* is the swan song of a tired romantic who has had quite enough of his own ego.

Histoire de Paola Ferrani is a refusal to be many things, but, first of all, it is a refusal to be Paul Morand. In his last chapter, "Return," the author autocriticizes with his usual frankness: "The preponderance of the intellectual over the visual causes me to be attracted less by what is new than by what has been brewing for centuries in art and literature. . . . For certain writers, traveling is a hand-to-hand fight between a man and a monster, a fight in which the man must be naked. But I am not an explorer and never will be. The monster would have made short work of killing me with boredom by depriving me of intellectual nourishment." Lacretelle has no desire to record the spirit of contemporary Italy; rather, he would seek its more timeless aspects and travel through it spiritually in the company of that wanton admirer, Henri Beyle, alias Stendhal. Vesuvius may leave him cold, Pompeii may even seem a shapeless pile of bricks bearing witness to the limited horizons of a mercantile civilization; but the sight of the Bay of Naples inspires him because Stendhal deigned to describe it and because, from a respectful distance, it looks like a sketch by Ingres.

Probably the only Italians from real life are the *entremetteurs* who tempt the tourist in the first chapter and whose venal presence is necessary to give that atmosphere of sensuality essential to the violence of Italy as Lacretelle sees it refracted through the work of Stendhal. Lacretelle's real purpose is not so much to recapture Italy as it is to recapture Stendhal, in whose *Rome, Naples et Florence* he has found an example of the same mixture of fiction and personal digression which he has been practicing. As he travels about Italy he interrupts his casual narrative to tell the same kind of rapid, violent anecdote which dispenses with all of the accessories of what we call the art of the short story. Two such very brief anecdotes in the beginning of the volume are typically Stendhal. The story of the husband who disguises himself as a priest in order to stab his wife as she confesses is suggested by one of Count Vitelleschi's numerous adventures in the first volume of Stendhal's work. Also Stendhalian, though its source is not certain, is the story of the defender of the Castel del Uovo who kills his mistress because, knowing of the impending attack, she has lured him away from his duty.

On the whole, however, Lacretelle tends to go further than Stendhal in developing his stories. That is true particularly of "Histoire de Paola Ferrani," the keynote story of the book, which is typical Stendhal in the violence and in the straightforward narration but yet turns out to resemble more closely a story by Stendhal's disciple Mérimée. The latter's brutal tales about Corsica never surprise the reader by their brutality but rather keep him in suspense concerning what particularly barbarous form the final violent act will take. While unfolding his narrative with a Mérimée dry candor, letting the characters act for themselves, Lacretelle introduces one of his own psychological subtleties by providing the key to the final violent act in a previous behavior pattern. To protect her son from the violence of her husband, Paola is on the verge of murdering her uncouth and unfaithful spouse; years later, when her son has grown into a beast like her late husband (murdered by someone else), she becomes demented, and the whole scene is repeated, with her son ending up as the victim. It is a good story, by far the best in the volume, but lacking the psychological depth and aesthetic subtlety of the stories in *L'Ame cachée*. This is because the whole volume is conceived in the spirit of a pastiche: a pastiche of *Rome, Naples et Florence* in the travelogue part; an overt pastiche of Stendhal's novel *Armance* in a selection called "En Marge d'Armance"; and an unconscious pastiche of Mérimée in the story "Histoire de Paola Ferrani" in which the author seeks to recapture on a fictional level the spirit of Stendhal's Italy.

The subjects of the other stories in the book are typical Lacretelle, rather than Stendhal or Mérimée, but, related with the same economy of detail, they are inferior to the usual Lacretelle narrative and, lacking vividness, are also inferior to "Histoire de Paola Ferrani."

Only one of these stories, "Addio," really acquires any shape. Its subject is banal, even sentimental; yet Lacretelle possesses the art of saying simple things with taste and artistry. While honeymooning in Sorrento, the young French bride falls ill, and her husband summons the aged Dr. Sammartino, who discovers he had known the bride's grandmother years before when she, too, came to Sorrento. How intimately he knew her, he never says; but his sentimental attentions are so annoying to the young couple that they decide to leave. The morning of their departure they learn that the old doctor has just died while attempting to rewrite his will.

Another story, "La Porte de Cipolin," is interesting for reasons extraneous to its subject, for nothing is more commonplace than the story of this bored French author who befriends a young compatriot in an Italian pharmacy, reminisces in a flash back about a former mistress and then discovers a week or so later that the young compatriot's "friend," who has meanwhile died, was his ex-mistress. The story stands apart from the others because it is the only one in which the author abandons the simplified narrative technique (except in the abrupt denouement) and enters into the sensibility of a character. The French author, Antony Morot, is one of these semiautobiographical characters like Damville or like the narrator of *Le Retour de Silbermann*—which Lacretelle is now finishing more or less simultaneously with his Italian stories.

The least interesting of the stories, because it lacks a plot and denouement, is "Naissance de Sapho"; it has, however, some typical Lacretelle complexities in the psychological pattern: Dora becomes a Lesbian because of her affection for her sister; the proof of this is her periodical dream in which she sees her sister upside down, the result of a childhood game of looking at each other through their legs.

As a travel book *Histoire de Paola Ferrani* is far superior to *Lettres espagnoles* because it captures the spirit of the country, but as fiction it is inferior to Lacretelle's usual production. The inferiority of the fiction may be partly due to the fact that Lacretelle is trying so hard to be Stendhal that he is no longer himself. He has strayed far from the spirit of *Dix Jours à Ermenonville*.

Unlike *Dix Jours à Ermenonville*, which was composed on the spot, the book on Italy was written later on French soil, for Lacretelle tarried in only one place in Italy long enough to write anything. While at Capri he penned a very rudimentary short story, *Virginie ou les manies,* about a provincial girl living chastely in

Paris Bohemia and making a specialty of flattering the conscious or unconscious foibles of her male entourage. Among these males there is a narrator resembling Damville. The short story had no connection with *Histoire de Paola Ferrani*, and Lacretelle published it separately in one of Edouard Champion's plaquettes in 1927 and also in *Candide* on December 27th of the same year. The story reappeared in a "gallant aphabet," *D'Ariane à Zoé*, published by the Librairie de France in 1930.

Although subjective in form, *Histoire de Paola Ferrani* was not really subjective in spirit. In the intellectual journey from Ermenonville to Athens, Lacretelle has reached a half-way station. However, the account of the itinerary from Ermenonville to Naples is not complete, for we still have to consider *Le Retour de Silbermann*, written during this period.

9

SILBERMANN COMES BACK

SILBERMANN disappeared "like a prophet who ceases to be visible to the eyes of humans to whom he has just brought a warning."[1] After this ascension, only Alexandre Dumas or some modern author of serials would have had the temerity to bring him back to earth again. As a serious author, Lacretelle was obviously taking a calculated risk in writing *Le Retour de Silbermann.*

Since the writing of this novel occupied most of Lacretelle's literary itinerary from Ermenonville to Naples, we shall rediscover along the route the same check points as in the two preceding chapters. Despite the fact that, in order of publication, the new novel comes after *Histoire de Paola Ferrani*, it originates in Ermenonville rather than Naples and must not be thought of as a new departure after Naples.

Le Retour de Silbermann, as it appeared in *Candide* from May 9 to August 15, 1929, was quite different from the epilogue to *Silbermann* which was to bear that name in book form. Although conceived and written as one unit, it was divided, even in the original version, into two distinct parts which were artistically so unrelated that it was a relatively simple matter to separate them subsequently into two novels: *Amour nuptial* and *Le Retour de Silbermann.* The first required almost no alterations to become an autonomous text, whereas the second involved considerable rewriting, largely stylistic rather than structural.

The part of the novel subsequently called *Amour nuptial* had a major plot not concerned with the character Silbermann, and a minor plot, the only function of which was to make the second half of the novel possible. Only a minor character Hélène Mossé held the two parts together. The ease with which Hélène Mossé vanished shows how superfluous she was and how right Lacretelle was to disregard the advice of Jean Paulhan, who, speaking for the Gallimard publishing house, had urged him to publish his novel without alteration. At that time, Paulhan had written to Roger Allard: "There is no reason to hesitate; it should be published as is. It is even excellent Lacretelle. I could perhaps have done without Mlle Mossé and especially her milieu; however, I should not like her to disappear from the main narrative; the narrator would lose part of his verisimilitude."[2]

Gallimard accepted Lacretelle's revisions, however, and *Amour nuptial* appeared under his imprint without benefit of a limited edition in 1929. *Le Retour de Silbermann* came out almost simultaneously in a limited edition under the imprint of Le Capitole and reappeared the following year in a regular Gallimard edition.

The simplest method for understanding the original version of *Le Retour de Silbermann* and the changes which occurred to make the two published volumes is to consider first the text of *Amour nuptial* in its final form, since this text is the major portion of the first half of the original novel. Then we shall take up the discarded fragments of the first half which dealt with Hélène Mossé. Finally we shall turn to the published volume called *Le Retour de Silbermann* and compare it in detail with the original text.

The central character of *Amour nuptial* is a narrator who has the misfortune to be without a name. We can refer to him only as "the narrator," which is a disadvantage when dealing with so distinct a personality. In the fiction of *Amour nuptial*, he is supposed to be the same person as the narrator of *Silbermann* and to have written a novel by that name. Except for minor details to substantiate the fact that the narrator of *Amour nuptial* is the narrator of *Silbermann* grown up, there is no reference to Silbermann himself either in the first half of the original text or in the published volume. *Amour nuptial* is concerned secondarily with the literary career of the narrator and primarily with his marriage to a Protestant girl Elise Mérillier, to whom he was first attracted for purely sensual reasons. Elise loves her husband, but her excessive puritanism soon annoys him and causes him to take refuge in vice. Every attempt which she makes to win his affection only provokes further revolt on his part. Throughout all this, he, as the narrator, displays a strange lucidity; he knows precisely what is happening and is yet unable, by the exercise of his will, to prevent his wife's death from a broken heart.

Amour nuptial is an extremely tense psychological novel, as simple and as direct in style as *Silbermann*. Although there are only slight resemblances in plot, one thinks of that classic in the art of the French psychological novel, Benjamin Constant's *Adolphe* (incidentally one of the favorite books of the narrator of *Amour nuptial*).

By his own account, Lacretelle began the active writing of the first version of his novel in 1926 after his return from Italy. The earliest printed allusion to the subject is contained in the short story *Virginie ou les manies*. The Damville-like character, who is the narrator of the short story, says at one point:

> At that time, while thinking of writing, I despised invention. One can depict nothing, said I to myself, unless one has felt or seen it.
>
> That is how I came to make use of Virginie. I had in mind the subject for a novel: the story of a man endowed with so contradictory a nature that a virtuous life made him into a creature addicted to vice, whereas, once a prey to vice, he became a saint. Since the second part interested me more, I began with the end.

These aesthetic considerations and this typical Lacretelle antithesis are the central ideas of *Amour nuptial*.

The text of *Amour nuptial* itself provides a very tangible clue to the genesis of the novel. There the narrator tells us that *Les Rêveries du promeneur solitaire* stimulated him to complete his novel *Silbermann*. Although this detail is fiction rather than fact, this is the strongest indication, borne out furthermore by the entire structure of the novel, that *Amour nuptial* originates in the aesthetic considerations of *Dix Jours à Ermenonville*. In writing this new novel, Lacretelle was returning to the principle of a personal, lyrical *témoignage*. In the conceptual process, a mere antithesis could not have been the point of departure, since the novel springs full-blown from *Silbermann* itself, which, in turn, benefited from all of the imaginative thinking of the "Roman protestant."

Further evidence in the novel shows that it developed parallel to many of the works already mentioned. What the narrator has to say on several occasions about the manner in which his imagination works repeats the considerations of "Le Rêveur parisien." The closest tie-up with another text is the narrator's plan for a story about "a widow who, after having suffered cruelly from her husband and after having directed to her son all the tenderness in her body, found again in this son, as he grew up, the image of the man she had detested"—all of which is obviously the "Histoire de Paola Ferrani." It seems likely, after weighing considerations of chronology, that this passage is the genesis of the short story rather than a reference to a text already composed. (To complete the record at this point, we shall note, in anticipation of a later discussion, that the parts of the second half of the *Candide* version, which were discarded, recapitulate the pattern of *Mort de la jalousie.*)

A blurb (never reproduced subsequently) in the first number of *Candide* in which the novel began to appear, announced the new work as the "intimate biography of a man of letters of the twentieth century." This was its true subject, and the return of Silbermann in the original version was to have been subordinated to the central theme. To some extent the desire for self-examination manifest in *Dix Jours à Ermenonville* had already worn off when Lacretelle began his new novel—which turned out to be hardly more confessional than *Silbermann* itself. The narrator of the new novel, in his emotional life, is not a whit more autobiographical than he was in *Silbermann*. Lunel still figures as Aiguesbelles; the narrator is momentarily an unsuccessful banker like the author; the mother is still too concerned with material success, a tendency inspired by Mme de Lacretelle's admonitions to her son to undertake a remunerative career; and above all the narrator has many of the attributes of Damville, who is ambiguously autobiographical (especially with regard to gambling). But the resemblance to reality stops there. Certainly the author, still a bachelor, has not experienced any of the marital problems which are the subject of *Amour nuptial*. The new novel, considered autobiographically, is not a moral but an aesthetic re-examination; in this respect, at least, it is faithful to the principles of *Dix Jours à Ermenonville*.

In the more articulate stages of his career, the narrator was a Proustian seeking his subject exclusively in his personal experience (there is no mention of Proust, however, in the novel); yet, whenever he counted most on reality to furnish usable materials, the result was disappointing. "Then I understood the role of imagination in the novel," he adds. Further on he explains: "I understood that the best novel is one in which, by a miraculous and unforeseen alliance, the grafting of memory on imagination succeeds the best and establishes between these two faculties a constant continuity." All this we know to be an accurate account of Lacretelle's experience of writing *La Vie inquiète de Jean Hermelin*, just as his statement that to finish *Silbermann* he needed "a denouement which would show the principal characters with a definitive seal," corresponds to our previous conclusions regarding this novel.

What, aesthetically, is the lesson of *Dix Jours à Ermenonville* in all this? That essay had led us to expect something new. But instead of renouncing the principles of *La Bonifas*, the narrator applies somewhat anachronistically to the writing of his *Silbermann* some of the very same ones that went into the making of *La Bonifas*. For example, he says, speaking of his *Silbermann*: "These characters obeyed laws of physical and moral determinism so well concerted that in order to describe them I had almost more need for logic than for imagination." And again: "Novelistic characters take on a new dimension as soon as one has studied in them the relationship between the physical and the moral." This leaves no doubt that Lacretelle's fundamental concept of psychological structure in the novel has not regressed and that he intends, as much as ever, to be an analytical novelist. Even though the narrator alludes to the catalytic effect of *Les Rêveries du promeneur solitaire*, the conclusion is inescapable that much of the Ermenonville inspiration has been lost or, rather, adulterated and that adherence to the principle of the first person narrative is not so much a matter of policy as it is the inevitable result of the choice of subject.

As long as Lacretelle persisted in his plan to write a sequel to *Silbermann*, his chief problem was to recapture the inspiration of his earlier novel. That inspiration was predominantly Gidian. Willy-nilly, he had to become a Gidian all over again; he thinks now that the reading of *Si le Grain ne meurt*, published in 1926, helped to put him in a Gidian frame of mind. As he wrote his new novel, in addition to returning to the Gidian principle of a *témoignage* and to the favorite Gidian subject of Protestantism, he went right to the heart of the Gidian problem, the individual's revolt again social morality. The narrator of *Amour nuptial* is an immoralist. Gide himself remarked in his *Journal* on the resemblance to his own novel, *L'Immoraliste*. It almost seems as if Lacretelle intentionally set out to show that the problems of marital relationship would remain the same under identical conditions if heterosexuality were substituted for the homosexuality in Gide's novel. In both novels there is revolt on the husband's part against the wife's moral principles and then physical infidelity. As a result of the husband's immoralism, the wife pines away and dies. There are essential differences, however. Marceline, the wife in Gide's novel, is a Catholic, and also her attitude is entirely passive, whereas the Protestant Elise makes an active attempt for a time to retrieve her husband's soul. Furthermore Gide's novel is a vindication of revolt, while Lacretelle, more of a novelist than Gide, is primarily concerned with the psychological conflict between his characters.

In creating his narrator for *Amour nuptial*, Lacretelle imagined a very different character from the narrator of *Silbermann*, who was altruistic and virtuous. All that is left of the narrator of *Silbermann* in the character of the narrator of *Amour nuptial* is an occasional itching of the Protestant conscience which produces a temporary duality of character. After relating his degrading attempt to cheat at cards and his sordid night with a prostitute, the narrator of *Amour nuptial* says: "In an instant, while I was experiencing a sort of pleasure in degrading myself, something in me revolted against my acts, and my imagination, recreated in evil, caused me to fly upward toward the good and the beautiful." Without *Silbermann* to account for the itchings, this duality would be almost inexplicable. By referring back to the earlier novel, we are sure that the metamorphosis of the narrator dates from his resolution to make friends again with Robin because he has concluded from the example of his parents that life on this planet is possible only by sacrificing principles. In *Amour nuptial* Lacretelle comes back to this idea when he describes the death of the narrator's father, the judge, who is stricken with apoplexy during a trial after being accused of dishonesty. In narrating this episode, the narrator leaves no doubt that he considers his father to have been guilty.

As a logical structure, the character of the narrator of *Amour nuptial* is a convincing prolongation of the original, and yet the inspiration which produced the two essentially different facets of the character is seemingly not the same. Just as Jean Hermelin contributed to the creation of the narrator of *Silbermann*, so the nondescript character of Damville, who parades at this time through the minor works, contributes to the inner vision which produces the narrator of *Amour nuptial*. Although in neither case is the character really autobiographical, he has nevertheless grown up as a secondary personality within the imagination of the novelist. The imaginative depth of both narrators—who are really one, just as Lacretelle the adolescent and Lacretelle the mature novelist are obviously the same person—is manifestly the result of this symbiosis.

The narrator of *Amour nuptial* does have depth, as does every Lacretelle character after we acquire a second sight permitting us to see beyond the logical framework. On the surface, there almost seems to be something arbitrary in this ill-fitting Protestant conscience; or, since the novel is really a confession, like the Rousseau text which was partly responsible for it, and like the Gide novel which it parallels, perhaps we should consider it to be a rationalization on the part of the narrator in an attempt to prove that there is some righteousness in his soul. However that may be, the narrator is still a bundle of complexes which go deep into his Protestant heredity and which cannot be explained away as the natural reaction of anyone who chances to marry a bigoted wife (such an error would be the result of failure to see beyond the logical framework). As an intellectual and as a lucid novelist claiming to be an analyst of human conduct, he attempts to reason out his attitude toward his wife and to act with intelligence and decency. Not only does he fail in this, but his wife never even profits by the momentary twinges of conscience which are his puritan nature coming to the surface. There are subconscious forces at work in the character (obviously the lesson of *Le Christ aux bras étroits* has not been lost) which cause him to do evil when he has intellectually resolved to do good. His wife's attitude may aggravate these tendencies, but it does not explain them, because this character is more than a geometric theorem or a problem in checks and balances.

It was not through decency that the narrator finally consented to marry Elise Mérillier; it was only because, after their encounter with lovers in the grass when she reacted with instinctive signs of prudishness, he was fired with a desire to violate this citadel of puritanism, "to know these lips, to pluck from them this bubble of purity." Such physical attraction could not last, and soon his physical relations with his wife were to become an impossible burden. He might seek to admire the moral virtues of his wife, even to the point of becoming envious of her goodness, which reminded him of the purity and idealism of his own childhood and adolescence; but he could not help revolting against the servitude of this well-regulated existence.

Although there is no record that he ever destroyed the innumerable clocks, the symbolism of which is only too obvious, he did eliminate by an act of will that paragon of oppressive virtue, Mlle Marchal, his wife's governess, and then proceeded to break his wife's spirit by denying her the one thing she craved, his affection. Every attempt she made to draw near him was bound to abort: changing their mode of living, even trying to emulate his mistresses. The only way he could wash himself clean of her virtue was to plunge into the foulest debauchery. But even this escape was ineffectual, since his puritan conscience pursued him everywhere, finally taking the form of a fellow frequenter of brothels who reminded him with revolting bestiality: "What a wonderful life we have!" Only when he has killed his wife's spirit, broken her body physically and turned her love to despair, does he arrive at what he egotistically calls his "spiritual nuptials."

When Elise dies a physical death, the author leaves a great blank in the narrative. This may be due partly to his desire to leave an impression of the aridity of the narrator's soul and partly to the technique which he developed in writing the short stories of *Histoire de Paola Ferrani*. In the *Candide* version, Elise's death is the end of an episode, and there is a further evolution of the narrator's character to come. In *Amour nuptial*, this is the end of the novel, except for a brief episode which is really the final pages transplanted from the *Candide* version. The effect of this juxtaposition of the death of Elise and of the final pages of the *Candide* version is to heighten the feeling of emptiness and futility created by her death. One is persuaded that the narrator has gone selfishly and unconsciously through a life not worth mentioning in further detail. At last he begins to feel something of his own unworthiness and even sheds a tear when his dying mother reserves all her affection for her grandson, ignoring her own son. Even his attempts to educate and mold his son have failed because his own character was so shapeless as to leave no impression on the next generation.

A Jewish critic has said that the subject of *Amour nuptial* strikes no chord in the heart of the average Frenchman because the drama is so exclusively Protestant.[3] Obviously the endorsement of such a proposition would automatically condemn a large part of Gide's work on the same ground. What is striking, in comparing *L'Immoraliste* and *Amour nuptial,* is the more universal character of Lacretelle's novel. Its Protestant background serves only to emphasize some of the mechanics of the psychological relationships, which may still be defined as the human drama of the virtuous and monogamous wife who has the misfortune to marry a morally unstable and basically polygamous husband. There is no reason to believe that this particular husband would have behaved any differently toward a less puritanical wife, provided she were virtuous and loving. The Protestant ramifications only heighten the drama, but do not create it.

If there is a truly tragic character in Lacretelle's work, it is Elise Mérillier.[4] But there is a limitation in Lacretelle's art. He can perceive the outward manifestations of great emotional depth and can explain with great finesse the reasons for it; but he will never attempt anything like Phèdre's soliloquy in Act I, scene 3. In *La Bonifas* there was tension and at times emotion, and yet there was no great tragedy—nothing comparable to the cold, methodical and medically perfect but starkly tragic agony of Emma Bovary. André Vignet, Rose-Marie and Elise Mérillier, though tragic in essence, are observed characters, and their tragedy is always sifted through the somewhat impersonal observation of the narrator. To assuage Elise's sorrow at the thought of losing Mlle Marchal, the narrator becomes suddenly tender and says: "Try to understand why I ask this of you, Elise; it is because I want to love you." This inadvertency reveals to her the real indifference of her husband. Her awareness of her husband's attitude hastens the progress of her emotional disintegration.

How coldly analytical is the following scene and yet how adequately it suggests with the impersonal detachment of the objective novelist the tragedy of reality. Elise has just fled from her husband after he has blamed her for all that is evil in him, and now he (the narrator) is observing her from outside through the window:

> Her gestures seemed to obey a fatal and absurd mechanism, as in the case of all people we observe without their suspecting it; and the pane of glass which separated me from her added to this strange vision something frozen and distant. From time to time I saw her lips open, her eyelids blink with fright, and I had no difficulty in recognizing in this upset state the still stinging effect of my words. One of these expressions was so touching that I almost gave a slight call to reveal my presence to her with the idea of consoling her and trying to erase the harm I had done. I started to make a gesture toward the window.... But this tender intention broke against the idea that all I had said was true, that I could take none of it back, could change nothing in the certainty that I had given her.
>
> ...And I left without a sound, happy to go away from Elise with the memory of the vision which had brought her near me again....

So, supreme egotist that he is, he goes on recording with the reliability of a moving picture camera this suffering which is really greater than anything he can imagine.

Amour nuptial is a novel of analysis, less vivid than *Silbermann* and very incompletely orchestrated as compared with *La Bonifas*; and yet there is a marked progress in the subtlety of Lacretelle's art. Although the narrator of *Amour nuptial* is painfully lucid, like the analytical novelist that he is, there is no feeling that his knowledge is transcendent, as it tended to be in the case of Antoine in *Le Cachemire écarlate*. He rationalizes his own conjugal infidelity by claiming that it is the appeal of the unknown, the novelist's professional urge to know other souls, which impels him to change women with the frequency of changing linen. Even the primary explanation he gives for his behavior—that his wife's virtue drives him contrariwise to vice—is proffered in a spirit, not of confession and atonement, but rather of revenge and spitefulness. He formulates such an idea only to hurt his wife more, and not because he is concerned with convincing the reader. And what shall we think of this rationalization:

By an anomaly of my mind, an aspiration toward good never manifested itself in my case except at the sight of evil or in the momentary abandonment to a degrading action. Scarcely had I touched or breathed evil than I was spurred by a mad desire to offset it. It was this reaction, and not the sight of virtue, which spawned good in me.

The narrator considers himself to be capable of explaining everything. In reality, as we have said, he is the unwilling and occasionally unconscious victim of contrary forces in his nature. Despite the unfavorable picture which he gives of his wife's virtue, we realize that she is not a hypocritically good person *à la* Mauriac (like the heroine of one of the projected novels which the narrator describes to his wife); instead, we come to understand that she is entirely absorbed in her love for her husband, that all her attempts to reform him are desperate though awkward maneuvers to bring out some of the goodness which she still believes to be in him, and, finally, that her love withers and dies because she is incapable of inspiring a similar love in the perverted soul of her husband. By contrast with her, we see what the narrator lacks.

Although all this is still typical Lacretelle psychological analysis, the absence of formulas leads one to believe that, in keeping with his Ermenonville program, the author, like the narrator, is seeking to emulate certain English novelists who "know so well how to create the illusion of life and to represent its tragic side simply by the succession of the most minute details. . . ." *Amour nuptial* represents greater flexibility in an art which could be quite rigid, as it was in the case of *La Bonifas*, and is a step in the direction of *Les Hauts Ponts.*

Strangely enough—since literary theory is generally obtrusive in a novel—the narrator is convincing even in his role as a novelist. As we have said, he behaves like one with his wife, and his vocation serves only to increase the complexity of his character. He may not be the most appealing Lacretelle character, but, along with Le Maistre of *Le Pour et le Contre*, he is the most subtle. A modern intellectual is likely to be a much more complex character than a simple provincial like Marie Bonifas or Lise Darembert, whose reactions, in their limited surroundings, are reduced to certain more elementary patterns.

In *Amour nuptial*, even the problem of integrating the vocation of the novelist in the action of the story has been successfully surmounted; the narrator's discussions and arguments with his wife on literary problems are an integral part of their domestic drama. When the bitter conclusion of *Silbermann*, written by the narrator to defy his wife's idealism, comes at the moment when Elise has just given birth to her son, it breaks them asunder at the very moment when they should have been closest together. No doubt some of the discussion about good and evil in the novel seems academic, but it fits in perfectly with the Protestant background of Elise.

Dix Jours à Ermenonville and the other "reveries," which succeeded it, signalized a revival of lyricism in Lacretelle's work. We have already noted how Lacretelle tarried at length over one "Proustian" episode in *Les Rêveries du promeneur solitaire* in which Rousseau sought to register a sensation directly. *Amour nuptial* contains some additional theorizing on the subject:

> "It seems to me that translating what I see into words gives me a profounder understanding of this scene. The expression is like a key which I hold between my fingers and which I can turn."
>
> "That is so true," I continued, "that very often I have chanced to stop before a landscape, a tree, a piece of sky, and gaze at them first of all like indecipherable mysteries. But, if I tried mentally to describe them, it seemed to me immediately that I penetrated into something of the mystery; it seemed to me even that if, perchance, I had succeeded in finding the most appropriate epithets, perhaps a unique expression, I would have been successful in elucidating completely the mystery of this tree or this sky. That is why I want to write."

Obviously, this is straight Proust—the steeple of Martinville. In returning to the principle of Gidian authenticity, Lacretelle is, at the same time, trying to recapture some of his early Proustian lyricism. There is not much but still enough to underline the essentially lyrical nature of the original conception. The opening pages of *Amour nuptial* are an invocation to memory and a patchwork of sensation:

For, to be alone on the terrace of Aiguesbelles, when the sun has gone down around the roof of the *mas*, gives me a happy plenitude. At the sight of the cocoonery and its grilled openings, at the sight of the vineyard and the scrub-covered hillside, memories crowd back into my mind. And it is not, as at midday, the disordered rush of images, the burning so blinding to the mind that it no longer distinguishes anything. At this time, on the contrary, when I lean on the stone, which now gives off only the warmth of ashes, each object before me lets itself be captured easily, unloads its weight of memories, then flies away with serenity.

Then the family fig tree appears, a symbol of the good which lies in the narrator's past and also an admonition for the future; it will reappear at the end of the novel, destroyed not by the narrator but by his son, who sees life from the point of view of a new generation. It is less a philosophical symbol than a lyrical element designed to give an artistic unity to the book. It was an easy matter to transplant this tree from the end of the *Candide* version to the end of *Amour nuptial.*

So far we have been describing simultaneously *Amour nuptial* and the first half of the *Candide* version of the original *Retour de Silbermann*, for the texts are practically identical. Now we shall turn our attention to the omitted portions of the original text.

The rewriting of *Amour nuptial* involved only a few deft cuts with the scissors and the writing of three new paragraphs in the epilogue.[5] In this part of the original novel, Hélène Mossé was only an episodic character, the "nurse" still mentioned in the text on page 73. Mlle Marchal, in one of her periodic attempts to find specimens of virtuous people, had engaged her because she "had, with a savage zeal, cared for a companion who was sick and even a little crazy,"[6] quite overlooking the fact that, "companion" being a synonym for "lover," the relationship between nurse and patient was scandalous by all standards of puritan morality (evidently the author does not consider it to be scandalous, since he passes up the incongruity of the situation without comment). That is all we or the other characters in the novel are permitted to know about her. Her mysterious manner intrigues the narrator, who, seeking to draw closer to her, lends her the manuscript of his new novel

Silbermann to read. Instead of returning the manuscript in person, she gives it to a servant the next morning at an early hour and then simply vanishes.

In the second half of the *Candide* version, after an interval of several years, the narrator accidentally encounters a David Silbermann who turns out to be a cousin of the hero of the novel. This David Silbermann is able to tell the story of the other David Silbermann only up to the time the latter returned to France from America. In order to satisfy his curiosity—for it must be no more than that since there seems to be no question of a resurgence of his youthful altruism—the narrator eventually tracks down Silbermann's mistress, who proves to be none other than Hélène Mossé.

Hélène Mossé's function was to integrate the posthumous return of Silbermann more fully in the novel. To justify the long digression necessary to finish Silbermann's story, this posthumous intervention had to be of some consequence in the narrator's life. Lacretelle's solution to this problem was to use again the behavior pattern of *Mort de la jalousie* (suggested, as we have said before, by Mme de La Fayette's *Zaïde*). Hélène Mossé becomes the narrator's mistress, but he grows increasingly jealous of Silbermann and finally obliges her to tell him all of the details of their liaison. As his jealousy increases, even though she has finished Silbermann's story, the narrator alternately abandons her and takes her back so many times that, in complete boredom, she eventually leaves him forever.

In giving Hélène Mossé an active role in the novel, the author tried to conceive of her as balancing Elise, since she is a sensual and mysterious character, a kind of *femme fatale*. On top of this was the suggestion, never thoroughly exploited, that she instinctively hated Gentiles and, in her heart of hearts, remained faithful to Silbermann, which would explain her promiscuous indifference to matters sexual. As Jean Paulhan remarked, Hélène Mossé was distinctly a drawback in the novel. That was really no fault of her own. The fault lies rather with the narrator, who is so phlegmatic that he is incapable of projecting his emotions outward and of experiencing that elementary but altruistic emotion called love. To be sure, he says almost naïvely: "Before knowing her, I had experienced neither these vague aspirations, independent of the flesh, which sometimes made me a child again, nor that vital force which impelled me to hope, in spite of everything, for the future of our love."[7] The one or two statements of this kind at the very end of the *Candide* version leave us skeptical, because the emotional tension in the second half of the novel is nothing in comparison to that in the first half. It is a weak ending for what set out to be a strong novel.

This lack of balance was undoubtedly due to the disproportionate amount of space assigned to the narratives of David Silbermann, the American cousin, and of Hélène Mossé. The focus is so clearly on Silbermann in the second half that the narrator slips down to the level of an inorganic Damville, having no more reality than the narrator of *Lettres espagnoles* or of "La Porte de Cipolin." The subterfuge for integrating the posthumous return of Silbermann in the structure of the novel had failed because the author had become bored with Hélène Mossé, whose original intervention in the novel had been too melodramatic to suit his exacting artistic taste.[8] It was obvious that he had returned to the subject of Silbermann with considerably more interest than he was capable of showing at that point in Hélène Mossé. Furthermore, there was an unconscious reorientation in the creative process as he turned away from the Damvillesque projection of himself and tried once more to imagine a character outside himself.

Considerable rewriting was required to erase all trace of Hélène Mossé and to demote the narrator to the rank of an impersonal *enquêteur*, and yet the parts retained and revised are so close to the original in spirit and tone that one can easily say that *Le Retour de Silbermann* is really contained in its entirety in the *Candide* version. In the rewriting, Lacretelle yielded altogether to this new compulsion toward objectivity and so successfully eradicated the subjective elements that it is now hard to believe that *Amour nuptial* and *Le Retour de Silbermann* were once part of the same novel.

In *Le Retour de Silbermann*, Hélène Mossé of the *Candide* version becomes Simone Fligsheim (in the *Candide* version, Simon Fligsheim was one of the benefactors of Silbermann's review *Les Tables*). Married to a Gentile and anxious to hide her past, she has lost all of her glamor and mystery: "She was a woman of about thirty-five, whom one might have called ugly, but whose face, somewhat too thin, bore rather unbecoming marks of febrility. She reminded one of those figures one glimpses in a doctor's waiting room, bending convulsively over an old magazine." In this passage one feels that the author is taking revenge on the defenseless Hélène Mossé. Except for frequent stylistic improvements and the addition of several pages of matter-of-fact narrative to explain how the narrator, with an old address sent by the American cousin David Silbermann, was able to find Simone, *Le Retour de Silbermann* comprises David Silbermann's account and then Hélène Mossé's (that is to say, Simone's) account as they are found originally in the *Candide* version.

The principal omissions, then, from the *Candide* version were the story of the beginnings of the narrator's liaison with Hélène, corresponding chronologically to the new pages which relate the tracking down of Simone, and the final story of the narrator's jealousy, corresponding chronologically to nothing in the new novel, which ends with the conclusion of Simone-Hélène's narrative.

The new novel therefore puts the spotlight exclusively on Silbermann. It had originally been postulated in *Silbermann* that Silbermann was a romantic Jew lacking in true originality, but there was still some small margin of doubt. The whole purpose of *Le Retour de Silbermann* was to prove that the narrator's first diagnosis was correct. Having failed in the jewel business because of his contempt for such base occupations, having failed in the book business apparently for lack of conviction, Silbermann intentionally pulled the temple of his ambitions down on his own head by alienating the sympathy of his uncle, the one person in the world left to help him—and all that because of a "secret admiration for the misfortunes of his race." Thus is the first point made.

When Silbermann returns to Paris, he founds the literary periodical *Les Tables*, which has only one subscriber, who takes it under the misapprehension that it is a spiritualist publication. The periodical fails because Silbermann lacks originality, as the narrator discovers when he examines Silbermann's historical study of the Dreyfus case:

> Whereas Silbermann had so many times made us marvel, in his schoolboy essays, at his supple and skillful language imitated from the best masters, he had expressed himself this time in long and heavy sentences, loaded with disordered metaphors. I

began to think that his old style was perhaps only a skillful pastiche, and that his true soul had delivered itself up in this piece of writing swollen with imprecations and prophetic visions.

Before his death Silbermann himself had recognized his lack of genius when he discovered the book which Leboucher, the schlemiel of Janson days, had written:

"It is because I was only one of those precocious little rabbis who, at ten, know the Torah by heart and are capable of copying it entirely and of discussing for hours a single word. That is why I was four times ranked first. But when it came to creating something, to writing a book—nothing, nothing at all. It is the Christian who did it."

Thus is the second point made.

This dogmatic insistence on these two aspects of Silbermann's character has not increased his literary stature. There was something great in him as the symbol of a persecuted race. Lacretelle was not satisfied to leave him as a symbol but yielded to a desire, expressed several years before,[9] to make an individual out of him. There is no reason to conclude that he intends to generalize, since he carefully shows us, in Silbermann's uncle, a Jew who has successfully adjusted to American society and, in Herfitz, a Jew of genius who has surmounted incredible adversity and aggressively risen to the top. The germs of Silbermann's failure are purportedly in his nature and not in the misfortunes which were his lot at Janson; when the persecution has ended, his misfortunes only increase.

On closer examination, one sees that there is also a third and more plausible explanation for Silbermann's failure. He says:

"I never truly had any admiration for the Jews, I never had any faith in their future. As soon as I began to reflect and to judge the beauty of things, as soon as I glimpsed, through the history of civilizations, the great trajectories of human thought, I felt myself drawn outside my race. In the *lycée*, I had only one ideal: to get away from the Jews and to imitate others. All that

> I said about us and against the Christians was because I was attacked, and I defended myself with the weapons at hand. But I did not believe what I said. And if I had had a chance to change blood, I would have accepted with joy. Later, in America, when I tried to retrace my steps, it was too late. I could think only of what I had learned and loved in France, and that rose up between me and my life as a Jew."

This is a strong statement and one that is undoubtedly tinged with the bitterness of later life, since it completely distorts Silbermann's noble program to be "a Jew and a Frenchman"[10] enunciated in the first novel. Moreover, it seems to imply that the persecution at Janson did have something to do with Silbermann's character after all. In neglecting to expand this idea and in overlooking all that he had said in the first novel about the evolution in Silbermann's character as a result of persecution, the author of *Le Retour de Silbermann* singularly restricts the universality of his novel.

Although the stature of Silbermann is somewhat diminished by the methodical psychological analysis, he is still, in his words and deeds, a compellingly tragic character fully sustained by the imagination of the author. It takes a little time for him to re-emerge in this light. First David Silbermann relates his cousin's failures in America, and then Simone Fligsheim tells how her lover attempted to make a new start in France with *Les Tables* and how he also achieved a moral victory over the Vicomte de Montclar-Lagrange who had married Silbermann's mother after her husband's death and who had cheated his stepson out of some money that should have come to him. Both tales, up to this point, are so secondhand and so laconic that the reader is unmoved. But gradually Silbermann comes to life as Simone continues her narrative by telling how her lover began to lose faith in himself.

First he discovers that he is incapable of writing French; then he reads in the newspapers of Leboucher's success and is convinced of his own lack of genius. His vital spark quenched, he now seeks every means of degrading himself. He lives in squalor; with soap he writes on the mirror "Death to Jews—Down with Silbermann"; and finally he forces his mistress to unfaithfulness with his friend and protector Herfitz. By these desperate acts he rises once more to epic heights, and his end is worthy of his beginning:

Nevertheless, one night, in one of those last convulsions in which the human soul seems to drive away its most tenacious devils, he was literally lifted up by delirium. Calls, hoarse cries, imprecations, came out of his throat, through which little sound had come for a long time; then he began to utter sentences, bits of poems, entire tirades, in which his companion recognized with stupefaction famous passages which he had not read for years and which she did not know were in his memory.

At the same time, as she related this scene to me, she showed me a portrait which she had kept of Silbermann. His gaunt, bearded face is frightfully thin. The protruding cheek bones, the ridge of his bent nose, the elongated cranium, all the bony structure sticks out under the skin like a rock.

And as I gazed upon this face of so strange a form I began to think that the devils which had left the brain of Silbermann at the supreme moment were our Racinian princesses and a whole procession of legendary heroes dressed in the French manner.

The morning which followed this night he calmed down. When sunlight had come, his companion took advantage of his tranquillity to part the curtains, and rays of light erupted into the room. Then he half opened his eyes. He perceived thousands of atoms which, astride the rays, slid down toward his bed and advanced in columns on the sheets. What terror came back to his memory? He made a gesture as if to protect himself. It was his last movement.

The preceding passage is not in the *Candide* version of *Le Retour de Silbermann*. As Lacretelle rewrote his novel the character of Silbermann grew on him once more and he succeeded in bringing him to life again. Assuredly these last pages compensate for whatever was coldly analytical or matter-of-fact in the beginning. With Hélène Mossé removed, *Le Retour de Silbermann* possesses all the artistic unities which we are accustomed to find in a Lacretelle novel. The continuation is an interesting commentary on *Silbermann* for those who may be devotees of this work, but it inevitably dissatisfies those who may prefer the greater ambiguity of the earlier Silbermann. In any case, the final version of *Le Retour de Silbermann* is infinitely superior to the second half of the *Candide* version, and, Paulhan's advice notwithstanding (Maurois echoes

Paulhan's opinion in the preface to Lacretelle's *Morceaux choisis* in 1938), Lacretelle was certainly right to leave Hélène Mossé for the literary historians and to deny her a permanent place in his work.

Amour nuptial and the de luxe edition of the rewritten *Retour de Silbermann* appeared almost simultaneously in late 1929. In the critical reception, the latter novel got lost in the shuffle. Few critics received the de luxe edition, and the regular edition managed to come out at the same time that Lacretelle was awarded the Prix du Roman of the French Academy for *Amour nuptial* (that was in June 1930). On the other hand, enthusiasm for *Amour nuptial* was extraordinarily great for a novel which seems to us, in retrospect, to be thin and undramatic, despite its subtle psychology. André Thérive, Abel Hermant, Gabriel Marcel, Albert Thibaudet and John Charpentier extolled it, and Gilbert Charles became ecstatic about this work which "has rivaled the creation."[11] On the excuse of the resemblances to Gide's *Immoraliste*, Henri de Régnier praised Lacretelle and attacked Gide.[12] Robert Bourget-Pailleron, Ramon Fernandez and Jean Vignaud, although paying homage to Lacretelle's skill in analysis, criticized the novel, however, for lacking emotion.[13] André Rousseaux was alone in saying that *La Bonifas* was better.[14]

René Doumic, who, according to insinuations in the press at this time, was running the French Academy to suit himself and who was therefore responsible for giving Lacretelle the prize—after having refused it to him the preceding year for *L'Ame cachée* —said on the cover of the *Revue des deux mondes*: "In awarding to M. Jacques de Lacretelle the Prix du Roman, the Academy intended to reward much less a particular book than the continuity of effort of a novelist faithful to the genre of the novel."[15]

Surprisingly the criticism of this period is much less concerned with examining *Amour nuptial* in particular than with heaping praise on Lacretelle's total literary output. The Academy award did not initiate but rather confirmed this spontaneous tribute to Lacretelle as a novelist. The round of eulogies began even before the publication of *Amour nuptial* with an article by André Rousseaux on *L'Ame cachée* in 1929 in which the critic placed Lacretelle "in the rank of our best writers."[16] Similar expressions came to the pen of Firmin Roz, Gilbert Charles and André

Thérive, and Philippe Amiguet wrote: "... a page of Lacretelle offers to our minds, tired by the 'planetary' literature of our times, a very special pleasure almost unsurpassable."[17] At the same time, Thibaudet was defining Lacretelle's new novel as "Marcel Proust written by André Gide."[18] Lacretelle's continuing success as a novelist is obviously due to the same factors which explained the success of *Silbermann* seven years before. His works have a modern appeal because of their themes, but they also provide a classical refuge from the more eccentric forms of contemporary literature.

In ten years, Jacques de Lacretelle had risen to the summit of contemporary French literature. Twice (by Paul Reboux and by Gilbert Charles) he had been mentioned as a likely candidate for the Academy.[19] In the preface to the de luxe edition of *Le Retour de Silbermann*, Ramon Fernandez had remarked that French literature falls naturally into couples: Corneille and Racine, Lamartine and Hugo, Lacretelle and Mauriac. And André Rousseaux wrote in *Candide*:

> In the domain of contemporary letters, one might notice—as one does the path of the Philosophers at Chantilly—a place that one might call the garden of intelligence. It is a place provided less with natural beauties than with the improvements of human art: Everything in it is willed by the mind; the park of Versailles itself would appear to be overflowing with phantasy and unexpectedness, compared to this garden laid out according to the most rigorous mathematics. Moreover I do not know exactly how it is made and whether, as in gardens so conceived, one sees ponds, staircases and balustrades. What I know is that this garden is dominated by two busts: one a poet's and the other a prose writer's, opposite each other. One is sculptured in the image of M. Paul Valéry, the other of M. Jacques de Lacretelle.[20]

10

ATHENS

SOMETIME in 1926 Lacretelle received a surprisingly literate fan letter from a female admirer. Perhaps it would have been the better part of discretion to let a secretary answer it, but he had no secretary. A voluminous correspondence ensued, the only one in which Lacretelle has been known to engage with such consistency. It now appears that his letters have been lost, which is regrettable since they would provide a valuable record of his literary activities. Soon the two correspondents met in Paris, and Lacretelle made the acquaintance of Madeleine T. Guéritte, a married lady much older than himself. A resident of England, she was a frequent visitor to Paris and carried on correspondence with Duhamel, Valery Larbaud, Gabriel Marcel, Ravel, Debussy and Albert Roussel.[1] Sympathetically but still not altogether flatteringly portrayed as Catherine Galea much later in Lacretelle's novel *Le Pour et le Contre*, she appears to have been a lady with literary ambitions who would have been pleased to guide the destiny of an important literary figure.

In *Le Pour et le Contre*, the hero resists the attempts of Catherine Galea to dominate him. Whether it ever came to that in real life is not known, but it is nevertheless a fact that Madeleine Guéritte did have an uncommon influence over Lacretelle's literary destiny since she persuaded him to help her translate Mary Webb's *Precious Bane*, called *Sarn* in the French version. The assistant translator, who eventually became the head translator, was inspired to emulation of the English novelist, and a major Lacretelle novel, *Les Hauts Ponts*, was presently to result.

Lacretelle states that his collaboration with Madeleine Guéritte began in late 1926 or early 1927, although the translation did not appear in print until 1930. In order to finish, Lacretelle finally spent a month in the Guérittes' home at Surbiton near London.

The year seems to have been 1929 because Lacretelle recalls that he answered from Surbiton a poll of *Les Annales* on the "dream of my life."[2] This poll appeared in December of that year. However, his sojourn at Surbiton must have occurred before July 24, 1929, which is the date of a letter from Pierre Brisson commenting on the finished translation.

Sarn proved to be so un-French that no periodical would take it for a pre-publication run. Brisson said in the letter just mentioned that the novel was too slow for the readers of *Les Annales*. In a letter of August 10th, René Doumic expressed willingness to see the manuscript. What sort of reply he gave we do not know, but at least he did not take the novel for the *Revue de deux mondes*. Both of these editors displayed a surprising lack of foresight, for *Sarn*, published in book form by Grasset, has gone through innumerable printings, including four illustrated de luxe editions,[3] and has become a major source of income for Lacretelle.

In the preface to the translation of *Sarn*, Lacretelle wrote: "Beneath the novel of human beings as it unfolds, there is the novel of fleeting time, the story of the days which pass and disappear with their indifferent, serene or tragic visage." The narrator of *Amour nuptial* expressed a similar idea after his trip to London, when he spoke of finding the "illusion of life" in English novels. Mary Webb—or was it Madeleine Guéritte?—now taught Lacretelle to look closer for the illusion of life.

On April 8, 1927, André Rousseaux had published in *Candide* "Un Quart d'Heure avec Jacques de Lacretelle." The excuse for the interview was the publication of *Aparté*, but its interest for us lies in the discussion of the novelist's future plans. *Le Cachemire écarlate* and *Le Christ aux bras étroits* are about finished; he must write a book about Greece and, at Gallimard's request, a life of Racine; but, above all, he would like to get to work on a new novel called "Recouvrance." "I should not like it to be composed," he says, "like *La Bonifas*, in terms of one principal character. In my next book, I want the reader, at least in the beginning, to be unable to guess, among several characters, who will become the most important one. I do not know, moreover, whether I shall succeed. I mistrust my natural tendency to organize everything in relation to one principal line of development." Obviously the novel which he has in mind is not the still unfinished first version of *Le Retour de Silbermann*. It is something which is seemingly very different, a vast fresco fusing nature and life, a recovery of something—perhaps the recovery of Cormatin, in other words the tetralogy of *Les Hauts Ponts*. Whether or not he had really conceived the subject of *Les Hauts Ponts*, "Recouvrance" is unquestionably the seed for his major literary endeavor of the thirties.

Before attempting this enormous novel, he had to finish not only the literary projects which were the subject of the preceding chapter but also the book on Greece, which was to be based, he said in the interview, "on a trip to Greece which I made last year." (Incidentally, we never hear of the life of Racine again.) Actually, he was to make three trips to Greece before the book appeared: September 1926, April 1927 and August 1927. *Le Cachemire écarlate* contains an enthusiastic allusion to one of these. More time elapsed, however, before he was able to get down to writing the book on Greece. In an interview he granted to Raymond Millet in *Gringoire* for December 20, 1929, we find that he is at last composing *Le Demi-Dieu*—"The Demigod, because a mortal, under the sky of Hellas, feels that he becomes a superman."[4] According to the author's account at a much later date, he composed the book without any literary interruptions, partly in his house at Montfort-l'Amaury and partly at Tamaris on the Côte d'Azur in the house which Edouard Bourdet was in the habit of lending him periodically. (In *Edouard Bourdet et ses amis*, Denise Bourdet describes how they sometimes returned to their house and found a hirsute Lacretelle living in a world remote from reality.)

Le Demi-Dieu, ou le Voyage de Grèce appeared first in *Les Annales* from March to July 1930, reappeared in a de luxe edition with engravings by Gallibret the same year, was reissued by Grasset in an ordinary edition in June 1931 and by Ferenczi in a cheap popular edition in 1936, and finally reappeared in 1955 with revisions and additions under the Fayard imprint with a new title, *Le Voyage de Grèce*.

Lacretelle had lived with this book for four or five years before it appeared in print. No one but himself was aware of this hurdle he had to cross before he could undertake his major work. In the *Gringoire* interview of 1929, he even seems to be chafing at the bit when he alludes to the necessity for writing *Le Demi-Dieu* before beginning a big work—which sounds more and more like

Les Hauts Ponts. One could easily fall into the error of considering *Le Demi-Dieu* a *pensum* when it was really an act of faith. Mary Webb notwithstanding, Lacretelle was still looking to the classical tradition for his inspiration. He had gone to Greece the first time with fear and trepidation—fear that the land of the immortals might turn out to be a succession of fly-infested, dusty donkey trails leading up to a few broken stones and uncomfortable lodgings; trepidation that somehow his literary gifts might be unequal to the task of rendering the beauty that was Greece, should he chance to discover it somewhere along his road. To use his own expression, the "marriage" took place naturally and spontaneously. The result was one of Lacretelle's most fervent books. It was, indeed, the accomplishment of a spiritual journey which started in Proust's Combray and ended in Pericles's Athens. *Le Demi-Dieu* was a necessary and fruitful prelude to *Les Hauts Ponts.*

Ostensibly relating one trip to Greece, *Le Demi-Dieu* combined all three. Here is Lacretelle's reply to our request for information on this subject: "The first itinerary corresponds to that of the book. Embarkation at Venice, landing at Bari, at Santi Quaranta, sojourn at Corfu, then Patras and Olympia before Athens. From there, the classical visits (Peloponnesus, Delphi), but not the islands, which date (including Crete) from the second trip. In the course of the third, I filled in my gaps by making some secondary trips (Epirus) and by revisiting what I had already seen. I wanted to go to Bassa (temple of Apollo in the Peloponnesus), but a storm, which made the roads impassable, forced me to turn back."[5]

Le Demi-Dieu, among all Lacretelle's writings, comes closest to being a pure travel book; it lacks particularly the fictional tangents which were the real subjects of *Lettres espagnoles* and *Histoire de Paola Ferrani*. Abandoning his introspective, fictional world as much as it was possible for him to do, he set for himself the new task of describing Greece. This was the result not alone of an exceptional enthusiasm for his subject but, even more, of an intimate persuasion that something had heretofore been lacking in his literary art. He calls this new attitude an awareness of nature, and we have only to return to his preface to *Sarn* to realize that he owes these new perceptions to Mary Webb. In the preface, he says: "I went forward slowly before the landscapes of the book. As I searched for and studied the words, these landscapes became engraved more forcefully in me than others which I had seen a thousand times; the return of the seasons, so well observed by Mary Webb, showed them to me from all angles; it seemed to me that I had acquired a piece of land and was clearing it." In *Le Demi-Dieu*, he alludes to "these strange refusals which so long kept me from nature" and then adds: "The lines, the forms, the colors of nature, became perceptible to me after I learned by groping the equilibrium of a sentence and the musicality of a word."

Lacretelle was really doing himself an injustice in saying that he had hitherto been impervious to nature, for *Dix Jours à Ermenonville*, among other writings, is there to prove the contrary. In fact, he says in that work that he had already formed years before in Cambridge the habit of looking at things "for the effect that they might produce if I were to give a picture of them." He had also discussed thoroughly in *Amour nuptial* the problem of representing the "mystery" of an object. Having once absorbed so much of Proust, Lacretelle was keenly aware of the aesthetic principle of the transformation of an object through art.

In *Le Demi-Dieu* he stands in ecstasy before a mere olive: "All my thought gravitated around it, and not in the heavy attraction of a dream, but in a sparkling game which showed me the heads and tails of arguments, the resemblances and dissonances of images, an entire singing swarm of ideas." And later, in the same book, there is a reaffirmation of the aesthetic principle: "We sometimes chance to look with sudden delicacy at the corolla of a flower or the body of an insect which we have seen a thousand times and which we thought we possessed thoroughly. And this minute object begins to shine so hard that it casts great lights into all corners of the mind." *Le Demi-Dieu* is an attempt to express on a very conscious level—for Lacretelle's art is eminently lucid—this communion with objects. The object this time is Greece. Because he has such a poetic, even surrealistic, understanding of the function of description, Lacretelle's book is a long-drawn-out metaphor rather than a Baedeker.

On account of the time which elapsed between the three trips to Greece and the writing of *Le Demi-Dieu*, it is obvious that there is large degree of literary arrangement in the final record of Lacretelle's observations in Greece. There are moments—like the time when he describes impressionistically the light effects as the ship nears the coast of Greece—when the imitation of nature appears to be altogether a conscious process; but even in such cases, there is a new vividness and attention to reality. To be sure, we find typical Lacretelle moods. Arriving by the two A.M. train in the sleeping town of Olympia, he imagines behind each closed door a funeral wake around the body of a girl "veiled in white." And one may easily sense a certain degree of romantic embellishment in scenes like this description of Delphi: "This little platform backed up between a ravine and vertical rocks which have a burned color, these bristling and crevassed peaks around which great birds fly peacefully—all that composes a picture almost foreign to the mind, especially if one imagines the vapors which formerly escaped from the ground and the earthquakes which shook it frequently."

Lacretelle's descriptive qualities reach their highest development in this book when he ceases to write literature and focuses his attention on the challenging problem of representing what he has seen in a manner which conveys both an accurate image and an affective impression capable of rendering the intrinsic beauty of the object. Such a challenge comes in dealing with the Acropolis of Athens. It would necessitate quoting many pages of this beautifully written book to show how Lacretelle rose to the challenge; let us be satisfied with this one passage from his description of the portico of the Propylæa:

> The marble of the Propylæa has, for the eye, the substance of a fruit, the grain of a white and unctuous flesh which a knife has just divided. One is surprised, when one's hand comes to rest on the surface, not to feel it yield. And, closer up, one understands whence comes its whiteness. This surface, so thoroughly worked over that the joints of the blocks are invisible, is not however polished to excess; it has been able to retain an impalpable dust of crystals which holds the light.

In all of this description Lacretelle was not seeking the picturesque, the particular, so much as he was the universal. At least three times he upbraids Barrès, one of his earliest competitors along the well-beaten path from Paris to Athens (see Barrès's *Voyage de Sparte*), for his "fetichism" in seeing little more in Greece than a few romantic feudal ruins dating from the French conquest. On another occasion he expresses satisfaction that the Parthenon has lost its gaudy glory of the age of Pericles and become instead a living symbol of the harmony of the classical mind. He says: "This Parthenon which they wish to show me is precisely the edifice arranged for the common practices of man, that is to say delivered over to vanity and superstition. The one before which I find myself today has returned to its intact principle; all that was destined to perish has perished. . . ."

As a former hater of Gothic cathedrals[6] and as an enemy of all the disorders of the mind, Lacretelle imposed a certain perhaps even arbitrary harmony on the country of his predilection. Very likely, he did not really see it as it was, and yet his vision of eternal Greece penetrated to the very heart of his subject because the pattern of classicism was already in his own mind. It is particularly noteworthy that he derives this harmony from a contemplation of the plastic arts rather than from an analysis of Greek literature, to which, however, his allusions are frequent. From time to time, with a certain willfulness which he owes to his reflections on Mary Webb, he transfers this harmony from the plastic arts to the natural setting. But never does living man, in other words a contemporary Greek, upset this balance. All fisherwomen are Nausicaæ, all shepherds strike regal and harmonious attitudes; and that is not so much because a linguistic barrier shuts off the traveler from the contemporary Greek as it is because Lacretelle has always been incurious about the lives of others, preferring to leave such intimate details to his imagination. Although *Le Demi-Dieu* comes closest of all of Lacretelle's works to embracing real objects, we readily see how, in the last analysis, it remains a work of introspection.

At the end of the road to Athens, Lacretelle really found more of himself than of Greece. His trip to Greece, or perhaps more properly the writing down of his trip to Greece, since we cannot overlook the lapse of time between these events, was a spiritual experience comparable to his ten days at Ermenonville. The second experience was in some measure the answer to the first; whereas Ermenonville affirmed a belief in the spontaneous and the individual, Athens reaffirmed a belief in polished art and in universality. In Greece, Lacretelle had sought and found the certainty which he needed to write his new novel. In *Le Demi-Dieu* he says with conviction: "... my destiny as a writer is linked to my will...." However much he may broaden the base of his art by annexing Mary Webb's nature, he will not sacrifice perfection and universality to mere spontaneity. His will be a vibrant and a sober art: "... an art which would offer the counterpart or the parallel of certain faculties for reasoning without ever breaking with nature has always appeared to me to be the highest region in which the human mind may move." And further on in *Le Demi-Dieu*, when he is drawing his final conclusions regarding his Grecian experience, he says again: "Noble enthusiasm, I thought, the kind which gives substance to a work of art by separating it from a dream, must always be governed, in an artist, by his critical faculties." Greece, he concludes, has become part of him. He had stated much earlier in the book: "I am so made that the more colors and changing images I see, the more columns are necessary to me." That is really what he found in Greece: the confirmation that he wanted columns to support his work.

Le Demi-Dieu was (and has continued to be, since it remains in print) a very successful book, perhaps for reasons which were extraneous to the subject. As Edmond Jaloux said in *Excelsior*: "... what interests us in this book is M. de Lacretelle and not Greece."[7] And apropos of Lacretelle's book, Albert Thibaudet was impelled to speculate what Gide would have written about Greece if he had gone there: "With both Gide and Lacretelle there would be the kind of intelligence which goes to the root of things, measures them and envelops them, to be sure, but which always comes back to the pronoun *I*, to a concern for perfection and acumen."[8]

In 1932, to compensate the Editions de France for not receiving a book on Greece, as stipulated by contract, Lacretelle scraped together a number of miscellaneous stories which appeared under the title *L'Enfance d'une courtisane* in a lurid six-franc collection called "Le Livre d'aujourd'hui." Most of the volume was composed of the already twice-published fictional parts of *Histoire de Paola Ferrani*, but the lead story was new—at least in a sense. Although it was less than a year old, it had also appeared twice: in the *Revue de France* for April 1, 1931, and also in a de luxe edition published by Trémois with the date 1931 and the title *Luce, ou l'Enfance d'une courtisane*. Since the de luxe edition nevertheless bears the *achevé d'imprimer* of September 17, 1930, one must assume that the story was written before that date and not in 1931. It may even go back to 1926 or 1927 (a hypothesis which the author considers quite plausible) because of the similarity of title to *Virginie et les manies* and because of a reference to Angers, where Lacretelle wrote *Lettres espagnoles* in 1926.

In view of the probable date of composition, it is not at all surprising to note that *L'Enfance d'une courtisane* displays the same adherence to the principles of coherent psychological structure as the short stories of *L'Ame cachée*. The author appears not to have the slightest desire to achieve that new kind of spontaneity which, around 1930, he considered to be lacking in his work. As a young girl, the unnamed narrator and heroine (one might be justified in calling her Luce after the title of the Trémois edition) is threatened with a dull marriage to a newly acquired stepbrother. At the same time her new stepfather is seriously threatening her virtue, though she is still too innocent to realize it. To save herself from marriage with her stepbrother, she suddenly has the wicked idea of accusing her stepfather of having seduced her. Thereupon it dawns on her that her lie is the truth, in a sense, and that, if she does not keep her wits about her, she will always fall victim to predatory males like her stepfather. Henceforth she turns the tables by exploiting the predatory male, and thus the professional courtesan is born. Because of the subtlety of the analysis, this story, now out of print, is Lacretelle's best short story since *L'Ame cachée*; it deserves to be resurrected.

For some reason the courtesan occupied a very prominent place in Lacretelle's minor works at this time. In *Le Divan* for June 1930, he published two sketches of *demi-mondaines*, "Alice" and "Fiasco." These were part of a collection of such sketches written as "illustrations" to a series of lithographs by Marie Laurencin which appeared the same year as a volume entitled *Pressentiments*. Two of the stories bore the characteristic double title "Rose ou la femme d'amour" and "Christine ou l'Amazone."

All of this has little or no relation to the main works of the moment, except that there will be in *Les Hauts Ponts* a courtesan named Lili who follows Virginie's system (from *Virginie ou les manies*) based on the principle "that one succeeds in keeping them by their idiosyncrasies."

II

LES HAUTS PONTS—ELABORATION

LES Hauts Ponts is the saga of a provincial family at the end of the nineteenth century. In the *Gringoire* interview of 1929,[1] Lacretelle spelled out very plainly the idea for his novel: "I should like to set forth the history of a family while avoiding the bad habit which consists—*La Bonifas* is an example of it—of studying the characters in terms of a central hero. I want to create in a single novel a collection of human beings animated by their own individual life." Retrospectively, in 1933, he gave this additional information about the development of the main plot: "I had had for a long time in my mind a subject for a novel: the story of a woman marked by her attachment to a family estate. Not a harsh and narrow-minded attachment but, on the contrary, one nourished in her by the imaginative faculties and the poetic treasure of her nature. If one wishes, a case of the spell of the land."[2]

In its completed form the tetralogy tells the story of three generations of the Darembert family who lived originally in the château of Les Hauts Ponts in the vicinity of Fontenay-le-Comte, a town in Vendée. The first volume, *Sabine*, centers around the mother, Sabine Darembert, and her ineffectual attempts to escape from the boredom of provincial life and from her uninspiring husband, Alexandre. For a time she seems to be on the verge of an affair with a neighboring landowner, Jean de la Fontange, who proves to be as ineffectual as her husband. When this prospective liaison comes to naught, she falls ill, and her husband sends her to the Riviera with her daughter, Lise, to recuperate. In the boarding-house she has one last sentimental adventure with a young man of Spanish extraction, Olliès, who vanishes after embezzling all her available cash. The adventure now seems to her so grotesque that her illness recurs, and she dies shortly thereafter. Meanwhile Alexandre Darembert loses his small fortune at the hands of a dishonest lawyer. After Sabine's death, he sells the Hauts Ponts and goes to live with Lise in an ordinary bourgeois house at Vertes, where he presently dies, leaving his now grown daughter to her own devices.

Unlike her mother and father, Lise is a strong-willed person with one ambition, to get back the Hauts Ponts at any cost. *Les Fiançailles* deals with her abortive attempts to find a husband, first in a local boy named Jacques Monnet and then in a second lieutenant named Philippe Gillin du Boiscourbeau, who also slips through her fingers despite her more aggressive tactics. Finally she falls back on Jean de la Fontange, her mother's ineffectual admirer, whom she seduces in an hotel room at Fontenay, the reader being spared the details. Jean would like nothing better than to run off with her to Canada, deserting his wife Berthe; but Lise will not leave the vicinity of the Hauts Ponts, which she still covets. She has, in fact, achieved her purpose, since Jean is forced to settle a sum of money on the illegitimate child which she is going to have. With this money she hopes to be able to buy back the château which the Moussière family purchased from her father.

The first half of the third volume, *Années d'espérance*, is essentially a novel of adolescence since it deals largely with that period in the life of Lise's illegitimate son Alexis. He is a maladjusted and unworldly child whom she first sends to school at the Institution de Saint-Juire in Paris and then brazenly puts in the *"lycée"* of Fontenay-le-Comte. At the age of nineteen, Alexis has an idyllic love affair with a peasant girl named Marie Plannier, whom Lise presently uses as bait to set her trap. Since Lise learns that the new owner of the Hauts Ponts, Hubert de Prieix, is a lecherous young widower, she contrives to send Marie to the château to be a maid, with the result that the *châtelain* attacks the girl. Lise has been doubly successful since she has rid herself of Marie, whom Alexis ceases abruptly to love because the attack has inspired him with such loathing, and since she now has the means of blackmailing Hubert. Thus she drives Hubert out of the château and is able to buy it herself with her son's money. She may have the château, but she has little satisfaction in her triumph; her son has no interest in these unfamiliar surroundings, and she does not have enough money to live in the grand style of her childhood.

The final volume, *La Monnaie de plomb*, opens with Alexis at

Monte Carlo passing himself off as Count Alec d'Arembert and living with a courtesan Lili on the money which keeps flowing to him from the scheming notary Filluzeau back in Fontenay. Without his mother's knowledge, he has given the château as security. Too late, Lise discovers what her son has done, rushes to Monte Carlo and brings him home. Temporarily she manages to stave off the sale of the château, while, on the advice of her priest, she sends Alexis to a Catholic rest home run by a devout layman, M. Francisque. In this atmosphere Alexis discovers his religious vocation and decides to become a priest. His mother pursues him to the seminary of Gheel in Belgium in a vain attempt to save her son for herself. When she returns home in defeat, Filluzeau gains control of her castle, and she goes to spend a senile old age at the farm of La Huttière with her old maid Francine.

Les Hauts Ponts, next to *La Bonifas*, is the least autobiographical of all of Lacretelle's major works, and yet the elements of the plot come from the annals of the Lacretelle family, or more correctly of the Verne family, to which Lacretelle's grandmother, Marguerite Verne, belonged. Jacques never knew his grandmother, who was the first wife of Henri de Lacretelle, because she died twenty-eight years before his own birth. Among the Lacretelle family papers, however, there was a document which eventually came into the hands of the novelist; it was a memoir written during the last years of the reign of Louis-Philippe by Florianne Verne de Besseuil, the mother of Marguerite, and it read thus:

> My Grand Father was very rich, that is to say he left more than two million to my Father and Aunt. He had bought the domain of Cormatin and Uxelles from M. de Beringhen, who had inherited it from the Marshal of Uxelles, his Relative. My Grand Father had married Mlle de la Fin d'Oise, who had been brought up by Mme de Beringhen but who had no fortune. Her Grand Father had been raised to noble rank by Henri IV. My Grand Father made the trip to Italy with M. de Beringhen when he accompanied Mesdames de France, the daughters of Louis XV. In Rome he had his portrait painted, the one which is over the fireplace in the gold room. He rarely came to Cormatin, to which his wife came only once, but nevertheless he caused some extensive works to be undertaken, among others the terrace along

the river. The castle was surrounded by moats, which were filled in by my Aunt, who had received the domain of Cormatin at the death of her Father, and my Father [had received] some important properties, such as the buildings of the Little Stables of the King, where lived M. de Beringhen, Grand Equerry of France. The domain of Cormatin comprised twenty-five villages, of which the proprietor was lord. The Marshal of Uxelles had had the castle constructed, the one at Uxelles being too small and not being commensurate with his fortune which was immense. My Grand Father caused a magnificent market to be constructed in the village and had the mountain of Saint-Roch planted with walnut trees, but the municipality has now seized it as well as the meadow which it has made into a common. There was a charming chapel, painted with frescoes, inside the castle. The arms of Uxelles which were over the doors were destroyed in the big revolution of 'ninety-three. The present orchard and shade trees were planted by my Aunt. The main façade was on the north and the garden on the same side. It was only a vegetable garden. My Aunt had married M. de Sercy, lieutenant of the states of Burgundy. He was the owner of the domain of Sercy, so that at the death of my Grand Father, she found herself the owner of the three castles of Cormatin, Uxelles and Sercy. She was obliged to sell the last one, her husband having left her only debts. She also had at Mâcon the magnificent hôtel on the embankment, now the Hôtel du Sauvage. My Father lived in Paris. He had married my Mother who had no fortune. He had bought for a hundred thousand francs the office of secretary in the king's council and had taken the name of Besseuil from a fief belonging to the domain of Cormatin. All of his fortune being in *assignats* at the time of the revolution and having sold all his properties in Paris, he found himself ruined.

My Aunt had made a second marriage with M. Dezoteux, who had played a part in the war of the Vendée as a royalist, an amiable and witty man, but one who wasted the fortune of his wife, who was obliged to separate from him. He left very sad memories at Cormatin.

All of the land on the other side of the river as far as Contremson was in timber trees and the bridge opposite the castle led to the castle of Busomesnil which was opposite. It was carried away by the ice. My Grand Father liked the arts very much and encouraged artists. I once saw six, seven or eight portraits of him and of my Grand Mother also. There was the original of the one showing both of them, which was by Roslin and was of great value, and which, through unbelievable forgetfulness, was forgotten in a town house in Paris. The copy which we have was done by a young lady and was given to the Grand Father of M. Gormand, who was my Grand Father's business manager and lived at the castle. His children returned it to us, perhaps to get rid of a memento which reminded them of their original station.

As Jacques de Lacretelle read over this document, he could see his ancestor's immense pride in Cormatin, and he must also have sensed her deep humiliation, because he knew the essential facts of her life which she purposely omitted from her memoir. What she did not say was that her aunt, Mme Dezoteux, had been obliged to sell Cormatin but that she, Florianne Verne, the poor girl who had continued to live on in a room in the château, had brought the estate back into the family again. She purposely did not publish to her Lacretelle descendants, for whom she intended this memoir, that her own daughter, Marguerite, who married Henri de Lacretelle at the age of fourteen by a special dispensation from King Louis-Philippe, was illegitimate; nor did she mention that Marguerite's father was Charles Brosse, the widowed and otherwise childless owner of Cormatin who died in 1832 when his daughter was only three.

Florianne Verne left a few other things unsaid. For some reason, she boasted only about her grandfather's money and not about his ancestry; in fact she forgot to mention his name, probably because he was not of noble birth.* And did she know the rumor about Catherine-Guy de la Findoise (as the historians call her)? According to this rumor, which remains as an oral tradition in the Lacretelle family today, Catherine was also illegitimate and was really the daughter of the very noble Marquis de Beringhen, grand equerry of France. According to this version, the sale of Cormatin to Jean-Gabriel Verne was only a pretext for the Marquis, who had no other children, to bequeath his fortune to his illegitimate daughter.

* See the "Genealogical Notes."

In *Les Hauts Ponts* Florianne's memoir becomes the memoir on his estate which Alexandre Darembert leaves for Lise. But it must also be apparent that the plot of the novel comes rather from what Florianne intentionally leaves out of her memoir. The Lise Darembert who sacrificed her virtue to get back the Hauts Ponts stands for Florianne Verne de Besseuil, who might have recovered Cormatin in the same manner. In the novel Lise gets the idea for her unconventional act from the story which her mother, Sabine, told her about an ancestor, Mme du Foussais, who regained title to the Hauts Ponts shortly after the Revolution by having an illegitimate daughter with the owner of the château, a Revolutionary profiteer named Vignemale. Although this is really the Florianne Verne affair narrated twice, it is an allusion to the Catherine de la Findoise affair as well. The initial letter of Vignemale suggests that Vignemale might somehow stand for Jean-Gabriel Verne, who might very well have been some kind of pre-Revolutionary profiteer; but the fact that Vignemale had promised to marry his mistress before his sudden death identifies him, in this respect, with Charles Brosse, who, according to another legend in the Lacretelle family, was planning to marry Florianne Verne when he died unexpectedly.

In all likelihood it was the letter of Jacques de Lacretelle's mother, quoted much earlier (in Chapter 2), which first gave the novelist the idea of telling the story of the Vernes and the Lacretelles. In that letter she went on to say: "For the first ten years of our marriage, he hoped to keep Cormatin. These old stones, the memories of his mother which were there attached him strongly and he wished to keep it—then when he saw his health decline and the financial position of his father getting worse and worse, he told me: 'If I die before my father, Cormatin will have to be sold.' But he added: 'Who knows whether someday one of our sons will not buy it back?' "[3]

There is no proof that Jacques de Lacretelle ever seriously considered burdening himself with an incommodious castle in Burgundy far from the amenities of Paris or that his mother ever tried to inculcate in her two sons this tradition of the reacquisition of the family lands, but there can be no doubt that the origin of the fiction of *Les Hauts Ponts* is a nostalgia for Cormatin. Reviewing the third volume of the tetralogy a few years later, Henri de

Régnier, who had by that time become a personal friend of Jacques de Lacretelle, indicated that he understood the essentially autobiographical nature of the work, in spite of its apparent objectivity, when he said: "It is a search for what no longer exists, a vain hope to make 'lost time' live again, to revive extinguished joys, at least the impressions of yester year, so fleeting and nevertheless so desperately durable in ourselves."[4]

The elaboration of *Les Hauts Ponts*, which signifies by its very name a "castle in Spain," smacks strangely of Pirandello, for it is the case of a castle looking for an author or more exactly of an author with a real live castle in his baggage but with no place to put it. Determined to avoid autobiography, Lacretelle had uprooted the Burgundian castle of his childhood, but now the question was where to plant it again. In an interview with Robert de Saint-Jean in the *Revue hebdomadaire*,[5] he had claimed to be working on his novel in February 1930. Evidently he got nowhere until he set out in August with Mme Serge André (at whose salon he had been a frequent visitor) on an automobile trip through Berry and Poitou in search of a timeless region, unaffected by wars or by the agitation of the metropolis.

To say that he was looking for the castle itself would be entirely erroneous. No real castle could be equal to this imaginary one. Why then did he travel at all, since it would have been more convenient to remain at home at Montfort-l'Amaury and climb occasionally to the ruined castle of Anne de Bretagne which Victor Hugo had honored with an ode? The answer is Mary Webb. He felt the need for a more poetic region which would bring him even closer to the good earth, its seasonal rhythms and its occult inspirations. Feeling the lack of a communion with nature in his work, he had decided to make up for this deficiency by direct communion.

As he crossed a forest in the course of his travels he opened his guidebook and learned "that this great forest of Vouvant was considered to be the cradle of the fairy Mélusine, the patroness of dreams, of the imagination, of chimeras. This legend had left its imprint on all the country round about. Mélusine had built there dungeon towers, churches, castles. This apparition released the thunderbolt of inspiration. The dream rooted in the land, that was the whole subject of my novel."[6] Nothing could be closer to Mary Webb than the fairy Mélusine. It was Mary Webb, disguised as

Mélusine, who caused Lacretelle to stop in his travels and to take up residence in a comfortable inn (now closed) called Le Rouet d'Argent at Fontenay-le-Comte in Vendée.

A note on the manuscript of the first volume of his tetralogy tells how long he stayed there: "I worked on this first part of the *Hauts-Ponts* [*sic*] for ten days in the month of August 1930 at Fontenay-le-Comte. Then, again at Fontenay, the setting of which I needed, I continued for almost two months, from October 15th to December 10th. I went back to work on it at Montfort-l'Amaury, from January 10th to the end of February." Asked whether he had covered the Fontenay region in detail, Lacretelle replied: "I traveled about very little in the region of Fontenay-le-Comte. When I did so, it was either by renting a car or by going with friends passing through. Thus I went through a rather beautiful forest, the forest of Vouvant. I remember that I went alone to the ruins of the abbey of Maillezais, and another time I spent the night in a rustic restaurant. Next day, a pilgrimage started out from that spot to a grotto where once lived a hermit, Père de Montfort. A detestable night, moreover, and not a well-patronized pilgrimage. But I made use of these memories for a passage of the *Hauts Ponts* when Alexis is an adolescent."[7]

An anecdote which Robert Bourget-Pailleron related in the *Revue des deux mondes* in 1933 is apropos here: "Jean Tharaud, passing through Fontenay-le-Comte, saw some notables of the town. 'Jacques de Lacretelle has lived among you,' he told them. 'You must know him. This is where he assembled the documentation for his latest novel.' 'Know him?' they answered with astonishment. 'Why during more than six months that he spent here, he was never seen to speak to anyone—except to the newspaper woman.' "[8]

As much as Lacretelle needed Fontenay-le-Comte in the beginning, this initial immersion was enough to keep him going for the next five years. He seems not to have returned to the town until 1950 or 1951, when he lectured there. Only once after leaving Fontenay did he return to the Vendée in search of local color. That was sometime in the summer of 1932, when, seeking a new inspiration to rewrite the end of the second volume, he went back to Niort. At that time he wrote in a letter: "I am going to leave Niort for a greener spot. There is right near here a region called the Poitevin Swamp. It is a river, the Sèvre, which divides into a hundred canals, so that there is no road and one communicates between villages by boats. There are many trees. All that appears a fine place for me to situate the end of my book, that last part about the love affair between Lise and Jean, which was so incompletely developed in the review version."[9]

Many years later, he related what happened after that:

> I went to spend a week near Niort, in the swamp. No hotel. I lodged with peasants and took my meals in an inn where the only food was fresh water fish, carps, tenches, pikes, etc. I had rented a boat and would go along the river between the islands of the swamp. As at Cambridge, some twenty-five years before. I wanted to give the final touches to the passage where I showed Lise living with her lover. My hosts, chosen at random or rather pointed out to me by the innkeeper, formed a typically French couple. She, delicate in spite of her calling, sensitive, clean; he, a worker always talking politics, proud of being a socialist and always returning home drunk in the evening. They had with them a girl of sixteen, either a daughter, a daughter-in-law or a niece, with whom the father joked in a shocking manner. One evening, when I was returning home, I saw her struggling to escape from the drunkard. The wife, in consternation, was a witness to the scene. As chance willed it, I had to leave the next day, and I shall never forget the humiliated expression of this woman, who attributed my departure to the scene of the evening before."[10]

It is significant that none of this episode, which apparently made such a strong impression on the author, has crept into the novel. However, the literary result of this sojourn was one of the most lyrical and delicately done parts of the novel. Undeniably a certain exuberance came from this contact with nature, and one can well imagine that the author felt the same exuberance in his initial discovery of Fontenay-le-Comte.

The writing of the four volumes of *Les Hauts Ponts* was to account for the major part of Lacretelle's literary activity for the next five years. There is no record of where the other three volumes were written, but they were obviously sandwiched in between other events which we shall come to presently. Under the simple title

Les Hauts Ponts, the first volume was serialized in the *Revue des deux mondes* from June 15 to August 1, 1931, and it reappeared with a Gallimard imprint as *Les Hauts Ponts I: Sabine* in February 1932. There were some minor alterations in the text. The second volume, *Les Fiançailles* (the generic title, *Les Hauts Ponts*, remains, of course, throughout the series), was serialized in the same periodical from April 15 to October 1, 1932, and, in February 1933, was reissued by Gallimard with extensive alterations. From June 6 to August 22, 1934, *Années d'espérance* came out in the new weekly *Marianne* (to oblige the owner Gallimard) in a version slightly shorter than the final version bearing the Gallimard imprint and the date of February 1935. *La Monnaie de plomb*, the last volume of the tetralogy, appeared in the *Revue des deux mondes* from July 1 to August 15, 1935, and was published by Gallimard in September with only the most minor changes and the restitution of the remark "Je suis vierge,"[11] which the prudish periodical had deleted.

How necessary were the town and region of Fontenay-le-Comte to the creation of *Les Hauts Ponts*? In the methodical files in which the author assembled ideas and scraps of paper to assist in the elaboration of his novel are to be found a map of the region, notes on local dialects from the *Mémoires de la Société des Antiquaires de l'Ouest*, pictures of peasants in Vendean costume and post cards showing the ruins of Maillezais, ecclesiastical edifices at Luçon, natural sites and ruined castles in the forest of Mervent (which, with some justification, Lacretelle always calls Vouvant[12]), and finally numerous inhabited châteaux of Vendée. Very little of this material, however, passed into the book itself. Maillezais is the only one of these localities described in the novel, and further evidence in the files shows that the description is based rather on notes scribbled at the spot. Not even the place names on the post cards survive in the novel, with two possible exceptions: the Château de la Loge seems to have become the Château des Loges, perhaps by confusion with a locality Les Loges east of the Mervent which also provides Fontenay with a street name, the rue des Loges; and the relatively modern château of L'Hermenault, northwest of Fontenay, which seems to have become a medieval ruin, the Tour de l'Hermenault, somewhere in the Vouvant.

None of the post cards resembles the Hauts Ponts, nor can the fictional castle be located with certainty on the map. In *Sabine* we learn eventually that it is upstream from Fontenay on the Vendée River, near the forest of Vouvant. Elsewhere in the same volume is the information that two roads, a high road and a low road, lead from there to Fontenay; and a variant in the manuscript states that this route is a short cut to Parthenay. Comparing all this information, one may conjecture that, in the author's imagination, the Hauts Ponts was originally situated on G.C. 49 north of Saint-Michel-le-Cloucq and only eight kilometers from Fontenay. Since the parsimonious Lise Darembert never walked that distance but took the stage or blackmailed her friends into driving her, the impression created by the novel is that the Hauts Ponts is considerably farther out of town, especially when we are told that Vertes, the hamlet to which Lise and Alexandre move, is between the Hauts Ponts and Fontenay near the equally fictitious village of Grosbreuil.

In the files there is an old map of Cormatin calling attention to two bridges, neither of them very large in reality. More than likely this is the origin of the two bridges mentioned in *Sabine* as explaining the name of the estate. Subsequently in *Sabine* (p. 73), one of these bridges is said to have three arches; in *La Monnaie de plomb* (p. 48), however, we are told that it has five arches and that the second bridge lies in ruin further upstream. There was originally an allusion to this second ruined bridge in the manuscript of *Sabine*. In *La Vendée*, Louis Chaigne writes: "At the village of Ouillères, one comes upon a curious five-arch bridge of the eighth century of which Jacques de Lacretelle speaks in his novel *Sabine*. . . ."[13] Despite the slight error in referring to *Sabine*, Chaigne was probably right in supposing that Lacretelle was thinking of the bridge at Ouillères, which is near the grotto of the Père de Montfort.

Along with rough sketches of bridges in the files, there is also a rough map of the domain of the Hauts Ponts. If the map is to be oriented in the conventional manner, the Hauts Ponts is on the left bank of the river facing the stream. The road from Fontenay comes in behind the estate, follows around the right edge of the map and then crosses the river on the "old bridge." The "new bridge," in ruins, is further upstream. The iron grill, through which Lise was wont to view the castle in later years, is situated on another road which runs between the castle and the river which it parallels; it joins the other road near the bridge. Across the river from the castle is the farm of La Jolletière. To the right of the castle are the stables and the vegetable garden as well as "the little gate through which she comes back" (quoting the notation on the map). The castle, as at Cormatin originally, is in the form of a horseshoe with the prongs pointing toward the river. The orientation of the Hauts Ponts is therefore exactly opposite to that of Cormatin, which turns its back on the Grosne River.

In the first few pages of *Sabine*, the château of the Hauts Ponts is described in enough detail to provide an accurate, though hardly a vivid, picture. Its construction had been undertaken "shortly after 'eighty-nine, and the façade, with its ten beautiful windows and its stone steps forming two curved stairways, dated from this period." The two wings, completed during the Restoration, were smaller, less pretentious, the result of enforced economy; and "the tile roof, which was supposed to rise high and give to the habitation its sign of nobility, was greatly flattened out." Fragmentary information spread through the four volumes provides some vague notions on the position of the dining room and Sabine's sitting room with relation to the terrace; and, in due course, we learn that most of the furnishings are contemporaneous with Louis-Philippe. In the face of this meager and generally uninspiring evidence, it is hard to understand why the Abbé Faralay is so impressed with the Hauts Ponts.

The apparently insignificant detail of the low roof is a conscious or unconscious symbol. The Hauts Ponts is obviously not the noble Cormatin built by Jacques du Blé with its high roof and Renaissance turrets, but the bourgeois Cormatin which came into existence when Jean-Gabriel Verne acquired it on the eve of the Revolution. By denying the existence of all the pre-Verne history of Cormatin, Jacques de Lacretelle has written it off as uninteresting and inconsequential. The Hauts Ponts has no history, for the hiding of a few royalists in subterranean passages, the existence of which is problematical as far as the novel is concerned, is hardly worth mentioning. The same is true of the inhabitants. Although Mme du Foussais is allegedly of noble origin like Catherine de la

Findoise, she comes about by a kind of parthenogenesis just like Jean-Gabriel Verne.

Except for references to a few well-known localities such as Velluire and Niort, the geography of the hinterland is extremely vague. Nuaillé does not occur on any available map of the region, but Serzay does have a definite situation, being located east of Saint-Hilaire des Loges, which makes it east of the Mervent. Although used for characters and not as place names, Foussais and La Moussière are in reality small towns on the perimeter of the Mervent.

Surprising to say, while Fontenay-le-Comte is present on almost every page of the novel, it never assumes any definite shape. No street has a name; no public building is identified by anything but a generic term: the church, the city hall, the palace of justice, the theater, the *lycée* (called correctly a *collège*[14] when it is first mentioned in the novel). In the entire novel the only building at Fontenay which is described for as much as five lines is the old town house in which Maître Viet has his office; the information is so meager as to make identification impossible. Because Lise spent the night in a hotel which had formerly been a private dwelling, it must have been the Rouet d'Argent, 45 rue de la République. Alexandre might have spent the night at the Hôtel de France in the rue du Dr Audé, since it is said to be across the street from the post office. In *Années d'espérance*, we learn for the first time that there is a broad main street which runs from the public garden at the high end of town to the station, bisecting the town; this is the rue de la République, the most recognizable feature on the city map. This main artery seems not to be the street referred to in *Sabine* as the "rue Grande," to which the notary's street was parallel; more likely this is a reference to the Grande-Rue, the old main street of the Renaissance part of the town. Both Alexandre and Lise seem to have visited the tree-enclosed Place Verdun on the south side of town, one to peer over the parapet of the river in the direction of the estate he was about to lose, the other to glimpse through the sensuous twilight the lovers in the grass.

Aesthetically, this meager information adds up to a negative result. Fontenay-le-Comte is definitely not a pretext for local color, although it is difficult to understand how the author could have resisted describing the picturesque Renaissance houses around the

Place Belliard, the sumptuous castle of Terre-Neuve which Rapin built in 1595, or the medieval ruins which recall the past glory of this romantic town, long before it became the prosaic "Fontenay-le-Peuple." One is reminded of Lacretelle's diatribes against Barrès's Middle Ages in *Le Demi-Dieu*. Evidently he willfully shut his eyes to this picturesqueness, for he said to Robert de Saint-Jean in the 1930 interview: "I never consider the setting to be a motif which requires treatment for its own sake."[15] In all probability there is also a psychological reason which is related to his refusal to project the history of the Hauts Ponts and the Darembert family back beyond the Revolution. But the primary reason is aesthetic. In the development of the novel, Fontenay-le-Comte has an anti-realistic function; its existence as a real town relieves the author of the necessity of creating it fictionally, as he had to do in the case of Vermont in *La Bonifas*. The presence of the town is felt throughout the novel, even in the absence of any detailed description, because the fictional characters are projected against a real background to which allusion can be made without undue digression.

Unanimistically speaking, Fontenay has less personality than Vermont because there is no collective action, even against the socially ostracized Lise Darembert. However, the reader does form a mental image of the personality of the town which contrasts strangely with the real Fontenay-le-Comte, should he chance to visit it. When he alights at the almost deserted station after slow progress up a seldom-used branch line, he finds the town to be a provincial backwater quite different from the Athens-on-the-Vendée which it seems to have been in the days of Lise Darembert (although Jacques Monnet and Jean de la Fontange claimed to chafe at the bit, anyone of average intelligence was quite satisfied with the cultural advantages of Fontenay). Asked to comment on what seems to be a fictional embellishment of Fontenay, M. de Lacretelle has written: "The town of Fontenay-le-Comte was certainly more animated and more cultivated formerly, even without going back to the Renaissance. There are a library and a theater which bear witness that in the nineteenth century it was an isolated spot in the provinces which maintained its past tradition."[16] In partial corroboration, there is Ardouin-Dumazet's characterization of Fontenay as an "intellectual center" in 1898.[17]

Now let us see how the novel took form. In a radio interview in 1935 with Frédéric Lefèvre, just before the publication of *La Monnaie de plomb*, Lacretelle said: "I have no other method than to bring into realization an outline which is in my head, but I should be lying if I said that this work is uniform, continuous and easy. There are rose-colored days and black days. When things are not going right, my method of work consists of forgetting as much as possible my career, my profession, I should even say my exact identity, and of going walking in the streets or along the roads in an effort to capture in flight the secrets of a face, of a tree, of a cloud. These are moments that count, and one is especially surprised on returning to see how these chance contacts enrich the literary creation."[18] The importance of spontaneity is obvious, but, as usual in Lacretelle's case, we cannot overlook the concerted and systematic effort which precedes and also channels the spontaneity. The existence of an early outline for the entire *Hauts Ponts* in the files shows that the author had from the outset a very clear idea of where he was going.

This outline leaves no doubt that Lacretelle, from the start, conceived his novel as a *roman-fleuve*. In another radio interview on March 23, 1935, he said: "At bottom, it is an ambition which comes to every novelist at the turning point of his career. He has made use of his personal memories, he has described an adventure, done a full-length portrait. But, he says to himself, why not aim higher, why not embrace several destinies tied together by the mysterious laws of heredity and opposed by social evolution? The task will be bigger, it will require more wind, the present-day necessities of publication will doubtless oblige him to publish in fragments. No matter. The enterprise is worth the trouble."[19] In an interview with Marcel Augagneur in *Gringoire* in 1932, he had pointed to the precedent of Proust, Romain Rolland and Roger Martin du Gard at an earlier date.[20] In the 1930's, the *roman-fleuve* seems to have been particularly in the air. The year Lacretelle published the first volume of his novel, Jules Romains came out with the first volume of *Les Hommes de bonne volonté*; that year also Georges Duhamel published the last volume of his *Vie et aventures de Salavin*, only to begin again the following year with the first volume of his *Chronique des Pasquier*; and in 1936, Roger

Martin du Gard resumed *Les Thibault*, after an interruption of eight years, with the fifth volume, *L'Été 1914*.

It seems certain that Martin du Gard had a large part in Lacretelle's decision to undertake this major work. Praising *Le Christ aux bras étroits*, the author of *Les Thibault* had written him in 1927 to warn him against his habit of "dressing up second-choice pieces in valuable materials."[21] In 1930, while giving polite praise to *Le Retour de Silbermann*, he admonished, underlining this sentence: "You owe us fruits which are richer in vitamins."[22] Finally, in *Le Demi-Dieu*, Lacretelle related how he indiscreetly told some Athenians the plot of the sequel to *Les Thibault*. Obviously he and Martin du Gard had been discussing the *roman-fleuve*, and even if the latter had not exhorted him to imitate, that is precisely what Lacretelle proceeded consciously or unconsciously to do.

Strictly speaking, because of its smaller dimensions, *Les Hauts Ponts* is a *roman-cycle* rather than a *roman-fleuve*. In this area, Lacretelle must have been very much aware of the example of his friend and mentor, Abel Hermant, whose *Cycle de Lord Chelsea* in four volumes appeared in 1923.

In the list of Lacretelle's works opposite the title pages of *Les Aveux étudiés*, a collection of miscellaneous articles which Lacretelle published in 1934, three unpublished volumes of *Les Hauts Ponts* are announced: *Années d'espérance*, *Alec d'Arembert* and *La Huttière*. In reality, this information concerning a five-volume work tends to confuse our understanding of the original structure of the novel, since this arrangement does not correspond to the first outline. This outline is divided into four, not five, parts, but these parts do not correspond to the final division into four volumes. The first part covers Lise's life from the age of thirteen to twenty-one (she was born, says a note, in 1861): "Childhood; the love of the mother; the ruin; the death of the mother in Algeria far from the father; the sale; the death of the father." Except for the shift of locale from Algeria to the Riviera and the apparent emphasis on Lise in the first volume, this is the plot of *Sabine*. The second part, taking the heroine from twenty-one to twenty-six, is roughly the plot of *Les Fiançailles*. The third part, from the age of twenty-six to fifty, includes both the repurchase of the estate and the Monte Carlo episode which results in the loss of the estate again. Thus it covers *Années d'espérance* and the first portion of *La Monnaie de plomb.*

The fourth part diverges considerably from the rest of *La Monnaie de plomb*, although there are obvious common elements, and gives us some idea of the proposed plot of *La Huttière*. This is the outline for this part: "Return to the old servant. Attempt to marry her son. Refusal of the son. His trip to Belgium. Departure of the son. Her life with the old servant. Death of the servant from whom she inherits. She goes to live in the house of the servant right near the estate. Death of the son. She becomes governess of the child who lives in the house in order to get back into it. Her love for this child. Dotage. She dreams of marrying him. She becomes the washerwoman. They drive her away. One night, half mad, she tries to get some laundry to wash it. She goes through the gate known to her as a child. She falls and dies. It is freezing; spots on the rich earth." In the final version she becomes, not the governess, but only the washerwoman at the Hauts Ponts, and when she comes back to die, she slips through the bars in the main gate and not through the special gate provided in the outline and in the map of the estate. In spite of these differences, this is so obviously the conclusion of *La Monnaie de plomb* that it is apparent here, as it was in *La Bonifas*, how important the conclusion is in the thought processes which go into the making of a Lacretelle novel.

From a comparison of manuscripts, first printed version in periodicals and final versions, one finds few major deviations in plot arrangement and characters. The most striking fluctuation, an idiosyncrasy found in most Lacretelle manuscripts, is the change of names for characters. The original family name was Daremberg, which must have seemed geographically misplaced in the Vendée; hence the change of final "g" to "t." Sabine was originally Edmée (Lacretelle had an aunt by that name), which was perhaps discarded because it suggested a misleading analogy with George Sand's Edmée de Mauprat. In the manuscript, Lise was called Paule, which was then scratched out to Berthe. Both in the manuscript and in the *Revue des deux mondes* version, the de la Fontange family is known as de la Moussière, and Mme de la Moussière of the final version is called Mme de Cholais. The latter's daughter is known as Jeanne instead of Solange. Between the manuscript and the *Revue des deux mondes* version, Berthe (that is to say Lise) and Madeleine de la Moussière (that is to say Berthe de la Fontange) traded names, becoming for the time being Madeleine Darembert and Berthe de la Moussière. Among the minor characters, Froberville (a Proustian name, incidentally) is Frobert, Papin is Ouchard and Olliès is Carlo Reyes. In the manuscript of *Les Fiançailles*, Lise is known as Madeleine, and the Fontanges are still Moussières (the Monnets, introduced here for the first time, are Goads), which proves that this manuscript antedates the publication of the volume *Sabine*, wherein the names are already changed. In the remaining two volumes, there are no variations in the names of characters.

The variations in plot are more interesting but do not correspond to any radical changes of direction. In the manuscript of *Sabine*, Madeleine de la Moussière (Berthe de la Fontange) has a nephew and a niece, Henri and Geneviève Chassanon, who visit at Serzay. Henri, both a poet and a Saint-Cyrien, falls in love with Berthe (Lise), but Alexandre is opposed to the marriage because the suitor has no money, and Berthe calls him contemptuously a "handsome ninny." The development of this secondary plot requires many pages of manuscript and, by its recurring intervention, tends to detract from the unity of the main plot. Because Berthe's attitude is ambiguous throughout most of the affair, her character, which is vital to the success of the larger novel, fails to emerge with clarity. The removal of these episodes strengthened the plot of *Sabine* and reduced the eventual heroine more definitely to the rank of a secondary character until she was ready to expand naturally under the stress of significant circumstances, namely the death of Sabine and the sale of the Hauts Ponts, and to carry henceforth the burden of the action. The strange antithesis in the character of Henri Chassanon accounts for the subsequent division of the "aborted marriage," already foreseen in the outline for the second volume of *Les Hauts Ponts*, into two episodes in which Lise's first potential victim, Jacques Monnet, is a poet and her second victim, Philippe Gillin du Boiscourbeau, is a second lieutenant. Another noteworthy change in *Sabine* is the suppression of the doctor who visits Sabine in her final illness; the absence of a doctor in the final version renders Lise even more ferocious, which is doubtless what the author intended.

Changes in *Les Fiançailles* were more considerable. The surviving manuscript, labeled "second manuscript," tended to bog down first in trivialities consisting of a long series of relationships with Mlle Carria, a visit to Vertes, parties at Fontenay, all of which were subsequently eliminated. Originally, it was Carria who suggested that Lise call on Blanche Monnet. In broad outline, the plot elements remain the same in the final version, but their arrangement is different. The most significant changes serve to point up characters and plot and to set up those almost mathematical relationships so characteristic of Lacretelle's manner. In the manuscript, M. Monnet merely offers to drive Lise home; in the final version this episode serves as an example of Lise's machinations. Jacques is not a poet (maybe Henri Chassanon still existed at this time), and his only attitude toward Lise is general boredom; the poetry and Lise's letter to him are the result of later expansion. Lise had set out with the idea of winning him even before she saw him; in the final version she sees him first in the street and subsequently has the idea of a visit to Blanche, the reader being left to establish the relationship between the two events.

The most interesting changes in *Les Fiançailles* occurred between publication of the *Revue des deux mondes* version and the final version, when the author went back and lived for a few days in the swamp of Gallans. In the *Revue des deux mondes* version, reference is made to a house belonging to Jean near the swamp where they meet occasionally, but no particular action takes place there. All the psychological and lyrical development associated with the house at Gallans is missing from the *Revue des deux mondes* version; scarcely does even the psychological conflict arise when Jean exposes his "Tolstoian" ideas, as this version says, with respect to his proposal to flee to Canada. Her refusal to go with him is, in the *Revue des deux mondes* version, a shock to him; in the more subtle final version he anticipates resistance but tries just the same to convince her. In both versions Lise makes her desperate expedition to the ruins of Maillezais to inform her lover of her interesting condition, but with some important differences: In the original version, he brings up the flight to Canada again, whereas in the final version he remains cold, aware that he has been led into a trap. Likewise the scene wherein Berthe de la Fontange calls upon Abbé Faralay for help in solving the family scandal comes vigorously to the point in the final version, whereas it began originally with an enormous circumlocution about an anonymous friend, behind whose fictitious identity Berthe maladroitly took refuge.

In order to make the Abbé a more distinct character, the author went back to the beginning of *Les Fiançailles* (being unable to retouch *Sabine*) and at each reappearance of the character's name, introduced an additional sentence or two about his bogus archaeological research in order to prepare the long digression in which the Abbé is summoned before the Bishop of Luçon to explain why he perpetrated the hoax. It is directly after this scene that the Abbé, reduced to human proportions, must resume his sacerdotal mission in counseling Berthe de la Fontange. In the original version it had been intimated that the Abbé was unduly inquisitive about the private affairs of a great lady; this remark was the pretext for expanding him into a realistic character, but neither the incidents of his humiliating adventure nor the further insight into his character in any way affect the main direction of the novel.

In the case of *Années d'espérance*, the final version appears to be not a rewritten but an expanded form of the *Marianne* text. Large portions of this added material are found, however, in a manuscript labeled "first manuscript," which leads to the conclusion that the original text was cut to make the *Marianne* version. The only significant passage not occurring in either the "first manuscript" or the *Marianne* version is the three-page digression serving to expand gratuitously the characters of M. de Saint-Juire and his wife.

Changes in *La Monnaie de plomb* are rare and insignificant.

The imprint of Mary Webb on *Les Hauts Ponts* is inescapable, particularly in the systematic attention to the theme of the return of the seasons. Lacretelle's use of this theme is different, however. In *Les Hauts Ponts* the seasons march inexorably onward, aging the characters and changing their outlook on life; they register a psychological time accessible to human reason rather than a fatalistic force which precipitates man to a tragic doom as in *Sarn*. As in Rousseau, Lacretelle's seasons are really settings for states of mind. Taking spiritual leave of the Hauts Ponts, Lise walks along the river:

> For years, no finer harvest had been seen in the countryside. Good rains came regularly to soften the earth when the sun threatened to dry it out; and everything started over again, trees, plants, bushes, as if each fortnight were a new season. The river was up to a medium level, without much current, which gave the shady spots a more poetic appearance than at the period when it flowed high, forcing along its troubled waters; sometimes, where it formed an elbow, there was a little round lake which one could see on the edge of the meadow; and on the surface of these stagnant waters, motionless bubbles grouped together made one think of wild hemlock blossoms thrown from the bank by some idle hand.

It is true that the harvest has no life-giving meaning for Lise, since her economic well-being is not directly related to the success of the crops, as it is in the case of Prue Sarn, but she is still attuned to its poetic significance even though her roots are not actually in the soil.

By selecting characters tainted with typical bourgeois attitudes, Lacretelle raised an initial barrier to the full realization of his back-to-nature program. Mary Webb writes about simple peasants who, although they are contemporaries of Wellington, have anachronistic *mores* and live in a social organization which is two hundred years out of date. Between Lacretelle's main characters and the good earth there continually lies a gulf which all this poetry cannot bridge. He uses Mary Webb's nature to his own ends, as a backdrop for "those great moments of solitude when the mind, solicited at the same time by the most vast problems of the universe and the smallest hopes of our lives, really creates its precious materials."[23] In imitating Mary Webb, he is characteristically Lacretelle, the author of *Dix Jours à Ermenonville*.

One long segment of *Années d'espérance* which deals with simple peasants is very consciously modeled on Mary Webb's novel. In addition to similarities in plot we note a very particular effort to introduce occult elements. However reluctant Prue Sarn, the narrator, may be to accept irrational explanations for phenomena apparently supernatural, a sense of the occult hovers over Mary Webb's novel, with its sorcerers, its superstitious peasants, its hallucinated characters and its almost incredible sequence of events which, no matter how much they derive from the actions of the characters themselves, seem to be linked together in some supernatural order. Lacretelle must have felt that this occultism was really inseparable from Mary Webb's poetry.

That is undoubtedly why the name of the fairy Mélusine stopped him initially in the vicinity of Fontenay-le-Comte. Twice, in *Sabine*, Lacretelle introduced the name of Mélusine, as though the mere mention of it would work some magic charm; instead it strikes the uninformed reader as the flattest kind of literary allusion. In *Années d'espérance*, Alexis remembers a story about Mélusine which Francine used to tell him in his younger days. There is no allusion in the novel to the basic legend of the noble lady of Melle and Lusignan (hence Mélusine) who could change herself at night into a snake and who, until the seventeenth century, was accustomed to appear in the form of a snake whenever danger threatened a member of the family of Lusignan.[24] In short, Mélusine failed to work the literary miracle which Lacretelle expected of her, and he had to turn back to Mary Webb as the exclusive source for occultism.

It is only in *Années d'espérance* that, according to plan, this occultism emerges as a theme, since it serves as a background to the moody character of Alexis. In the episode dealing with his idyllic love affair with Marie Plannier, the knife-and-scissors-grinder Plannier is a mysterious and malevolent creature: "On his gnome-like face, lighted up by the moon, one could distinguish a curious expression, both innocent and rascally, as though he were the dupe of his own tricks." Potentially, he is a source for evil, a romantic villain, whose only villainous act, however, is to send his daughter to work as a servant at the Hauts Ponts, but then only at the suggestion of Lise, who is the real villain in the piece. In other words, his villainy is wasted. Why then is he a villain? The only explanation is that he is a transposition of Mary Webb's Beguildy, who, upon discovering that Sarn has consummated a marriage with his daughter out of wedlock and has thus thwarted his plan to derive profit from her chastity, sets fire to Sarn's harvested crop and precipitates the tragedy. Beguildy is a practicing sorcerer. If Plannier is not Beguildy, why is he a manner of sorcerer, with his mysterious observatory in the Bois de la Salle, where the scheming Lise goes to find him in the dead of night? The only function which all this sorcery and villainy has in *Les Hauts Ponts* is to provide a romantic contrast to the sweet, innocent and ultimately unfortunate daughter of Plannier. And if this symmetry in the characters is not already proof enough that Marie Plannier is Jancis Beguildy, one may mention that both Marie and Jancis commit suicide after they have been abandoned by the men they love. Mary Webb is certainly responsible for this poetic interlude, but there her responsibility ends, for the novel as a whole is conceived quite differently.

The true spirit of the novel is realistic rather than occult. Shortly before rusticating in the swamp of Gallans, Lacretelle had written in a letter: "I read very little. Criticism especially. Sainte-Beuve, Amiel. When I take up a novel, I say to myself: 'I know that sauce.' And I feel a slight disgust which is harmful to what I am doing."[25] Being in a realistic frame of mind, he obviously feels the need for more authentic sources of inspiration than fiction can provide. He turns to the critics for their humanism, not for guidance in the art of writing. Even more, as miscellaneous scraps of paper in the files of *Les Hauts Ponts* testify, he seeks authentic accounts of human action: in George Sand's correspondence and her *Histoire de ma vie*; in the *Mémoires de Mme d'Epinay*; in the works of Taine and Diderot—and so the list continues.

Among all the possible sources, we have so far found only four which bear directly on the novel. The description of Lise's body, which is said, in *Années d'espérance*, to have aged much less than her face, comes from the *Journal des Goncourt*, where it applies, however, to an old maid. The minerva, the instrument for holding young girls upright mentioned in *Sabine*, comes from the *Souvenirs* of the Comtesse d'Agoult. The account of how Alexandre Darembert succumbed to a scratch from a cane-sword, which he had drawn grotesquely to threaten his former tenant Chaffaroux, has its medical justification in a clipping from *Le Temps* in 1930 which relates how Albert Henry Washburn, United States minister to Vienna, died suddenly from blood poisoning caused by a superficial wound which he had ignored. Another clipping from *Candide* reviewing a book by Vayson de Pradenne, *Les Fraudes en archéologie préhistorique*, obviously has some connection with all the changes made in the character of Abbé Faralay.

In the files there is also a mine of unused information. For example, there are never-used notes on the hardening of dog's feet which are supposed to serve for a provincial conversation; reminders to write about hay carts passing through the streets of Fontenay; a passage on the Vendée from Stendhal's *Mémoires d'un touriste*. The function of the files was to store up ideas long in advance of their possible utilization, and in the creative process they were not always consulted. However, they do serve to underline the essentially realistic approach which Lacretelle is taking to the art of the novel.

Echoes of Lacretelle's previous writing inevitably creep into this new novel. The walk along the river in *Sabine* harks back to a similar walk in *La Vie inquiète de Jean Hermelin*; Marie Plannier commits suicide by jumping out of a window, just as Reine did in *La Bonifas*; the amorous couples in the grass in *Les Fiançailles* disported themselves previously in *La Vie inquiète* and *Amour nuptial*; and perhaps the bizarre graveyard in *Sabine* has something to do with the eccentric gravestone which Marie Bonifas erected on the grave of Claire Allandier. Certainly, the narrator of *Amour nuptial* has made a direct contribution to the sexually perverted Hubert de Prieix, just as the *lycée* episodes in *Années d'espérance* owe much to *La Vie inquiète de Jean Hermelin* and to *Silbermann*.[26]

In addition to Mary Webb, there are various literary influences in *Les Hauts Ponts*. From Jean Schlumberger's *Saint-Saturnin*, a novel about another fight to save a family estate, Lacretelle took a very minor episode—the scene in which Hubert de Prieix makes the servant girl parade in his dead wife's dresses. Memories of Daudet's *Jack* still linger on in the similarity between Le Gymnase Moronval and the Institution de Saint-Juire, both situated at the dead end of an alley and protected by an iron grill and a nondescript sign. Balzac also enters into the picture, for no one can deny that Mme Désormeaux, the proprietor of the Oasis in *Sabine*, is another Mme Vauquer straight from the pages of *Le Père Goriot*. Stendhal may have something to do with the fact that Alexandre's anger evaporates at the sight of a rusty sword, for there is a similar situation in *Le Rouge et le Noir*. André Thérive has pointed out an analogy between Jean de la Fontange and M. de Nemours in Mme de La Fayette's *La Princesse de Clèves*.[27]

But, most important of all, Flaubert continues to be, as he was in *La Bonifas*, the strongest literary influence in the novel. The restless and ill-mated Sabine is a simpler and more human Emma Bovary; as in the case of Emma at Vaubyessard, her imaginative and her sentimental life come into balance only once under the spell of the glittering ball at Nuaillé; like Emma, she falls ill when she gives up hope that her inarticulate and Platonic lover will ever tamper with the boring *status quo*. After her death, her equally inarticulate husband ruminates over his memories, just like Charles Bovary.[28]

12

LES HAUTS PONTS—ANALYSIS

SIMILARITIES of plot to Flaubert would be inconsequential in *Les Hauts Ponts* if they were not symptomatic. Lacretelle has decided, not so much to imitate Flaubert specifically, as to return to the fundamental principles of the French novel. Although he has never expressed it in quite those terms, the Flaubertian novel manifestly appears to him as the classical period of the French novel, comparable in importance and spirit to French classicism of the seventeenth century.

In *Le Demi-Dieu*, Lacretelle's remark about letting noble enthusiasm be governed by the critical faculties is an affirmation of his belief in the necessity for classicism in art. Without a doubt, he went to Fontenay-le-Comte on the rebound from his Grecian experience, which was a purification for the task ahead.

On the surface, there seems to be a definite antagonism between the Flaubertian point of view and the rudimentary principles set forth in those early interviews when *Les Hauts Ponts* was still "Recouvrance." At that time, Lacretelle spoke of his desire to write a saga, to confuse the reader by hiding the main character behind a multiplicity of characters, to combat his natural tendency to construct his characters with too much logic. In *Les Hauts Ponts* there is no confusion or lack of logic—quite to the contrary. Nevertheless, in the perfectly unified and ordered pattern of the novel, these disruptive principles remain as an aesthetic illusion. Life may be disordered, but its representation in the work of art must be subject to the critical faculties without which there is no art.

In *Les Hauts Ponts* there is, first of all, none of the intentional symmetry in chapter organization which we found in *La Bonifas*. Breaks in the chronology of the narrative occur whenever convenient and even several times in one chapter, so that the chapter is frequently no more than an arbitrary unit and will vary in arrangement between the first version published in a periodical and the final text. The chapter or subdivision of a chapter never fails, however, to taper off in typical Flaubertian fashion with the action fading out in the memory of the character, and one senses the ever-present hand of the artist. Usually one episode glides imperceptibly into the next, which in turn opens up on the Mary Webb theme of the passing of the seasons.

Twice in the novel there is the old romantic shift of scene technique when two important events are occurring simultaneously; such is the case in *Sabine* when Sabine is dying on the Riviera while Alexandre, at home, is making ineffectual attempts to ward off financial ruin; and such is again the case in *La Monnaie de plomb* when Alexis is squandering the family fortune on the Riviera while Lise, at home, seeks to ward off disaster. There are other symmetrical episodes which are even symbolical in their symmetry: Lise pursues her son to the Riviera when he is in the clutches of Satan (never named, however) and then pursues him to Gheel when he is about to dedicate himself to God, the idea being that, in her egotism, Lise makes no real distinction between Satan and God. Shift of scene, without this close relationship of parallel action, is also common because of Lacretelle's habit of expanding secondary characters in the novel. Naturally, there is nothing new in all this, since these are the time-honored techniques of the traditional novel.

The only structural technique which could be considered in the least modern is Lacretelle's frequent use of reminiscence, but only once does this system really affect the structure of the novel. That is when Alexandre re-creates in his imagination the character of his late wife and she lives again projected in a new dimension which is distinctly Proustian. Without having done violence to the traditional chronology, since this remembering takes its chronological place in the events of the last days of Alexandre's life, this part is in effect a modern flash back and was undoubtedly conceived as such in the general plan of *Sabine*. Impressed with the success of this episode, Lacretelle returned to the same technique once more with Hubert de Prieix, who re-creates Solange in his memory while she is dying in another room. In fact, this whole episode is so distinctly an echo of the end of *Sabine* that Solange, while dying, has the same sensations and hallucinations that Sabine had in her last moments. The effect of this variety in structural techniques is an impression of flexibility, serving to mask momentarily the structural balance of the novel.

The division of *Les Hauts Ponts* into four volumes is not arbitrary, since each volume heads toward a climax of its own: the loss of the Hauts Ponts in *Sabine*; the pregnancy of Lise in *Les Fiançailles*; the repurchase of the estate in *Années d'espérance*; Lise's loss of her son to the Church in *La Monnaie de plomb*. Although the novels are far from tense, they do progress coherently toward these climaxes and possess a distinct unity of plot, with the one exception of *Années d'espérance*, in which the plot takes shape only in the "Second Part." The first part of *Années d'espérance* is a *Bildungsroman*, apparently digressive since it contains the long and unrelated episode of the death of Solange de Prieix, the only function of which is to animate the character of Hubert for future use; it appears to be about to end in some form of climax when Alexis, after the excitement of hiding in the subterranean passages of the *lycée* (psychologically linked, of course, to the subterranean passages of the Hauts Ponts about which Lise had told her son), first runs away from the *lycée* and then anticlimactically returns to it. The entire narrative of *Les Hauts Ponts* does not build up to one master climax, however, since Lise never quite goes down in defeat, the idea of defeat being so foreign to her nature. Because of this failure to focus on one extraordinary episode, the reader feels that the plot has a neat arrangement but that the true unity of the novel is not in this plot arrangement.

The real architecture of the novel lies deep in the psychological framework. One character dominates the novel and holds it together, not as a tenuous thread or as mortar of any kind, but as its subject, its plot, its harmony of rhythm. This point may well be missed because the focus of the first volume seems to be on Sabine and because this first volume appears to be an autonomous novel which can be separated with impunity from the rest. In reality, this is not so. Sabine is not so much a character as a poem serving as an overture. Nothing really happens to Sabine until she is about to die; then the novel comes to life as Lise springs into action. In more prosaic terms, *Sabine* defines the forces of heredity and environment which make the character of Lise (and subsequently of Alexis). Although one's sympathies lie with Sabine, it is Lise who stands out vividly, because of her more salient traits, her egotistical devotion to the Hauts Ponts, her cruelty to her mother, her indifference to her father, whom she finally comes to look upon as a useless burden and an obstacle to her plans.

Subsequently, she may prove to be somewhat disappointing because, by reason of the consistency of her character, she contains no more surprises. But in *Sabine* she comes to life and remains alive to sustain the next volume, *Les Fiançailles*. At the end of that volume, having achieved her immediate objectives in life and being free to concentrate all her energies on recovering the Hauts Ponts, she loses all human attributes and becomes a kind of automaton unleashed for the destruction of others. Even then she remains the unifying force and, because of acquired momentum, continues to dominate the novel. Her son Alexis never quite materializes (except possibly in one scene in *La Monnaie de plomb* when he reveals his lifelong quest for his father) but remains somewhere beyond our grasp, just as he remains beyond his mother's grasp. Ultimately Alexis fades completely out of the picture, not through death, as originally planned, but through his emergence to a fuller life into which neither we nor his mother will ever penetrate. We then realize that the only person who was truly present to us throughout the novel was this shriveled old woman, lying dead with her arms outstretched toward the Hauts Ponts. The novel was not written about anyone else but her.

In getting his characters onto the printed page, Lacretelle shows that he has not forgotten the lessons he learned ten years before in shaping *La Vie inquiète de Jean Hermelin*. A short character sketch, always accompanied by physical details, will be set in motion in true Flaubertian fashion by some characteristic gesture such as Mme du Foussais' habit of jumping up to kill a clothes moth or Maître Maingret's broad mechanical smile. Realistic scenes, complete with setting, physical details of characters, dialogue and psychological impact of these details on the observer, are common in the novel and serve to give it a momentary vividness. The description of the crowd outside Maingret's office after the lawyer has absconded with his clients' funds is an example. Lacretelle obviously would have been able to construct the entire novel according to the compact realism of *Le Belle Journée*.

The 1927 interview with André Rousseaux shows that Lacretelle set out with the avowed purpose of disrupting the formula of the traditional French realistic novel with respect to the central intelligence. Even realistic novels written from the point of view of the omniscient author tend to have a central intelligence, one character whom the reader is permitted to see both inside and out and in whose cosmos all other characters have only limited orbits. Such central intelligences are Rastignac in *Le Père Goriot* and Julien Sorel in *Le Rouge et le Noir*. In *Madame Bovary* there is a distinct shift of focus from Charles to Emma after Chapter VI of the first part. Lacretelle's plan called not so much for disruption of the traditional formula as for its multiplication by attempting to elevate numerous characters to the position of central intelligence. Of course, the reader is always certain that a character has been raised to the rank of central intelligence if he is able to penetrate into his thoughts and sensations; as to be expected, Lacretelle makes frequent use of his lyrical analysis to accomplish this purpose. It may have seemed to him that he had arrived quite independently at his system of multiplying the central intelligences as a result of his own experimentation with the realistic novel, but actually he was imitating Tolstoi, whom he had so admired in his own formative years.

When Jean de la Fontange first appears in the novel as a visitor at the Hauts Ponts, he is a completely objective character, that is to say seen from the outside alone. But when he rides off on his horse, the mental optic follows him as he meditates on his conversation with Sabine and his place in life. Lacretelle applies this Tolstoian method with striking consistency to Alexandre, Abbé Faralay, Hubert de Prieix, Solange de Prieix, Marie Plannier, Jean de la Fontange and Berthe de la Fontange, as well as to Sabine and Alexis, who contend with Lise for a place as the true central intelligence of the novel. There is no doubt that it is a definite method, almost a formula for bringing more life into a scene. As we noted in comparing the *Revue des deux mondes* version and the final text of *Les Fiançailles*, the author promoted Abbé Faralay temporarily to the rank of central intelligence in the Luçon episode so that he would be more than a mere sounding board in the capital scene in which Berthe calls on him for help; a similar digression with the focus on M. and Mme de Saint-Juire is added to *Années d'espérance* in order to infuse additional life at a point where *Les*

Hauts Ponts had lost momentum because of a major gap in the chronology. In fact, it is difficult to find even minor characters who do not benefit in some degree from lyrical analysis—Mlle Carria, M. Monnet, for example. Some very live characters like Blanche Monnet and M. Francisque still manage to remain on the objective level. Two villains, Olliès and Filluzeau, never benefit by any form of sympathetic analysis because they must remain on the villainous level to be in keeping with the old tradition handed down from the romantic to the realistic novel.

Lacretelle's lyrical analysis we once called a Proustian device to express the complete monadism of the individual. In the letter Proust wrote to compliment the young author of *La Vie inquiète de Jean Hermelin,* he noted the protagonist's futile attempts to break out of his chrysalis, his desperate attempt to communicate with other people. That was the whole drama of Jean Hermelin's life, and in *Les Hauts Ponts* the same drama is at the center of Sabine's existence: "She had her eyes as though fixed on a screen on which she distinguished images, scenes, and when, through certain flashes of lucidity, she had the presentiment that she was mistaken, that all that was only an illusion, she would say to herself: 'But why should now be the time when I am mistaken?' And she would give up looking beyond the screen." This screen, which is a figment of her delirious imagination as she lies dying, obviously symbolizes that she had lived her life behind such a screen. Her inarticulate lover, Jean de la Fontange, had also been hiding behind a screen, so that finally she had given up hope of piercing two screens and had confessed to her husband to break the monotony. Her grotesque affair with Olliès was her last attempt to grasp at the reality which was slipping through her fingers. It was a reflex action which did not implicate her entire being, and yet her delicate soul was mortally wounded by the hideousness of this last experience.

Sabine is probably Lacretelle's most subtle literary creation, for reasons which are entirely foreign to the structure of the novel. That is because Lacretelle had to do violence to himself to create Lise, whereas he had only to be himself in being Sabine. In her there is none of the wantonness of autobiography but rather an inner melody which results in the transposition of emotion to a pure art form. The first volume which bears her name is the most outstanding example of art for art's sake in the contemporary French novel.

However, the multiplication of lyrical analysis in *Les Hauts Ponts* produces a peculiar result, already noticeable in the first volume. It is a common and seemingly inevitable trait for all characters given to the habit of inner scrutiny, which accompanies lyrical analysis, to be conscious of their isolation; and this universal trait may expand to the detriment of other distinguishing traits. Originally, Alexandre is an unimaginative and ineffectual, though not brutal, husband occupying the same psychological relationship to his wife as Charles Bovary to Emma, whereas Jean de la Fontange is poetic and not concerned with material things—in short a much more congenial Léon Dupuis. There is supposed to be a certain antithesis between these two men occupying opposite corners of Sabine's eternal triangle; but when Alexandre awakens spiritually after the death of Sabine and shuts out all material considerations, he becomes a greater poet than Jean de la Fontange ever hoped to be. Emotionally, he seems to have changed places with Jean. We suspect that the author did not really intend to create such an illusion, because much the same thing happens to Hubert de Prieix, the egotistical sensualist who coveted Solange only because her dog desired her but who, from time to time, acquires unexpectedly some of Jean's poetic nature.

Thus there is obviously a danger in the over use of lyrical analysis because it produces a certain similarity of character as well as the impression of a strange static world. The only character who appears to have escaped from this static world is Alexis, whose symbolical dash for the tram to overtake Abbé Feuillard in order to convince him of the sincerity of his religious vocation marks presumably his passing into a world of action and reality. The changes made in the manuscript to reduce or suppress lyrical analysis show nevertheless that the author was fully aware of the dangers of his method but, far from abandoning it, was continually striving to perfect this tool. The aesthetic reason is obvious. Lyrical analysis was Lacretelle's vehicle for a return to nature.

In the center of this static world there is a much more dynamic character, Lise Darembert. Like so many Lacretelle characters, Lise tends to be a geometrical theorem for which we find the postulates in the original notes: "Hard parts: tenacity, will to indoctrinate, no pity, avarice, ambition for her son. Tender parts: her first love, love of flowers (all her life), senile love for the child of the last owners of the château." Obviously Lacretelle wants to create neither a romantic monster like the Heathcliff of *Wuthering Heights* nor a moral monster like a typical Mauriac or Bernanos character. Even when Lise tends sometimes to emerge as a force of evil, a romantic villain obsessed with the desire to recover her castle at any cost, Lacretelle inverts the force of evil so that she really destroys herself. What was potentially a romantic situation becomes a subject for character study. Lacretelle hopes to avoid the pitfalls of this latent romanticism by this antithesis between the "hard parts" and the "tender parts." As a realist his primary concern is to make Lise as human as possible. Writing in *Le Figaro* in 1935 an essay entitled "Mélisande ou Salammbô," he set forth the principle in these terms: "It seems to me that the great progress in the novel in the last twenty years has been to suggest that good and evil are not two unshakable fortresses and that subterranean ways link them together."[1]

To humanize Lise, Lacretelle resorts precisely to the same technique of lyrical analysis as in the case of the other characters. The following passage describes, not Sabine, but Lise:

> She stopped before the most beautiful corolla, and, continuing to dream, she had in a sort of keen ecstasy the idea of the life concentrated in this white pulp, so similar to human flesh. She perceived the shivers of dawn, she imagined the burning unfolding of midday, the exquisite somnolence of evening, and the presentiment of all these secrets put a kind of fire into her throat. Oh! how she would have liked to know such happiness, so simple, so peaceful, and to know only that! She put a finger toward the flower in a gesture of unpremeditated desire.

Probably Lise's most human moment occurs after Philippe has jilted her and she wanders about in a daze, finally picking up a discarded frying pan. Lyrical analysis has definitely added something to her, but, at the same time, it has slowed her dynamic character down to the more somnolent rhythm of the book. It is difficult to decide whether this is really a gain or a loss for the novel. Perhaps the result would have been better if the reader had been allowed more frequently to penetrate into her thoughts in her more disagreeable moments.

In his radio interview with Frédéric Lefèvre just before the publication of *La Monnaie de plomb*, Lacretelle said: "It is a task for me as a novelist to show in my little models and through my characters in what respect a character apparently so difficult to unravel, is logical and natural."[2] In the light of all that we already know about Lacretelle's literary methods, we hardly need this reminder that the character of Lise Darembert is really a psychological edifice. All of the building stones are in place and still visible if one looks closely. The difference between this novel and *La Bonifas*, however, is that the architect does not flaunt his plans in our face. At the base of the edifice are those "mysterious laws of heredity," to which he referred in the other radio interview. Lise is obviously a throwback to the imperious Mme du Foussais, although the author makes a point of not telling us so; and similarly, her son inherits the dreamy nature of Sabine and Jean de la Fontange.

Initially, throughout *Sabine*, there is a certain rigidity and oversimplification in Lise's character, as so often happens with Lacretelle characters in the expository stage: ". . . the fairyland invented by her daughter was quite different. It was not a matter of childish patter improvised with a butterfly or a caterpillar. It was an ambitious love which seized hold of the castle, of the woods, of all the family possessions and made them grow in her hands."

In a similar manner, Alexis suffers from oversimplification when we first encounter him in boardingschool and learn that he gambles and spends his gains on religious post cards. This is a clue to the antithesis in his character and presages the denouement (note that the origin of the antithesis must be Pascal's wager, which has created a peculiar association in the author's mind between gambling and godliness, although the metaphysical problem never comes out in the novel).

Both of these characters later expand. In Lise's case this happens in *Les Fiançailles*, wherein the analysis becomes so subtle that the reader is never more sure than she apparently is about her conscious motivation. She purposely misses the stage in an uncharacteristic moment of recklessness, but she cannot foresee the consequences of her action; yet things work out to her advantage, and the

Monnets, father and son, drive her home. Is it an accident when she slips and falls headlong into the presence of Philippe Gillin? Did she really foresee the outcome of a liaison with Jean de la Fontange when she lured him into her hotel room? In due course she has accomplished all of her human functions and is free to devote herself to her all-consuming ambition—having got rid of her lover just as "the bee, once fecundated, gets rid of the male who has assured the future of the hive."[3] Then her character resumes a certain rigidity, but we are still obliged to deduce the motivation. Obviously, the flight of the first housemaid from the lecherous Hubert de Prieix gave Lise the idea of using Marie Plannier as bait. But we are certain of this only retrospectively when we learn that Lise later sent anonymous letters to finish off her victim. The logic of this behavior pattern is basic to the art form itself, that is to say to the traditional realistic novel. The novel must be either admired or rejected on these terms, as Roger Martin du Gard so aptly put it in the letter accompanying his criticism of the manuscript of *Les Fiançailles*:

> . . . I do not wish to enter into a discussion of your book, because it is done, finished, because it is part of a whole, and because it is an honorable work in which all your qualities as a writer and as a psychologist have had the opportunity to come into play. It goes without saying that I make a heap of reservations. On the genre. But that would get us too involved, and fruitlessly. Moreover, my reservations would have to do not so much with that book, which is completely successful, as with the road you are following.[4]

By definition, the realistic novel is not philosophical, except as the attitude of determinism may be implicit in the art form itself. However, Lacretelle was too much of a theorist in the novel to pass up the opportunity, at least once, to make his deterministic attitude explicit. In a lyrical analysis of Lise when she stops in the Luxembourg on her way to bring Alexis home after the first educational fiasco, he says: "The notion of fatality reigned over her consciousness, reigned everywhere she cast her eyes, expressing itself in the chirping of the birds, the lively fists of the children, and even in inanimate things such as this stone queen or that flag hanging limply from its staff." In a similar frame of mind, Lacretelle had written in a personal letter in the summer of 1931: "So in my novel you do not like the sad fate of Sabine. That is because I wanted to make a woman with so pure a nature that she acts and chooses maladroitly each time she yields to a desire. Moreover I have never tried to imagine characters altogether happy. I have the feeling that by showing them touched and defeated by fatality they will be more interesting and bigger."[5] Writing during this period an essay on the "Dangers of an International Literature," he attacked the notion of a didactic or moral literature, maintaining that a novel will be great only if the author "carries in his head the idea of fatality, that is to say an unhappy combat with superior forces."[6] Never does this sense of tragedy develop into metaphysical anguish, perhaps because, like Flaubert, he satisfies his quest for the infinite in the perfection of the art form.

There is no other infinite in Lacretelle. If, for example, Alexis becomes a priest, it is for Lacretelle only an interesting psychological problem related to that of escape from maternal domination and a sense of deflation when his father refuses to receive him. There is no evidence in the novel that the basic Lacretelle has in any way changed from the man who said in *Dix Jours à Ermenonville*: "If someday I seek out a priest, it will be because he resembles the Old Vicar." That seems to express the neutral attitude which he takes toward religion in the novel; there is no implied criticism of Alexis's vocation or of those who, like M. Francisque or Abbé Feuillard, influence his decision. The Abbé Faralay and the Abbé Bourrasseau are represented as human beings with decidedly human weaknesses; nevertheless, they undoubtedly represent for Lacretelle the sympathetic figure of the clergy of France, to whom he refers with a certain nostalgia in *Le Demi-Dieu* after an encounter with their slovenly Grecian counterparts.

Lise is the only character not above reproach. She expects God to serve her interests and calls upon Faralay, as His minister, to prevent the sale of the Hauts Ponts; and throughout the novel she makes use of the Church, never doubting the sincerity of her own faith, but never conceding the right of the Church to take her son from her. Despite faint echoes of Mauriac in all this, one never feels that Lacretelle steps out of his accustomed role of disinterested observer. His disinterestedness surpasses that of Flaubert, who certainly took a malicious delight in the dispute in *Madame Bovary* between the pharmacist and the curate. Obviously, we must take Lacretelle's realistic novel on its own terms, and those terms are not metaphysical.

A French realistic novel must ultimately be judged by the degree to which it accurately represents life. As one reads on in the essay on the dangers of an international literature, Lacretelle's meaning is clear when he concludes: "... the *character*. That is what one must seek above all and put above everything else in a work. That is the truly fecund seed. He who gives it to others can say anything, dare anything; he is assured of serving, more than anyone, the moral and intellectual perfecting of humanity."[7] The accuracy of the realist's observation is his interpretation of life. However, two different criteria exist for judging the human qualities of the realistic novel. Originally dynamic with Balzac, the realistic novel has undergone a slowing-down ever since Flaubert's *Education sentimentale*; Proust's work was the quietus to the realistic novel of analysis as well as its logical conclusion. Because of its Proustian inspiration, the Lacretelle novel, given to the analysis of minutiae, tends to be static. To be successful, the static novel must turn the reader inward and cause him to exclaim that life, as described in the novel, is truly his own pedestrian existence. According to this criterion, *Sabine*, the overture of the tetralogy, is eminently successful; but the remaining three volumes do not possess this quality of empathy to the same degree.

The reason for this difference may be apparent if we judge *Les Hauts Ponts* in terms of the tragic qualities of the characters. Lise Darembert's passion for a piece of property to the utter exclusion of all other emotion (even when she imagines herself to be in love, she is still scheming) is so unusual an attitude as to exclude it from the common range of experience. Furthermore, with his notion of "fatality," the author tends to give her semiheroic proportions. Her whole life is a dynamic effort to recover the lost estate, and it leads to a tragic climax when her son destroys the work of a lifetime and simultaneously escapes from her forever. This is not the fatality of Greek tragedy or the absurdity of the existentialists; it is the fatality of French classical tragedy in which the character makes his own destiny (but not his character). Thus the conception of the character is dynamic, but the structure of the novel is still static. The tetralogy does not build up to the climax; in fact, the climax, which we assume to be Lise's interview with the priest at Gheel when she realizes at last that she has been defeated, is singularly undramatic.

Very probably this antinomy between the static and the dynamic in the last three volumes explains why some readers are not altogether satisfied with Lise. She is not human enough to be a static character; she is not heroic enough to be a dynamic character. This does not mean that there are no moments of tension in the novel. On the contrary, there is excellent dramatic tension when Lise is battling with Blanche Monnet for possession of Jacques's soul; when she is to meet Mme du Boiscourbeau at the theatre and be judged; when the orderly brings her the farewell message of Philippe; and when she pursues Jean de la Fontange at Maillezais. However, all of these episodes are in *Les Fiançailles*, and the next two volumes decrease in tension. Only three moments stand out: the arrival of Marie Plannier at Vertes after the attempted rape, the sale of the Hauts Ponts when Lise triumphs, the impact of her son's profligacy on Lise. Of minor dramatic importance are Alexis's visit to his father and Lise's two pursuits of her son, first to Monte Carlo and then to Gheel. Certainly the novel had all the plot elements for heroic and dramatic action. If the action is frequently engulfed by the static qualities of the novel, it is undoubtedly because the author intended it that way.

Lacretelle did not really intend that we should read his novel for the dramatic action but for the psychological analysis. The true literary achievements in the novel are not so much the dramatic scenes as those subtle moments when Sabine confesses to her husband and then is annoyed by his inability to comprehend; when Alexandre re-creates Sabine in his imagination after her death; when the love of Lise and Jean perishes through natural disenchantment in the cold swamp-dank dawns of autumn; when Alexis turns away in indifference at the sight of his disheveled sweetheart. Among all these scenes, perhaps the greatest is Alexandre's posthumous creation of Sabine. Only Proust, who undoubtedly provided the inspiration, has ever represented more intensely the emotional life of the individual entirely divorced from the contingencies of reality, or has ever succeeded in projecting on the screen of the memory a more convincing image of another human being. In such passages, while conforming outwardly to the tradition of the psychological novel, Lacretelle is still a man of the introspective twenties.

If Benjamin Crémieux had not finished his *Inquiétude et reconstruction* before the publication of the first volume of *Les Hauts Ponts*, he might have classified Lacretelle's novel as an example of the classical revival in literature—the reconstruction following the anxiety of the twenties. Lacretelle certainly wrote his monumental novel in that frame of mind. In studying the principles of his psychological analysis we are even more keenly aware of the extent to which he turned his back on the twenties. Facetiously, in his notes on the manuscript of *Les Fiançailles*, Roger Martin du Gard had remarked: "After having given us so many minute scenes, the usefulness of which was not always obvious, now you avoid the difficulty and refuse us the scene of the rape. Zut! We had certainly earned it." He might have protested with even more reason Lacretelle's failure to describe what happened when Lise lured Jean de la Fontange into her hotel room. Lise has no overt sex life. Once she was known to stare at her body, but that was all. Is she frigid? That is a question of primary psychological importance even in the passage later added to *Les Fiançailles*: "They stopped, stretched out on the ground, and she said to herself, when she felt the warmth of another body spread through her limbs, that it had to be thus. She was aware of accomplishing part of her destiny, and she abandoned herself to this idea as another allows herself to be conquered by the flesh."

Lacretelle has gone so far out of his way to avoid any Freudian themes in his novel that he denies us a total understanding of her character. Her seduction of Jean de la Fontange is a crucial scene. Was it the call of the flesh following the discovery of lovers in the grass as she walked around Fontenay? Was it an act of desperation, of defiance against society? Was it a final bid to achieve her goal by extraordinary means when conventional means had failed? The failure to answer these perplexing questions may be explained by an essay on "Le Réalisme dans la littérature," in which Lacretelle condemned eroticism in *Lady Chatterley's Lover*, adding that the "act of possession, unless it is represented on a mental level, has the coldness of a copy or, what is more vexatious, the comic of the *graffiti*."[8] Although this was an attack on Lawrence rather than on Freud, criticism of Freud is also implicit in it since Freudianism is so thoroughly excluded from *Les Hauts Ponts*. In this respect, Lacretelle was much closer to his times when he wrote *La Bonifas*.

However, *Les Hauts Ponts* was far from being an act of defiance or a gamble. In writing his monumental novel, Lacretelle must have felt that he was crowning his literary career with an artistic achievement which would bring out the true originality of his art and that his intentions would be recognized by a respectable number of his contemporaries. Perhaps the emphasis should be on the word "respectable," for it is certain that Lacretelle's work was designed to appeal more particularly to the conservative defenders of French literary tradition to be found on the benches (the so-called armchairs being a misnomer) of the French Academy or among the highest-paid literary critics on the leading dailies and periodicals.

Yet the criticism which he most valued was not to come from the greybeards of the Academy but from the leader of his generation. On September 6, 1931, André Gide wrote to him:

My dear friend,

I am sad to think that I shall not have been one of the first to congratulate you on your book. At least I console myself a little for not having been able to know it before its publication in a magazine, by the thought that the only remarks which I might have made would have been praise. I have not had the patience to wait for the book. I read it in the Pullman which brought me back from Marseille four days ago (and which I had taken in memory of our trip together, for ordinarily I take the night train). But I had only the first three installments. They are supposed to send me the August 1st number. Already I can judge that you have written nothing better. This novel remains so perfectly objective that I wonder what drove you to write it and by what mysterious link to attach it to your intimate being. The umbilical cord is so well cut that one looks in vain for a trace of the navel. If I find you everywhere in it, it is because you alone were able to write it. You alone were capable of such delicacy of sentiment and of delineating the characters in a manner so subtlely precise. Had I read it in manuscript, I would not have thought of advising you to modify anything—but the first sentence, the "resembling those of the preceding month, would be . . ." seems to me illogical. One must understand: "would be in the likeness of . . ." And I believe that I would have written: "that this first day of May would be grey and wet like the days of the preceding month."—This to spice up my praise a bit.[9]

Dutifully, Lacretelle altered his first sentence in the way Gide suggested.

In the critical reception, *Les Hauts Ponts* suffered a fate common to many *romans-fleuves*. Since the articles were spaced over three years, the impetus of fresh impression was completely lost by the time the last volume had appeared and no critic really sought to evaluate dispassionately his piecemeal impressions. Whereas *Sabine* was greeted with much fanfare, *La Monnaie de plomb* received only respectful attention. Robert Kemp, who had hitherto never written anything really enthusiastic about Lacretelle, said of the heroine of the first volume: "I have liked Sabine more than I could possibly say."[10] And André Thérive wrote from his place of eminence in *Le Temps*: "I believe sincerely that the new novel of M. Jacques de Lacretelle is going to occupy an important place in our literature."[11] Henri de Régnier, Marcel Prévost, Henri Martineau and Ernest Seillière also rated *Sabine* a masterpiece. Apropos of the second volume, Eugène Marsan spoke of the spell which the novel cast over him; and apropos of the third volume, Louis Gillet and Gabriel Marcel continued to praise Lacretelle as the outstanding representative of the traditional French novel, which they continued to defend as a literary form.[12] Apparently one convert was made to *Les Hauts Ponts* in the course of publication; although Pierre Lœwel disagreed with Thérive's opinion about *Sabine*, he said he was won over by *Les Fiançailles*.[13] From the outset, however, Edmond Jaloux and Benjamin Crémieux were critical of a certain willfulness in Lacretelle's manner, although Jaloux gradually came to be more receptive after encountering the character of Alexis.[14] When *La Monnaie de plomb* appeared, only two defenders of the novel remained articulate, Robert Kemp and Auguste Bailly.[15] That does not necessarily mean that the other defenders had recanted but, failing to write articles at this time, they were not at the finishing line.

Lacretelle himself must have been impressed with an increasing severity in the criticism, and perhaps it was for this reason that *Les Hauts Ponts* eventually had only four volumes instead of the five announced in 1934. As a character, Sabine had a very strong appeal, but Lise aroused little sympathy (Chaumeix was an exception to the rule since he found her "moving"), probably because she was less close "to the heart of M. de Lacretelle," as Marcel Arland pointed out by way of criticism.[16] André Thérive felt the same way about Lise; but when he encountered the "schizoid" character of Alexis, this erstwhile defender of Lacretelle raised cries of horror and accused his favorite author of adopting "tricks which have been serving M. Green and others for the last ten years."[17] The third volume was the most severely criticized; André Billy objected to certain gratuitous developments in the plot and to the "lack of emotional involvement"; André Rousseaux, once a staunch supporter of Lacretelle, said that he had never had much enthusiasm for *Les Hauts Ponts*; Robert Brasillach accused Lacretelle of writing in an outmoded nineteenth century manner; and Marcel Arland charged that in the third volume Lacretelle was only "filling the canvas which he has set for himself."[18] A more polite attitude toward *La Monnaie de plomb* (Charpentier's remark that we should admire the "harmonious proportions" was typical) did nothing to redress this unfavorable balance.[19]

Except for Jean Baudry, who wrote a very poor article,[20] no critic attempted to view the novel as a whole, and none has since. *Les Hauts Ponts* has not been a popular novel, and, although it remains in print, it has never been honored with de luxe editions, as *Silbermann*, *La Bonifas* and *Le Demi-Dieu* have been since the Liberation. Unquestionably, it was a casualty of changing literary tastes and was already quite dated when the last volume appeared. That is indeed ironical, since it was written in a classical spirit with the avowed purpose of transcending contemporary idiosyncrasies. There is a definite need for a re-evaluation of this monumental novel—the *Jeune Parque* of the contemporary novel, to use Gillet's expression.[21]

13

THE PUBLIC LETTER-WRITER

ON March 26, 1931, a tall, distinguished man of forty-seven, who certainly did not look his years, was seated opposite a young lady of eighteen and her grandmother as one of the new Pullman trains sped southward toward Marseille. Whenever the grandmother's glance was averted, his eyes would fasten on the girl. On leaving the train, he surreptitiously slipped her his personal card on which was penciled this note: "Shall I not be able to see you again someday? I know very well that I should not ask in this manner. But how? If this request displeases you, forgive me and forget me. If not, try to inform me that I have not annoyed you by looking at you all day long. I shall be back in Paris on April 18th."[1] A telephone number followed.

The young lady had had the audacity to return all his glances, although she was hardly the frivolous type, because she had the advantage of knowing his identity. His portrait was in the *Nouvelles littéraires* which she had bought at the station.[2] The distinguished gentleman was the author of the recently published *Le Demi-Dieu, ou le Voyage de Grèce*, who, after an interval of four years, was making another pilgrimage to Attica.[3] The young lady, whose name the author had no way of knowing, was Yolande de Naurois. For purely professional reasons it might have interested him to learn that she was descended from Racine, whose granddaughter had married a Naurois d'Ablancourt. The Naurois family no longer had any literary pretensions or interest and, for generations, had been serving incumbent French regimes in a military capacity. One might say that the only thing which the gentleman and the girl had in common was a little *particule*. Everything else, beginning with the gap in ages, argued against any sequel to this mute flirtation. On both sides there was a heavy heritage: on one, an intellectual tradition of liberalism coupled with indifference to all forms of mysticism; on the other, a record of adherence to the most conservative political principles and of devoutness in religion.

She neither telephoned nor wrote, being a proper young lady, but managed to meet him through mutual acquaintances in June. Almost from the first, whenever they were alone, they talked of an eventual marriage. A passage in one of his letters to her at this time alludes to the difficulty of reconciling romance with literary production: "I had thought of going to stay near you in September, but that would mean giving up my work. We have such difficulty arranging our little meetings that one can scarcely imagine any other occupation. And then I should not desire any other, and to see you a few minutes I would spend two hours in front of the station post office. The Hauts Ponts would collapse."[4]

Her family did look askance at this projected union with the author of *Amour nuptial*, or with any author, for that matter. The only thing to do was to wait until she was twenty-one. On Thursday, April 6, 1933, in the church of Saint-Philippe-du-Roule in Paris,[5] they were married with a minimum of ceremony. Henri de Régnier was one of the witnesses. After the wedding came a honeymoon at Majorca, chronicled by an impersonal travel article in *Les Annales politiques et littéraires*,[6] and then a visit to Mme Amaury de Lacretelle at Cap-Ferrat in the south of France. In September the newly-weds made a trip to Holland. In October 1933, Jacques de Lacretelle gave up his *garçonnière* in the Avenue d'Eylau for a second-floor apartment at 49 rue Vineuse with a view onto the Place du Trocadéro.

A month before the wedding, Roger Martin du Gard had written Lacretelle a card which probably summarized the viewpoint of his friends: "Well what can I say? Fiat! My word, you have reflected as long as necessary to avoid committing an act of folly, or at least committing it consciously."[7] In reality, this marriage was no act of folly but a turning point in his emotional life, a settling down to a meaningful existence after the profligacies of Damville. One might even presume that it was the end of a quest for emotional stability which began when an adolescent escaped from school to go to the races and continued when a young man worked his way through all the jobs of the Banque Française pour le Commerce et l'Industrie because his mother did not understand him. Such conjectures are not altogether gratuitous, since they are based on the fictional record of his marriage, the enormous novel *Le Pour et le Contre*, whose main plot is built around a similar kind of marriage.

Of necessity, marriage brought an entirely new manner of living into the existence of this rank individualist and confirmed bachelor. It was not so much a problem, in this case, of living with another person and making the necessary concessions in the intimacy of home life as it was that of accepting the type of conduct which society forces upon the individual who has both a fancy social position to maintain and a public rôle to play. In *A la Rencontre de France* (a little book on his reminiscences of Anatole France, published in 1930) he had written: "Gracious! What a terrible custom conversation is! Solitude is a liberation." During his courtship, he had expressed the same idea to his fiancée: "Society is terribly stultifying to the mind. No one seeks it less than I. I flee it even with joy, and nevertheless, when chance wills that I remain in it for some time, my mind becomes well furnished with these futilities and is amused by them. Without suspecting it, I must be flattered to relate such and such a little anecdote, a very insignificant one but one in which I manage to insert a name or an advantageous scene. I probably did that with you. You must forgive me. It is not at all my true nature."[8] How many times, in daily life during the years to come, he was called upon to tell his little anecdotes and put up a social front! Not only that, but how little time there was left for serious work! He had never been able to write in Paris, and he still had to seek out the anonymous hotel room or take refuge in Montfort-l'Amaury. Now the opportunities for such escape were to become more and more rare.

A daughter, Anne, was born to the Lacretelles in 1934 and a son, Amaury, in 1937. The arrival of children, however welcome they were in the household, certainly did not free any more time for writing.

If home life and social obligations interfered with literary production, it was through no fault of Mme de Lacretelle. She quickly became a faithful amanuensis and literary advisor. It was she, henceforth, who typed out her husband's manuscripts. In 1937 she collaborated with him in translating Emily Brontë's *Wuthering Heights* under the title *Haute-Plainte*.

The change of habits did not affect *Les Hauts Ponts*, the last two volumes of which appeared in record time. With characteristic impatience to be on to another major work which would be, aesthetically, the antidote to the previous one, he had no sooner finished describing *La Monnaie de plomb* in the pre-publication interview with Frédéric Lefèvre,[9] than he launched into a description of his new novel, for which he had already found a title, *Le Pour et le Contre*. In 1936 he mentioned it again in an interview with Gaëtan Sanvoisin in *Candide*[10] and, in another interview with Marina Paul-Bousquet in the *Nouvelles littéraires* in October of the following year, he said: "...I have just begun *Le Pour et le Contre*, a novel which takes place in Paris and which will comprise, I think, several parts but in a single volume."[11] In a brief interview in *Les Annales* in late 1937, he said: "I certainly expect that it will appear next year."[12] That was an optimistic prediction, for it was far from ready even the next year and was to undergo the same fate as Proust's *A la Recherche du temps perdu*—to be interrupted by a war and then to expand further as a result of the delay in publication.

These were busy years even if there was less time for pure literature. There was still time for "impure" literature, the journalistic variety, which could be written in Paris between interruptions. Beginning in 1925 Lacretelle had ceased contributing his occasional review to the *Nouvelle Revue Française* and had concerned himself almost exclusively with writing books, big and little, fine editions and popular editions. Of course most of these appeared at some point in the periodical press, but they could not properly be called journalism—with the possible exception of the three articles on his trip to the Wagner festival at Bayreuth, which were done for *L'Intransigeant* in 1927 and appeared the next year in a de luxe brochure as *D'une Colline*. Nor do the articles "Les Joies du traducteur" in the *Nouvelles littéraires* in 1930 or "Retour en Grèce" in *Gringoire* in 1931 constitute a significant breach in his purely literary activity. It is only after he agrees in late 1932 to participate more actively in *Les Annales politiques et littéraires* and in Gallimard's new literary weekly *Marianne* that the dikes are down. Actually *Les Annales* gets little more than thumbnail reviews of current books, whereas it is *Marianne* which encourages the journalistic habit of writing on any and all subjects: literary generalities, personal experiences and impressions, and finally politics.

The evolution from a literary to a political figure is an easy one in France, where writers are invited to contribute *chroniques* which are prominently displayed on the front page of the leading newspapers. The name of the writer rather than the subject guarantees that the article will be read. The subject may be trivial on one day and serious on the next, and the fact that the author is not a political analyst in no way precludes his emitting a well-turned opinion on the most controversial issues. Such literary journalism explains the evolution of François Mauriac from a psychological novelist to one of the most widely read political commentators in France. Although he never went as far as Mauriac in this direction, Lacretelle was already acquiring the habits of a *chroniqueur* in *Marianne* and the *Nouvelles littéraires* and became a full-fledged practitioner of the art when he began contributing to *Le Figaro* in 1934.

The year 1934 saw the publication, by Gallimard, of a volume of Lacretelle articles entitled *Les Aveux étudiés*. Little more than half of the texts were of recent date (they all bore honestly their original date, which is not the common practice in such volumes), the others being reprints of articles going as far back as 1923 and of the following texts which had already appeared in limited editions: *A la Rencontre de France* (1930), "Le Rêveur parisien" (1927), *Mélanges sur l'amour et les livres* (1925) and *D'une Colline* (1928). There was very little straight literary criticism and nothing tendentious in the two articles reviewing books on political subjects.

In 1936, Gallimard published another volume of Lacretelle articles under the title *L'Ecrivain public*; this new volume was composed entirely of recent articles, some of them important definitions of Lacretelle's literary art, and tells us as much about the workings of their author's mind as *Aparté* told formerly about his personality.

The literary articles of *L'ecrivain public* represent a codification of the principles which went into the making of *Les Hauts Ponts*. The cornerstone of the system is an article entitled "Les Romans de La Rochefoucauld," first published in the *Nouvelles littéraires* in 1934 but actually written for Gallimard's *Tableau de la littérature française*, which was not issued until 1939.[13] As one might anticipate because of the epigraph from La Rochefoucauld on the title page of *La Bonifas*, the main idea is that vice and virtue have subterranean links which it is the novelist's function to observe without regard for conventional right and wrong. But he adds: "I know no biography so black that it does not inspire pity in the long run." By practicing the art of the "moralist"—which is very distinct from that of the "moralizer"—the novel transcends good and evil and rises to the higher plane of truth. Thus the novelist is an observer, and that is why La Rochefoucauld is a novelist: "It is because he exploits his daily capital just like a novelist." In the process, he arrives at certain psychological truths: "What makes the interest of a psychological truth is its force of penetration and its originality, and both disappear as its application is extended." Vauvenargues had contemptuously written in the margin of La Rochefoucauld: "a maxim for a novel." For this eighteenth century moralist, his predecessor was falsely ascribing universality to a particular observation. For a novelist like Lacretelle, it is the particular observation which counts. As we have had occasion to note so many times, the observation has greatest validity for Lacretelle in the form of an abstraction. His function is to see but then to understand. It is amusing to note, in his essay on La Rouchefoucauld, the scenarios which Lacretelle outlines on the basis of a maxim, for we have seen him develop his novels in much the same way.

The ultimate in the art of the novelist is this total understanding of a character. Physiology, he says in a preface to Henry Mark's *La Fondrière*, is the "great conquest of the modern novel."[14] And he continues: "It is a kind of *magma* in which are found heredity, the innate penchant, the ineffaceable imprints received in the first ages of life, the obscure progression of sensuality, in short, all the secret forces which weigh on the will. In summation, it is the *fatum* of the Ancients, the great law which dominates human acts without controlling them openly; and one can say that the essential element of ancient tragedy has of necessity reappeared in the modern novel." Thus is the novel equated to tragedy and placed on the same level as that genre in which the French consider that they have achieved their greatest literary triumph. In the essay "Mélisande ou Salammbô," he introduces his favorite word *fatality*: "To show all the powers of a human being and to show them at the same time bent under a superior law of which he is unaware, is to make him benefit by a long tragedy which began with the first man and will doubtless end only with the species."[15]

Though rooted in observation, the novel is essentially a creation of the imagination, he says in "Bons et Mauvais Sujets," insisting on the futility of translating a *fait divers* into literature (Stendhal made that mistake in the denouement of *Le Rouge et le Noir*).[16] In "Le Musée d'Alphonse Daudet," he again returns to this point which he had once explored so thoroughly in *Amour nuptial*, when he writes: "I have often questioned myself on the miracle which ends in the creation of a type character. . . . To imitate nature is an insufficient means. One must both copy life and deform it, make use of the present and reject what is perishable, be realistic and imaginative, precise and immoderate, trivial and lyrical. One must, in short, by a willfulness which has to remain imperceptible to others (or else it is the proverbial Epinal picture), seek a public."[17] This public, he goes on to say, is not situated in time, for the artist must compose with eternity in mind.

The style must be eternal as well, or the author runs the danger of not being understood. In "Le Réalisme dans la littérature," he doubts whether Céline's *Voyage au bout de la nuit* or James Joyce's *Ulysses* possesses these eternal qualities, since their originality is based on verbal eccentricities.[18] An enduring style also requires dignity in the treatment of subject matter, a realization by the author that he dwells on a plane higher than his subject. Too much complicity on the part of an author is what he finds in D. H. Lawrence's *Lady Chatterley's Lover*, which, according to Lacretelle, adds therefore nothing to our understanding of human nature.

There is a certain danger of pontification in exercising the trade of a *chroniqueur*. Instead of saying how he wrote a novel, Lacretelle was tending to legislate on the writing of novels in general. For this reason it is refreshing to discover an essay entitled "Académisme," published in *Le Figaro* in 1936 and never reprinted, in which the novelist frankly admits that his point of view may have limitations:

> . . . I am going to make an admission, at the risk of being marked with infamy in the opinion of my colleagues: I write because others have written before me.

If, in the presence of a landscape, or a work of art, or a conflict of the heart, I desire to express what I feel, it is because others have done so and have opened the way for me.

It is not a matter of copying, nor more often, alas! of competing, but rather of communicating with minds which, in the presence of analogous phenomena, have felt the same emotion and the same desire....

As for the concern with perfection, is it, as certain people claim, the excuse of impoverished minds? That is possible. Nevertheless one has it by birth, and one never acquires it....

In my opinion, the most dangerous academicianism is that anchylosis which pervades us almost without our knowledge by making us the slave of our own prejudices and habits.[19]

Keenly aware of such dangers confronting the artist, he had written in 1931 in "Grands amateurs": "After a few years of production appears an evil fairy, the fairy Facility, who knows our penchants, our capabilities and, while appearing to aggrandize us, extinguishes the breath of another fairy, Inspiration."[20]

Once again, as at the very outset of his career, certain doubts creep in as to whether he is not dangerously out of step with his times. In the last paragraph of "Le Réalisme dans la littérature," he expresses a certain nostalgia for the kind of literature which he had chosen not to write: "And, if one may speak for onself, may the fathers of these monsters know that those who have come to artistic creation by way of classical culture and love for the Greek column go dreaming sometimes, with devious covetousness, before the blocks of Easter Island."[21] Not only is there covetousness but also, as he said in the preface to Henry Mark's book, direct inspiration from these irrational sources: "For my part, it is these researches, these plunges into the depths of our shadows which gave me a taste for writing novels."[22] Flaubert notwithstanding, the debt to Proust is ever present in his mind.

In the roaring twenties it was easy to be out of step and not notice it, since every marcher was his own platoon. In the social-conscious thirties it was not so easy to ignore the rhythmic goose steps or the clenched fists raised in coordination. In the new literature of this new decade, Lacretelle feels out of place. Eventually, as he expresses the idea in *Le Pour et le Contre*, he discovers a real solidarity with his generation of individualists, against whom this new generation reacts so violently; but now he feels only his isolation, particularly since Gide himself seems to have taken a one-way ticket to Moscow. In 1932, in a review of Albert Thibaudet's *Idées politiques de la France*, he insists on the incompatibility of political action with the modern aesthetic founded on individualism. And, in the essays "Esquisse du génie français,"[23] "Dangers d'une littérature internationale"[24] and "L'Ecrivain et la vie publique"[25] (which got him into a controversy with Julien Benda), he continues to resist the infiltration of politics into literature, until finally, in 1935, he finds himself attacking even Gide in "Autre Défense de la culture."[26]

But, in the meantime, he was becoming inconsistent, for in "Objecteurs d'intérêt" in November 1933, he had given vent to his indignation over the parliamentary chaos.[27] The Stavisky scandal two months later made an irreparable breach in his ivory tower, and he wrote at that time "La Dernière Prophétie de Gobineau," in which he called for the abdication of reason before a myth:

> Yes, a myth, but which one? Religion, national tradition, dynastic principle, socialist gospel? The misfortune is that as soon as you seek and discuss, reason comes into play, balks, makes its conditions. Then, if a myth is really needed and time is pressing, you want to say for once: "We will verify afterwards."[28]

What myth will he accept? That of the marching men whom he saw the other day "coming down in columns from all points of Paris, without community of class or opinion." The next year, in "Les Deux Cortèges," he seems to have accepted a new discipline:

> ... if there is a method incapable of curing the present unrest in the world, susceptible even of aggravating it, it is certainly the free discussion of ideas.
>
> ... to dominate the rude shocks of war, strong governments are required. Much better to admit it among ourselves, within the limit of the national temperament, rather than to lose our time through fetishism for a word seeking an attenuated formula in the Codex of Homais....

> Liberalism . . . is an agent of decivilization in periods of disturbance . . . this doctrine becomes the refuge of individual egotism and of governments without ideas.[29]

These are sorry times, Lacretelle concludes. The fault is not with liberty but with the men who have degraded it.

He has decided to give the marching men his moral support from the ruins of his ivory tower. More than that is out of the question. To go down into the street is not in his temperament; even to call names like an ordinary polemicist is something he will never resort to. In a letter to Colonel de la Rocque, published as "Ligne de conduite," he calls for the rejection of internationalism (the Communist line of the moment, of course), for a rebirth of civic consciousness, and for support from writers, who should "contribute to a sort of moral education which reassures the individual and regroups the country."[30] His letter is hardly incendiary. It is only by implication an endorsement of the Croix de Feu movement, since he seems to propose a program rather than to subscribe to one.

Sometime in early 1933 Lacretelle had met Lieutenant-Colonel Count François de la Rocque at a luncheon attended by Giraudoux, Morand and Drieu La Rochelle, and had been impressed by this retired soldier "who demilitarized himself in order to become interested in social problems."[31] Although his enemies have represented him as a crafty demagogue, La Rocque certainly did not produce that impression on the English journalist Alexander Werth, who described him after the dissolution order of 1936, in this way: "He is personally charming and simple in his manner, and one wonders whether his extraordinary lack of bombast was not one of the reasons for his setbacks. He was clearly not a demagogue or a great leader, in spite of his 800,000 followers, and he was totally unlike the bogyman of the Communist posters. Even on an occasion like this he could not find anything dramatic to say."[32]

Lacretelle was definitely not interested in demagogues; on the other hand, he could not fail to take kindly to this mild-mannered man who claimed to be above partisan politics and who proclaimed, as his one purpose, the restoration of the civic conscience in France by a union of all Frenchmen without distinction of class or political affiliation (Communists, of course, not being rated as Frenchmen). Whether consciously or not, Lacretelle overlooked that other aspect of the Croix de Feu movement which made it a potential storm-trooper organization, threatening the very existence of the Third Republic. One could easily explain the occasional outbursts of violence as the sporadic activity of certain radical elements in the organization (Lacretelle, we repeat, remains silent on this subject). Without attempting to whitewash La Rocque, who was not altogether above strong-arm methods (one of his earliest acts when the Croix de Feu was still exclusively a veterans' organization, was to break up a pacifist rally at the Trocadéro[33]), it is possible to see his failure to intervene at the crucial moment as the refusal to compromise his *mystique*. On February 6, 1932, although La Rocque's cohorts were in a favored position to storm the Palais Bourbon from the rear, he did not act; nor did he do anything when Doumergue fell, after having failed in his attempts to revise the Constitution along authoritarian lines; and finally La Rocque accepted, without lifting a hand, the decree of 1936 dissolving the Croix de Feu.

Historians may look upon La Rocque as a weakling who missed his opportunity or as a well-informed politician who realized that his movement was not yet strong enough for a *putsch*. The rank and file of his organization, recruited among the small-bourgeois class who sought only security and who might have been capable of defensive, but not offensive, action against the Left, could only view this tergiversation as the wise counsel of someone who meant all of the ideology which he preached.

Lacretelle was one of those who viewed him in this light and who rallied openly to the cause only when the Croix de Feu became the Parti Social Français after the dissolution of 1936. It seemed to Lacretelle that in spite of this decision to engage in political action, contrary to the original premise of the movement, the purge of the storm troopers was a decided improvement. That is why he contributed to the new party in 1937 a forty-seven page brochure, *Qui est La Rocque?* La Rocque, he says, is not a potential dictator, since events have proved the contrary; nor is he someone who missed his opportunity: "Say, rather, that there is in his character a strength for withdrawal which you lack and also that power of fraternity which always shows him his adversary in the guise of a man he might love as much as his best supporter." An intellectual can conscientiously support La Rocque because the latter believes in allowing the "intelligence to move about freely."

La Rocque's mysticism of the union of all Frenchmen, continues Lacretelle, has always translated itself into a form of social action which is very different from the class struggle at the basis of socialist and communist doctrine. Even André Gide, whose *Retour de l'U.R.S.S.* has just appeared, has seen the errors of the intellectual *tabula rasa* accomplished in Russia: "If there is a country where the solution of the *tabula rasa* is useless, it certainly is ours, which has always disseminated liberal ideas to the four winds and organized on the surface of the earth the laws of democracy." France, now in the control of the "artificial block" of the Popular Front, is already experiencing the despotic domination of one class, which is what La Rocque opposes.

In conclusion, Lacretelle praises La Rocque's moderation in the recent strikes, an attitude which was disappointing to "professional agitators" and to those "who nourish little tenderness for the Republic," but which can be applauded by those who link "the conduct of politics to the moral development of the individual."

To some, this fascistic democracy advocated by Lacretelle may seem like just so much double talk, yet there is no doubt that he is sincere, since only a short time before the publication of his brochure, he had referred with pride, in the interview with Gaëtan Sanvoisin, to the liberalism of his grandfather and great-grandfather.[34] The best barometer of his changing attitude is his opinion of real dictators. One of his earliest political articles is "Néo-Nationalisme allemand," in which he condemns Hitlerism.[35] His attitude toward the German dictator will never change. In 1935, discussing "L'Italie heureuse,"[36] he tries to see in this country of his predilection a kind of La Rocque Utopia, making immense progress because of a common spirit of sacrifice. In the course of a trip there, he claims to have met a Garibaldi republican who regretted the loss of his personal liberty: "What is this vain regret over an idol become dangerous, over a fetish, over a word? What is important in an individual is the belief in an ideal." The same year, in response to a poll on pedagogical reform, he defends the Italian system: "Discipline does not suppress characters."[37] This is the theme also of the essay "L'Exemple de Rome."[38]

In 1937, however, his attitude has changed. In "La Fête du travail à Rome," he compares the dignity surrounding work in Italy and the discredit into which work has fallen under the French Popular Front, but he obviously has misgivings about the rest. Is statism good for literature? He answers as though trying to convince himself: "... but I didn't at all have the impression that the writers with whom I conversed ... were the slaves of this regime." Liberty? "No one prizes more than I this notion of liberty ... but in the measure that it leads to the moral elevation of the individual and produces results fruitful for all."[39] A month later, in "Les Six Jours d'un conférencier," which chronicles a trip to Belgium, he notes that the Rexist leader Degrelle, viewed in private life, made a good impression on him, but, in the next breath, he registers his antipathy to dictators, particularly to Mussolini, whom he saw in action at Stresa: "At heart, I am one of those who will doubt the god because of the high priests."[40]

The next year, in "Quinze Jours au Portugal," he prefers to Mussolini an enlightened and self-effacing dictator like Salazar and regrets that France does not have such a leader: "Imagine a fête at Arles, the land of color and good humor, to celebrate, in our country, an authority restored within the framework of the Republic."[41] In 1939, in "La Croisière en eaux troubles," he praises a similar benevolent dictatorship in Greece but foresees the decline of Mussolini because he has lost contact with his people in his search for glory. It is the dictators who foment war for their own aggrandizement.[42]

Actually Lacretelle's support of the Parti Social Français was little more than moral, although he did speak to a few student groups. His support fell into the category of too little and too late, for the La Rocque movement was on the wane even before the political party was founded. Determined to prevent any manifestations, even under the new label, the government had already made 1,150 arrests on October 4, 1936, when the P.S.F. tried to parade down the Champs-Elysées.[43] But the severest blow came in the summer of 1937, when the rightist papers *Le Jour* and *L'Action française* took umbrage because La Rocque had transformed the lowbrow *Petit Journal* into a competing rightist organ. In *Le Jour*, Tardieu accused La Rocque of having accepted secret funds from the government during his and Laval's incumbency. Denying the charge in court, the Colonel "cut a rather poor figure," according to Alexander Werth; and he added that La Rocque "from a budding and almost blossoming dictator in 1935 had now degenerated into a not very competent newspaper editor."[44]

During all this, Lacretelle continued to support La Rocque, if the kind of articles which he contributed to *Le Petit Journal* can be called support, for the first was called "Le Tourisme, agent de liaison entre les nations,"[45] and all but one continued in this vein. The lone political article which he gave *Le Petit Journal* was a mild-mannered one called "Contre la Guerre civile," in which he reiterated the official La Rocque attitude on this subject, presumably apropos of the Cagoulard plot of 1938, although there is no direct reference to events.[46]

Lacretelle did not completely abandon his Croix de Feu point of view in his writings until the Liberation. His political position during the war was still conditioned in some degree by this attitude.

14

AMONG THE IMMORTALS

THE brochure on La Rocque in 1937 was signed "Jacques de Lacretelle de l'Académie française." The year before he had been elected to the Academy, not for his political views, of course, but because he had just completed a major novel in four volumes which, added to his other works, made him one of the most worthy representatives of the literary generation which was just then beginning to knock at the portal of the "palace of the immortals." Urged by Hermant, Régnier and Mauriac, Lacretelle had been a candidate for the *fauteuil* of Paul Bourget after the latter's death in 1935, but it had been reserved for Edmond Jaloux. After the death of Henri de Régnier in 1936, the mantle of the symbolist poet-novelist, who had long been a personal friend, fell quite naturally on Lacretelle's shoulders.

Lacretelle was fully prepared, though a novelist, to accept the "legacy of symbolism," as he said at this time in a lecture translated and published shortly thereafter by Clive Bell in the *New Statesman and Nation*.[1] Symbolism, according to Lacretelle, was more than a group of poets; it was a mode of thought which, in the novel, included Proust and, after him, most of Lacretelle's contemporaries. When Lacretelle defines the symbolist novel, he is, quite intentionally, defining one aspect of his own: ". . . it forebodes and suggests more than it states; and it finds its richest material in that secret monologue which each one of us holds with himself, in that spidery arabesque which is our subconscious reasoning."

Thus Lacretelle was elected in the name of symbolism to replace a symbolist, but one suspects that it was rather the name of Flaubert, so often invoked, which made this young upstart of forty-eight acceptable to the venerable company. It might also have been to a small extent his "academic" ancestry, well known to the Academy, no doubt, but seldom called to the attention of the general public (the only one to allude to it before André Maurois's biographical article in the *Nouvelles littéraires*[2] after the election was Gilbert Charles[3] in 1930). In *Marianne*, Paul Brach called Lacretelle "the first of our generation to be admitted under the cupola."[4] This was hardly correct, for François Mauriac, only one year older, had been admitted in 1933. However, to become momentarily the youngest member of the Academy was no mean achievement.

There was one person who could be expected to take special pride in this accomplishment. Mme Amaury de Lacretelle wrote to her son at this time:

> Your success at the Academy is a great joy to me. Immediately the thought of how proud your father would have been came to me, and my happy emotion is doubled by it. . . .
>
> What is Poucette going to say when she sees her father in Academic costume? In these hard times which we are experiencing it is going to be expensive! And to think that in the family, at Bel Air as well as at Cormatin, they used to dress up in uniforms half destroyed by moths for charades or plays! In any case the tradition continues, and in some sixty years Poucette's children will do what your aunts did.[5]

Although elected to the Academy on November 12, 1936,[6] Lacretelle was not formally received into the illustrious company until January 27, 1938. The delay is customary to allow for plenty of homework in preparation for the speeches. At some point during the interval, the new Academician wrote to his wife:

> Next a long interview with Hermant. He had read my speech and had found it to be, in spots, not Academic enough in tone and too close to an ordinary lecture. That is precisely the effect I was trying to get, knowing how boring that tone can be. He asked me to take out two or three things: the captain of *cuirassiers* (which I shall do), the reminiscence from Régnier's speech on the Virtue Prizes, that is to say, the little story from Tallemant (I shall not do it), and also to modify my first sentence "Now is the time to pay," which, so he claims, can be interpreted as "Now comes the irksome task." I have only to put "Now is the time when audacity pays for itself."

But for him, with so free a mind, to have become so meticulous, so scrupulous, and to seek what is so stilted, it must be that the Academy ruins people. Let us beware. I believe also that he is in the position of a sponsor who wants his junior, whom he has gotten into the club, to observe rigorously a tradition for which he doesn't give a hang.[7]

It would appear, from an examination of the printed text of his speech, that he finally changed only the first line. Still in the text are the captain of *cuirassiers* (Albert de Mun of the Academy, in reply to Régnier's acceptance speech, claimed that the new member's novels made even the captain blush), and Tallemant's story about Bautru, who tipped his hat to God (a passing funeral) but did not speak to Him; and there is an even more un-Academic story about Régnier's grandfather, who, at fourteen, slept between two female traveling companions to quiet their fears. In such terms did audacity pay for itself. "In the middle of a pit full of grey beards, of pink craniums, of red sashes and ribbons, he looked like a pupil from the philosophy form who had got loose on the dais of the professors," wrote André Rousseaux in *Le Figaro*.[8]

The speech was typical Lacretelle, contrived in a genial manner which seemed to ramble without the least sacrifice of logic or unity. As was customary in his critical utterances, Lacretelle quickly made the subject personal by telling how, as an adolescent, he first visited Régnier to ask for a *dédicace* and how, a few years later, he could not screw up his courage to ask him to read the manuscript of *La Vie inquiète de Jean Hermelin*. Then, as he developed his subject he did full justice to Régnier's poetry in appreciative criticism. About Régnier's novels he had more original things to say because of his recent reassessment of the symbolist movement: He defines Régnier as the precursor of the "Freudian novel." The attitude of the symbolists is a way of life which he is now prepared to defend, he indicates in veiled remarks in his introduction, addressing the Academy: "You are making yourselves seem a little strange in these times, I realize, because you are cooperating in a collective task which is called culture, without giving in too much to the pressures of the present and without yielding any of your individualism. That is a tradition which is vanishing, a liberty which has been breached. I assure you that both tradition and liberty will henceforth count among you another defender."[9]

In all of Lacretelle's speech, Flaubert was not once mentioned. It was Abel Hermant who, in reply, presented his young "godchild" as a Flaubertian classicist who, by his "clear and coherent expression," had escaped from the prejudices of the literary schools which condemn fine writing in the novel. In conclusion, he maintains that Lacretelle approaches the novel on the highest moral plane: "To be sure, you do not moralize; but you let it be seen in spite of yourself that you have a sense of sin, that you have a doctrinal understanding of it, and that you have neither the taste for it nor a dangerous dilettantism toward it." Hermant overlooked this new definition by which Lacretelle had made himself a symbolist.

On the whole, the press was also satisfied to define him as a classicist. In *Marianne*, Benjamin Crémieux paid him this compliment along with others more equivocal. "To be sure," he said, "vigilant friendships, the complicity of a few literary salons, rather than his merit, opened the doors for him. But his merit could and should have sufficed. . . ."[10] And he added a personal grievance: "He was romantic only once in his life, the day when unfiltered passion made him greet Colonel de la Rocque as a messiah. We wager that he will not do it again."

Shortly after his election to the Academy, Lacretelle accepted the position of literary critic on the daily newspaper *L'Ami du peuple*. From December 26, 1936, to May 23, 1937, he knew the servitude of supplying a weekly column. At the end of that period, realizing how stifling this was to his own literary production, he gave it up; and subsequently, until the war, the only literary criticism which he wrote was an occasional brief review for *Candide*, "La Lettre de Jacques de Lacretelle."

As the literary critic for *L'Ami du peuple*, Lacretelle had no mission, literary or political; his only purpose was to write an equitable and interesting review of the books (he usually reviewed several at a time) currently on his desk. His attitude might be summarized by the remark which he made in *Le Petit Journal* a few months after he had begun his column in *L'Ami du peuple*: "The day I no longer desire to read a new book or, if it has pleased me, to serve it by word or pen in the feeble measure of my ability, that day I shall doubtless have no longer any desire to write."[11] To attempt to summarize this criticism would be futile and meaningless since there is no central theme or doctrine. These articles lack both the dogmatic point of view in literary matters and the conservative political point of view which were characteristic of the articles collected in *L'Ecrivain public*. Lacretelle seems to have reverted politically to a much more liberal attitude. If one did not go beyond this evidence, one would conclude that our author had altogether lost his Croix de Feu bias.

His first review, devoted to Roger Martin du Gard's *L'Eté 1914* (the continuation of the latter's *roman-fleuve* entitled *Les Thibault*), is a tribute to the sobriety of his friend's art and quite overlooks the leftist political attitudes expressed in the novel.[12] Even greater impartiality marks his review of Gide's *Retour de l'U.R.S.S.*; now that Gide has recanted his communistic views, Lacretelle praises his sincerity and places his opinion far above that of the political polemicists of the Right.[13] Reviewing *Notre Ami Psichari* by the arch-Rightist Henri Massis, Lacretelle shows his true colors once more as a nineteenth century liberal when he criticizes the priest responsible for the conversion of Psichari: "To save this soul was right, but to hope that Renan, attacked in his descendants, might be finished off by his grandson, is a vindictive attitude hardly compatible with the Christian spirit."[14] And Lacretelle adds that he anticipates that Massis will not like his "Renanian interpretation of the Faith." One senses that Lacretelle is not at all at home with his subject in reviewing Massis's book, and one understands with what predilection he seizes upon the opportunity to review René Dumesnil's *Le Réalisme* and to praise once more the objectivity of the nineteenth century realists and of Flaubert in particular: "And when one starts to look over this century, one says to oneself that it is certainly Flaubert, this tormented Atlas, who holds it on his strong shoulders. For his enthusiasm, his scrupulousness, his power of sincerity, his irony, his gifts as an artist and his will to accomplish, what a model for all of us!"[15]

During this period Lacretelle was becoming more of a European than ever. "To travel," he said in 1938, "is a little like making up a play oneself, like changing one's character temporarily, like adopting other muscles and another costume."[16] To chronicle accurately all of his geographical movements would be fastidious and difficult. However, he did leave the printed trail of some of his travels: Belgium and Holland in 1935 (articles in *Le Figaro*[17]); Egypt in 1936 for a lecture tour (articles in *Excelsior*[18]); Belgium in 1937 for lectures ("Les Six Jours d'un conférencier" in *Candide*[19]); Rome in 1937 to attend the Fiesta del Lavoro (article in *Candide*[20]); Portugal in 1938 to participate in the jury for the Camões literary award for the best foreign work about Portugal ("Quinze Jours au Portugal" in *Candide*[21]); Greece in 1939 ("La Croisière en eaux troubles" in *Candide*[22]).

"Les Six Jours d'un conférencier," "Quinze Jours au Portugal," "La Croisière en eaux troubles" and "Une Visite à Stendhal" (*Le Figaro*[23] in 1939) were combined in 1939 to make a volume called *Croisières en eaux troubles*, published by Gallimard. Full of the personal digressions which constitute the charm of such Lacretelle texts, the volume is particularly interesting in retrospect because it records the European state of mind on the brink of war. The odyssey of the *Champollion* on a pleasure cruise to Greece while Albania is being invaded has some of the nightmarish qualities of the odyssey of the *Achios Nicolaos*, that other ship which they encountered loaded with displaced Jews trying to make a clandestine entrance into Palestine. One never learns whether the Jews, for whom the French passengers of the *Champollion* took up a collection, ever reached their destination; but Stromboli erupting in the darkness makes the reader feel that catastrophe is at hand. Lacretelle is now convinced that dictatorship does not lead to a fuller life: "The end which we seek is accord, stability. If the dictators agreed to it, that would be their death sentence."

Meanwhile the changing international scene had already begun to interfere in Jacques de Lacretelle's personal life. His mother had died in 1938 from a heart attack attributed to anxiety over the likelihood of another world war.[24]

Since 1938, as though nothing were going to happen, Lacretelle had been making plans to lecture in the United States. Finally, earlier plans having come to naught, on August 12, 1939, he embarked for Canada on the *Empress of Australia* as the official delegate of the French Academy to the twenty-fifth anniversary celebration of *Maria Chapdelaine*. Lacretelle subsequently described for the readers of *Le Petit Journal* his discovery of Old France in the New World: his ship slipping through the Newfoundland fog in the wake of a welcoming iceberg; the eighteenth century city of Québec clinging to the cliffs stretched out like the prow of a ship into the river; the slow intonation of the Québecois, who reminded him of the peasants of Guernsey; the low whitewashed farmhouses roofed with wood made to look like tiles; the villages clustered around their tall-spired churches, whose interiors made him think disagreeably of Saint-Sulpice. Part of the celebration included a speech at the "Université de Québec" (presumably Laval), in which he paid tribute to another "dreamer," Louis Hémon, and concluded with an exhortation to the French Canadians to draw nearer to contemporary France, defined by Lacretelle in terms of nineteenth century realism:

> If it is a matter of literature, you see our present-day novelists attack subjects or scenes which, not long ago, would have caused a scandal. That is because we wish to see clearly; we have the pretension, no doubt audacious, of unraveling human secrets; and we think that even if Providence regulates the course of our destiny, there is not one of our acts which cannot be studied in the light of reason. . . .
>
> Must one judge on that account that our literature is in decomposition and our art degenerate, as our enemies proclaim?
>
> No, Gentlemen, for these researches follow a great principle—what am I saying?—an old tradition, which we shall never disown: that which says that the individual is free. Free to choose his religion, his system of government and his trade. Free to affirm his personality.[25]

The celebration, appropriately, moved in due course to Péribonka on the shores of Lac Saint-Jean, where the French delegation met the originals of Louis Hémon's characters and were served a meal by none other than the original Maria, who was then (and perhaps still is) the curator of the Hémon museum. At that point, so Lacretelle wrote later, the news of catastrophe reached them:

> It was that evening that our little group found out what was going on in Europe. We had gone around the Lac Saint-Jean, a veritable inland sea fifty kilometers wide. It was for the purpose of going to a place, Pointe-Bleue, where the Indians are allowed to come during the summer season to sell the produce of their

> winter hunting. We walked around their camp, we visited their tents, we looked down with pity at the children lying on the ground in the midst of débris of all kinds. All these faces were inoffensive; they expressed neither hate, nor fear, nor curiosity; in truth one read in them only one sentiment, but an irreducible one: the refusal of our civilization. And it was there, before these unexpected witnesses, that we received, from a Canadian come from the neighboring city, the news of *our* world, of *our* civilization. A pact signed between Germany and Russia; Poland, encircled, was having to stand up to increased demands; war seemed inevitable.[26]

The Lacretelles—for in his travels he was usually accompanied by Mme de Lacretelle—hastened to Montréal and spent their days listening to the news broadcasts in the studios of Radio-Canada. They had booked passage on a French liner for September 6th, but on September 2d, Lacretelle wrote to his friend Maurice Coindreau, professor at Princeton University, from Pointe au Pic, County of Charlevoix, Québec:

> I have decided to prolong my sojourn in Canada because of events and especially because I have been assured that the *Champlain* will not leave on the 6th. So I have preferred to await the turn of events at the house of Canadian friends who offered us hospitality. Nevertheless I certainly intend to leave by way of New York as soon as ship departures are certain. . . .
>
> We are so overwhelmed by the news received and awaited in a foreign land that I lose my head a little and busy myself only with the present, with what must be done just to get along.[27]

On September 17th, a post card to Coindreau announced their arrival in New York with the prospect of a fortnight's wait. During this time Lacretelle lectured at the French pavilion of the World's Fair and then, one day during the first week of October, embarked with his wife on the *Washington*. All of these events were presently to supply a denouement for *Le Pour et le Contre*, and momentarily they provided copy for *Le Petit Journal* and for a brochure entitled *Le Canada entre en guerre*, published in 1940.

They landed in an English port, which remained anonymous in the *chronique* which he wrote shortly thereafter for *Le Figaro* to relate his impressions of wartime Europe and to express his confidence, which never seems to have wavered, in England.[28]

That winter the Lacretelles borrowed her mother's villa at Cabourg, which, as it happens, adjoins the hotel which Proust has immortalized as the Grand Hôtel of Balbec. In this Proustian atmosphere, with a daily walk along the *digue* (the local "boardwalk") and a view of the inmates of the hotel looking like fish in an aquarium behind the great plate glass window, he continued to work on *Le Pour et le Contre*. In February 1940, he wrote to Coindreau:

> Is this strange *status quo* going to last? No one knows. One would accept it wholeheartedly on condition that Germany exhausts herself....
>
> I was disappointed to see that the Finnish affair had, in the long run, aroused nothing more than Platonic indignation in the two worlds. I would have thought that America, the Scandinavians, then all the neutrals, would stick together.
>
> ...I have worked very slowly at my novel. But I am going to pursue it with fewer interruptions, for we are leaving in a few days for the Midi. Here is my address: Les Héliades, Avenue Louis Sorel, Le Mourillon, par Toulon, Var.
>
> ...I received last week a telegram from Bédard asking me if I was disposed to make a lecture tour in the United States next spring.[29]

Pierre Bédard was the director of the French Institute in New York. On May 15, 1940, Lacretelle again wrote to Coindreau from Paris to ask his advice on the three lectures which he planned to give in English, but he expressed doubt that he would get to America: "...I am writing to you on a day when we are listening to the radio with anguish. We had become accustomed to an inert and distant war. The awakening is harsh. And suppose this were to be the decisive clash. But, alas! it is only the beginning of the true war."[30]

A few days later Lacretelle took his wife and two children to Montfort-l'Amaury. In the midst of the "exodus" with refugees cluttering the roads in every direction, they took refuge with friends in Brittany, but left presently for the Bordeaux region. Lacretelle went into the city of Bordeaux to obtain permission from the refugee government to continue with an official mission to represent the French Academy at the fourth centenary of the "Portuguese World" in Lisbon. The journal which he kept at this time records an amusing interlude in the troglodyte existence which he was experiencing for the first time. While he was staying at the apartment of Abbé Mauriac, brother of the novelist, the air raid warning having sounded, he took refuge, clad in pyjamas, in the shelter. Everyone rose as he entered, and the housekeeper of the Abbé announced solemnly: "Monsieur le Curé is not here; it is Monsieur who is replacing him."[31]

Authority was granted to continue with the mission, although Henry Bordeaux and Jérôme Tharaud, the other official delegates, did not accompany him, and he spent the next three months with his wife and children in Portugal. During this time he read English newspapers avidly, and his journal records great sympathy for England. He does not approve of collaboration with the Germans, but, on the other hand, he is critical of the anti-French attitude of De Gaulle, whose activities, he thinks, should be limited to heading a French legion in the service of the British. On July 8th, he wrote to Coindreau from Estoril, Portugal:

> You don't know with what words to begin a letter in these times. You have lost the thread of your ideas, you can no longer get your bearings. Each day brings a disconcerting bit of news. You thought, at the end of the war, that you had reached the bottom of the well, and now this Franco-British tension is raising doubts about everything, even honor. I shall say nothing about recent events, or rather I shall say only this: A capitulation by arms is admissible, a moral capitulation not. And I wonder what generation of men they hope to prepare if they teach them with so much celerity to go back on their decisions, to disown their friends and their ideals. . . .
>
> I have been in Portugal for a fortnight. With all my family. The Academy had sent me as a delegate. . . . If there is not too much of a fracas in France (morally and materially), I shall return in a few months. If not, I shall remain here, preparing

these lectures which I certainly expect to give in the United States in the spring.[32]

On August 7th, he wrote to Coindreau, again from Estoril:

Today we learn that the attack against England is being prepared. Germany has positions so advantageous and a war technique so powerful that it does no good to make of one's admiration for England an article of faith; one trembles for her....

I accept very gladly the end of the Third Republic and of parliament, on condition that what replaces it should take its inspiration from a national idea and from French personality. Up until now, also, the government in power has been taking measures with a knife at its throat.... In short, there are moments when one is overcome with emotion. Continuing my novel—as I am doing at present—gives me the impression of writing in the moon and for the moon.

Nothing from Bédard since his cable. I think it will be necessary to give up the idea for next spring. But I remain on the list for 1942. It would be the worst possible thing if France had to give up reproducing herself abroad.[33]

In the United States, French lecturers, of course, were a dime a dozen with no one willing to pay a nickel to hear them. In the report which he subsequently sent to Marshal Pétain (his colleague in the Academy) because of his inability to communicate with André Bellessort, the secretary of the Academy, Lacretelle expressed the hope that the government would presently subsidize lectures in the United States.[34] It was a vain hope.

After a difficult trip of eight or ten days across a Spain still suffering the effects of its recent revolution, he reached Toulon and settled down in the house of his brother-in-law, too weary, as he was to say later, to think of returning to the Occupied Zone to defend his personal possessions: "Personal goods seemed to me so inconsequential in comparison with what was lost!"[35] He continued to go through all the motions of his normal existence, at the center of which was his unfinished *Le Pour et le Contre*; but as he wrote, taking refuge in art as the true reality, he would frequently be assailed by doubts. Was he not like the "manipulator of marionettes who shakes out the wrinkles in his dolls' dresses and, in spite of hard times and empty benches, continues to pull the strings and to repeat the old grimaces."[36] More serious still, he came to doubt his art: "Henceforth, after the deep cracking which had shaken the foundations of my country, I wondered if I had not accorded too much admiration to art themes, which never give, after all, anything but a transposition of vital problems."[37] Outside his window, as he works, the sun shines down on the blue harbor of Toulon, where an occasional French warship goes through wartime maneuvers, kindling a glimmer of hope in the observer, and, in the garden, his children, who have known the hardships of the exodus, the screech of sirens, the hiding in cellars but who have never been so close to danger as to see it as anything but an exciting game, engage in this conversation:

"Rico, do you want to play war?"
"I don't know."
"Why yes, you know. It's like the story of my dwarfs."[38]

The ivory tower dweller wonders whether it is right to leave them in their state of innocence.

Once, at the time of Dakar, he got into a dispute with a naval officer and left him to his bouillabaisse with the parting remark: "Whatever happens in the course of this war, I shall never be able to separate the fortunes of France from the fate of England."[39] Occasionally he went to see Gide and Roger Martin du Gard, who were at Nice, and when a Gide lecture was canceled, he sent him this quatrain:

La défaite rapide
C'est la faute à Gide.
Nos mauvais généraux
C'est la faute à Malraux.[40]

As long as there remained a Free Zone in France, Lacretelle continued to write articles for the newspapers. Pierre Brisson, having escaped from a German prisoner-of-war camp, had re-established *Le Figaro* at Lyon, and Lacretelle had become one of the directors of the newspaper. Really a De Gaullist at heart, according to Lacretelle, Brisson "supported Marshal Pétain to the extent—

which became more and more feeble, alas!—that he repulsed German demands."[41] Lacretelle himself has never claimed to have been a De Gaullist at this early date. The only contemporaneous evidence which we have of his opinions (the preceding quotations being taken from *Libérations*, which appeared in 1945) is in the articles which he published in *Le Figaro*, *Le Petit Journal*, *Candide*, *Présent*, *Le Journal de Genève* and *La Gazette de Lausanne*. A few of these articles reappeared immediately in *L'Heure qui change*, brought out by the Geneva publisher Le Milieu du Monde in June 1941, but most of the new volume was composed of the articles which had appeared several years before in *L'Ami du peuple* and *Le Petit Journal*. Although a large number of Lacretelle's wartime articles were collected in a postwar volume, *Idées dans un chapeau*, others have never been republished.

Some of these wartime articles are typical Lacretelle *chroniques* on miscellaneous subjects: the art of writing novels, family reminiscences, painting, recent books. There are no book reviews as such, but frequently a book serves as the excuse for a digression on Baudelaire, Mallarmé, Ramuz, Colette, the Goncourts, Lamartine, Mme de Genlis. Other articles are commentaries on problems of living in a changed world, such as "La Femme seule," which records the disappearance of special compartments for lone women in French trains and the psychological implications thereof.[42] A large number of the articles are written with a definite purpose: to support the Pétain regime, or to argue for the restoration of certain intellectual values which the Pétainistes have excluded from their program, or to incite resistance to the Occupiers.

There is no denying that Lacretelle placed all his hopes in the Pétain regime in the beginning. In "Les Racines du nouvel état français," published in *Le Petit Journal* in 1941 and never reprinted, he pointed out that Pétain's motto "Work, Family, Fatherland" was borrowed from the Parti Social Français. And he concluded: "Thanks to the Marshal, there are no longer any partisans. There are only the artisans of a great work of reconstruction."[43] In his article "Les Enfants et les nains," he went out of his way to say: "One admires everything which is being accomplished in France at the present time. The respect for the individual, but making him subservient to a higher interest; the importance given the family while inculcating the notion of sacrifice; a realistic political policy which seems not to overlook the fact that History is made of successive realities—to all that one subscribes fully. For years people had been hoping for this census of good wills, this national communion, this death of the sectarian spirit."[44]

Lacretelle unquestionably felt that his contribution to the rejuvenation of France would be in the maintenance of the permanent values of French culture. Imitating the luxury trades which, so as not to lose their skills, continued to produce useless but beautiful objects while the lines grew longer in front of the bakeries, he might have gone on discussing such a subject as "Le Paysage dans notre littérature"[45] (on which he spoke for the Marseille radio), but he soon discovered that his personal cultural tradition had antagonists in the highest places and would not survive if he remained passive. The difficulty was that he was still a nineteenth century liberal, and he was now rubbing elbows with the same faction who had lately been proclaiming "the stupid nineteenth century" and who were now adding something about the gangrenous twentieth.

Throughout these first two years he clings to the forlorn hope that the new regime will accept his definition of French culture as "the taste for the individual attempt, the study of the human condition, the free exchange of thought."[46] How can one talk of rebuilding France on traditional foundations, he asks, when one rejects the foundation on which all French culture has been built:

> . . . an attitude of humiliation is incompatible with this vigorous recovery effort which is demanded of the Frenchman. For the present, I put aside the question of agreement with the victor. That is a matter of vital necessity which the evolution of our relationships will settle for better or for worse. But if each one of us goes repeating that the character of the Frenchman, his superciliousness, his imprudence, have been the cause of our defeat, that our decadent literature and our anarchistic art have contributed powerfully to it, on what note can one sound the rallying call and what is the use of doing it?[47]

How frequently he returns to this theme! He even writes his review of Colette's most recent book in such a way as to be able to say: "But one hopes that the France of tomorrow, young France, will have a level enough head to leave to literature all its liberties."[48] He is right in defending *l'art gratuit*, he says triumphantly in "De la Vraie Culture," when he notes how the public is rushing to see Molière: "People very seriously criticized the princesses of Racine and the Cornelian heroes for never having talked about a square meal. Today there are no square meals, and people are fighting to listen to Molière. Let future generations remember."[49] In lectures at Geneva and Lausanne in April 1941 he defends the not-too-stupid nineteenth century and even has a good word for Gide and Romains. The Swiss newspaper *Le Peuple* thanks him for "what would have been, scarcely two years ago, banal declarations, and what is today a courageous affirmation."[50]

In June he repeats these ideas at length in "Position de notre littérature," two unreprinted articles in *Le Petit Journal*[51] which he refurbishes the next year for *La Gazette de Lausanne* as "Littérature d'hier et de demain."[52] We quote from the latter article, also not reprinted: "To claim that the curiosities and the bold innovations of the literary generation to which I belong have marked a decline and have taken the edge off the national resistance is an absurdity to which history will do justice if it has not already done so. There was on the contrary a boiling up of sap and a spurt which are proof that a country vibrates to everything and lives generously."

Lacretelle was safe in his iconoclasm, because book-burning did not take place in the Free Zone until the Germans moved in on November 11, 1942. The doctrine which Lacretelle was attacking was not official dogma. However, he did dare to criticize official dogma on one minor, but related, issue in a series of articles, parts of an extensive controversy arising from his "Le Français, langue unique" in *Le Figaro*.[53] He begins by opposing the government's decision to encourage, if only on an optional basis, the teaching of dialects as part of the program of return to the soil. The originator of the idea, Véragnac, and Maurras attack, but Lacretelle remains adamant, pointing to the danger of separatist movements and the even greater danger to the national patrimony if the French language is allowed to deteriorate in any way. In unequivocal words, he even accuses his adversaries of undermining this patrimony with an "ideology loaded with dynamism,"[54] such as one finds among certain "neighbors." And he remains incorrigible:

"It may be professional deformation, but the day someone demonstrates to me by *a* plus *b* that Gutenberg has corrupted humanity, I will answer: 'So what?' "[55]

Lacretelle made one gross error, and that very early in the game, when he heralded the reappearance of the *Nouvelle Revue Française* under the direction of the arch-Collaborator Drieu La Rochelle. Deceived by the names of Gide, Alain and Giono in the table of contents, he calls the first number worthy of the best Jacques Rivière tradition and better than recent prewar numbers, in which Julien Benda "had reached the point of wanting to make the world turn according to his system of antipathies and personal rivalries."[56] He hopes that the new *N.R.F.* will rediscover the spirit of the original review, that it will remain above polemics and will become "a laboratory in which every writer, preferably young, is invited to make his experiment, provided that he does not yield to a taste for publicity and that he relies on a sincere faith."

All of this wishful thinking is in accord with his cultural program, of course, but the discordant note is the accolade which he gives Drieu La Rochelle, whose only fault, he says, is to write novels without believing in the genre. He continues:

> As for Drieu's career as a political writer, it is worthy of respect, for—with that temperament somewhat distrustful of itself which I have just noted in the novelist and amidst innumerable anxieties attributable to the complex misfortunes of France—it follows one road: patriotism and the greatness of our country. . . . A supporter of Doriot, attracted by the social revolution which was being accomplished in Germany, he struck up, before the war, an interested curiosity about the Hitler movement and wrote a few months ago, in the *Nouvelle Revue Française* to be exact, an admirably clairvoyant article on the blunders of French policy and temperament.

Apparently Lacretelle soon recognized his mistake, but he waited until 1945 to correct it in print.[57]

Because he fancied the Pétain regime to be a La Rocque Utopia, he was perhaps unaware of his fundamental ideological opposition. Not so with his opposition to Hitler. Ever since his article on "Néo-Nationalisme allemand" he had been berating Hitler in digressions such as those to be found in "Le Miracle hollandais" (1938) and

"Les Suisses et nous" (1939), unrepublished articles which appeared in *Le Petit Journal*.[58] In 1941, again in *Le Petit Journal*, he published an article in two installments on "Les Etats-Unis et l'Europe" which is so incredibly frank in its anti-German attitude that it is amazing it passed the censor.[59] First comes praise for the United States: "Civilization, liberty, Rights of man, are terms universally revered." English resistance has now fired the American imagination; the United States has buried Jefferson's will (he means the Monroe doctrine) and has vetoed the extermination of England: "One can imagine that the entry of the United States into the war would assure Great Britain of at least a compromise peace." He might have borrowed M. Jourdain's words and said: "I cannot speak more clearly."

Most of his allusions to the Germans, however, were more guarded. In the form of seemingly innocent reminiscences about his former travels, he focuses attention on Crete, Alexandria, Rhodes, Malta, as they become Hitler's targets.[60] "L'Index de 1940," published in Switzerland, is an enumeration of the books banned in the Occupied Zone in which he seems to be making light of serious matters when he says: "Not just anyone is persecuted."[61] And one had only to turn another statement inside out to detect his real meaning: "But for over something like ten years, our writers have been dismayed not to find on the German side a work which makes possible the initiation of a moral penetration between the two literatures."

In "Notre Culture," written for *Candide* in 1942, he said:

> I was reading recently an affirmation proclaimed outside our country by a mind which, so it appears, has charge, in his country, of youth and education: "Modern intellectuals are unaware of Faith, unaware of Sacrifice, Duty, Respect, Fidelity and Honor, which are values of the soul. They have no ideal."
>
> A Frenchman would have had a great deal of difficulty putting that sentence together, and, finally, he would probably not have written it. First of all because of Péguy, but also because he would have had the feeling of betraying the European spirit.[62]

Even without knowing the name of the author of the quotation, anyone might have guessed that it was a Nazi. When reprinting the article in *Idées dans un chapeau*, Lacretelle added a footnote to identify the writer as Baldur von Schirach, head of the Hitler-jugend.

When Hitler was embarking on his Russian adventure, Lacretelle published an article entitled "1812" in the *Journal de Genève*.[63] Ostensibly this was nothing but a review, without contemporary implications, of a Russian history of Napoleon's campaign. But, just as though the contemporary analogy was not obvious, Lacretelle added: "And Napoleon no doubt drew the moral of the adventure, if not of his entire reign, when he wrote: 'Great powers die of indigestion.' "

In July 1941, shortly after "1812," Lacretelle asked for and, to his surprise (after all, he was a director of a newspaper which still maintained a notorious independence of judgment), obtained an *Ausweis* to cross the line of demarcation to attend a session of the Academy. For several anxious hours, his train was sidetracked at the line of demarcation, but apparently neither Napoleon nor Brisson had anything to do with the delay, for presently the train continued and reached Paris after curfew. Passengers had to spend the night on the train. The next morning was a grim one in the empty spaces of Paris. Lacretelle lodged with Anne de Biéville-Noyant in the latter's *garçonnière* on the rue des Saints-Pères since his own apartment had no furniture—his mother-in-law having sent it to a warehouse in the nick of time to avoid having it requisitioned by the Germans. When presently he visited Montfort-l'Amaury, he found that his larger house—one originally bought by his wife's grandmother in 1933 and then given by her to his wife—was in a shambles, having been occupied by the Germans. Furniture was missing, particularly numerous bureau drawers. The housekeeper explained that the German soldiers, when going on leave, took the drawers with them as suitcases.[64]

In the course of his Paris sojourn, Lacretelle saw Drieu La Rochelle and, as he related four years later in *Libérations*, discussed with him frankly his attitude toward Germany:

> He hoped—oh! stupidity—that France, carried onward by this force and paired with it, would derive some advantages, but we had to deserve them.

"It is serious, Drieu," I said, "to follow, without any assurance, men who have always hated us and are today the stronger."

His glance vacillated a moment. It is certain that he was not consciously betraying his country. But his was a female-brain which had always allowed itself to be seduced by the myth of strength.

The Paris expedition provided grist for three articles. "Devant une Armoire pillée" relates how "someone I know well," having long neglected to read some old papers in the family archives, returned one day to find his house looted and the old letters destroyed: "Kneeling before these letters, he found fragments which appeared to him to be marvels of emotion and ingenuousness; he saw expressed in them authentic and truly felt sentiments, in short all the palpitating subject matter which he is striving to discover in people. It was there and was only waiting to deliver up to him its secrets. But he had neglected it, and now it is too late."[65] The same episode is related in *Libérations*. It took place at Montfort-l'Amaury; the letters were some which Mme Amaury de Lacretelle had not destroyed when she was going through the old papers after her husband's death.

The second article, "Images de Paris," published in *Le Figaro* and not reprinted, recorded surface impressions of Occupied Paris: the crowds in the métro and the difficulty of finding your way if you are one of those unfortunates who have "neglected to find out until now where the Place Ballard and the Porte des Lilas are"; the absurdly tall feminine hats; the material hardships and the lady, surrounded by luxury, who shows him "the room where we shall stay this winter."[66]

The third article, "Paris et la collaboration," published in *Le Journal de Genève*[67] and likewise not republished, attempted to scratch beneath the surface. The Germans, he said, remain aloof, either because of stricter military discipline or because of "a certain automatism of thought." The French have no profound animosity toward Germany, even accept the inevitability of an understanding with her, but cannot be expected to like the Germans because they must "undergo" them. There are no clashes, he continues, except on the part of terrorists, "of whom everyone disapproves." And finally he does not mince words: "As long as Germany is in a position to exert pressure on France, as long as she does not seek loyally, in broad daylight, the assent of the nation, it is to be feared that the new order, the greater Europe, these ideas to which the Chancellor wishes to attach his name, will remain suspect to the country, and public opinion will accept them only with reluctance." This was outspoken criticism, and it is not astonishing that the article took a week to pass the censorship in France. It finally appeared in *Le Figaro*[68] with the note "copied from the *Journal de Genève*," as though to unload the responsibility on the Swiss.

An interview in the *Courrier de Genève* indicates that Lacretelle was in Geneva in March 1942.[69] Shortly after that, he transported his entire family back to Paris because his wife was expecting another baby and he wanted her to get the best medical attention. Another reason for returning was his concern over his possessions and the simple fact that at the large house in Montfort-l'Amaury "the vegetable garden and the lawn where a cow was pastured were, at that time, things which one could not neglect."[70] However, he also kept his Paris residence at 49 rue Vineuse; this he doubled in size by taking over the palatial ground-floor apartment with a garden overlooking the rue Franklin. It had belonged to the late Marcel Prévost. Lacretelle's second son, Didier, was born at a hospital in Boulogne-sur-Seine on April 15, 1942.

"Littérature d'hier et de demain" was Lacretelle's last important wartime article. After that he wrote only a few articles on neutral subjects, mostly in the Paris *Comœdia*—in fact, most of them were reprints of previously published articles. *Le Figaro* and *La Gazette de Lausanne* got only one article apiece. With the merging of the two zones, *Le Figaro* vanished and with it the remnants of a free press. For Lacretelle the long night had settled down.

Actually he spent the "long night" in pleasant enough surroundings, his wife's large house in the center of Montfort-l'Amaury, with its ample grounds, affording typically French suburban privacy. Living in Paris was too complicated because of the scarcity of food, but he still went there frequently and even by bicycle after trains and buses had stopped running. In 1943 he was joined in his Montfort house by a German officer and four men. With these uninvited guests, silence was the rule, but the Lacretelles, like everyone else, continued to listen to the B.B.C. It was a long night, broken only, as far as the printed word was concerned, by his report on the "Virtue Prizes," the oration which Lacretelle gave at the Academy in 1943 and which was published in *Présent*.[71]

In August 1944 the little town of Montfort-l'Amaury was in the fever of excitement:

> The cry, "They are here," which spread one fine day in the sunlight, through the streets of the village, turning the faces of the girls crimson, causing the young men to gesticulate and the old men to weep, still resounds in my head. And—comedy nestles always beside grandeur—I cannot forget either the astonishment of a good woman, whilst she remained planted before these men of another world, whilst she fingered their weapons, examined their net-covered helmets. "They keep eating," she said, with increasing admiration, "they eat all of the time." For it is true that the Yanks, even when on the alert with their tommy guns in their fists—they knew that the enemy was not far off—continued placidly to chew their chewing gum.[72]

As so often happened, the liberation was not definitive the first time. No sooner had the American soldiers left than twenty beaten Germans emerged from nowhere; but the Americans returned in time, killed two of them and put the others to flight. Two days later the Germans were back, burned six houses and bayoneted four inhabitants in reprisal.

This second episode is related in *Libérations*, whereas the first episode is to be found in an article "Ils arrivent," which appeared in *Le Figaro* on September 1, 1944. One assumes that the return of the Germans occurred after Lacretelle had taken his article into Paris. Paris was free. *Le Figaro*, with Pierre Brisson at its head, was back on the streets. The long night was over, and Lacretelle, in "Ils arrivent," took advantage of the opportunity to spell out his obituary of the Pétain regime, which had once deluded him as it had deluded so many Frenchmen:

> By what stubborn aberration did a man of state and by what stupid isolation did a marshal of France not feel that this force of resistance was the true virtue of the country, the only one which was in conformity with its tradition of heroism, the only one which might assure its recovery? . . .

Those who, in 1940, had accepted the armistice with a gnashing of teeth, but with the hope that under an organized power the country would more quickly remake its vital blood, have seen this power go through a series of abdications. Lack of character? Desire to remain in place? Both no doubt.

The lie about the famous "changing of the guard," the breaking of the armistice agreements and the brutal dissolution of the army, the official patronage accorded to deportations and to bloody repression, the banishment of our statues both literally and figuratively—all was sanctioned, accomplished, without any other mitigation than a senile benediction. To their own resignation the rulers of Vichy have always preferred the resignation of France.

However great their name was *before*, they have stricken it from the annals of the nation. They will no longer be for posterity anything but the men of the German Occupation.[73]

15

LE POUR ET LE CONTRE—DRAMATIS PERSONÆ

ON August 3, 1945, Jacques de Lacretelle wrote to Maurice Coindreau: "... I have finished my novel and now have nothing but trifles on my work table." The manuscript, neatly typed by Mme de Lacretelle, is dated June 24, 1945.

Ten months had elapsed since the liberation of Paris when Mme de Lacretelle closed her typewriter. They had been busy months, not altogether given over to the writing of the novel itself. Lacretelle was taking advantage of the new freedom to move around the world once more. An article in *Le Figaro* in February 1945 records his visit to bombed-out London.[1] In the spring of that same year he was lecturing in Canada and the United States.

Just after the Liberation it appeared that Lacretelle might resume his prewar activities as a *chroniqueur* in *Le Figaro*. During September and October 1944 five of his articles were prominently displayed on the ridiculously small sheet on which *Le Figaro* was forced to appear because of the paper shortage. It seemed for the moment that he might begin to alternate with François Mauriac, who had suddenly emerged as the most widely read political commentator of the post-Liberation period. But, after these five articles, Lacretelle stopped all systematic writing for *Le Figaro*, and although he has continued to contribute articles at the rate of five or six a year right up to the present, these have been only random musings or accounts of his travels. Only once, in an article "L'Intérêt de la France" in *Le Figaro* for October 2, 1945, did he make any further comment on current events. On that occasion he took a mild stand against the nationalization of industry.

It would be idle to conjecture what political views Lacretelle might have expressed if he had continued to write. No matter what they might have been, he would have had difficulty making people forget his previous affiliation with the Croix de Feu. Colonel de La Rocque, having been "liberated" by the American army from a German concentration camp, was under arrest and would have been brought to trial subsequently if he had not died. Having never been identified in any way with the underground, Lacretelle made no attempt—as so many of his contemporaries did—to get on the Resistance band wagon. For a time he probably thought that his sincerity would be sufficient and that he could wipe the slate clean by disavowing the Vichy regime, which had so sorely disappointed him. At least it must have been clear to him from the start that he could not hope to gain the same prestige as Mauriac, who had been involved in clandestine literary activities during the war.

Nevertheless, there is no reason to suppose that Lacretelle's failure to write more political articles in 1944 and 1945 was the result of an immediate appraisal of his situation. It seems logical to assume that he simply did not have the time, with his enormous novel to finish, his travels, his lectures and his family obligations. At some point, however, the appraisal came. Very likely it was after his American trip.

During this American trip he discovered that someone or some group in France was actively working to discredit him, because, without explanation, several of his American lectures were canceled. He asked Maurice Coindreau to investigate, and, after returning to France, he wrote to him:

> I owe you a thousand thanks for the little investigation I asked you to make. By the way, do you know the name of my enemy? It is good, in life, to know where one treads. I suspected that this series of amiable and evasive refusals came from the cabal which was organized against me a few months ago by a man jealous of the mission which had been formed in Paris. The article attacked ["Paris et la collaboration"] had been skillfully tampered with and truncated. It dates from September 1941 but was so little favorable to collaboration and Vichy that *Le Figaro*—a newspaper which hated the Germans and made wry faces at Laval—had succeeded in getting it through only with great difficulty. They had to battle for a week against the censorship. The reproduction of it, made in America to do me a disservice (be sure to say so when the occasion arises), purely

and simply suppressed the conclusion, which showed the inanity and the danger of a policy of collaboration. That is the exact version. I am anxious that [André] Morize and others, who were disposed to show me interesting things in the United States, should know it. And I shall speak no more of it. The incident is forgotten.[2]

Despite his desire to forget, this experience was enough to give him pause and to dampen some of the enthusiasm with which he had greeted the Liberation—for there is no doubt that he had been enormously enthusiastic during those heroic days of August 1944. A month after the Liberation he penned an enthusiastic preface entitled "A la Gloire de Paris"[3] for a pictorial history of the uprising in Paris which Fasquelle published the following year under the title *La Libération de Paris*; and his American lectures, "La Nuit longue" and "Paris occupé, Paris libéré," were particularly eloquent. During his American trip he had given Brentano's the text of these lectures, as well as the clippings of his first four post-Liberation articles and the text of another lecture "Le Sentiment national dans la littérature," dating from the Occupation, and, in July 1945, the American publisher brought out a new Lacretelle volume entitled *Libérations*. The only one of these lectures which the French, themselves, were to see in print was "La Nuit longue," which appeared in 1945 in *Les Œuvres libres*.

After his unpleasant experience in America, Lacretelle had begun to lose some of this enthusiasm. Among the French, he was not alone in feeling that somehow the post-Liberation period had failed to fulfill its promise. The material discomforts, even worse than those under the Occupation, only aggravated this disappointment. On December 15, 1945, Lacretelle wrote this discouraged letter to Coindreau: "I am writing you on the evening of a most somber day. Somber not only because of the cold and the darkness (there is no electricity in Paris) but because of the horribly severe sentence given this poor Lord Chelsea. Life imprisonment for a man of eighty-four who had no influence over any minds, whose articles no one read. What madness!" Lord Chelsea was, of course, Abel Hermant. Lacretelle did not protest at this time in print but published two eulogies of Hermant after his death in 1950.

On April 29, 1946, he again wrote Coindreau: "... and I try

not to put my finger in the political pie, as long as I find my place neither among the fanatics of the extreme Left nor among the blind men of the Right. . . . Sunday we vote. I fear very much that this Constitution thrown together at the last minute, antiliberal, dangerous for the present and the future, may be ratified by the referendum." If he had ever thought of trying to influence public opinion at the time of the Liberation, by 1946 he had decided to withdraw into his familiar ivory tower.

In this atmosphere of growing disappointment, *Le Pour et le Contre* went to press. Since the novel itself ends on a pessimistic note which is very significant because of the autobiographical nature of the work, it is important to determine whether this pessimism in the novel dates from the post-Liberation period. The evidence is not absolutely decisive. An undated newspaper clipping, which has slipped into Lacretelle's papers and which can be dated *after* October 1940 and *before* March 1942 because of a reference to his current lecture subject "Le Sentiment national dans la littérature," states that his novel is two-thirds finished. Page 215 of Volume II was probably written after February 4, 1942, because it contains the same quotation which appeared in Lacretelle's *Candide* article on that date.[4] At least one can say with certainty that before February 24, 1943, pages 225 to 346 of the second volume had not been written, because that is the date of an article in *Chantiers d'art* serving as the primary source for the *Sel de la terre* episode. This episode, which convinces the autobiographical character Le Maistre that he is out of step with his times, is the beginning of the pessimistic theme on which the novel ends. The theme is so unrelated to the existentialist point of view of the young post-Liberation writers that, although it would have been anachronistic to look ahead in the novel, it still seems impossible that Lacretelle could have conceived his concluding pages in these terms if he had written them after the Liberation.

These conclusions are not intended to prove that the entire novel was completed before the Liberation, for Lacretelle has said in conversations that this was not the case.

The manuscript was enormous and was to make 664 pages of text in the first edition. *Les Hauts Ponts* had made 1045 pages but in a much smaller format. It was the author's plan to publish *Le Pour et le Contre* all at once because fragmentation would produce a confusing effect on the reader. On May 26, 1946, Lacretelle wrote to Coindreau: "Paper is still lacking in France. *Le Pour et le Contre* has been printed (first printing) in an edition of 17,000 copies. In France friend Gaston would have been gracious enough to print me in 7 or 8 [thousand copies]." *Le Pour et le Contre* had appeared in two volumes in Geneva under the imprint of Le Milieu du Monde, which had previously published *L'Heure qui change*. Subsequently a Canadian edition, published by L'Arbre, appeared in four volumes, in spite of the author's reluctance to adopt this segmentation. These extraterritorial transactions annoyed Gaston Gallimard, and publisher and author remained estranged for the next few years.[5]

Le Pour et le Contre is the life story of an author, Olivier Le Maistre, beginning apparently *in medias res* but with frequent flash backs to his youth. It follows him through his literary career, from a distance, and through his amorous affairs, based for the most part on physical attraction. For years he is attracted to the enigmatic Bali—until he discovers her shallowness. When he is in his forties, he suddenly embarks in all seriousness on marriage with a girl hardly out of adolescence (she is seventeen when they meet), and apparently he makes a good husband. Misunderstandings occur now and then but do not last until the wife, Chantal, discovers under melodramatic circumstances in 1939 that he has held back the secret of a previous marriage. She runs away, unsuccessfully tries infidelity for twenty-four hours, rejoins her husband in New York (he is on a lecture tour), and they sail for France. In the midst of a reconciliation, their ship is torpedoed, and Olivier Le Maistre is lost at sea.

Since the novel ends in 1939 and, to unravel the plot, makes use of historical events which occurred after Lacretelle had started writing it, it cannot be claimed this time that he had the complete plot in mind in the beginning. In the extant notes there are no outlines or embryonic manuscripts, nothing which illuminates the genesis of the novel. The only surviving manuscript is the 1945 typewritten copy, which contains some interesting variants about the character of the editor Laume but which otherwise shows little divergence from the printed version. The few interpolations add nothing to the plot, and the change of proper names is characteristic of all Lacretelle manuscripts (Stubel is first called

Maynard, then Rolland; Fabrecoul is Bénédict; Bali is May; and the geographical place Yvelines is Chevreuse).

The only significant evidence in this problem of genesis is in the descriptions of his novel which Lacretelle gave from time to time before and after he had begun writing. In his radio interview with Frédéric Lefèvre in 1935, when he first mentioned the idea for the novel and announced its title, he said also:

> [LACRETELLE]. I should like to put in it much of my personal experience and even mix the plot up with the literary world in which I have lived.
>
> LEFÈVRE. A novel with characters keyed to real people then?
>
> LACRETELLE. No, not at all. I have never been interested in novels which copied reality too closely. They lack thickness, resonance. I believe that to create a good fictional character twenty living characters are needed.[6]

In late 1937 he described the novel further: "The action will take place in Paris, immediately after the war; it will be a painting of modern society and particularly of literary circles, and at the same time the biography of a writer. This work will involve many characters, and one will find in it personal observation especially."[7] When the novel was nearly finished, he said again: "It will be the sum of my personal experiences. . . . I could not better define it than to appropriate two very accurate remarks of Goethe: 'Nature and art are too great to have purposes,' wrote the German poet in his correspondence; and his Memoirs contain moreover this parallel thought: 'A work of art can have and doubtless will have moral consequences. But to require of the artist a moral purpose signifies the perversion of his trade.' "[8] Thus we see that the best definition of *Le Pour et le Contre*, the idea which was present from its very inception, is that it is the sum of Lacretelle's mature personal experience and a broad panorama of his times. Whether or not he was influenced by Albert Thibaudet's prediction in 1930 that he would eventually continue with his "one great supple novel . . . half autobiographical and half imaginary,"[9] this was in effect, what he had decided to do.

Whenever he wrote for publication, however, Lacretelle continued to define the art of the novel in terms of *Les Hauts Ponts* and said nothing about a change of heart—unless it was that apparently irrelevant remark about envying the creators of monsters.[10] That is probably because he still does not recognize any dichotomy in his work, although, for us, the new novel is just another example of this oscillation from objectivity to subjectivity. After *La Bonifas* comes *Amour nuptial*; after *Les Hauts Ponts* comes *Le Pour et le Contre*; no formula could be more simple or more obvious. Not only that, but *Le Pour et le Contre* is clearly the result of a desire to take up again the two main themes of *Amour nuptial*, a literary career and a marriage relationship. He seems to feel that he has something more intimate and more sincere to say on the subject.

Le Pour et le Contre has been variously compared to Thomas Mann's *Magic Mountain*,[11] to George Meredith's *The Egoist*,[12] to Voltaire's *Candide*,[13] to Lesage's *Gil Blas*,[14] to Drieu La Rochelle's *Blèche*,[15] to Oscar Wilde's *Intentions*,[16] to Flaubert's *Education sentimentale*,[17] and to the work of Aldous Huxley in general.[18] Lacretelle apparently invited the Flaubert comparison, since it is mentioned in a "To appear" notice,[19] based on publicity which he probably approved. It is nothing short of astonishing that no critic mentions *A la Recherche du temps perdu* or *Les Faux-Monnayeurs*. The reason may be that the references to these works were so pointed that critics feared to be taken in by discussing the obvious. The problem of influences in Lacretelle's novel is intricate because the work is, intentionally, a mosaic of all of the author's aesthetic experience. No single work explains the genesis of *Le Pour et le Contre*, but all of contemporary literature, plus some literature that is less contemporary, makes its contribution.

Because of his intention to make this novel a *summa* of his essentially intellectual personal experience, Lacretelle has produced a work hovering between the essay and the novel and between memoirs and fiction. It seems almost as though the so-called novel were a hybrid consisting of an apparently discursive, digressive and totally unsystematic discussion of ideas, which slows down the action to the vanishing point, and a subterranean and almost invisible plot structure, which now and then causes the outcropping of the action that one normally expects in a novel. This is a superficial impression which does not stand up under close examination.

As a *summa*, the novel is first of all historical; not predominantly so, of course, but yet so obviously so that there is no need to belabor the point. Olivier's unconsummated marriage to an American with a spot (*avec tache*), more for the nonconformity of the thing than for financial gain; Ranouche's visit in a piquant bathroom scene in which her virtue is seen to be part affectation and part inability to come down to earth; the superbly grotesque luncheon in the tree house in Robinson during which a dypsomaniac nobleman, descended physically from Jeanne d'Arc and morally from Arthur Rimbaud, celebrates his marriage with his not unsullied mistress in an orgy of wit, horseplay and scabrous allusions in the presence of a fallen prince (who, incidentally, is alleged to be copied after a real prince, notorious in Parisian society), a stupid and conceited bourgeois, an amoral son of the people, a Jewish scapegoat, and a drug addict who is also a shoplifter whom two moronic detectives are following—all this is obviously the hilarious, roaring twenties. History of the cut and dried variety is not present simply because an awareness of history would be incongruous in this pleasure-loving age. Except for those who disintegrate like Malebrèche, the noble descendant of Jeanne d'Arc, or Frederica Watson, the drug addict, these characters survive long enough for history to catch up with them. The Jewish scapegoat, having reappeared as a bibliophile, evolves into a statesman.

Without descending from his ivory tower, Olivier is forced to note what is happening when his newly acquired in-laws, industrialists or professional military, discuss the aftermath of February 6, 1934, and when the rising literary generation, to Olivier's dismay, takes up the cudgel for one side or the other. Finally the dictators rattle their new armaments, and Olivier begins to take a lively interest, for fear of what may be the outcome rather than through any desire or ability to do something about it. As Europe slides down the greased plane toward Munich and a declaration of war, historical events assume contour and begin to guide the destinies of the novel. Almost unintentionally, Lacretelle winds up with a historical novel, which is all the more convincing because he is concerned only with the psychological impact of events. When he first conceived his novel in 1935, he could hardly have foreseen the vital role which historical events would play in it.

In the early days of the Robinson brawl, Olivier was already saying, "What a novel one could write on our period!"—as though there were something beautiful in the debauched twenties. In fact, it was Malebrèche who, in a more sober and hence incongruous moment, kept insisting that Le Maistre would one day make their luncheon into a novel. There are many things which we have to take for granted in Olivier Le Maistre, because he is never the subject of omniscient analysis but, rather, unfolds gradually in small fragments. One of these things is the creative urge; whence it comes and why the reader never learns. Suffice it to say that it is there and that he writes a first novel which is not, however, the great novel "on our period." Like any French intellectual who writes novels, he gets involved in literary movements, and henceforth his ideas make sense only when he is put in his proper place in the literary firmament.

This literary firmament is a fictional creation of no small magnitude and requires extensive comment to be fully understood. Initially, it is limited to an eclectic group collected around a publishing house, Les Nouvelles Editions des Jeunes, which has its own review, *Messages*. On page 115 of the first volume of the novel, Stubel remarks that "*Messages* no longer exists," but on page 238 of the same volume Laume says: "We must enlarge *Messages*." There seems to be some inadvertency here on the author's part. In any case, the publishing house continues throughout the novel, whether the periodical does or not.

Among the notes for the novel, there is this revealing one: "2d part. The N.E.J. Gallimard, Jacques Rivière. Morand, who drops out. Artaud. Schlumberger, who made up the title. Prévost, Arland, Dabit. Vildrac, who goes to live as a savage, gives up writing when he feels he has nothing more to say." If it were necessary to prove that *Messages* and the Nouvelles Editions des Jeunes is the *Nouvelle Revue Française* and the Librairie Gallimard, something which is obvious to anyone informed on contemporary French literature, this scrap of paper should settle the matter. In spite of what Lacretelle said about not wishing to write a novel with keys to the characters, he has obviously done so—but with very decided limitations. It is never correct to conclude that the fictional character *is* a real author. From time to time the character will possess a distinctive trait identifying him with a real author, or often he will possess several distinctive traits apparently identifying him with different authors. This seems to be partly a private game in which Lacretelle indulges and partly a method for presenting a fictional literary group enough like the original N.R.F. to convey a feeling of authenticity to the informed reader. Curiously enough, the note quoted above also gives a number of false leads, since many of these real authors do not seem to have found a place in the firmament of the N.E.J.

Since the N.E.J., like the N.R.F., is an eclectic group, there are as many tendencies represented as there are individual writers, and the reader is likely to lose his way in this labyrinth of secondary characters. In elucidating this point, it may be useful to run through the entire *dramatis personae* of the N.E.J. and to collect together the dispersed information pertaining to each individual author.

Borger. He is the first practicing author to appear in the book and comes on the scene before the N.E.J. is mentioned. Among the notes for the novel, we find this description: "A character who has a syphilitic heredity and knows it, is haunted by the pox. He is a man of letters and believes that the legacy has changed in his case into genius.—How to make him die? I have imagined that he has had all his life a swollen arm like Constantine III. Is it possible? And is it within the bounds of probability to speak of caries?" As planned, Borger does have a swollen arm and does die of caries; syphilis is not mentioned by name, but the author clearly has this in mind. In addition to his swollen arm, which leads him to assume frequent Byronic poses, Borger may be identified by a cane which once belonged to Barbey d'Aurevilly. He is the contemporary Barbey and, being an anachronism, has no significant spot in the literary firmament of the N.E.J. A journalist rather than a creative writer, he has initially some vague ideas about a contemporary novel, in which case he merely serves as a sounding board for Olivier Le Maistre. His real ambition is to write biographies of romantic authors, and, very belatedly, we learn that he has produced a biography of Byron.

He belongs to the genus *type character* and does not represent any significant tendency in contemporary literature. The fact that he writes romantic biographies suggests that he might stand for André Maurois. However, an allusion to the fact that he is writing "un de ses billets" (one of his notes) brings him closer to the journalist Gérard Bauër, who was the author of the *Billets de Guermantes* and who also wrote a biography of Byron.

MARCENAT. He, likewise, is unimportant for the development of ideas but is a vivid type character. He is the publisher of the N.E.J. who goes over his literary archives like a miser and pounces upon new literary prospects with a flair for originality which explains the enormous financial success of his literary enterprise. Kind and considerate about the well-being of his authors, he is also capable of maliciousness and has inherited the sensuality of his father, who reputedly treated himself to two *pucelages* a year. In the fictional literary group of the N.E.J. he occupies the same position as Gaston Gallimard in the N.R.F. Furthermore, those who know M. Gallimard in real life find some resemblances in the physical portrait.

LAUME. He is the editor of *Messages* and the moral force behind the N.E.J. Entirely lacking in distinguishing physical traits (nothing whatever is made of the "provincial correctness" of his accent), Laume is the first of the disembodied spirits who stand for a literary idea rather than for an individual author. To the neophyte Olivier Le Maistre, he appears as a pillar of strength when he encourages the aspiring young author to write about his childhood. The prerequisite for great writing, Laume says continually, is sincerity toward oneself, and, at the time of his death, we learn that he once wrote an *Essai sur la sincérité*. But from a pillar of strength he presently changes into a pillar of salt as he is immobilized by the very eclecticism of his literary doctrine. Encouraging genius in others, he remains impotent himself and is incapable of going beyond his first work, *Formes de la vie intérieure*. Signs of his bewilderment are evident in his debate with Torral on the subject of Proust, whom he limply defends as one of the "primitive voices" bringing a new literary ethic. When Torral loudly proclaims, "And I refuse to seek man in the placenta of Dr. Freud," Laume has no reply, because he is manifestly struggling within himself. Presently, he announces his intention to write "a book on the senses, a natural account devoid of all eroticism, which no one has dared to do."

When he next appears in the novel, he is dying offstage of some cerebral fever, caused presumably by the "intolerable duality of mind" of which he had once complained. Shortly before, Torral and Charmery had exerted all the moral persuasion possible to prevent him from publishing his confession. His death is a case of moral disintegration and conforms to Lacretelle's intention, recorded in the notes for the novel, to describe the "madness of an intellectual, that is to say the state of a man who little by little loses his footing through an excess of intellectuality." In the novel, the case against Laume is never summed up, but one might presume that it is primarily the failure to establish any artistic standard and secondarily the fact of having evolved a doctrine which is more self-indulgent than truly critical.

In the Laume who brings out the best in the young men grouped about him, one has no difficulty in recognizing Jacques Rivière, the editor of the *Nouvelle Revue Française* who also wrote *De la Sincérité envers soi-même*. The quotation on page 18 of Volume II, purporting to be from Laume's *Essai sur la sincérité*, is taken with only slight alteration from Rivière's essay. Given Lacretelle's admiration for Rivière, one wonders why he condemns Laume to such an ignoble death. The answer is that in the subsequent evolution of the character, Laume has ceased to be Rivière. Freud, of course, was Laume's undoing. It is a fact also that Rivière was interested in Freud and that he gave a series of lectures published posthumously as *Quelques Progrès dans l'étude du cœur humain: Proust et Freud*. However, it is not known that he ever planned to shock the world with any sexual revelations, as Laume did, and certainly he did not receive a visit from the flesh and blood equivalents of Charmery and Torral, attempting to dissuade him from publishing his book; for this episode is directly inspired by a passage in Gide's *Journal* wherein Maritain tries to prevent the publication of *Corydon*.[20]

Obviously, Laume is writing some kind of *Corydon*, and he has therefore ceased to be Rivière and has become Gide. Laume's interest in Russia likewise points to Gide. Although *sincérité* is Rivière's word, it is quickly apparent that Lacretelle uses it rather in the sense of Gide's *authenticité*, and, at the time of Laume's death, we learn retrospectively that the word *authentique* did occur in Laume's *Essai sur la sincérité* (but it is not to be found in Rivière's *De la Sincérité envers soi-même*). Laume's *sincérité* is not an approach to religion, as it was in Rivière's case; it is dangerously close to hedonism. As an aesthetic principle, Olivier Le Maistre finds it to be a good thing since it teaches him originality, but it is a bad thing for Laume because it is the basis of self-indulgence. Warned by Laume's example, Olivier never makes this his way of life, which is tantamount to saying that Lacretelle rejects the basic principle of Gide's doctrine.

Unlike Rivière, Laume is not a religious person. The allusion which Lacretelle makes to Gide's *Journal* seems to conjure up so many unpleasant images in his mind that he creates the episodic character of Laume's bigoted brother, a professor at a Catholic university, ready to swoop down on Laume's manuscripts to distort the true picture of his personality (perhaps this is meant to suggest the notorious case of the Rimbaud manuscripts). Here, Lacretelle is definitely taking sides in the struggle between Maritain and Gide. Rivière is completely out of the picture at this stage, and, queried on this point, Lacretelle has said emphatically that he remembers Rivière only for "his curiosity, his delicacy, his fraternal heart, his desire to extract from others what was best in them without influencing or guiding them."[21] In other words, he does not subscribe to the main thesis in Martin Turnell's recent *Jacques Rivière*, in which the English critic asserts that "his influence seems to have been deplorable."[22]

CASTELLI. He has restless eyes and a few other physical features which belong to René Crevel, but otherwise he is an abstraction standing for Cocteau. "Art," says Castelli, "makes a good companion for all that is lazy, along with grass, the moon, cats. I can very well do without the scissors and paste pot of old man France." When Olivier sees him on his first visit to the N.E.J., Castelli has just published *Robinson 1920* (the title seems to be an association of ideas between the events which take place at Robinson at the beginning of *Le Pour et le Contre* in the roaring twenties). A few years later the book is outmoded, and Olivier draws the moral that a work of art should never be dated. At another stage in his career, Castelli writes *Vert et blanc*, a title which came from the fact that the manuscript was tied with a green string. Obviously, Lacretelle sides with old man France in this matter of artistic standards. Laume's inadequacies as an artist are due entirely to his sponsorship of writers like Castelli, for he is no longer able to distinguish true art.

MALOUIN. He is the author whom Le Maistre admires from a distance on that memorable first visit to the N.E.J. The antithesis of Castelli, he stands for stability and down-to-earth intelligence. Without his blue scarf and horn-rimmed spectacles, "he would have simply resembled a foreman drawing up the plan for his task." In the beginning only his boorishness stands out, particularly when he barricades himself in an office of the N.E.J. during a reception in honor of his literary prize. At one point he says disparagingly of himself: "On the few occasions when I happen to be intelligent, I am intelligent only before facts, in the presence of concrete things or authentic images." Although he quotes Taine in support of realism, he says further: "For me, to stick to facts is to escape as much as possible from systematic views; it is to renew oneself constantly through experimentation, to live between open windows."

Malouin seems to be Roger Martin du Gard, who won the Nobel prize and who has always shunned the spotlight. The advice which he gives Stubel about the danger of constructing his novel according to a predetermined mechanism is almost a quotation from Martin du Gard's letter on *Les Fiançailles*. Later, when he stresses the importance of the ear for judging style, he borrows an idea from Duhamel. It is probably because Duhamel and his friends founded the Abbaye de Créteil that Malouin discusses, but never pursues, a plan to found a similar cooperative institution in the country.

At first Malouin seems somewhat obtuse, but only because we do not know him. After the death of his wife, he turns on life with a lucid ferocity and expresses himself in a pithy style reminiscent of the most truculent Huxley character. He sees man as the dupe of his own myths: "Man, by dint of having invented and reasoned in all domains, of having decreed the mysteries of the Holy Trinity and that a little rectangle of paper is worth a thousand francs, impresses me as a madman who stumbles at every moment against reality and, when he rubs his eyes, throws himself angrily against his neighbor."

The drama of Malouin's life is this relentless lucidity, beginning with his ill-considered but reasoned act of getting married because "he had wished to get rid of it all so as no longer to have to think about it." Because his wife was devout, he tried to meet her halfway on the terrain of liberal Christianity, but the bigotry of her unreasoned faith made all compromise impossible. He entrusted the truth of their relations to his journal, which she eventually read, with tragic consequences. Finally Malouin fell a victim to the two primary irrational tendencies in so-called civilized society, religion and war, the first being symbolized by his daughter, who left him to become a nun, the second by the false rumor of war which spread through the village and caused him to commit suicide. One recognizes here certain elements of the plot of Martin du Gard's early novel *Jean Barois*, in which an impenitent Dreyfusard, married to a bigoted provincial, has a daughter who becomes a nun. It is not clear whether Lacretelle is alluding to this novel or to some event closer to the personal life of Martin du Gard. *Jean Barois* is written with such fervor that one suspects that it corresponds to something real in the intimate life of the author.

Aesthetically, Malouin stands for realism; philosophically, he is killed by realism. At first glance, he seems to have failed in life because he compromised his aesthetic principle, which he once defined thus: "At the basis of an idea I must feel a breath of human life or at least perceive the imprint of life." But that is where the dilemma begins: how to represent life without understanding it? The realist is doomed to be the judge of humanity, and it takes superhuman courage to maintain one's equanimity. Malouin, the pinnacle of strength, lacks this courage; in fact, no character in the novel possesses it, particularly not Olivier Le Maistre, who is beset with the same problems (note the parallelism: He has drifted into marriage with Chantal because he was in a marrying mood, and he has never shared her religious sentiments) but never quite faces them head-on because he is not given to strong decisions. If Olivier were a strong character, one would concede that he has succeeded where Malouin has failed. That seems to be what Lacretelle intends to say; solicited alternately by the pro and the con, Olivier lives on the human rather than the philosophical level. Perhaps that is the way life should be led, but it is also evident that, at heart, Le Maistre is a realist and that it would not take much prodding from life to drive him to an attitude of intransigent realism. In that light, Malouin seems to be a projection of Olivier beyond the point where his life is interrupted by enemy action.

STUBEL. Another realist, friend and disciple of Malouin, whom he succeeds in Olivier's esteem. Eventually, he withdraws to the outer suburbs and finds a rewarding literary inspiration in a simple rural life. Despite Stubel's frequent appearances in the novel, the author never delves very deeply into his aesthetic or philosophical problems. The main idea is that Stubel's successful marital life is an example to Olivier that even a realist can take a wife with impunity.

Although there are no salient features to make identification obvious, Lacretelle has said that he had Marcel Arland in mind. Stubel also stands remotely for Lacretelle himself, since he receives from Malouin the same criticism which Lacretelle got from Martin du Gard: too much rational organization in the novel. A manuscript variant also states that Stubel was writing a Protestant novel, and at the end of the published version of *Le Pour et le Contre* he is reported to be doing a critical edition of Flaubert, two facts which also relate this character to Lacretelle himself.

BOËTTE. A minor literary figure distinguished at one point by his "systematic sarcasm which is cultivated at Normale." He seems to be Jean Prévost. Like Prévost, he succeeds in writing only one novel, *Le Coron*, which is probably an allusion to Prévost's populist novel *Les Frères Bouquinant*.

QUARRIZ. The composer who has "cut his connection with youth" and who is wrong when "he breaks deliberately with the human person and seeks all his sustenance in solitude." Though there might be some utilization here of the original note on Vildrac, the author is very positive in identifying him as Ravel, and his *Rocking Chair* as Ravel's *Bolero*. Just as Ravel frowned on Poulenc's Ecole des Six, Quarriz frowns on the Ecole de Romme; like Ravel, he was born a Basque and lives in solitude near the fictional town of Yvelines in proximity to the central character Olivier Le Maistre, just as Ravel lived near Montfort-l'Amaury.

CHARMERY. François Mauriac remarked in a letter to Lacretelle, after the appearance of *Le Pour et le Contre*, that Charmery changes heads in the course of the novel.[23] At the outset he is clearly recognizable as Jean Schlumberger in the thumbnail sketch which, contrary to his new technique, Lacretelle gives when he first introduces Charmery. In quick order we learn that Charmery was one of the co-founders of the N.E.J. with Laume, as Schlumberger was a co-founder of the N.R.F. with Gide; that Charmery practices his art with such scrupulousness that his creative vigor is somewhat impaired, a description which would also fit Schlumberger; and that Charmery has withdrawn to his Normandy estate, where he classifies "his woodman's sensations as his grandfather, the notary, once did the accounts of his farm rents." This last is an allusion to Schlumberger's preference for his Normandy estate and the fact that he was born into a rich bourgeois family—of industrialists, not farmers.

But Charmery changes, and inconsistently. He is the one member of the N.E.J. who does not break with Torral and who in due course is converted to Catholicism, to the great distress of Laume. Now he has become Charles Du Bos, whose conversion was of such concern to Gide. It was Charmery who accompanied Torral in his attempt to silence Laume, an allusion to the moral pressure which Du Bos also tried to exert on Gide. At his last appearance in the book Charmery has sunk to an even lower level in the implied scale of moral values because he writes novels about "the cult of the body," which may be an allusion to Montherlant (rather than Crevel). None of this fits Schlumberger, who is still a Protestant writer faithful to the antiauthoritarian doctrine which he and Gide placed in the original cornerstone of the N.R.F.

TORRAL. The arch-villain of the piece who nevertheless remains extraneous to the action of the novel and who indeed resembles a villain with his "black and dry hair which added something Moorish to his Spanish type." Appropriately a Spanish type, he is the Grand Inquisitor, who would probably take pleasure in burning all the Laumes, Malouins and even all the Olivier Le Maistres in this fictional cosmos. Despite the absence of any physical resemblance, Torral becomes Henri Massis when he brands Proust as "the man crucified by an eroticism which he cannot satisfy"; for that has been the basis of Massis's attack on Proust these many years. In due course, Torral founds his own review, which we can easily assume to be, in real life, the *Revue universelle* of Jacques Bainville. Though Torral exists as a potential source of evil because he contributes to the moral disintegration of Laume and, much later, aligns himself with Charles Maurras and founds a phalanx of storm troopers in blue berets, he never develops beyond the level of an abstraction as far as Olivier Le Maistre is concerned.

He is one of the ideas which solicit Olivier's attention and which arouse only antipathy in him. After his unreasonable attack on Frène, the contemporary exponent of the classical novel in the manner of Mme de La Fayette, Torral appears to be a greater threat to Olivier, because in this attack he emits a diatribe against the literature of analysis and introspection which "rejects Catholic experience." But the danger never materializes for Olivier. From this, one may conclude that Lacretelle does not feel at home among the ideas expressed by Torral but that he does not view them as a significant threat to his own intellectual independence.

DESTOILE. During the golden age of the N.E.J., he is a misfit who has the "shoulders of a soldier on leave with nothing to do" and who bores people with the war, especially in a long forthcoming volume of verse, *Diagrammes* (manifestly an allusion to Apollinaire's *Caligrammes*). After the 6th of February, Ravenez mentions, along with the Camelots du Roi and the Croix de Feu, the "party of Destoile." Near the end of the novel, he has become the chief advocate of Franco-German *rapprochement* and is seeking to revive a moribund France with a transfusion of Teutonic bellicosity. His poetry, such as it was, has dried up, and he has been a miserable failure as a novelist, a playwright and an essayist; these successive failures explain the instability of his gaze, and his bitterness. One has no difficulty in recognizing Drieu La Rochelle, whose literary and political career parallels exactly that of Destoile, except that he did not found a party. Probably Doriot is meant in that case.

ETIENNETTE FABRECOUL. Because she runs a bookshop where the intellectuals of the N.E.J. gather, she will inevitably be compared to Adrienne Monnier, whose Maison des Amis des Livres in the rue de l'Odéon received, among others, Valéry, Schlumberger, Gide and Lacretelle. But the resemblance goes no further, for Etiennette, instead of being an abstraction like the writers of the N.E.J., is a fully developed fictional character, whose amorous adventures are also entirely fictional. The spirited side of her character comes from an entirely different person, Marie-Louise Bousquet, at whose salon, it will be remembered, Lacretelle was a frequent visitor.

JACQUES FRÈNE. This "young owl" is conceived in the image of Raymond Radiguet: "In spite of his youth, he had a motionless mask and a complexion without freshness, the color of horn, like the frame of his big spectacles." He is ill at ease in literary circles because he feels incapable of producing the flow of anecdotes and puns which people expect of him. According to his announced intention, he eventually rewrites *La Princesse de Clèves*, an obvious allusion to Radiguet's *Le Bal du Comte d'Orgel*. Olivier is not particularly taken with him until he becomes the butt of Torral's attacks, an entirely fictional situation. As Etiennette's lover, Frène is also a fictional character.

FOULQUE. He keeps reappearing in the novel, sometimes saying something serious, but generally as a buffoon. His verbosity and nocturnal habits give him a certain notoriety which serves him in lieu of a literary reputation. His masterpiece, *Promenades magnétiques*, the title of which everyone knows, will never be written. The only thing of consequence by him which will ever be published is his correspondence with Laume, who tricked him into writing under pretext of offering aesthetic advice. The correspondence is a vivid record of literary impotency. Lacretelle has produced a reasonable facsimile of Léon-Paul Fargue, with some injustice to Fargue's real literary importance. The correspondence, however, stands for that which Rivière exchanged with Antonin Artaud and which was published in 1927.

RAVENEZ. He represents the beginning of a new literature opposed to the individualism and introspection of the N.E.J. What is wrong with literature, he says, is that "it dissects cadavers, whereas a new world is in the making, the heroism of which escapes us." With his fair hair coming down over his ears, with his frequently unshaven face and with his aviator's jacket, Ravenez is a man of action. He has been in the Orient. Presently he goes to Russia and returns to become the adversary of Torral. If anyone has any difficulty recognizing André Malraux in this portrait, Lacretelle states near the end of the novel that Ravenez has written a long novel about the Reds in Spain, an allusion to Malraux's *L'Espoir*. As the representative of the new literature of action, Ravenez absorbs Antoine de Saint Exupéry as well, since he alludes to a time when he was an airline pilot and made night flights.

Malouin had once expressed this idea: "The drama of our times is that no one is interested any longer in the human condition for what is enduring in it. To it people prefer myths, parties, opinions." At the point where it occurs in the novel, the remark is anachronistic, for Ravenez and the new tendencies which he represents have not appeared on the scene. It is to be expected that Le Maistre, the disciple of Malouin in so many ways, will be hostile to Ravenez; and one is sure that he will endorse the observation of the omniscient author, who says: "One was never sure of Ravenez, for his will to destroy at times turned on his own ideas. . . ." However much Olivier may feel out of touch with Ravenez, he does not react as strongly to him as he does to Torral.

LE SEL DE LA TERRE. The *Sel de la terre* group is the rising generation. Logically, it ought to grow out of Ravenez, but, if it does, there is no visible umbilical connection. Lacretelle has yielded here to his habit of collecting little scraps of paper and turning them into fiction. Almost at random he picked up in 1943 two numbers of a typical "cabbage leaf" periodical, *Les Chantiers d'art*, particularly distinguished for the violence of its language and lack of a coherent program. Who has ever heard of this periodical since, or noticed the names of the signers of its manifestoes, Maurice Langlois or Jean de Beer? Since *Le Sel de la terre* is the reaction to *Messages*, that is as much as to say that *Les Chantiers d'art* is the principal reaction to the *Nouvelle Revue Française*—which is a historical absurdity. In any case, situated in the fictional world of *Le Pour et le Contre*, *Le Sel de la terre* seems to be the epitome of incoherence and absurdity, as though Lacretelle were venting his spleen.

If there is any spleen, it is entirely vicarious, for all the violence of language in *Le Sel de la terre* is an exact, though not verbatim, transposition from reality. Lacretelle's two copies of *Les Chantiers d'art* are thoroughly annotated with the names of his characters, as though he originally intended to quote these texts without alteration. On second thought, he kept only the style. Here is a sample from the original *Chantiers d'art*: "We are revolutionaries against them because, if they were able to entertain us for a time, nothing today attaches us to them. They no longer amuse us. And, we say in a loud voice, we no longer understand them. We are brutes. We make no sense out of their hocus-pocus, their images, their shades of meaning, their refinements, their 'harmonics,' their 'mystical exercises,' their poetic anatomies."[24] This new group, which has "never digested the poems of Jean Cocteau or the eggplants of

M. Matisse,"[25] is just as eager to attack Mallarmé, Claudel and Gide. The difficulty is that these eager youths have no idea what they will put in the place of these "pissers of ink," as they so elegantly call their predecessors.

Not knowing personally the writers of *Les Chantiers d'art*, Lacretelle has to imagine them, and therefore he sees them standing in the same relation to each other as the writers of the *N.R.F.*, or rather the N.E.J. The leader is Delestang, who is another Laume, fostering eclecticism and manfully trying to get his rebellious followers to respect tradition. Then there is Vollemin, whom Olivier dubs the "Copeau" of the group, forgetting that Copeau was in the N.R.F. but not in the N.E.J. He thinks of another as the "false Boëtte" because he is opposed to Maurras. Haubourdin, although not so identified, would appear to be Ravenez since he proclaims that gratuitous art is dead and that his generation is anti-Proust: "The intermittences of the heart no longer interest us; it is permanent feelings that we wish to know and emphasize." Peyruis, who is a more violent Haubourdin, concludes the debate in the style of *Les Chantiers d'art*: "This literature for the people and by the people will upset your so-called audacities and your heresies. No longer will one see anarchistic *little bourgeois* suppressing punctuation and capital letters if they are poets and deliberating on the prettiest way to open their flies, if they are moralists or novelists." Thereupon he draws a pistol, like Jarry in the banquet of the Argonautes in Gide's *Les Faux-Monnayeurs*, and the party breaks into a brawl.

Le Maistre. Olivier Le Maistre is the most elusive of the literary personalities in the novel because he is the least dogmatic. The allusions to his literary career are so indirect as to delude the reader into believing that he is an abject failure because he never succeeds in writing the great novel *Le Pour et le Contre* (remember that the manuscript is lost at sea and that there is never any question of retrieving it). On one hand, one thinks of Frédéric Moreau in Flaubert's *Education sentimentale,* the greatest character—artistically speaking—in all realistic literature to whom nothing of consequence ever happens and whose life is meaningless; and, on the other hand, one thinks of Edouard in *Les Faux-Monnayeurs*, who will apparently never succeed in writing his "pure" novel, as he calls it, about the counterfeiters. Immediately, in the reader's imagination, Frédéric Moreau and Edouard submerge the character of Olivier Le Maistre. Undoubtedly, the author intended it that way so that he might say: This is not I but rather Frédéric Moreau disguised as Edouard. If the reader reads more carefully, he will soon discover that the author is not infrequently saying: Do not be anyone's dupe; this is really I and not Frédéric or Edouard.

This handsome young man about town, this tall chap who awakens like Proust through a dislocated dream, turns on the faucets of his bath, unscrews his razor, exhibits "more nerves than muscles" when he has taken off his pyjamas, and revels in the joy of being master of his own destiny, is certainly none other than Jacques de Lacretelle in his *garçonnière*, which for fictional purposes has moved only a few blocks from the Avenue d'Eylau to the rue Spontini. Whether or not Ranouche calls and scratches his nose for him while he is still in his bath is an irrelevant detail for the speculation of future biographers.

In a series of Proustian flash backs we are enabled to piece together his biography. His father, now dead, was an "important liberal functionary," and his family, "friends of the Renans and the Berthelots, were the great anticlericals of the West." Read "Lamartine" for "Renan and Berthelot," and substitute "Alexandria" for "Rhodes," where Le Maistre's father was consul, and you have two salient facts in Lacretelle's biography. Inevitably, as a boy, Olivier attended Janson and played hooky, taking refuge, of course, in the garden of the Trocadéro. Later he went to Cambridge. At twenty-five he is frequenting *Le Bœuf*, where Proust is to be seen now and then.

His mother, suffering from heart trouble, has retired to the country and left him independent; she is an understanding mother but according to that overbearing female, Mme Galea, she is nearly as blind to his literary gifts as Mme Aupick was to Baudelaire's. About the mother there is also this curious passage: "He wonders whether his mother has not suffered in secret from having broken with her family at the time of her marriage; whether, now especially, she has no regret and is not attracted again to the more ancient cult." In context, the word "cult" does not refer to a religion; out of context, it is an allusion to the autobiographical elements in the plot of Lacretelle's "Roman protestant." Surreptitiously, in the novel, the author keeps referring to things and events in his own childhood: his father's eyebrows; Cornegliano, *fotografo d'arte*, whose real habitat was Alexandria, not Sicily; the *meuble empire*, which is the ornate cabinet standing today in the antechamber of 49 rue Vineuse and which, unknown to the casual visitor, is bursting with unclassified manuscripts; the heliotrope which he remembers so well, although he has forgotten his grandparents; Tante Marcellin, who owned a letter from Vallès, who was a friend of Clemenceau, who was always making war on the "petticoated men" and who was, in real life, Mme Ménard-Dorian —these are some of the allusions which are easily detected, and doubtless there are many more.

Of course, it may well be argued that such personal allusions are not without precedent in the novels of Lacretelle and that in the cases of the narrators of *Silbermann* and of *Amour nuptial*, the connection with the author was only secondary. However, the opposite is true of Olivier Le Maistre: He comes amazingly close to being Lacretelle himself. Partly to avoid interloping readers and partly because fiction interests him, whereas autobiography does not, Lacretelle takes refuge behind a third person narrative and the same kind of psychological formula which was the cornerstone of his objective characters. With his usual alacrity, he launches the formula on the fourth page of the text when he says of Olivier: ". . . there are beings who have the privilege of seeing the contrary image appear immediately behind each object or each figure." This obviously explains the title of the novel. But even this apparently rigid formula contributes to the subjectivity of the character this time, for, oversimplified though it may be, it tends to summarize Lacretelle's own intellectual attitude.

If Olivier Le Maistre is judged from the Olympian position of the omniscient author and the critical reader, there may be a certain irony in his family name "Le Maistre." His failure to write *Le Pour et le Contre* causes us to lose sight of the fact that Olivier is commonly considered to be a successful author by his literary colleagues and by the public and that he has apparently achieved that position rapidly and without difficulty. At the time of the N.E.J. reception in honor of Malouin's prize, in other words not too far from the beginning of the novel, Joachim Ravier, a minor character, remarks: "Monsieur le Maistre, you are no longer the unknown. I have read all your books." Well along in the second volume, we learn that he has written twenty books, and that may not be the final total. Although there is irony again in the banquet of *Le Sel de la terre*, it should not be forgotten that it is given in Le Maistre's honor. By human standards Le Maistre is a successful author; by Olympian standards he is not. This is the most human and most personal thing which Lacretelle says in his entire book, and therefore we see that the theorizing about Laume's *sincérité* was not idle speculation.

In the work of Le Maistre, Lacretelle is surveying his own work; and even though he maintains a certain superiority because, after all, he did succeed in writing *Le Pour et le Contre*, the most casual reader senses that he shares Le Maistre's misgivings about his ability to achieve Olympian stature. Such an attitude is rare on the part of an artist, to be sure. To those who know Lacretelle in real life or through his work it is clear that he has given a realistic portrait of himself. When one scrapes through the veneer and dignity of one of the most impressive members of the French Academy, one still finds Jean Hermelin. In private life as well, he is capable of writing something like this: "I have definitively broken off with ******** . I called him a crook, and he answered that I had no talent whatever. As we are both right, there is no reconciliation possible."[26]

Only a careful reading of the text of *Le Pour et le Contre* will corroborate the contention that the twenty or more volumes of the writings of Le Maistre are really the work of Lacretelle. The youthful *Carnet d'Ombre noire*, in which Le Maistre later detects the influence of Huysmans and Laforgue (from the description, however, one would say that it is Rimbaud's *Bateau ivre*), corresponds to nothing real except that Lacretelle's first novel was written in notebooks. However, it is an obvious allusion to the adolescent Lacretelle's interest in the symbolists. From this same period of his life, Olivier later finds a miscellaneous page of imprecations against the "prejudice of filial love," which tends to make Olivier a Gidian *avant la lettre* but is really related to a similar theme in *La Vie inquiète de Jean Hermelin*. Somewhat tardily, like Lacretelle, Le Maistre begins his literary career with a novel which relates his mother's life story as seen through his own adolescent eyes. The novel therefore stands for *La Vie inquiète de Jean Hermelin*, with an additional allusion to those letters which Mme Amaury de

Lacretelle burned and those which the Germans defiled at Montfort. After that first novel, Le Maistre's problem is to break out of the subjective into the objective novel, and he exclaims to Laume: "I can invent nothing. It seems to me that I shall never be able to write anything which does not come from within me." Apparently he did become an objective writer, but direct allusions to his work are vague indeed. Ravier mentions that he has written a novel about castle owners in Anjou, which must be an allusion to *Les Hauts Ponts*. Much later, discussing Laume and sexuality with Mme Galea, Olivier refers to the time when he was interested in sexual motivation as a literary theme; unquestionably, *La Bonifas* is meant. At this point, the text again alludes to *Les Hauts Ponts*: ". . . he had entered more fully into country life. It seemed to him that the great mystery resides in these calm skies and the visible structure of things. Just as the destinies of people with a straightforward gaze appeared to him to be the most ticklish to describe." All other allusions to Le Maistre's literary activity likewise lead back to Lacretelle. The study on La Rochefoucauld is either the 1934 article "Les Romans de La Rochefoucauld" or the preface which Lacretelle finished in 1948 for an edition of the moralist; the book published in Belgium which is a masterpiece of typography must be *Mort de la jalousie*; the translations must be Mary Webb and Emily Brontë. In other words, the author leaves us no choice but to suppose that the entire mature work of Olivier Le Maistre corresponds almost exactly to the mature work of Jacques de Lacretelle.

The same parallelism is striking in the broad outlines of Le Maistre's life after he becomes a literary figure. He buys a house at Yvelines, which is a "*burg* hugolien" two kilometers from the station. The description would have fitted Chevreuse; by changing the name to that of a small locality near Montfort-l'Amaury the author invites more positive identification with the latter town—also two kilometers from the station and even more "hugolien" in appearance and associations. Autobiographical also are the public lectures which Le Maistre gives in the provinces and his marriage to Chantal. Of course, the meeting of Olivier and Chantal in the course of one of the lectures (at Dôle, says the text, but at Pontarlier says a note, indicating that it must be a reminiscence of an actual lecture) is much less romantic than the real story, as if the author did not wish to overtax the credulity of his readers. He even indulges in a little private humor when he makes Chantal the niece of Mme Galea, for that has the effect of making him the nephew of Mme Guéritte in real life. After the marriage, there are other autobiographical episodes: the trip to Austria, Mrs. Otis' ball, and, to be sure, the concluding events of the novel, which follow closely the Lacretelles' trip to the New World in 1939.

Olivier Le Maistre insists so much on his own tergiversation that we are likely to take it for granted. First, the omniscient author says: "Never has he given his entire support to such and such a form of existence or even to such and such of his penchants. . . . If there is in him a note which is worth being heard, it is precisely the one which expresses these discordances and the restlessness of which they are the cause." Later, Olivier himself says of the central character of his work in progress: "It appears to you altogether natural to admire Italian primitives and the *Bœuf écorché*, a Holland landscape and a desert view, the music of Rameau and that of Beethoven. But transport the antithesis into another area, moral, philosophical, and you have to make a choice; take or refuse, praise or condemn. Well, that is what my character intends to avoid doing." That is why Le Maistre never assumes a trenchant attitude toward the literary figures of the N.E.J., who represent the possible choices in the domain of the intellect. He never gets into an argument with Torral or Ravenez. In a way, he seems to admire Ravenez for being able to do something new, just as he would ask nothing better than to be admired himself by the idol-wreckers of *Le Sel de la terre*.

He is indeed so pliable that not only does he admire Chantal's spontaneity, which is so different from his own reflective nature, but he respects her religious sentiments in spite of the fundamental opposition between them. This opposition is symbolized, on Chantal's side, by the fact that she was born "miraculously," as Mme Galea says sarcastically, while her mother was on a pilgrimage to Paray-le-Monial, and on Le Maistre's side, by Tante Marcellin sitting firmly astride the family tree to prevent any idolaters from clambering aboard. Because his mother was also religious, he came "the nearest he had ever been to faith for many years" and even tried to persuade Malouin to forgive his daughter for taking the veil.

In politics he inclines more to the Right than anything, since he says to himself, comparing Destoile and Ravenez: "He [Ravenez] also said the same thing about Moscow. Curious this need Frenchmen have for praising force and discipline elsewhere than at home." One concludes that he would not be averse to a little order at home; however, when pressed for an opinion about the *Esprit social* (obviously the Parti Social Français), he made a laconic answer: "It gave the impression of an Epinal picture, he declared. One could not see where they were going. In short, he did not believe in it." When the Munich crisis comes, he seeks the counsel of Guastaud, the socialist, of whom he says: "He is sincere. Or at least he *sees* all that he says." Nevertheless, he subsequently admires certain conservative attitudes in Canada, to the annoyance of his more liberal friend Brusagier. On the whole, he seems to take the attitude that all holders of political opinions are opinionated and that they are responsible for the sorry plight of the world. As a reasonable person, he shies away from politics.

That is partly because the *chose littéraire* interests him infinitely more and partly because politics threatens the very survival of literature. Yet, about literature itself, he does not seem to be too articulate. *In camera*, he is eloquent, especially as a young man discussing literature with Borger and then with his mother; but whenever more than two people are assembled, he takes refuge in small talk or simply listens. However, this listening is accompanied by cogitation from which emerges a definite aesthetic serving him in lieu of a philosophy of life. Because of the consistency of this aesthetic, he never heeds the solicitations of other aesthetics, however tolerant he may claim to be of them. For example, he is never interested in Castelli, and he refers later to the outmoded *Robinson 1920* only to corroborate an opinion which he had held from the start. From this start, that is to say from the very first pages of the novel, he is a realist; his ambition, he tells Borger exuberantly, is to become a twentieth century Balzac: "Everywhere there is a character in being, a type." And again: "The world, even represented as it was there, in its most humble reality, had the effect on him of a nest of boxes; one always finds another one to open." Borger cautions him that he is still too much the accomplice of his age to be its judge; when Le Maistre sticks too closely to externals, his novel about the affair with Mariette aborts, for he has neglected the real problems of psychological realism.

Even before he began to write about Mariette, Le Maistre had entered upon a most useful apprenticeship from which he was not capable of profiting immediately. Any reader of *Le Pour et le Contre* is inevitably struck by what seems to be a pastiche of Proust in the beginning of the novel, and his opinion that it is a pastiche is later reinforced by the overt pastiche of Gide in the *Sel de la terre* episode. If he thinks it is only a pastiche, he has overlooked the significance of the "Proustian" experiences which Olivier undergoes, for the experiences are obviously self-induced. Lacretelle took care to point out seventeen pages earlier that Le Maistre was keenly interested in Proust. In his creative exuberance, Olivier imagines himself to be Proust. He sees a woman at a window who reminds him of someone; he concentrates on the mental image, and, to his great annoyance, remembers an insignificant provincial cousin: "The disparity between Olivier's desire and his fine discovery made him burst out laughing." But he tries again, and, with the help of Easter eggs in a *bistrot* window, he succeeds in recalling a fragment of his own childhood in Rhodes. This is not a mysterious summons from the subconscious to create; it is only an indication that Le Maistre is very consciously experimenting in preparation for the great novel which he is determined to start immediately. Because he cannot reconcile realism with introspection or, more exactly, because he has not served an apprenticeship, the great novel about Mariette aborts.

Thereupon, encouraged by his mother, he begins his apprenticeship in introspection and writes the novel about her. He is on the right track because he is developing his own originality without concern for externals. Even then he remarks: "And what an error to believe that an authentic memory, the emotion reported directly, triumphs always over literature." Subsequently, he laments to Laume that "this *I* does not always have something to say." Though not a realist himself, Laume gives this advice: ". . . banish the *I*, report events in an objective manner, but in the measure that your characters have been the spectators of them."

This is the first step in the evolution from introspection back to realism; and although the passage is really an allusion to the aesthetic structure of *Le Pour et le Contre*, it is at the same time a recapitulation of the aesthetic problems which beset the narrator of *Amour nuptial* and which the latter solved in the same manner. The details of this evolution are not clear because of the gap in the narrative at this point; after the gap, Le Maistre has already reached his mature stride.

All we can say with certainty about this mature stride is that it is realistic. The evidence is fragmentary and widely dispersed. At one point Le Maistre agrees with Charmery's idea that "notes resemble little mollusks which are delectable when raw but are worth nothing in a sauce." Like Stubel later on, he disagrees with Malouin and defends the value of generalizations: "If there is in each one of us a permanent psychological truth, and not lifelike, intermittent states, one can discover it only by grazing the surface and then by deep soundings. The facts, that is to say our acts, are perhaps not the most significant part of ourselves. —And that everything can be explained I admit. . . . But do not proclaim it as a system, or else the mystery and illusion will crumble, no more enchantment is possible, imagination becomes superfluous." A moment later he says: "Reality must not be a screen which shuts out the view." He is in complete possession of his aesthetic when he says to himself in the next chapter: "One notion counts, one alone, and it is superior to styles, it is valid for all temperaments: It is that there are two worlds which must be joined—poetry and logic. And when one succeeds in doing so, one becomes a god." Later he defines his method as a combination of "memory and will." All of this obviously fits in with Lacretelle's own theories on the art of the novel.

The striking thing about this intellectual self-portrait is its earnestness. It is difficult to decide whether Lacretelle is merely caricaturing himself because, initially, he saw certain minor resemblances between himself and Frédéric Moreau, or whether he is judging himself in retrospect. There certainly seems to be judgment in Le Maistre's disapproval of the Esprit Social, and hence this sounds like self-censure for the part which Lacretelle played personally in the Parti Social Français. For this reason one is tempted to assume similar self-criticism in the fact that Le Maistre is as taciturn as an Anglo-Saxon and seeks his real intellectual sustenance in solitude. Hitherto, Lacretelle has looked upon this attitude as a virtue. Could he now mean that this inarticulateness is connected with Le Maistre's inability to create a great work? Instead of attempting to answer this question loaded with psychoanalytical implications, the better part of wisdom would be to concede a greater measure of autonomy to Le Maistre and to conclude that his personal defeat is fictional rather than autobiographical.

There are cogent reasons for conceding this autonomy. One is that it seems highly improbable that Lacretelle could have imagined a novel of personal defeat at the very time that his literary career had reached its apotheosis with his reception at the French Academy. The other reason is that the moral defeat of Olivier Le Maistre is part of a central theme which is the intellectual collapse of Occidental civilization. With this collapsing civilization Lacretelle feels a strong solidarity. That is the explanation of the peculiar symbolism of the characters in the *Sel de la terre* group. Le Maistre first imagines this generation to be similar to his own in its revolt against its predecessors and its search for individualism, but he soon discovers that it is really intent on destroying all the cultural values in French literary tradition.

Le Sel de la terre is only an indication of disintegration; the proof of disintegration is the outbreak of war itself. As the Red Star liner with Le Maistre aboard makes its last crossing, the great author muses: "Analysis, introspection, the light which glides along the walls of the cavern, the lead which dives down and clings to the depths—all that is just so many outmoded styles." If he ever finishes *Le Pour et le Contre*, he says to himself, it will only make people yawn. He expresses the idea in personal terms, but in reality no one has attacked him, no one has threatened to burn his books. It is his way of life which has collapsed; under the falling cornices and capitals lie buried Laume, Malouin, even Castelli and, in a larger sense, Gide, Proust, Claudel, Mallarmé and Valéry. In such company this is hardly a personal defeat. *Le Pour et le Contre* is the record of the defeat of 1940 seen from the aesthetic point of view.

In a sense, Le Maistre sought redemption in literature, and in a sense, literature failed to redeem him. At the age of twenty-five he turned away from the pleasures of his pleasure-loving times and sought to give meaning to his life by literary production. This may even have been a slightly bourgeois desire to be useful, just as a young man of good family might redeem himself by taking up diplomacy or even by reviving the declining fortunes of the family business. Nevertheless, under his calm exterior he continued to seethe, for his emotions were still unsettled. Like the *littérateur* that he was, he wondered "if the daily presence of the same woman was not a means of capturing the source of inspiration." Whatever he does, his ultimate question is whether it will perfect his art. Even the death of his baby son does not deter him, because he puts art on a higher plane than life itself; he even exploits his own grief. Chantal rebels at this inhuman attitude but a year later says repentantly: "You owed it to yourself to write that."

In the last Proustian illumination which presages the end, Le Maistre remembers how, on other ocean voyages, he used to look through a porthole and see a green ray: "Now he no longer expected the green ray through the porthole, but he still kept repeating to himself: 'There must be something else.' What? He would never know. Never would he reach his goal. But he said to himself that all the intensity of his existence came from this presentiment and this quest." Obviously, that something else was not God but the attainment of that super-reality which, as the symbolists and Proust alleged, lifted man to the level of the gods.

The quest for art is so fundamental to Le Maistre's character that it conditions his most basic attitudes, his sentimental relationships and even his sexual desires. Though he is egotistical, art forces him to look at other people analytically and hence with a certain indulgence which breeds sympathy. At the same time, the artistic outlook prevents him from acting with true spontaneity, because he is always an observer rather than a participant; only with Chantal does he make an effort to be human, and even there his attitudes are often so studied that it is obvious that this is the real cause of discord between them.

Occasionally the artistic principle intervenes directly in the action, as when Le Maistre suddenly loses interest in Bali because he sees at last the shallowness of her nature through the impossible novel which she has written "in the margin of *Le Côté de Guermantes*." All of the mystery in which he had hitherto enveloped her is suddenly dissipated, and seducing her with the conscious objective of getting her out of his system is ludicrously elementary. Of course, it must be added that the intuitive Bali has not read Proust for naught and that she limply gives in, sensing that if Olivier is able to set his trap so deliberately, she has somehow lost her power to attract him. On the whole, however, the relationship of the artistic principle to the plot is so subtle as to be almost intangible; in this respect *Le Pour et le Contre* is very different from *Amour nuptial*, in which the plot hinges directly on the narrator's vocation as a novelist.

16

LE POUR ET LE CONTRE—ANALYSIS

LACRETELLE has never been an obscurantist, not even in *Le Pour et le Contre.* The complexities which he has introduced into his novel, though suggested by more obscure modern novels, serve the exclusive purpose of greater realism. This is probably a second reason why Lacretelle invited comparison with Flaubert's *Education sentimentale*, for, like Flaubert, he was trying to express the essential monotony of a real existence. It was in this very department of monotony that the modern novel since Flaubert had developed its originality, particularly with Proust. That is undoubtedly why Proustian themes come so readily to Lacretelle's pen and why, especially, he ties up the aesthetic pattern of the novel with the porthole scene in which an olfactory sensation enables Le Maistre to see his life in retrospect. Despite these occasional themes, the novel is not Proustian; the predominant technique is realistic, even when the modern innovations occur.

Lacretelle's notes for the novel show how he intended to modify his approach to realism. A scrap of paper says: "Let the brain of each character be a fictional hearth, and let the novel develop thus, almost by itself." Although, in the novel, the remark is attributed with only slight modification to Castelli, we are reminded of a similar principle in *Les Hauts Ponts*. Furthermore, another scrap of paper expands this principle of reconciling spontaneity with the purposes of realism: "Never make the characters intervene for the purpose of the movement of the narrative. Let them adapt themselves the least possible to the story. Let each one of them have his own originality and interest, his *autonomy*. And the novel will advance." Before the discovery of these scraps of paper, but several years after the novel had been written, Lacretelle used the same language, in an interview, to define his intentions: "Cause the analysis to pass into the dialogue. Avoid following step by step a fictional plot. Let each character have a novel of his own."[1]

Dialogue does dominate the novel and even absorbs a large part of the action, though not at the most dramatic moments, as if the author did not have full confidence in the new technique. Characters reveal themselves, report on other characters and even refer to dramatic events, which inevitably lose some of their dramatic impact when woven into the pattern of a casual conversation. Lacretelle had long been preoccupied with this problem of dialogue and as early as 1930 told Robert de Saint-Jean: "I regret using analysis too frequently instead of letting my characters talk."[2] Of course, dialogue is potentially a dramatic technique in the tradition of French tragedy, but not so in this novel, for it is not in the nature of typical Lacretelle characters to come so openly into conflict. They tend to be monads who keep their feelings to themselves and who, when they do conflict with others, express themselves more eloquently in silence than in words. Instead of accelerating the action, as it might well do, dialogue in this novel only retards and obliterates it. This is a common occurrence in modern novels more concerned with the continuum of life than with dramatic values.

At the same time, reliance on dialogue causes Lacretelle to stay away from the omniscient point of view and thus to avoid his greatest pitfall: the tendency to fit his characters into formulas. With the exception of the literary characters whom he has conceived as stereotypes, most of the characters are free agents. Even Le Maistre escapes from the yoke of the formula which the author placed initially about his neck. Mme Galea goes her domineering way entirely uninhibited by the derogatory formulas which other characters propound behind her back. Like the free agent characters in Proust's great novel, these Lacretelle characters reserve many a surprise. A simple example is Guasto, the scapegoat, who emerges bookseller of N.E.J. Bohemia, who turns up later as Lady Mac-as Guastaud the statesman; or there is Etiennette Fabrecoul, the lagan, much as Proust's Odette de Crécy finally becomes the Princess of Guermantes. A more subtle example is Ranouche the lightheaded, the untouchable, who surprises Le Maistre by promising to spend the first night with him if she ever decides to deceive her husband and who eventually surprises the reader by taking life so seriously that she commits suicide.

The Proustian technique of retouching works admirably with another untouchable, Bali, whose enigmatic character is projected onto the stage of the novel long before she makes a physical appearance. Le Maistre is so taken in by the enigma that he fails to see her for what she is, a silly little sentimentalist who likes to brood in the charred ruins of her country house. Somewhat like Proust's hero Marcel with Albertine, he imagines some fearful secret between her and her brother Eustache de Pilorge. Only when she dramatizes this relation as incest in her impossible novel does Olivier realize that there was no incest and no fearful secret. Without the incest, she is a very ordinary person, and so she remains throughout the rest of the novel, becoming the mistress of a prosaic person like Guastaud. Seen through Le Maistre's eyes, however, she herself had been a very poetic creature, changing like the colors of the sunset, instinctive like the small animals of the forest. In short, she is one of Lacretelle's best fictional creations, a breath of poetry left over from *Les Hauts Ponts*. Lacretelle makes frequent use of this technique of developing character from hearsay, and some characters (Eustache de Pilorge, for example) never develop beyond the hearsay stage. The result is an impression of psychological depth which Lacretelle had never so consciously sought before in the novel.

The prominence of dialogue in the novel suggests no French author so much as the Englishman Aldous Huxley, of whom Lacretelle had written in 1939: "The reading of a novel of Aldous Huxley is a cause for wonder, at least for me."[3] Actually, when he wrote that, Lacretelle was reviewing *Those Barren Leaves* (called *Marina di Vezza* in translation), but, in the same article, he expressed his particular admiration for *Point Counter Point*. Lacretelle's title *Le Pour et le Contre* seems almost to be a mistranslation of *Point Counter Point*. Huxley also relies on dialogue to reveal character and plot, as well as to suggest what we have called the essential monotony of life. On the whole (an exception is Malebrèche's tirade on Nugall insecticide), Lacretelle's characters are far more serious and do not often indulge in that super-witty repartee which makes Huxley's characters so amusing and yet so unbearable. It should also be noted how frequently Huxley's characters are scientists or at least choose their metaphors in science; in Lacretelle's novel there is only one scientist, Elsner the psychiatrist

—a pseudo-scientist at best—and there is only one biological scene, the birth of Chantal's baby. Lacretelle had no idea of imitating Huxley; he had found in the Englishman's work a realistic principle which he intended to apply in his own way.

At the same time he had discovered in Huxley a kindred spirit, which is surprising since their natures are so essentially different. The following passage is typical of the kind that must have attracted Lacretelle's attention in *Point Counter Point*:

> And he had never even noticed there was a lamp post there; it simply hadn't existed until this moment. And now it was the only thing that existed. Spandrell looked at it with a fixed and breathless attention. This lamp post alone in the mist—hadn't he seen something like it before? This queer sensation of being with the sole survivor of the Deluge was somehow familiar.... Staring at the lamp post, Spandrell waited, agonized and patient, like a man who feels he is going to sneeze, tremulously awaiting the anticipated paroxysm; waited for the long-dead memory to revive. And suddenly it sprang up, broad awake, out of its catalepsy, and, with a sense of enormous relief, Spandrell saw himself walking up the steep hard-trodden snow of the road leading from Cortina toward the pass of Falzarego.

The opening and closing pages of *Le Pour et le Contre* are full of such episodes, which previously we called Proustian. Obviously, Lacretelle discovered Proust in Huxley—not a difficult matter because the Englishman mentions Proust frequently—and he took Huxley's example as license to exaggerate his own Proustian techniques. Olivier's musings as he travels through Paris can readily be compared to Walter Bidlake's musings on the underground at the beginning of *Point Counter Point*. With minor variations, the style of the two novels is the same, not convoluted like Proust's sentences but clear and succinct.

Lacretelle uses involuntary memory or uncontrolled musing to express psychological rhythms; Huxley goes even further, as in the passage above, and uses involuntary memory as a device for reversing chronology in the novel. Although Lacretelle did not imitate him so patently, he was impressed by the kind of psychological realism to be obtained from reversed chronology and resorted to it frequently. For example, the entire episode of Chantal's flight is related while Olivier is ostensibly musing after Chantal has returned to him and, still unreconciled, they are sailing for home. There are innumerable examples of such reversal of chronology in the novel; sometimes, faced with the necessity of relating an important event which happens to the main character Olivier, the author even prefers to narrate the action in reversed chronology, as though no direct action could take place on the stage of the novel.

In his subvocal musing at the end of the novel, Olivier describes his unfinished *Le Pour et le Contre* as "a novel written as one works at a tapestry." He must be thinking of the complexity of Huxley as he says this, though, unlike Proust's and Gide's, Huxley's name is nowhere mentioned in the novel. *Point Counter Point* is a series of tableaux occurring simultaneously, successively, or previously, sometimes with the focus on one character, sometimes, as in a group scene, with the focus shifting from one character to another; there is no main character, no single plot, but rather a multiplicity of characters and plots, running parallel, converging and seldom progressing. There are as many, if not more, characters in *Le Pour et le Contre* (to be exact, one hundred and fifty-three with names, ninety-one without names); a goodly number of them are prominent enough to be engaged in their own plots. When the novel is in full progress, the author tends to conceive his chapters as group conversations on a fixed stage, as Huxley does so frequently. Although Lacretelle never tries to build up an impression of simultaneous action, he fragments the action, and even many of the chapters, into little pieces which give an impression of discontinuity. Much of the action, sometimes alluded to subsequently, sometimes ignored altogether, takes place in the gaps. Such is the psychological pattern of life itself.

Lacretelle diverges from Huxley in putting the focus in *Le Pour et le Contre* always on Olivier. Even when Olivier is a silent observer, he makes his presence known from time to time with a trivial remark. Once, but only once, on the occasion of Chantal's flight to Washington, the focus shifts inadvertently, as it were, to her. What has become of Lacretelle's "fictional hearth" theory? He had already experimented with it in *Les Hauts Ponts*. This time it is only a way of looking at the characters before putting them down on paper, for with so many disruptive forces at work in the novel, the author is reluctant to sacrifice the artistic unity which he can achieve with a single focus.

Of course, Gide's *Les Faux-Monnayeurs* is also concerned with representing the complexity of reality by fragmentation and simultaneous action. However, there are two compelling reasons for seeing this complexity in Lacretelle's work as a Huxley influence rather than as a Gide influence. One is the absence of all Proustian themes in Gide; the other is Gide's concern with the contradictory aspects of reality: His chapters, organized as opposing concentric mirrors, are designed to show how different characters envisage the same event. There are no such considerations in Lacretelle's novel.

Nevertheless, in some respects, Lacretelle has purposely stamped his novel with the Gidian hallmark. The idea of a novel about writing a novel is certainly Gidian; though Olivier keeps no journal, all the N.E.J. episodes and literary discussions bear the same relationship to the main course of the novel as Edouard's journal does to Gide's self-writing novel. Certain other episodes also recall distinctly similar episodes in *Les Faux-Monnayeurs*. The banquet of *Le Sel de la terre*—as already noted—must be the banquet of the Argonautes; the life boat scene at the end of *Le Pour et le Contre* is probably inspired by the life boat scene after the sinking of the *Bourgogne*, especially since the clipping from *Le Figaro* for March 27, 1940, telling of the sinking of the first British ship in the Channel by a Heinkel bomber, and obviously kept for this scene, is altogether different; and finally, in the manuscript version only, the Polish psychiatrist Lubowska, under whose influence Laume falls, is in all likelihood Gide's Sophroniska.

Point Counter Point and *Les Faux-Monnayeurs* both avoid a unifying plot. *Le Pour et le Contre*, either because the author cannot resist the temptation or simply by way of reaction to these novels, has a tenuous plot which sets the novel in motion, then runs along for years as a leitmotiv and finally burst its bonds in a most melodramatic manner, as Randolph Lemaistre, the son of Dorothy Vambrace, to whom Le Maistre had unconscionably sold his name years before, turns out to be the kidnaper in a fictional version of the Lindbergh affair. The coincidence of Le Maistre's arrival at New York at this same moment is overwhelming. Lacretelle later had doubts "whether the denouement is not too unreal to life."[4] Yet he could not do without this ending because of the symbolic value of the idea. The reappearance of the theme of Olivier's marriage to a sullied American, destroying the one thing that counts in his life, his real marriage, is a kind of retribution for having placed artistic achievement above sincerity, in other words above life. Gide has set a precedent for the use of coincidence, and Huxley for a melodramatic ending. Manifestly, the modern novel, unlike the realistic novel, does not worry about *vraisemblance*. Almost in a spirit of antirealism, Lacretelle preserved this unreal denouement which had occurred to him when he was in New York and for which he carefully documented himself at the time. Furthermore, he was still enough of a traditional novelist to feel that he needed tension in these final pages to leave a strong impression on the minds of his readers.

In spite of appearances, there is nothing haphazard about this novel; its complexity is entirely reasoned, as can readily be seen from the structure. The novel falls into three parts, each designated by a title. Part One, the overture "The Beautiful Dawn" (this title has a double significance because *La Belle Aurore* is the inn where Malebrèche gives his luncheon), presents the main character, creates the thematic atmosphere of his generation and leads up to his first successful literary effort. Part Two, "The N.E.J.," resumes after an interval of ten or twelve years, although it takes the reader some time to realize that so much time has elapsed. The pursuit of Bali dominates this part; the futility and emptiness of this pursuit correspond to the void into which Le Maistre's literature has fallen. Ranouche's death, concluding this part, brings Le Maistre to an awareness of this void. Part Three, "The Jubilee," resumes after an interval of five years and covers the period of Le Maistre's authentic marriage, which makes him infinitely more human and seems potentially capable of rejuvenating his literature. Everything converges on his great crisis with Chantal when he fails in the test of true sincerity and, by the same token, never rejuvenates his literature. Each of the two main parts of *Le Pour et le Contre*, focused on a definite psychological problem and reaching a climax in terms of those problems, is almost a novel by itself.

It would be difficult and probably impossible to imagine a successful novel into which the reader could not project himself in some manner. In the overture of *Le Pour et le Contre*, such projection is simple and natural because the reader remains inside the personality of Olivier, sharing in his subconscious associations and the general flux of his emotional life, participating in his prejudices and his enthusiasms. In fact, the reader's interest may be momentarily caught up in the mechanism of two apparently conventional plots, one having to do with Olivier's marriage and the other with Malebrèche's marriage. One even expects some villainous interference from Toulomiès, the ex-diplomat who tries to involve Olivier in his shady dealings. Even when these two plots lead purposely into a cul-de-sac, the reader may go on having a naïve interest in Olivier's success story as a novelist. Although quite modern in its conception, the overture is contrived with just enough of the elements of a conventional novel to hold the reader's attention.

Beginning with Part Two, the real purpose of the cul-de-sac is apparent: Most of life's plots lead to a dead end, and life must be presented as discontinuous to resemble itself. To emphasize the discontinuity, this part begins with a chapter-long conversation in which Olivier no longer occupies the center of the stage; in fact, the author now calls him "Le Maistre" rather than "Olivier" to signify his momentary demotion from the rank of central intelligence. From time to time Le Maistre re-emerges as Olivier, only to slip back into the impersonal role again (the method of name-changing not being rigidly observed, however); and with each reappearance the plot of the novel progresses, for life really does have a plot which it is the duty of the realist to discern. Whenever the focus is on Olivier, he is carrying on a kind of inner monologue, like the typical Lacretelle character that he is. Since the entire plot of Part Two is centered around the enigma of Bali, the workings of Olivier's mind and emotions are of concern to the reader. Similarly, whenever Bali appears on the scene, this interest, which may have been lagging during the conversations, again revives, so that a conversation in which Bali participates has a fascination which the others do not possess. Despite the ramifications, fluctuations and frequent interruptions, Part Two is held together by something closely resembling the kind of psychological plot which we are accustomed to find in Lacretelle's novels; and this plot is certainly one of his best efforts in this domain.

Nevertheless, this main plot is so centered in the mind of the principal protagonist that it is devoid of action and conflict until the denouement. The only semblance of conflict occurs in a subsidiary plot in which Mme Galea tries to dominate Olivier, and then for a few pages *Le Pour et le Contre* reads like a typical Lacretelle psychological novel. Domineering and willful though she is, Mme Galea arouses all the reader's sympathy when Ranouche unintentionally discloses in her presence the secret that Olivier has made with Bali the trip to Holland on which she, Galea, had long been trying to take him herself. Then comes the epic showdown, when, parrying her reproaches, Olivier cuts her to the quick by diagnosing her as one of those women suffering from "hysteria of the soul." The only other psychological relationship (the word "conflict" is much too strong in this case) which stands out in this part of the novel is the episode in which Etiennette Fabrecoul, always refreshingly disarming in her frank approach to life, first lets down her hair, after Frène has left her, and then seeks solace in Olivier's arms. In fact, Olivier is so reluctant to play the role of consoler the second time that he unintentionally causes Ranouche's death. In the entire second part, real action intervenes only once in connection with Ranouche's suicide, and then for many pages *Le Pour et le Contre* reads like any realistic novel, particularly because of the caricatural gendarmes in the center of the action.

Part Three, held together only by the theme of Olivier's marriage, is a triumph in the application of the techniques of accidental realism with which Lacretelle had been experimenting but which he had not yet applied to the limit. The history of this psychological relationship serves in lieu of a psychological plot. There is no drama in the strict sense of the word, although the author, because of an ingrown habit of introducing a logical structure into his novels, blows up Chantal's flight to Washington into the proportions of one supreme crisis. Actually it is not the supreme crisis but rather a worse crisis than all the others. In spite of the artistic conclusion, the novel, as we have said before, ends arbitrarily in the midst of a reconciliation. From the point of view of plot, there is no factual relationship between the various crises; these arise rather out of the problems inherent in any marital relationship and also out of the characters of these two individuals joined in wedlock.

Without a plot, there is no conventional device for sustaining the reader's interest in the third part, which, incidentally, is as long as the other two parts taken together. The success of the enterprise depends entirely on the author's ability to make this marital relationship so human that the reader will project himself into the situation without the artificial device of a plot. A marriage in which the two participants continue to love each other is unique in French literary history if not in life itself. A marriage without a full-fledged adultery defies all the traditions of the French novel and theater. Yet Lacretelle was not attempting the impossible, because he was drawing on life itself for his subject. Before Olivier's marriage, Laume urged him: "What you did for your childhood you must do now for your life as a grown man." In spite of his age, Olivier reached maturity only after his marriage. Lacretelle must have had somewhat the same feeling with regard to his own life; *Le Pour et le Contre* is his attempt to translate this experience into literature. This does not mean that he transposes all of the major events of his story from life itself; much imagination certainly goes into the making of the major episodes in this part of the novel, such as the death of Chantal's baby and, later, her flight to Washington. But it is noteworthy that he preserves the discrepancy in age between the two characters, as though this were a unique situation offering great possibilities in literature.

It is a striking fact that Chantal has no face, although at one point her clothing is elaborately described. Furthermore, from time to time she usurps the function of a central intelligence, so that for a brief moment we see events as she envisages them. Two explanations for this suggest themselves. One is that the author must feel so close to Chantal that he unconsciously takes her place; the other is that this marital relationship is more subtle when seen from both sides. Chantal is not Bali, and the love which she inspires in her husband has nothing in common with his passion for Bali. Jealousy disturbs the relationship between these two individuals, but it neither makes this love nor unmakes it. The implication is that Proust was wrong in asserting that love is subjective and its permanency impossible for this very reason. Olivier mused thus four years after his marriage (Part Three covers these four years): ". . . he saw in it his one and only act of obedience to a mysterious order placed above him. Love alone, however suddenly it had burst forth, did not explain his willingness to tie himself down forever. Up until then, could not his sentimental life be summarized in two concurrent rhythms, pursuit and flight? Between Chantal and him there must be something else." This something else is Lacretelle's main interest in Part Three.

Olivier looks upon Chantal as his creation. In the early days of his marriage, he is grateful to her for stabilizing his emotions by returning full-fold the affection in which he envelops her; but at the same time he hovers over her in her sleep as though she were a fascinating toy. Her minor vexations worry him until he soon discovers that he can master them with a few soothing words. He becomes smug in his confidence that he can control this psychological mechanism, and that is one reason for their subsequent misunderstanding.

On the other hand, her love for him is more than admiration; there is a certain deliberateness in every one of her acts which shows from the start that her love is not infatuation. It is not worship of a tin god by an unsophisticated provincial girl which prompts her to tear up the letters of her first admirer Guilmur and throw them into the river. This is the gesture of a woman who knows what she wants and is certain that she has found it. With the same deliberateness, she goes to Olivier's *garçonnière*, not out of a spirit of bravado toward her sheltered past, but because she is so sure of herself that there is no reason why she should not go. Chantal is no one's dupe. If she loves Olivier, it is because she understands him with her woman's intuition. Understanding him, she cannot give him up; nor can she betray him to Guilmur (the Washington episode) even to the extent of talking about him.

But Chantal is human. In physical pain she is irritable and even unjust. The first real jealousy scene develops at Mrs. Otis' ball when she is already pregnant and, in this unflattering condition, has to meet the women whom she believes to have been her husband's mistresses before their marriage. Stoically, she had hitherto accepted this part of life as inevitable, especially since her husband apparently had made no secret about any of it; but now the reality of it all was too much. Later she blamed, rather unreasonably, the death of her child on this prenatal emotional upset. Because she is human, the death of her child takes something from her which she will never recover.

When they are together, their relations seem to be normal and affectionate, in spite of the tragedy. Nevertheless, at the very time when he is writing his chapter on the death of their child, while Chantal is in the country, he picks up a woman in the street, spends the night with her and then joins his wife, completely reinvigorated. The little adventure has had a therapeutic effect; he forgets it and Chantal never learns of it. Eighty pages later, when they are in Canada, Olivier is calmly discussing Ranouche's death with their host Brusagier, the man whom Ranouche might have married, when suddenly Chantal's pent-up emotions break forth. She reproaches him that night for living in the past with the memory of his mistress (to set the record straight, it should be noted that Ranouche never was his mistress), and, at the same time, she blames herself for not having given him a child. One thing leading to another, they get back to the subject of their separation the year before:

> "You did not understand why! You did not suspect that it was more than I could stand to see you describe the death of our child, to be plunged daily into this sorrow?"
>
> The tone of her voice had changed, had become both severe and overwhelmed.
>
> Olivier remained speechless and said no more, meditating. No, he had not suspected; he had thought it was a physical detachment. "It amuses her less," he said to himself in order to find an excuse, as he led away the woman whom he had met in front of Hermès's. . . .
>
> In the deep night, on the edge of this impenetrable forest, he was struck by the mutual incomprehension of human beings.

Nevertheless, he makes an effort; they patch things up and even make a new start.

This scene is capital because it lays bare the psychological mechanism. The final misunderstanding, the climax of Part Three, will originate in the same temporary incomprehension; except for the similarity of pattern, there will be no factual relation between the two scenes. When they reach New York, they are happy; there is no false front. Having bathed, Chantal joins her husband to admire the myriad lights from the window:

He adored these moments when she did not fight against a liberation which was all his doing and his alone. He felt pride at having attained the great purpose in his life. And this insistence which appeared then in her glance! . . .

"In New York," she murmured, drawing him near her. "It is too good to be true."

He took her in his arms and carried her gently into the bedroom. "To think that I so long believed," he said to himself, "that happiness was to enjoy everything, without ever possessing anything. It is the contrary which is true."

Once again this is the affirmation that Proustian psychology does not work in his case.

Shortly thereafter, Olivier discovers the real identity of the Farquhart kidnaper. This time Chantal suspects nothing, because she falsely attributes her husband's agitation to her telephone call to Guilmur to get his help in securing a steamship passage. Her thoughts are elsewhere on this anniversary of her son's death, and trying to draw closer to her husband, she offers to devote herself henceforth to his literature. In the presence of this outburst of sincerity, Olivier blurts out the truth. The shock of his apparent insincerity during the four years of their marriage is so great to her that she runs away from him, then repents and comes back in a spirit of forgiveness. He, however, is in a different mood since he suspects her of infidelity; and convinced once more of the validity of the Proustian theory of the impenetrability of human beings, he decides to give up his marriage experiment. The pages which follow are the most sincere in the book. Unable to bear his coldness any longer, Chantal gives full expression to her grief, whereupon her husband gives away his real feelings by exploding: " 'Ah! you are unhappy?' he cried in a voice which gave way to anger to hide his pain. 'And what about me? Do you think my heart is light when I repeat to myself that all is over and that you are no longer anything to me? Do you think that it doesn't make me want to dash my brains out against these walls?' " The reconciliation is well advanced when the novel ends.

To make Chantal's flight more justified, the author falls back on her heredity. It is not alone her husband's insincerity which causes her to flee; it is her Catholic point of view with regard to the institution of marriage. To be sure that the reader gets the point, the author arranges to have her express shock and indignation when, on her arrival in the United States, she learns that the natives condone divorce but condemn adultery; in her country the reverse is true. Her reaction to Olivier's first confession follows the same pattern: She would have helped him in his difficulty if Randolph Lemaistre had been his illegitimate son, but she cannot approve of divorce. Her behavior on the supreme occasion of her husband's supposed insincerity is not at all arbitrary but is the logical outcome of the reactionary side of her character, which all her efforts to accommodate herself to Olivier's way of life had not eradicated. In the final reconciliation, he tells her that during their courtship he tried to lead up to the subject of his divorce but that she stopped him (thinking, she then explains, that he simply wanted to tell her about his "affair" with Ranouche, about which she was forcing herself not to be curious). Obviously it is the reactionary side of her character which he feared all along.

Le Pour et le Contre ends on a high pitch of action and emotion. It would be idle to speculate what the novel would have been like if Lacretelle had consciously sought to introduce dramatic qualities into his work, for the absence of dramatic qualities was so manifestly part of the aesthetic plan.

In spite of the long-range symmetry of the structure of the novel and the occasional tendency to stereotype a character, which comes from long habit, Lacretelle tries for once to avoid the effect of conscious artistry. This is particularly noticeable in the style, which never seems to strive for artistic effect. Even the more literary (that is to say, nonconversational) passages are a kind of indirect discourse which preserves the rhythms and vocabulary of conversation. In this novel Lacretelle is no longer concerned with the search for the *mot juste* or the well-balanced clause, in imitation of Flaubert.

With all of its qualities, the novel has serious defects which the casual reader will probably summarize as monotony. The same reader might find monotony in *A la Recherche du temps perdu* or in *L'Education sentimentale*, in which case he could be accused of a lack of literary discrimination. Nevertheless, a discriminating reader of these novels of Proust and Flaubert may still feel that Lacretelle's novel lacks complete artistic integration. That is because the reader has difficulty projecting himself into the literary conversations. Such conversations do not have a direct bearing on the lives of the characters, nor are the ideas particularly startling in themselves. In the last analysis, a novel must produce an illusion of reality; whenever it fails to do so, it is defeating itself.

It almost seems as though no amount of fiction would be sufficient to counterbalance the intellectual discussions in order to make *Le Pour et le Contre* into a true novel. In any event, the main fiction concerned with Olivier Le Maistre is inadequate to the task. With *L'Education sentimentale* as a precedent, Lacretelle was fully aware of the problem of converting an essentially unsympathetic and ineffectual character into a human being. Flaubert had found the solution by recording every minor fluctuation in the emotional life of his hero, making ample use of the technique of "lyrical analysis." Quite naturally and from habit, Lacretelle used the same technique with his hero but tended to dwell more on trivialities. He expected lyrical analysis to bring his hero to life, and yet he did not often put his hero into a situation in which the latter would reveal his deeper emotions. As a result, Olivier appears as a very unemotional person; and even when he blurts out to Chantal the remark that he is suffering as a result of their misunderstanding, the reader remains, at that crucial moment, outside the character. In following the disruptive, impressionistic pattern of Huxley, Lacretelle has paid less attention to Flaubertian techniques. Hence there is a certain insufficiency in the character of Olivier, whom Lacretelle had conceived so much in the image of Frédéric Moreau that he was incapable of converting him into a Huxley character.

On the other hand, many of the secondary characters, notably the feminine ones, are very much alive. Bali the enigmatic, Ranouche the untouchable, Mme Galea the possessive feminist, and particularly Chantal, the intuitive wife, join the gallery of memorable Lacretelle women. Whenever they appear, the novel comes to life. In the case of Bali, Ranouche and Galea, the author has imagined them with such vividness that he has no need to analyze them particularly; they have merely to act in response to their cue. Like Charlotte Vignet in *La Mort d'Hippolyte*, they retain some of the advantages of being incomplete, though vivid; as long as the author does not say everything about them, the reader is free to fill in the gaps with his imagination.

Although less vivid, Chantal also benefits from this autonomy vis-à-vis the author; he does not presume to present her completely, as he does Olivier (for that is his intention, despite the inadequacies of his presentation). As a result of being married to Yolande de Naurois, there is no doubt that Lacretelle has been able to give a new dimension to his female characters which would have been impossible if he had remained forever Damville. This is not the same as saying that Mme de Lacretelle is Chantal; in our ignorance of details, let us say rather that, unquestionably, she has inspired the character of Chantal.

Le Pour et le Contre is then an uneven work. In some parts it has the qualities of an excellent novel, but, in others, it is less likely to interest the average reader. Even though it has inadequacies as a work of fiction, it ought to have a compensatory appeal as an experimental novel. One regrets that Olivier was not as eloquent as Gide's character Edouard in stating his intentions with regard to the art of the novel. In fact, one wonders whether Olivier, in writing his own *Le Pour et le Contre*, was aware of what Lacretelle was really trying to do in his. Olivier was never more than a realist, whereas Lacretelle was really pushing his realism to such extreme limits that it was beginning to border on impressionism. If Lacretelle had expressed himself more resolutely on what he was doing or if the experimental nature of his work had been more clearly apparent in the structure of his novel, the work would now have a greater appeal for readers interested in the technique of the novel. The novel has immense possibilities in this respect which are not fully realized. Nevertheless, a great deal can be learned about the art of the novel from *Le Pour et le Contre*, and also a great deal about human nature. This novel may not be Lacretelle's greatest literary achievement, but it deserves far more attention than it has received so far.

Olivier Le Maistre predicted that his own *Le Pour et le Contre* would meet with indifference in the postwar era, and that is precisely what happened to Lacretelle's novel as well. The silence of many publications may be attributed to the still chaotic condition of the press in 1946 and the fact that the novel was published in Geneva rather than in Paris; but much more significant is the lack of enthusiasm in most of the articles which did appear. Even from his own generation, Lacretelle received little support; his colleague of the Academy, Emile Henriot, in the most prominent article, called Olivier an "icy character" and objected to the literary conversations; Pierre Lœwel called the work "well done but rather indifferent"; André Rousseaux avoided any value judgments; and Louis Barjon, in the Catholic review *Etudes*, openly attacked for reasons which seemed almost anachronistic.[5] The lone Paris critic of established reputation who really liked the novel was Marcel Thiébaut, writing in the *Revue de Paris*.[6]

Surprisingly, since he had never admired Lacretelle hitherto without reservations, Edmond Jaloux was eloquent in his praise of the novel, but he wrote in the *Journal de Genève* and therefore reached few French readers.[7] However, André Maurois, in the journal of a Swiss tour published in the *Nouvelles littéraires*, did mention a conversation with Jaloux in Geneva in which they agreed that *Le Pour et le Contre* was Lacretelle's best novel.[8] Among the new postwar critics, only one, Armand Hoog, rose in defense of Lacretelle's novel.[9] Today there are many readers in France who are familiar with Lacretelle's work up to 1935, but few of them have even heard of *Le Pour et le Contre*. Although many articles have appeared on Lacretelle since 1947, there seems almost to have been a conspiracy among critics never again to mention the title *Le Pour et le Contre*.

17

FLAUBERT SEMPER FLAUBERT

THE ink was hardly dry on the proofs of *Le Pour et le Contre* before Lacretelle started a new work. In April 1946 he stated in a letter: "I have begun a long short story which will perhaps be a little novel."[1] In October he again wrote: "I have spent the summer in Switzerland, in the Engadine at Sils-Maria, where I timidly stepped in the footsteps of Nietzsche (his house can still be seen). I did not come back with *Zarathustra* but with a novel which is very different from *Le Pour et le Contre* and appreciably shorter. The title: *Deux Cœurs simples*. All things considered, I wrote it rather quickly, since I began it last December.[2] It is to have first of all a de luxe edition."[3]

But *Deux Cœurs simples* did not appear in print immediately. In the chronology of Lacretelle's published work, the next volume was *Idées dans un chapeau* bearing the "achevé d'imprimer" of December 1946 and the imprint of the Editions du Rocher of Monaco. This thickest of all Lacretelle critical volumes was largely composed of articles published during the war; there were a few prewar articles, two even coming from *Quatre Etudes sur Gobineau*, and a sprinkling of post-Liberation articles. *Idées dans un chapeau* lacks a central theme or doctrine and need not be discussed separately since these same articles have already furnished material for the chapter dealing with Lacretelle's activities during World War II.

As for *Deux Cœurs simples*, it was to suffer from a strange attack of "printeritis." The type for the de luxe edition, to be published by Cramer of Geneva, was set in 1947, and the volume bears this date; in reality this edition was not placed on sale until 1952. It took Valentine Hugo six years to do the illustrations, and publication of the popular edition was held up by a contract stipulating that it could appear only ten months after the de luxe edition. As a result, the ordinary edition was not printed until 1953, and it bears that date. Once again, Gallimard's imprint appears on a Lacretelle work; evidently the hatchet had been buried along with the corpse of a certain literary character named Marcenat.

In the interim, *Deux Cœurs simples* had come out serially in *La Bataille politique et littéraire* from May 7 to July 30, 1947, and had given rise to a threat of lawsuit, which Lacretelle subsequently described in another letter: "My imbroglio with Mme Lydie Demirgian, a violinist whose name I had inadvertently attributed to a character in my novel, has been settled. She is satisfied with a statement added to each copy in which it is said that she is an artist universally and justly famous."[4] For this reason, Lydie Demirgian has become Myriam Astegian in the popular edition, thereby losing her bid for immortality.

Deux Cœurs simples relates the misfortunes of two rather ordinary bourgeois women, Rose Bienaimé and Romaine Franchard, the first married to a minor official in an insurance company and the second to an unsuccessful art critic. Rose's husband, François, dies of consumption before the story has progressed very far. For a time Romaine's husband, Paul, occupies the center of the narrative with his literary failures and his affair with the Armenian, Myriam Astegian; then he commits suicide. Gille Franchard and Christine Bienaimé, the children of the two couples, grow up, marry and have a child, Agathe. The incompatibility of Gille and Christine causes the first rift in the friendship of Rose and Romaine. Christine disappears with a lover, Gille dies a drug addict, and the two grandmothers, who now hate each other, are locked in a fierce struggle for the possession of Agathe. Then Agathe's death causes Rose and Romaine to forget their differences, and they become devoted friends again.

Lacretelle himself has said that *Deux Cœurs simples* is more correctly a long short story, rather than a novel, and that it was originally to have figured in a collection of short stories: "... I had the idea in about 1937, when Europe was entering a trance, and had a presentiment of the coming war. The title would have been 'L'An Mil,' alluding to the panic which seized Europe in the Middle Ages at the approach of the millennium. I did not write the other stories but can tell you that one of them had to do with the exodus of an Austrian Jew, driven from Vienna by the

Anschluss and who, after having been a snob and a social figure, becomes again in exile the typical wandering Jew. All the traits which he had tried to dissimulate his entire life long now stand out and are aggravated. I am not too sure how he ended up."[5] As for the one story which he did eventually write, he adds: "It does not seem to me that *Deux Cœurs simples* changed very much in the course of execution. The narrative must certainly have developed with more padding, but I believe that the main lines were laid out as soon as the subject came into my head."

It is easy to see how the basic notion of "L'An Mil" came to be expressed in *Le Pour et le Contre*, but it is not immediately obvious what relationship this notion bears to *Deux Cœurs simples*. That is because the emphasis appears to be exclusively on individual rather than group psychology. On second thought, however, it seems certain that the eccentric behavior of Gille and Christine, not altogether explained by their heredity and home environment, may be taken as representative of the wartime generation. If there is a historical intention in *Deux Cœurs simples*, it is submerged in this return to Flaubert indicated by the title.

In *Deux Cœurs simples*, Gille Franchard, exercising his profession of manuscript reader for a publishing house, made this comment on a novel submitted to him: "The story is not true because it is well written." The publisher was evidently a reasonable man because he fired Gille forthwith. If given the opportunity, Gille would certainly have written the same remark on the manuscript of *Deux Cœurs simples*. Lacretelle obviously wrote this novelette in defiance of all the Gille Franchards of the present day.

In this novelette, perfection starts in the very first line. No realist, be he Flaubert, Maupassant or Daudet, could have achieved a more balanced combination of whimsical humor and vivid observation of setting and character, all with the strictest economy of words arranged in simple, harmonious patterns. This is how the story begins:

> The two young women came out almost together from the shop, brushing against the shafts of lilacs and the iris stems which sprang forth from each side of the door. On the doorsill each cast a glance toward the flowers of the other.

"Oh! my goodness, I don't have my parasol," exclaimed the one who had bought the carnations.

And she went quickly back into the florist's shop.

The other woman, interested by the misadventure, turned her head and stopped on the sidewalk. She watched the bunch of carnations come and go as it participated in the search. They were of such a provocative red that she had not dared choose them for her living room.

The parasol was found on a table. But also what an idea, said the red carnations, to have placed on top of it this big roll of paper which hid it! The proprietor, a little Southerner with a black mustache, apologized profusely and went as far as the street with much bowing and scraping.

The technique is typical realism *à la* Maupassant-Flaubert: a certain sentimentality, a certain preciosity, a blending of an emotional attitude with a suggestion of real things. Particularly one must note the black mustache, representing the distinguishing trait without which no realistic character can exist (incidentally, Lacretelle adhered strictly to the distinctive trait throughout *Le Pour et le Contre*, no matter how minor was the character).

The Flaubertian imprint is particularly noticeable in the symmetry of some of the paragraphs. In this respect, the style of *Deux Cœurs simples* doubles back to that of *La Bonifas* twenty years earlier:

She [Romaine] noticed also with melancholy the change in Paul with regard to her. He no longer asked for advice, even seemed to flee from her. Carried away by his new passion, he had come to consider this faithful partner as a maladroit accomplice and a compromising witness to his failures. Romaine's little tricks to bring him into the limelight, the old stories told again in the presence of a new visitor, no longer had any value in his eyes. She got on his nerves, and he made her be silent. He had borrowed from Myriam an expression which the Armenian used readily to condemn people: "He's missed the mark—she's missed the mark." And often Romaine, when she tried to be of use to him, read this same judgment in the provoked glance of her husband.

The same symmetry occurs in the organization of each chapter, which, as in *La Bonifas*, culminates in an action scene indispensable to the plot. Chapter I leads to the death of François; Chapter II, to Paul's suicide; Chapter III, to the separation of Gille and Christine; Chapter IV, to Gille's death; Chapter V, to Agathe's funeral; Chapter VI, to Romaine's confession. The only variation from the structural pattern of *La Bonifas* is the absence of a "tapering off" scene for each chapter; since *Deux Cœurs simples* was a novelette, there was no place for such elaboration. Even the method of getting into the story is the same as in *La Bonifas*: an action scene followed by a biography—or rather by two biographies this time, since there are two main characters to be accounted for simultaneously. One hardly need repeat that this is the old-fashioned realistic technique. To old-fashioned realism belongs also the observation which Romaine makes as, under great emotional strain, she rushes into the bawdy house where her son lies dying: "She made out, on the staircase, a great bronze chimera." Lacretelle has consciously abandoned every vestige of modern techniques and attempts nothing which is not authorized by the precedent of Flaubert.

The expectation is that *Deux Cœurs simples* is a rejuvenation of Flaubert's *Un Cœur simple*. One is therefore struck at first by the dissimilarity of the two subjects. Félicité, the simple-minded servant whose affections finally settle on a parrot and who dies, confusing the spirit of the dead bird with the Holy Ghost, seems to have little in common with Rose or Romaine, Lacretelle's more sophisticated heroines. On the surface, the only tangible connection between the two stories is that Agathe languishes, dies and is buried just like Virginie in *Un Cœur simple*. On closer examination, however, it is soon apparent that Félicité, Rose and Romaine, in spite of the difference in social station, are all three the same at heart since they aspire only to the simple comforts of life and would be quite content with the monotony of an everyday existence. Rose and Romaine would have gone through life exchanging bouquets and recipes, marrying their children and settling complacently into dull middle age if the other members of their families had left them peace of mind.

One can almost imagine Lacretelle starting his story in reverse, seeing Rose and Romaine as two senile women living together in childlike simplicity. Next, by way of antithesis, he imagines them as great enemies, and then, to give cogency to the enmity, he imagines them to have started as friends. Since they are simple souls, they are never the mistresses of their own destinies; and when they become mortal enemies, it will be entirely the fault of other people. So that they may not be exactly the same, Romaine will have a stronger will power than Rose and will tend to dominate her. With all that, both remain simple hearts. Little does it matter that Rose is physically unsatisfied in her relations with François (as her daughter will subsequently be with Gille) or that Romaine seems more intelligent than Paul. Rose will never be unfaithful, and Romaine will never do anything original, because her originality is entirely at the service of her *raté* husband. If left to her own devices, Romaine would be as satisfied to exchange recipes as she would tidbits about avant-garde painting.

A critic has found fault with this story for being too loaded with melodramatic events: a husband who dies of consumption, another who commits suicide, a son who collapses from drugs in a bawdy house, a daughter who is apparently murdered (in obscure circumstances far from the main plot).[6] If these events were actually the subject of the novelette, the criticism might be justified; but the subject is elsewhere.

Deux Cœurs simples is not the chronicle of two families but rather a psychological study of the two women characterized by the title itself. More exactly it is the story of their relationship with each other. In a sense, the dramatic liquidation of their husbands is only preliminary to the main plot. The two main characters really come to life on the occasion when Rose and Romaine are discussing the failure of their children to give them a grandchild, and Romaine, who has hitherto been all sweetness and light, blames her friend's daughter for not having conceived. The incompatibility of Gille and Christine, their infidelity to each other, and Christine's scheming to get a divorce so as to marry her American lover have only an anecdotal value compared with the repercussion of these events on the two surviving parents. The breakup of the marriage of their children is a severe blow to them, but it is almost forgotten in the rivalry which develops between them for the possession of the baby, Agathe. Here the subject reaches its fullest realistic development, since it derives its pathos, not from high tragedy, but from the irony of those little conflicts in life which Maupassant, in particular, knew so well how to depict. Finally Romaine loses the battle when, with her son dead and all her financial worries descending on her, she has to accept the advice of a scheming maid and yield custody of the child to the rival grandmother. This is the high point of the story; after that comes a tapering off with the funeral of Agathe and the eventual reconciliation of the desolate grandmothers. The crowning touch is Romaine's return to the Church, after a lifetime of freethinking, and her search in the confessional for a peccadillo which she finally decides is the harm which she once sought to do to her friend Rose. In this final note of sentimental humor one sees the hand of the traditional realist.

Artistically, one minor flaw in the story is the lyrical analysis of François Bienaimé as he spends his last days in a sanatorium. Momentarily, the focus shifts to him, and, as happened so frequently in *Les Hauts Ponts* but with greater justification because of the size of the novel, he is transformed from an inconsequential prosaic person into a veritable poet. It is easy to understand why Lacretelle turned his attention to François: His death figures as one of the major events in the novel, and also, for the sake of symmetry, it was necessary to finish the first chapter with an episode requiring several pages to narrate. Nevertheless, these structural necessities do not altogether justify this sudden emphasis on a character who is outside the main current of the story. The typical realist would have been satisfied to leave François as a prosaic bourgeois, particularly since this is the chief point of differentiation between the Bienaimés and the Franchards. Instead, the author makes him a typical Lacretelle character, and this is slightly confusing because the two other males in the story are also typical Lacretelle characters.

These two males have a perfect right to be typical Lacretelle characters, since their maladjustment and escapism are fully integrated into the story. Although the episode of Paul's death is still preliminary to the main subject of the novel, the events leading up to his suicide are handled with an exceptional mastery of technique. By a slow but graphic evolution, he becomes more and more detached from life with the failure of his periodical, and more and more involved with the scheming Armenian. Romaine's attempts to win him back bring him completely into the main current of the story. His son Gille is like him, only worse. It is easy to understand how Christine, already egocentric, unpoetic and sensual, is driven to exasperation by this husband who unconcernedly caters to her wayward habits and then shuts himself off from reality in his late father's studio. The skill this time consists not so much in drawing the picture of Gille, who is something of a stereotype (the anecdote about his dislocation of the mechanism of his watch fits him initially into a formula), as in interpreting Christine's resistance to him. The men in this story tend to be all of a piece; only the women are unusual fictional creations—as is so frequently the case with Lacretelle's characters.

Deux Cœurs simples definitely ranks with Lacretelle's finest work. One feels that he has poured life into an artistic mold but that it has lost none of its original flavor. There is symmetry not only in the narrative technique but also in the relationship of the characters to each other. The Bienaimés, unimaginative, orthodox bourgeois from morose Lorraine, counterbalance the Franchards, the frank, artistic, emancipated intellectuals from the sunny South. The Bienaimés have a daughter, the Franchards a son, for the obvious purpose that they may be married. The two fathers and the two children have to be liquidated so that the old women may be left with Agathe; then Agathe must die so that they may be perfectly destitute. Yet Lacretelle has handled his materials so well that the reader never feels that he has forced the issue. Except for the fortuitous fate of François Bienaimé before the novel is well launched, every character who dies has a good reason for dying and, with the exception of Agathe, is even responsible for his own death. Nor is the marriage of Gille and Christine, so important to the plot, at all unnatural, because it is brought about by the emotional maladjustments due to wartime conditions.

Nevertheless, in spite of this mastery of technique, the novel gives the reader only an intellectual and an artistic satisfaction. This may be the result of the essential banality of the subject—the friendship, rivalry, then friendship of these two women. Despite the deaths, the suicide and the murder, there is no dramatic action. This is the kind of banality which is traditionally the essence of realism but more properly that of the realistic short story than of the novel. The quirks of human nature make a good subject for a

Maupassant short story. Probably *Deux Cœurs simples* fails to satisfy as a novel simply because it is basically a short story.

Deux Cœurs simples did not attract very wide critical attention. In some cases, critics who praised Lacretelle's work seemed less interested in its intrinsic merits than in the opportunity which it provided to attack contemporary tastes. Such is the attitude of François Mauriac: "I fear that there are scarcely any critics, especially among the younger ones, who will discover that this story by Lacretelle, on its level and of its kind, is perfect. No matter what they may say, this perfection is the result, not of a 'manner' which they have gone beyond, but of a secret which they have lost."[7] Pierre Lœwel and Jean Nicollier, the latter writing in Lausanne, expressed much the same sentiment.[8] Most critics, Robert Kemp, André Billy, Emile Henriot, Jean Blanzat, found the new novel to be worthy of Lacretelle's prewar work but displayed more respect than enthusiasm for this type of writing.[9] Actually *Deux Cœurs simples* fared much better at the hands of the critics than *Le Pour et le Contre*, but again there was a significant silence in many quarters, notably in the *Nouvelle Nouvelle Revue Française* itself.

In May 1953, Lacretelle received from Roger Martin du Gard a letter which bears witness to the esteem in which his literary generation still holds him: "I admire above all the simplicity of your tools, the impeccable correctness of each touch, the sobriety of the commentaries, the sureness of the choice of details, this purity of the language, under which the presence of the author never stands out nor anything which makes one think of his complicity, his premeditation, his technical skill, or of an intentional maneuver. Ah! long live simplicity, dear friend! It is by her alone that one attains true greatness."[10]

Simultaneously with *Deux Cœurs simples*, Gallimard published an unproduced play by Lacretelle, *Une Visite en été*. No doubt it was anticipated that the two works would be reviewed together, but in almost every case the literary critic was reluctant to usurp the prerogatives of the drama critic, who, in turn, not having seen the play, felt no compulsion to express an opinion. As a result, a great silence has settled over this work.

When Lacretelle wrote the play, he had no intention of starting a new *Spectacle dans un fauteuil*. Like many a born novelist late in his career, he had the ambition of seeing his characters act on a stage. His correspondence with Maurice Coindreau provides a record of this abortive attempt to follow in the footsteps of François Mauriac. On March 23, 1948, he writes that he has just spent three months in Switzerland (at Montreux, specifies a later letter) and that he wrote there the first act of a play. On August 14th of the same year he tells of some of his problems in writing: "The second act (there are three) has probably been less easy to handle than the first. A play is always judged in the second act, the dramatists whom I know have always told me. That is probably true. Because the first act, the exposition, is easier. But I am anxious that the third, in mine, should show no sign of flagging and that the characters should have something more to reveal, some capacity to surprise. In France, in all the contemporary theater, the play is finished when the curtain falls on Act II, and Act III brings nothing new but the denouement. In my opinion, it is a mistake." On December 17th he states that his play is finished but that it still requires retouching. "Now," he says, "I shall have to make up my mind to show it to a member of this terrible species called actors and directors. Terrible because they all live a lie made of easy promises and speak a hyperbolic language which I do not understand."

As a form of relaxation, he translated a minor English novel, *Mrs. Loveday* by Robert Goodyear, in collaboration with his faithful amanuensis, Mme de Lacretelle; it appeared under the imprint of Robert Laffont in January 1949. It is not clear what attracted him to this novel which might be described as a rather vulgar, modernized version of *Sabine*. Then he went back to his play. In a letter of August 19, 1949, to Maurice Coindreau, he records progress in the search for a producer: "As for my play, Marchat might produce it, but only in March, and Hébertot wishes to impose on me a contract in comparison with which those of Gallimard are liberal and generous." On November 25th of the same year he reports no progress: "First of all nothing new concerning my play. Marchat doesn't have a penny and is putting nothing in production." And so the whole thing drags on. On December 5, 1951, he reports: "I have some minor news concerning my play. Stève Passeur, who read it a few months ago, has greatly encouraged me. Furthermore he gave me some useful advice which I followed. We even made several changes together. A strange team.

It is the marriage of Heaven and Hell. But his outbursts of anger, sometimes excessive in his own plays, were useful in mine." There is no record of what new attempts Lacretelle may have made to get his revised play produced. When he decided to publish it in 1953, he had obviously given up all hope of seeing it on the stage.

The play underwent considerable change, writes Lacretelle in answer to a query on this subject. He says: "*Une Visite en été* was rewritten several times. I had to shorten, condense. Stève Passeur, the dramatist, to whom I read my manuscript, made some useful remarks, all tending, in general, to make the dialogue more naïve. Finally I changed the denouement. Originally Michelle wanted to kill herself and, saved by her father in a somewhat grandiloquent scene, did not leave."[11]

Despite this effort to write a producible play, *Une Visite en été* makes no concessions to the tastes of the mid-century. Though purportedly taking place in the present, the play seems rather to be dated 1900, since the eternal triangle so dear to the dramatists of that period is prominently displayed in the plot. Love, divorce, adultery—to return to those outworn themes without an ample dose of existentialism, postwar cynicism and a certain primitivism *à la* Faulkner seems to be on the order of Don Quixote tilting at windmills. Perhaps there was some unconscious atavism on his part in this return to a theater so close in inspiration to the realism of Flaubert. However, it seems likely that Lacretelle was not attempting to imitate any theater whatever. His real purpose was to adapt his art of the novel to a play.

The essential problem for him was to conceive one of his novels in dramatic form with due regard for the dramatic unities. The title *Une Visite en été* immediately accounts for the unities of time and place. The real stumbling block was the unity of action, because typical Lacretelle characters do not come into conflict. Above all, he refused to think in terms of a plot which leads to an unusual denouement, and that is why, eventually, he was able to construct his play in such a way that it really mattered little whether Michelle left or stayed. The play is built entirely around the principle of the unfolding of character and not on the traditional notion of conflict. Furthermore, these characters are ordinary people beset with problems not at all out of the ordinary. Needless to say, the basic principle of the play is singularly undramatic.

While confining himself to the technical limits of a play, Lacretelle continued to imagine his characters as a novelist. They seem to have biographies rather than emotions. Instead of revealing themselves by the intensity of their feelings, they turn upon themselves and, in terms of their past, dissect their present and predict their future. François and Adeline were once happily married, then they separated; now their daughter has contrived to bring them together. The liquidation of the biographies of all three of them will occupy the first act; our understanding of these characters will be contingent on their understanding of themselves and will be largely based on elements which are outside the finite limits of the play.

Biography is only slightly less important in understanding Michelle, the daughter, and Jean, the married man who becomes the daughter's lover. Michelle may act with a certain ingenuousness because of her age, but she is far from being an ingénue; her character takes form only in her attempts at self-analysis. Since she has already been in love (and may even have had an affair, though this is not clear) and has had the additional experience of living under the same roof with her mother's lovers, she will choose her future course of action with disarming lucidity. Her biography is as indispensable to her as it is to us. Similarly, however incomplete our knowledge of Jean may be (for he is a more peripheral character than the three just named), it is obvious that Michelle has not broken up a happy home and that the real cause of Jean's behavior lies in his marriage with Colette. Even Colette, about whom we know still less, seems to act in her marital misfortune according to a pattern in which she has had previous experience. Perhaps she was right in claiming that her husband was a Don Juan, but she was obviously playing this card in desperation. Every character in the play is thus projected against a much larger screen as he acts within the confines of the stage. In the foreground there is a play; in the background there is a novel. This is another reason for the attrition in dramatic intensity.

The play is still far from static, because the characters discover themselves on the stage, and this progressive discovering leads to the denouement. It is, in fact, a remarkable tour de force to have built an entire dramatic structure around the principle of psychological analysis. Whatever its dramatic insufficiencies, the play is entirely original in this respect. Based on an awareness of the past, this psychological analysis is nevertheless concerned with the present, which may introduce new factors (as Adeline progressively discovers). The over-all pattern, laid bare in the first act, is the by now traditional Lacretellian theme of the inaccessibility of human beings to each other. With all his perspicacity, François fails to realize that this principle is two-way and that certain individuals like himself unwittingly create barriers around themselves while supposing that the barriers exist rather in others. This causes him to make an entirely incorrect diagnosis of his wife's "case" when he falsely attributes her departure to his failure (which he aggravated through spite) to achieve success as an author. Confronting his wife again over the interval of the elapsed years, he forces her to think over the whole problem; and she finally manages to express herself coherently in the image of the closed gate which barred her from her husband's estate: "I suddenly saw again the one and only purpose in my life. And I found myself again before this closed gate." Their reconciliation supposes that henceforth the gate will be open.

As the play develops, Adeline discovers that not only is the gate not open but new factors have developed. In the third act she tells her daughter that her present relationship with her husband is a travesty of their former love because he has been attracted to her as though she were a new mistress; he is immune to any deep emotion because he views her with enough detachment to be intellectually certain that she is incapable of ever making him suffer again. There is no reason to believe that this interest in his wife is anything but a temporary infatuation. Adeline is certain of this when she receives dog biscuits instead of gingerbread in the one touch of humor in this humorless play and understands that her husband has apparently not dismissed his interim mistress. From this she generalizes: "Men judge that all situations can be smoothed out provided that they still desire us." This goes back to the situation in *Le Pour et le Contre* wherein Etiennette forces Le Maistre to admit that because Bali had held him off during the trip to

Holland, he had satisfied himself with venal love. Such a thing would be impossible for a woman, said Etiennette, because once she is in love, a woman has "a bar across her stomach."[12] The idea seems to be that men are polygamous and women monogamous.

That is where matters stand at the end of the third act. It has taken three acts to arrive at this fundamental situation, and only a very short act is left to unravel the play. Adeline has every reason to leave her husband again. Michelle is prepared to leave Jean because she is convinced that her mother's generalization applies perfectly to her own case. If Jean has failed to keep his promise to solve their problem by some form of courageous action, it is because he is really polygamous like all men and is satisfied with the *status quo*. Here the element of surprise intervenes in the middle of what was originally the third act. In the final version, the curtain drops at this point to give a certain finality to the idea and then immediately rises again on what is now called the "fourth act." The last two acts taken together are actually no longer than the other two acts taken separately.

The surprise—which is doubly a surprise since the author is Lacretelle—is a certain release from determinism. First the drama breaks loose: Colette plays her final card by telling Michelle that she is pregnant, and Michelle is driven to desperation because this confirms the polygamy theory; François assumes the role of the irate father and will apparently drive his daughter to suicide if she doesn't kill herself simply because of the polygamy theory. In this tense situation, Adeline learns from her husband that her interpretation of the dog biscuits was false. At the same time, goaded into action, Jean has actually made up his mind to leave and is waiting for Michelle to join him. Failing to argue Michelle out of her sudden impulse to run away with Jean, come what may, François suddenly says: "Pass. You are free." Evidently he had read Sartre. Michelle seems to choose her destiny, just as, a few minutes earlier, her mother has elected to stay with François. None of this invalidates the inaccessibility theory or the polygamy theory; both Adeline and Michelle have chosen happiness while they can get it, realizing that it is something which they will have to go after aggressively. Like the existentialists, in whom Lacretelle apparently has never been even remotely interested, they will upset the mechanism of cause and effect as long as they can.

It might well seem to the average spectator that the burden of the plot is Michelle's affair with Jean and her dramatic rivalry with Colette. Colette's unexpected return, her bid to expel the interloper which is renewed in the fourth act, her allegation that her husband is a Don Juan and finally her revelation that she is pregnant provide a central core of dramatic action for the play. However, if the spectator focuses on this plot, he may even find it banal; that is the principal danger for potential producers of the play. Nevertheless, the success of the play depends entirely on the dramatic action which is packed into the roles of Colette and Michelle. It is very probable that on the stage Colette will be the most vivid character, because her drama is the most poignant: She loves her faithless husband and is defending her home and children. Beyond any doubt, some of Stève Passeur's anger has passed into the scenes between Colette and Michelle. These are the most dramatic scenes in the play, with the possible exception of the tense scene wherein, with Michelle offstage, it seems to be indicated that she will kill herself.

Jean is something of an enigma and also a contradiction. He passes off with a shrug of the shoulders his wife's assertion, repeated accusingly by his mistress, that he is a Don Juan. He refuses to explain who, if anyone, wrote the letter which Colette claims to have received. Apparently, he is the living proof that man is polygamous. Added to that, he is pusillanimous, and yet he finally renounces the material comforts of home and the children for whom he apparently has some affection. Why then does he leave? A free choice? A streak of romanticism? Has he been bullied into it by Michelle's attitude or François's intervention? Even François, who ought to know him better, is confused, since he speaks of him with admiration at the beginning of the play and sees nothing but cynicism in him at the end. An actor playing this part would certainly have to interpret the role.

Strictly speaking, Jean and Colette are only foils for Michelle. By contrast, the author concentrates so thoroughly on Michelle's character that he leaves no stone unturned. Moreover, he sets forth his intention quite clearly in the "blurb" on the cover of the play when he says that he "tried to show also, with the character of Michelle, the different metamorphoses of a romantic nature." One must add: the romantic nature of a girl who has had the misfortune to inherit her father's lucidity. The part should be played with ardor but not with complete ingenuousness; after all, she has tried to deceive Jean by hiding her first affair from him; and, as her father points out to her, she is really doing evil to Colette.

François and Adeline are not foils for anyone; they are main characters of equal importance who perform in a plot parallel to that in which Michelle is involved. They are definitely escapees from a Lacretelle novel, and François we have met many times: He is Jean Hermelin, Damville and particularly Olivier Le Maistre. More particularly, he is Olivier with a new profession, because he seems to have given up literature to manufacture paper. Whatever autobiographical significance this detail may have, it is a surprising combination which only serves to make the character more awkward on the stage. It is easy to see that, like Olivier, François is an introvert; that part is clear enough and could be represented on the stage. But there are also innumerable overtones, all having to do with François's profession as an author. It is agreed that he finds it necessary to analyze everyone including himself, and yet what is the full implication of this remark: "How many times I have remained silent, or even made the gesture which was destined to antagonize you, simply to see if you loved me enough to bear it!" François is full of false attitudes which seem highly artificial unless one is acquainted with the entire range of Lacretelle's work. He would be a difficult character to create on the stage. Adeline would not be so easy either, because she can be understood only as the victim of François's exaggerated attitudes. With her succession of lovers, she seems to be a wanton; with her one great love for François, she seems to be a romanticist in the worst way. This entire second plot (which might more correctly be called the first plot because it starts the play and provides all of the overtones for the other plot), so subtle in print and so much more original than the eternal triangle of the other plot, would probably appear colorless on the stage.

Une Visite en été, described in the "blurb" as being "as simple as Chekhov," is simple on the surface but really complex when one reads it with care. It is possible that it would fail altogether to impress an audience at a time when introspective literature is out of style. Nevertheless, it is technically a remarkable play since the technical difficulties are overcome in the face of an entire concept of literature which is radically antidramatic. The one person known to have read it with care, Roger Martin du Gard, said in his letter to Lacretelle: "The word 'masterpiece' is at the end of my pen, and if I refrain from writing it, it is because one always hesitates to use that word as long as posterity has not given its impartial ratification."[13]

18

PIERRES D'ATTENTE

IN the year 1957, Jacques de Lacretelle is a vigorous person who looks the same as he did seven years ago. Only his best friends and his biographer know that he is really in his sixty-ninth year, for anyone looking at him would take at least fifteen years off his age and call him young-looking at that. A study of his work, ending in 1957, can make no pretense of being complete. Like the architect who leaves *pierres d'attente* jutting out for the wing which some successor may build, the student of his work must write: *suite au prochain numéro.*

It has been four years since *Une Visite en été* appeared in print, and there has been no other volume since then bearing Lacretelle's name, with the exception of the new edition of *Le Demi-Dieu* in 1955 entitled *Le Voyage de Grèce*, published by Fayard. Doubtless there will be a new collection of critical articles one of these days, for there have certainly been enough of them since *Idées dans un chapeau* to make another volume. Most of these articles would be *chroniques* from *Le Figaro*, miscellaneous short pieces on literary subjects; there would be a major article on La Rochefoucauld which appeared in *Hommes et mondes* in July 1948, another on Stendhal which appeared in 1953 in the third number of the rejuvenated *Nouvelle Nouvelle Revue Française*, and still another on Valéry which came out in Italian in *Convivium* in 1955; and there would be travel articles like "D'Amsterdam à Lima," which Lacretelle published in 1955 in *Hommes et mondes*.[1] To these could be added an article on Radiguet (another preface, in reality, like the La Rochefoucauld and Stendhal articles) and the text of an illustrated volume on Paris which Lacretelle is even now preparing.

But there is no news that such a critical volume will soon be forthcoming, nor is there any evidence that Lacretelle is currently engaged in any creative writing. Correspondence with him over the past few years reveals, however, the existence of an aborted project.[2] On May 30, 1951, he wrote: "I should like to begin something important, without waiting for my play to be produced; and I am hesitating. I am afraid that a long novel, treated in my style, that is to say with care, advancing from one landing to the next, may hardly be suited to the tastes of the present day. So I shall work at some *short stories* which will oblige me to proceed quickly and will allow me to make incursions into contemporary reality." This idea did not germinate. On February 15, 1952, in a letter describing how his villa at Cabourg had been pillaged and gutted by fire (at the time it seemed to be some kind of personal vengeance, but it turned out to be the deed of a slightly demented local character), he added: "Now I ought to set about something new. Unfortunately it is the Cabourg detective novel which is plaguing me." Then, in August 1952, a post card from Lucerne said: "I am working at a novel. . . ." In subsequent brief conversations in 1952, he revealed that the novel was in progress and that it was giving him some trouble with reversed chronology. On October 20, 1953, when this study of his work was making slow progress, he wrote: "You amuse me with your fear that my novel may appear before you have finished. I am putting it to one side for the whole winter, and when I think about it, it does not please me. A bad sign for the future!" And on February 5, 1955, mentioning his most recent articles, he said: "But all that is *rubbish*. And I don't know at all when I shall start something longer. Perhaps only in another life."

This gloomy prediction should not be taken at its face value, for it is typical Lacretelle humor. Yet it seems fairly certain, from what Lacretelle has said casually, that he has not touched his novel for four years. One is reminded of Olivier Le Maistre's conviction in *Le Pour et le Contre* that he was out of step with the younger generation. Usually discreet about his feeling toward the new post-Liberation literature (one may read "existentialist," if one desires), Lacretelle's rancor burst forth in his 1953 essay on Stendhal:

> One is frightened to see today all these paper heroes, who are either dwarfs serving as spokesmen for an absurd philosophy or heads illuminated for an easy game of *massacre*.

What would Stendhal, he who fulminated against declamatory

characters *à la* George Sand, say about these funambulists without roots or civil status! The novelist of these days carries a distorting mirror along the road, and, in reality, this mirror catches only the coarseness of language and the erotic scene. The author thinks he has done his job.

Are there no stories to be collected on our planet that one must have recourse to these puppets? Or else are we so blasé that one must renounce simple biography and real characters if one wishes to please? These authors who practice "escape" with such ease are only fleeing cheerfully, in the last analysis, from the responsibilities of the novelist.[3]

This little outburst explains better than anything else why Lacretelle lost interest in the Lucerne novel. Like Olivier Le Maistre, he must feel out of step. Such a fate has overtaken many a writer because new literary generations are fickle and reject any author—whatever be his merit—whose aesthetic differs from theirs. Some writers persevere in the face of such opposition or indifference; others lean back on their laurels. Lacretelle wrote *Deux Cœurs simples* and *Une Visite en été*, of course, in the face of such opposition. He may yet return to the attack, especially since he really belongs to a generation of *isolés* who wrote primarily for themselves and pretended to scorn success.

In the single footnote in his Stendhal article, Lacretelle commented on the latter's habit of reading the *Civil Code*, and added: "For my part, I go even further. I need the *Chaix Timetable*. And that does not prevent me from returning to literature, like the dog of the Scriptures." This curious admission is another symptom of Lacretelle's inability to concentrate all his energy on literary production at the present time. One could almost say that he is assailed by a kind of wanderlust. The following is a nearly complete record of his travels since his American trip in 1945: Athens for the centenary of the Ecole d'Athènes in 1947, and also Portugal on an official mission the same year; Scandinavia, North Africa, Belgium, in 1948; Austria, Holland, Italy, in 1949; the United States, Haïti, Cuba, Puerto Rico, in 1950; England, Ireland, in 1951; England in 1953; Peru, plus all the itinerary to get there, in 1954; Belgium, Italy, England, in 1955; England again in 1956; the United States and Mexico in 1957, and then immediately to Switzerland and

Italy. In 1953 it looked for a time as though Indochina would be added to the list, and in 1956 Iran offered a strong temptation. For the academic year 1956–57 he sent his son Didier to Mercersburg Academy in Pennsylvania, where the latter became momentarily Americanized and had difficulty explaining to his classmates that the French Academy is not comparable in academic importance to Mercersburg.

Between trips, the Lacretelles have continued to live on in their flat in the rue Vineuse, where they lead the somewhat exhausting life of typical Parisians. Frequently rising late because of some social event, a concert or a play the night before, Jacques de Lacretelle usually spends the rest of the morning in his dressing gown while engaged in his incidental writing. Winter vacation generally finds the Lacretelles in Switzerland or Austria. While the rest of the family participates in winter sports, Jacques de Lacretelle takes advantage once more of the "anonymous" hotel room to write. Summer vacation brings the family to their villa Ker Kevin at Cabourg. For years the Lacretelles neglected Montfort-l'Amaury, where they had rented their two houses, but in 1954 they took back the smaller house, repaired it and began to make occasional sojourns there. Family concerns have undoubtedly absorbed much of the novelist's time, especially as his children approached the dreaded *baccalauréat*. The two elder are now over the hurdle, and the third has still to try it. This aspect of Lacretelle's life might well be called "Damville tamed."

Since the publication of *Une Visite en été* only three events in Lacretelle's biography—one political, the second personal, the third literary—seem important enough to be recorded here.

The first of these events occurred in 1954. On March 19th Jacques de Lacretelle received the Duke of Lévis-Mirepoix into the French Academy to replace Charles Maurras. It may well be that Lacretelle was carefully chosen for the delicate task of receiving a successor to a man whom both the Academy and the nation had branded a traitor. But Lacretelle was anything but delicate. Jacqueline Cartier, reporting the meeting in *L'Aurore* that evening, said: "The reception of the Duke of Lévis-Mirepoix under the Cupola will remain—let us hope—unique in the Academic annals. Never has the Cupola known such a tempest."[4] All the delicacy was on the side of the recipient. After the expected eulogy of Lévis-Mirepoix, Lacretelle launched unsparingly into Maurras. He had just begun to say: "That Maurras, in 1940, suffered deeply from our defeat, I am sure. But it was a victory for his doctrines."[5] At this point François Daudet raised his voice to intervene, but the imperturbable orator continued, and in due course policemen in mufti hustled the disturber out. Then Lacretelle went on to accuse Maurras of perverting the truth by subtle dialectics, and at this point Georges Calzan, the former leader of the Camelots du Roi, tried to interrupt but was also expulsed. And Lacretelle continued his accusations:

> After the defeat all Maurras's policy was to consist, not, to be sure, in preaching collaboration with Hitler, concerning whom I doubt whether he had many illusions, but in setting up a dam against the return of the Republic.
>
> All his sarcasm, all his violence, were for the men of the dissolved regime and for our allies to whom our hope clung.... For years he was going to persevere with the same violence of language without ever rectifying his judgment and without our being able to give him credit for playing the double game which was so very often visible in the deeds of Marshal Pétain.

In short, Maurras was more than a traitor; he was a dangerous fanatic because he perverted truth while pretending to appeal to reason. Lacretelle, the nineteenth century realist, detests fanatics.

As a reminder that Lacretelle is not given to histrionics or demagoguery, we may refer to what he wrote the next day to the author of this book: "It was a rare, if not unique, session of the Academy. But, as one of my colleagues wrote me this morning: 'Public exposure is better than somnolence.' I hope you are well. Here, aside from this escapade which has somewhat upset the household (for a week I have been guarded by policemen who protect the building, to the great joy of Didier, who hopes for pursuits and gunfire), winter is finishing calmly and in good health."[6]

The second—personal—event occurred in 1955, when the Lacretelles purchased the Château de Brécy. At that time Lacretelle wrote:

The Hauts Ponts have been bought back. Last summer, when we were at Cabourg, a very beautiful château in the neighborhood of Bayeux was pointed out to me as a good objective for an outing. We went to it and discovered a Louis XIII manor of imposing dimensions, with a superb portal by Mansard and terraced gardens, also by Mansard, decorated with balustrades, vases and lions, in short a complete Italian landscape the like of which is very rare in France—the whole thing somewhat abandoned and deteriorated as a result of the Occupation, but this abandonment added to the grandeur and charm of the spot. Well, this château was for sale, and we bought it. I must mention also that it is eight kilometers from Lantheuil, the estate of the family of Yolande, which is what impelled the latter to commit this folly which is really not so foolish.[7]

At the present time, Brécy is the all-consuming passion of the Lacretelles; whenever Parisian living grants them a respite, they rush to Brécy to attend to the restoration. Les Hauts Ponts seems definitely to have come to rest at last in Normandy.

The third—literary—event occurred in 1957 and has to do with a lecture by Lacretelle on Benjamin Constant; it is his most penetrating literary analysis in the last few years. In his whirlwind tour from Paris to Yucatán and back, and thence to Switzerland and Italy, he tarried long enough in Princeton to deliver it to an enthusiastic audience. When he repeated the performance a few days later in Geneva and Lausanne, the Swiss press was also enthusiastic about it and took the opportunity to pay homage to Lacretelle himself. The *Tribune de Genève* called it a "brilliant lecture," and the *Gazette de Lausanne* said it was a "remarkable" one.[8] Such enthusiasm for his lecture and his work in general must have given Lacretelle a particular satisfaction after some of the disappointments of recent years.

Apropos of the lecture, the *Journal de Genève* observed: "If M. de Lacretelle speaks with such finesse and warmth about the author of *Adolphe*, it is because he recognizes himself in him."[9] Concluding a study of the work of Lacretelle in 1957, it is most appropriate to record this identification with Benjamin Constant, which Lacretelle himself has suggested. In his method of relating introspection and objectivity, he is certainly the Benjamin Constant of the twentieth century. Strictly speaking, however, the comparison with Constant is valid for only one of Lacretelle's works, *Amour nuptial*, which is written in the first person, combines introspection with an unusual lucidity, and avoids the representation of external things. In the language of French critics, *Amour nuptial*, like *Adolphe*, is a "psychological" novel rather than a "realistic" novel and rejects all the techniques which the successors of Constant, beginning with Balzac, introduced into the novel.

There are so many facets to Lacretelle's work as a whole that the comparison with Constant may not be extended further. It would certainly be just as correct, if not more so, to call Lacretelle the Flaubert of the twentieth century. However one defines his literary manner, no definition is complete which does not attach Lacretelle to the entire range of the traditional French novel, almost a literary genre in itself, depending upon analysis, lucidity, objectivity and logic. This novel, so antiphilosophical in its aesthetic doctrine, represents unequivocally a way of life. Yet any way of life which is so sure of itself is, of necessity, a kind of philosophy.

This way of life has been so nearly triumphant in France for so long—one might say since the eighteenth century—that its exponents have become lethargic and only now and then, under the label of "liberals," rise to the defense of a deep-seated principle. In condemning the fanaticism of Maurras in the French Academy, Lacretelle manifested his allegiance to the belief that reason is man's highest faculty. This action on a political level has its counterpart in Lacretelle's definition and practice of the novel. If man believes fully in his reason, he is satisfied to observe the relationships of observable phenomena and rejects metaphysics as unworthy. That is precisely how Lacretelle sees life and also how he constructs his novels, which are intended to be the mirror of life. When he defines his characters as the result of "physiological fatalism," he has expressed a basic concept of nineteenth century realism. In remaining faithful to a larger tradition of the French mind and of French literature, he has also perpetuated a more specific tradition represented, in his own family, by the ancestor who pled the cause of the two Jews of Metz, by another ancestor who tried to expell the Jesuits from the university, by another who headed a revolution in Mâcon, and finally by a small boy, bearing the name of Jacques de Lacretelle, who became excited about Dreyfus.

Since the days of symbolism, there has been a continuing assault on this way of life in France. When he wrote *La Mort d'Hippolyte*, Lacretelle rejected once and for all, in his own literature, the irrationalism of his contemporaries. Doubtless he felt that there was some danger involved in taking such a stand, but certainly he did not feel that he was thereby ostracizing himself immediately and irrevocably. That was because he saw only the superficial and exaggerated form of this irrationalism taking the name of dadaism or futurism. What he did not foresee was that modern man was to become a prey to metaphysical anguish and would seek solace in religion or in the rationalization of irrationality called existentialism. In staying firmly entrenched in the position of nineteenth century realism, Lacretelle did not comprehend that his objectivity would appear to many outsiders as complacency and his lack of involvement as indifference.

Nineteenth century realism (or determinism) was once a militant doctrine, not without its fanatics. But a true realist abhors fanatics. Flaubert, the greatest of realists, demolished the fanatics of realism in the person of his character Homais. No one could call Flaubert complacent or indifferent. He rendered the greatest service to the fundamental principle of his way of life by avoiding fanaticism. In remaining a nineteenth century realist in his literary and philosophical attitude, while avoiding any show of fanaticism, Lacretelle has really taken an attitude of "engagement," although the existentialists, communists or neo-Catholics would probably not recognize it as such.

To a student of literature it should be a matter of indifference whether an author expresses a way of life which is antagonistic to some personal persuasion. He should be more interested in the expression than in what is expressed. Lacretelle's work must be judged independently of the prejudices of a given moment of history.

Undeniably a certain coldness results from a complete application of the realistic principle in literature. One has only to compare Flaubert with Tolstoi to see the difference. But this coldness on the surface is really a matter of aesthetic perspective. Surely Emma Bovary, when she takes her own life, suffers as intensely as Anna

Karenina; Flaubert keeps the reader more consistently outside the character, whereas Tolstoi plays on the reader's emotions. One approach is not necessarily better than the other; the real appeal of each work, though the perspective is different, is in the intensity of the human drama.

Only one work of Lacretelle reaches an intensity in the human drama in any way comparable to that in *Madame Bovary* or in *Anna Karenina*; that is, of course, *Silbermann*, Lacretelle's masterpiece. Such a remark seems to be tantamount to denying true stature to a novel which is not intrinsically dramatic, and perhaps, in the last analysis, that is how novels are judged by the popular reader. It should be noted, however, that the greatness of *Silbermann* is due not to the subject but to the treatment of the subject; without Lacretelle's method of analysis, *Silbermann* would not be a great work of art, for if we removed the analysis, there would be nothing left to the novel. If any other work of Lacretelle, for example, is to be judged inferior to *Silbermann*, it cannot be simply because he has used in it a method of psychological analysis; rather, it will be for some reason which is extraneous to the method.

No discriminating reader or critic would so restrict the domain of the novel as a genre as to insist that it be dramatic. Such a standard automatically entails the rejection of *L'Education sentimentale*, *A la Recherche du temps perdu* and the remainder of Lacretelle's fictional work. Some of the great novels are essentially antidramatic and seek only to be a facsimile of everyday life. Their value is dependent on the depth of their penetration into everyday life. In such novels, as well, a method of lucid analysis is essential if the novel is to appeal to the intellect. The difference between the *Education* and the *Recherche* is that Flaubert arranges his observation in a logical pattern, whereas Proust uses his intelligence on the detail but does not really master the whole. There is an analogous phenomenon in Lacretelle's work. In *Les Hauts Ponts* there is everyday life but in a logical arrangement, and in *Le Pour et le Contre* there is everyday life with much less arrangement. Since Lacretelle, like Flaubert, has a particular gift for logical arrangement, *Les Hauts Ponts* turns out to be a greater artistic achievement. If one rejects dramatic intensity as the principal criterion for judging a novel, *Les Hauts Ponts* is a very fine novel. *La Bonifas*—which Lacretelle personally prefers to *Les Hauts Ponts*—appears inferior to both *Silbermann* and *Les Hauts Ponts* since it lacks the dramatic intensity of one and the lifelike qualities of the other, being over-constructed to the point that the reader senses a certain artificiality.

Nevertheless, it is an injustice to any author to insist exclusively on the formal qualities of his work. Proust has said that every great author expresses a new vision of the universe. On the surface, such a statement seems to put a premium on originality at any cost, and that is certainly the emphasis which many modern authors have given to this notion. Lacretelle has never sought this kind of originality, except in *Le Pour et le Contre*, which is very interesting as an experimental novel but which has so many *longueurs* that it takes a special devotee of Lacretelle or of contemporary French literature to appreciate it to its fullest.

If Lacretelle does not necessarily have a new "vision" of the universe in some superlative application of the word, he does have his special way of seeing the world. The imprint of his personality is to be found everywhere in his work. He, himself, feels a very strong kinship to Proust in the sense that he relies as heavily on introspection as on observation. There is a personal theme which gives a definite unity of tone to all the works of Lacretelle, the theme of solitude. In fact, the Talvart bibliography of French literature lists a nonexistent volume entitled *Solitudes*, supposedly written by Lacretelle. It may well be that Lacretelle once contemplated writing such a volume, although he does not now recall any such intention.

The theme of solitude and incommunicability, which Lacretelle felt so strongly as he read *Du Côté de chez Swann* for the first time, became the central theme of the book in which Lacretelle reveals himself most fully, *La Vie inquiète de Jean Hermelin*. The human qualities of this first novel are undeniable. These same human qualities are transferred to *Silbermann*, where the theme of solitude and incomprehension is less strong but indubitably present; without this ability to identify himself with his characters, Lacretelle could never have created Silbermann or the narrator. Similarly, all that is human in the heroine of *La Bonifas* is again due to this concept of the solitude of the character. Whatever objectionable traits the narrator of *Amour nuptial* may have, his tragedy is his inability to break down the barrier which shuts him off from others. In *Sabine*, the theme of solitude, expressed more intensely than in any novel since *La Vie inquiète de Jean Hermelin*, gives this volume a certain depth which even *Silbermann* lacked. In the rest of *Les Hauts Ponts*, the heroine Lise Darembert is "saved" in the reader's opinion only because she too suffers from this inability to communicate. Inversely, the real inadequacy of *Le Pour et le Contre* is in expressing solitude more as an axiom than as a lyrical theme; here again the great problem of the hero's life is one of communication, but the reader does not participate often enough in Le Maistre's emotional states to feel that he knows him completely. Solitude is even more of an axiom in *Deux Cœurs simples*, and that is probably why this novel has less vitality than other Lacretelle novels.

Feeling a solidarity with both Proust and Gide, Lacretelle has always considered himself allied with the literature of the introspective twenties. This kinship to Proust and Gide explains his great popularity as a writer between the two world wars. He could hardly be called an anachronism in the face of such a success; whatever nineteenth century qualities have survived in his work, they are offset—if not obliterated—by distinctly contemporary characteristics.

Abstractly, purely as a literary problem, what makes Lacretelle's work particularly interesting to study is this vacillation between the nineteenth century and the twentieth century point of view in art. Continually the pendulum has swung back and forth from a subjective to an objective technique in the structure of his fictions, as simultaneously he continued to blend the two points of view into an organic whole. In *La Vie inquiète de Jean Hermelin*, *La Mort d'Hippolyte* and *Silbermann*, he uses either a direct first person pronoun or a narrator, one approach producing an illusion of subjectivity as much as the other. Then, in *La Belle Journée* and *La Bonifas*, he goes to the opposite extreme and adopts a third person technique with all the objectivity associated with the realistic novel of the nineteenth century. Tiring of this, he writes his essay, *Dix Jours à Ermenonville*, and decides that he will again return to the subjective principle of Gidian "authenticity." In this spirit, he writes *Le Christ aux bras étroits, Le Cachemire écarlate* and the first version of *Le Retour de Silbermann*—all of which, despite the subjective structure, turn out to be a little more objective and a little less authentic than the Ermenonville declaration led one to expect them to be. With *Les Hauts Ponts*, he returns in his structure to the third person and to a novelistic technique which, though very natural to him, is so distinctly nineteenth century that it seems, on the surface, to be a total rupture with the twentieth century. Thereafter, with *Le Pour et le Contre*, he turns back to the twentieth century in subject and in theme, although disguising the real subjectivity of his approach in a third person narrative. This third person approach and a similarity of subject establish in the reader's mind a momentary relationship with Flaubert's *Education sentimentale*, whereas the real relationship is with *Point Counter Point*, *A la Recherche du temps perdu* and *Les Faux-Monnayeurs*. Then, as though it were an act of defiance to the existentialist generation, he writes *Deux Cœurs simples* in his more typical objective manner, emphasizing those characteristics which could be considered most traditional.

The most enduring quality in Lacretelle's work is the style. There is nothing angular about this style, nothing which distinguishes it remarkably from the style of any other author who writes good French. The true quality of this style is precisely to remove from the reader's horizon all notion of style. Unless the reader stops to reflect, he is aware neither of syntax nor of vocabulary. Speaking of this style, a Frenchman will refer inevitably to its purity. Lacretelle seems to have staked his bid for survival on this style, and undoubtedly he is right. Anyone who has taught the French language to non-Frenchmen is aware of the far greater difficulty in dealing with the vocabulary and syntax of most twentieth century authors, as compared with the vocabulary and syntax of nineteenth century authors—or eighteenth century authors. One inevitably wonders, as Lacretelle himself did, whether such verbal eccentricities among twentieth century authors may not prove to be an insurmountable barrier to readers of the future. For the readers of Lacretelle, as long as the French language is spoken, there will never be any such barrier. And because of his qualities as a stylist, Lacretelle's nonfictional work will probably always count as a major part of his literary production, particularly *Aparté* and *Le Demi-Dieu, ou Le Voyage de Grèce*.

Very intentionally, Lacretelle sought to combine what he considered to be the permanent characteristics of French literature with modern themes. It was his choice to be both a modern and a classic, and the reader of his work must be sufficiently eclectic to appreciate both points of view. The road from Combray may lead to Athens, but it leads right back to Combray again.

GENEALOGICAL CHART

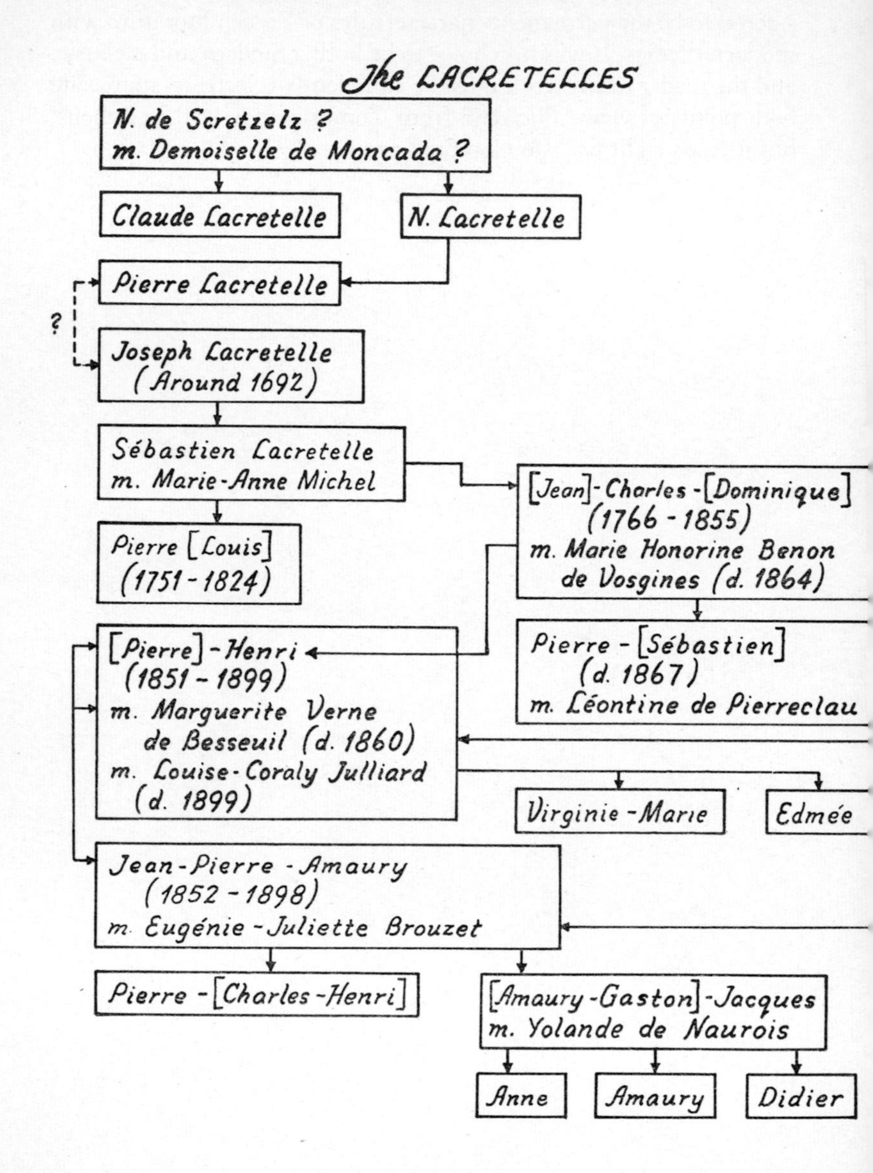

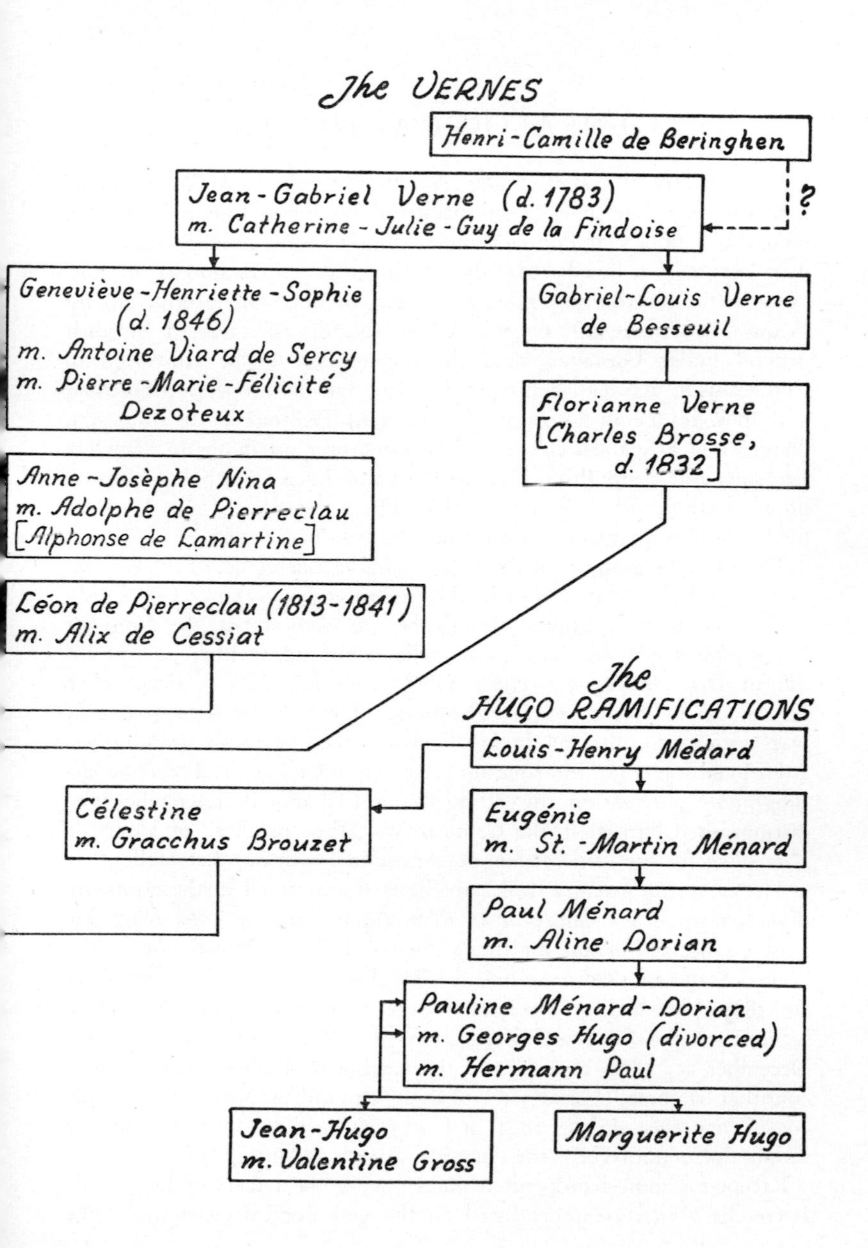
The VERNES
Henri-Camille de Beringhen
?
Jean-Gabriel Verne (d. 1783)
m. Catherine-Julie-Guy de la Findoise
Geneviève-Henriette-Sophie (d. 1846)
m. Antoine Viard de Sercy
m. Pierre-Marie-Félicité Dezoteux
Gabriel-Louis Verne de Besseuil
Florianne Verne
[Charles Brosse, d. 1832]
Anne-Josèphe Nina
m. Adolphe de Pierreclau
[Alphonse de Lamartine]
Léon de Pierreclau (1813-1841)
m. Alix de Cessiat
The HUGO RAMIFICATIONS
Louis-Henry Médard
Célestine
m. Gracchus Brouzet
Eugénie
m. St.-Martin Ménard
Paul Ménard
m. Aline Dorian
Pauline Ménard-Dorian
m. Georges Hugo (divorced)
m. Hermann Paul
Jean-Hugo
m. Valentine Gross
Marguerite Hugo

GENEALOGICAL NOTES

RÉVÉREND, in *Titres, anoblissements et pairies de la Restauration,* carries the Lacretelle family back only as far as Joseph Lacretelle, who was a notary at Pont-à-Mousson in 1692, and remarks that they were reputedly a Swedish family which settled at Dieulouard in Lorraine in the seventeenth century. A note, of uncertain origin, among Jacques de Lacretelle's papers, reads: "N. de Scretzelz, a Swedish general under Gustavus Vasa, having refused to be converted to Lutheranism, was banished from Sweden, had his property confiscated and took refuge in Lorraine. He married Demoiselle de Moncada, daughter of a Spanish colonel." The same note attributes to Scretzelz two sons and a grandson, bearing the name Lacretelle, but establishes no connection with Joseph Lacretelle. The Lacretelles of our day have made fruitless attempts to trace this Scretzelz in Sweden.

Thorough biographies of Pierre and Charles Lacretelle, of the Revolutionary period, can be found in the *Biographie universelle* (*Michaud*). Articles about them appear also in the *Larousse* and in the *Nouvelle Biographie générale*. Charles Lacretelle relates an exciting part of his life in *Dix Années d'épreuves pendant la Révolution* (Paris, chez A. Allouard, libraire, 1842). The biographical dictionaries give only brief articles for his son Henri de Lacretelle, Jacques's grandfather. Additional sources of information are given in Chapter 1. The *Nouvelle Biographie générale* errs in calling General Charles de Lacretelle, who distinguished himself in the Crimean war, the "brother" of Henri de Lacretelle, for the General has no connection with our Lacretelles.

The career of Amaury de Lacretelle is summarized in the *Annuaire diplomatique et consulaire de la République française pour 1897*. He was on special mission for the Ministry of Public Instruction to the United States in 1880; vice-consul, first class, at Varna, Bulgaria, May 19, 1885; detached as secretary to the management of the foreign sections of the Universal Exposition of 1889; consul, second class, December 31, 1888; chevalier of the Legion of Honor, May 6, 1889; consul at Salonica, February 10, 1890; at Alexandria, November 2, 1892; consul, first class, July 7, 1894; at Florence, April 16, 1897. A note in a family document records the date of his death as May 14, 1898.

Except for some handwritten notes among the papers of Jacques de Lacretelle which are reproduced on the genealogical chart under the heading "The Hugo Ramifications," the Lacretelles have no information about the ancestry of Juliette Brouzet. Dr. Gracchus Brouzet was a distinguished member of the Academy of Medicine of Montpellier and had an estate at Saint-Sauveur de Pourcils, which is now incorporated in the national forest of Mont-Aigoual in the Cévennes. Eugène and Emile Haag, in *La France protestante* (2d edition, Vol. 3; Paris, Librairie Sandoz et Fischbacher, 1881), list a Protestant family of Brouzet, also spelled Brouset and Brozet, many of whose members emigrated after the revocation of the Edict of Nantes; they list no contemporary Brouzets.

Le Château d'Uxelles et ses seigneurs, by Gabriel Jeanton and Jean Martin, is the authoritative work for the history of Cormatin. The same authors, listing themselves in reverse order, give some additional information on the Du Blé family in *Répertoire des familles notables de Tournus et de sa région*. François Perraud, in *Le Mâconnais historique; seigneurs, châteaux* (Mâcon, Protat frères, 1921) merely summarizes Jeanton and Martin, whereas *Les Châteaux de Bourgogne* (Paris, Vanoest, 1942), by Henry Soulange-Bodin, contains a certain amount of misinformation.

According to Jeanton and Martin, the present castle of Cormatin was begun by Pétrarque du Blé around the year 1616 and became the residence of two marshals of France, Jacques du Blé and Nicolas du Blé, who both bore the titles of Marquis d'Uxelles and Seigneur de Cormatin. In 1766, Jean-Gabriel Verne and Michel-Denis Péau de Saint-Gilles bought Uxelles and Cormatin from the Marquis de Beringhen, and, in 1770, Verne bought up his partner's share. Verne is described as "écuyer, conseiller et secrétaire du roi au Parlement de Besançon, contrôleur des équipages des Petites Ecuries du roi, seigneur de Cormatin, etc." Since Beringhen was "premier écuyer du roi," he was Verne's immediate superior at court.

Our attempts to trace the lineage of Jean-Gabriel Verne have been fruitless. Alexandre Estignard, in *Le Parlement de Franche-Comté de son installation à Besançon à sa suppression, 1674–1790* (Paris, A. Picard; Besançon, Paul Jacquin, 1892), mentions no such person. The *Dictionnaire de la noblesse* (3d ed.; Paris, chez Schlesinger frères, 1876), by De la Chenaye-Desbois and Badier, knows no noble family of Verne, nor does R. de Lurion, in his *Nobiliaire de Franche-Comté* (Besançon, Paul Jacquin, 1890), record anything but a family of De Verne or De la Verne which became extinct in the seventeenth century. One is therefore forced to conclude that Verne was a *roturier*.

His son, Gabriel-Louis Verne de Besseuil (who got his name from a dependency of Cormatin), was "procureur au Châtelet" and later "secrétaire greffier du conseil." He received as his share in his father's estate the Hôtel des Petites-Ecuries, in the rue Saint-Denis, which he sold to the king in 1784. He was ruined by the Revolution and ended his days as director of an educational establishment.

Cormatin went to Geneviève-Henriette-Sophie Verne, married to Antoine Viard de Sercy. Her husband died in 1783, the same year that she inherited Cormatin, and she was obliged to sell the castle of Sercy to pay his debts. This was the beginning of her financial difficulties, and her new husband, Dezoteux, whom she married the next year, remarked in a letter that she had "a brilliant fortune but very much embarrassed" and then proceeded to ruin her with riotous living at Cormatin. According to Henri Welschinger in *Aventures de guerre et d'amour du Baron de Cormatin, 1794–1812* (Paris, Librairie Plon, 1894), he managed to spend 700,000 francs of his wife's money before emigrating. However, he did one good deed by saving Cormatin from destruction when, in August 1789, he entertained a revolutionary mob at dinner while a messenger alerted the militia. He had been an officer with Rochambeau in America and then a major general commanding the Brabant frontier; during the Revolution he turned up in Brittany as the commander of the Chouans, made peace with Hoche and then put on such arrogant airs that the Republican general finally had him arrested. In 1802 he was allowed to return to Cormatin and to his wife, who had meanwhile divorced him. The divorce was annulled the following year, but she was forced to obtain a new divorce in 1809 to prevent him from squandering what money was left.

The divorce came a little too late, for she had to sell Cormatin and Uxelles to her friend General Etienne Maynaud de Lavaux, whose intention was to dispose of the property piecemeal. The crenellated ruin of Uxelles, uninhabited for two centuries, did not long survive this real estate operation, and Cormatin seemed destined to a similar fate when a falling beam crushed its new owner, Joseph-Laurent Salavin, a businessman from Lyon, who was transforming the building into a factory. Two thirds of the château thus escaped destruction, since the property reverted for nonpayment to the General, who gave it to his daughter. She was the wife of Charles Brosse, former aide de camp of Marshal Suchet. Mme Brosse died childless a year after her marriage. When Charles Brosse died in 1832, he left his estate to a common-law daughter, Marguerite Verne, who married Henri de Lacretelle.

Madame Dezoteux, née Sophie Verne, had a daughter Anne-Josèphe, known as Nina, who contributed as much as Dezoteux himself to the dilapidation of the Verne fortune. In a recent article ("Lamartine et Léon de Pierreclau," *Revue de Paris,* November 1, 1936), Pierre

[Charles-Henri] de Lacretelle told the story of her life. She married Adolphe de Pierreclau at Cormatin in 1807. In 1812 Lamartine was a frequent visitor at Cormatin, and it was really he who was the sire of Jean-Baptiste-Léon de Pierreclau, born the following year. Nina, having inherited her father's adventurous temperament, went to live in South America. She returned to France a few weeks after her husband's death, sold Pierreclos (the estate was spelled differently), and went to live in comparative poverty as the postmistress of Pauillac. At the death of Adolphe de Pierreclau, Lamartine adopted Léon. Léon fell in love with Alix de Cessiat, Lamartine's niece, and for a long time Lamartine, who had never admitted his paternity, opposed this marriage between first cousins. Eventually he gave his consent, and Léon was married in 1838, despite signs of tuberculosis. Léon died two years later, leaving a daughter Léontine, who, according to François Perraud (*Les Environs de Mâcon en Saône-et-Loire: Anciennes seigneuries et anciens châteaux*, Mâcon, Protat frères, 1912, p. 479), married Pierre [-Sébastien] de Lacretelle, the younger son of Charles de Lacretelle. This Pierre de Lacretelle died in 1867 without issue.

REFERENCES AND NOTES

1. CORMATIN

1. Vicomte A. Révérend: *Titres, anoblissements et pairies de la Restauration*. Paris, Champion, 1904. Vol. 4, p. 124.

2. *Ibid.*

3. *Nouvelle Biographie générale*. Paris, Firmin-Didot frères, 1861. Vol. 28.

4. François Perraud: *Les Environs de Mâcon en Saône-et-Loire. Anciennes seigneuries et anciens châteaux*. Mâcon, Protat frères, 1912. p. 479.

5. Pierre de Lacretelle: "Lamartine et Léon de Pierreclau (documents inédits)," *Revue de Paris*, Nov. 1, 1936. Although most historians and Lamartine himself spell this name "Pierreclos," Pierre de Lacretelle points out that family records say "Pierreclau" (the Marquis de Luppé, in *Les Travaux et les jours d'Alphonse de Lamartine*, Paris, Albin Michel, 1942, has also adopted this spelling).

6. *Les Cloches: Poésies* par Henri de Lacretelle. Avec une pièce en vers adressée à l'auteur par M. A. de Lamartine. Deuxième édition. Paris, Delloye, 1841. 277 [2]p. There is no first edition of this work in the Bibliothèque Nationale.

7. *Œuvres complètes de Lamartine*. Paris, chez l'auteur, Rue de Ville-l'Evêque, 43, 1860. Vol. 5, p. 206.

8. *Les Hommes d'aujourd'hui*. Vol. 3, no. 145.

9. Albert Thibaudet: *La République des lettres*. Paris, Bernard Grasset, 1927. p. 190.

10. Henri de Lacretelle: *Lamartine et ses amis*. Paris, Aurice Dreyfous, éditeur, n.d. (dépôt légal 1878). p. 146.

11. This information about Juliette Brouzet comes largely from interviews with Jacques de Lacretelle.

12. Juliette de Lacretelle: "Dans l'Intimité de Victor Hugo," *Le Figaro*, May 11, 1935.

2. "WHAT I LEAVE BEHIND HAS BEEN ONLY A GAME"

"What I leave behind . . . ." *La Vie inquiète de Jean Hermelin*, p. 235.

1. *Le Pour et le Contre*, I, p. 230.

2. Preface to Henry Marks: *Mère et fils*, Paris, Grasset, 1934 (*L'Ecrivain public*, p. 66).

3. *La Vie inquiète . . .*, p. 11.

4. Unpublished outline of "Roman protestant."
5. "Une Enfance en orient," *Nouvelles littéraires*, April 4, 1936.
6. Personal interview.
7. Unpublished letter of Mme Amaury de Lacretelle, dated Le Nid, Saturday, Nov. 8 (year not given).
8. Unpublished letter of Mme Amaury de Lacretelle, dated Le Nid, Nov. 12, 1936.
9. "Paysages," *Le Figaro*, Mar. 25, 1942 (*Idées dans un chapeau*, p. 68).
10. Unpublished letter from Madeleine Guéritte to Jacques de Lacretelle, Oct. 30, 1928.
11. "Paysages," *Le Figaro*, Mar. 25, 1942.
12. *Ibid.*
13. Personal interview.
14. In the most authoritative study of this problem ("Le Roman de Proust et le problème des clefs," *Revue des sciences humaines*, Jan.–Mar. 1952), A. Adam states categorically that Mme Ménard-Dorian could not be the original of Mme Verdurin and then contradicts himself slightly by admitting that since the Ménard-Dorian salon was so outstandingly Dreyfusard, it could have been a model for the Verdurin salon from that point of view.
15. "Hommage aux livres," *Le Journal*, Jan. 27, 1938 (*L'Heure qui change*, p. 11).
16. *Discours de réception de M. Jacques de Lacretelle*, p. 14.
17. "En Classe avec Bellessort," *Le Figaro*, Mar. 29, 1935 (*L'Ecrivain public*, p. 97).
18. "Un Critique en chaire," *Candide*, Dec. 31, 1941.
19. André Bellessort: "Silbermann," *Journal des débats*, July 9, 1931.
20. Preface by André Spire in Henri Franck: *Lettres à quelques-uns*, Paris, Grasset, 1926.
21. Henri Franck: *La Danse devant l'arche*. Paris, Gallimard, 1921. p. 82.
22. Letter to D. W. Alden, Nov. 13, 1954.
23. Maurice Sachs: *The Decade of Illusion*. New York, Alfred A. Knopf, 1933. p. 68. This book was published in French by Gallimard in 1950 as *La Décade de l'illusion*.
24. Unpublished letter dated Versailles, April 9, 1902.
25. Unpublished letter dated Versailles, April 14, 1902.
26. Unpublished, undated letter, one of a series from Guernsey.
27. Personal interview.

3. PROUST'S WAY

1. "Souvenirs sur Proust," *Table ronde*, June 1955.
2. "Les Clefs de Marcel Proust," *Nouvelle Revue Française*, Jan. 1, 1923 (repr. in *Trébuchet* and in *Les Aveux étudiés*, p. 33).
3. Henri Bardac: "Jacques de Lacretelle," *L'Eclair*, June 16, 1925.
4. *Dix Jours à Ermenonville* (*Aparté*, pp. 173–174)

5. Except as otherwise specified, all quotations in the remainder of this chapter come from the published version of *La Vie inquiète de Jean Hermelin.*

6. This text is in manuscript only.

7. On page 23 of the text Hélène is assimilated to Odette, since she is the object of a mild Oedipus complex on the part of the narrator and has acquired the sibilants.

8. This passage is not in original manuscript.

9. The incriminated passage is a variant in the manuscript now in the Princeton University Library, but it is not in the original manuscript still in the author's possession.

10. In *Le Pour et le Contre* (I, p. 99), Le Maistre follows *Messages* in the same manner.

11. Two anecdotes from this journal have been published, one in the *Journal de Colère* (*Aparté*, pp. 83–91) and the other in *Dix Jours à Ermenonville* (*Aparté*, pp. 178–183).

12. Fortunat Strowski: "Les Romans d'inquiétude et d'adolescence," *Renaissance politique, littéraire, artistique*, Jan. 15, 1921.

13. Henri de Régnier: *"La Vie inquiète de Jean Hermelin," Le Figaro*, July 11, 1920. Abel Hermant: *"La Vie inquiète de Jean Hermelin," Le Gaulois*, Aug. 21, 1920. Fernand Vandérem: "Les Lettres et la vie," *Revue de Paris*, Aug. 15, 1920 (pp. 855–856).

14. Jacques de Lacretelle: "Un Témoignage sur Proust," *Bulletin de la Société des amis de Marcel Proust*, no. 1 (1950).

15. *Marcel Proust et Jacques Rivière: Correspondance (1914–1922).* Présentée et annotée par Philip Kolb. Paris, Plon, 1955, p. 135.

16. Louis Martin-Chauffier: *"La Vie inquiète de Jean Hermelin," Nouvelle Revue Française*, May 1921.

17. Lacretelle, "Un Témoignage sur Proust."

4. HUGUENOTS AND HIPPOLYTUS

1. Unpublished lecture by Lacretelle on "Rencontres littéraires."

2. *Marcel Proust et Jacques Rivière: Correspondance* . . . , pp. 155–156.

3. "Portrait," *Nouvelle Revue Française*, April 1925 (repr. in *Trébuchet* and in *Les Aveux étudiés*, pp. 43–44).

4. *Journal de Colère* (*Aparté*, p. 123).

5. This name is transferred to Blanchod's guardian in *Le Christ aux bras étroits*, the later short story in which Blanchod reappears.

6. This manuscript is now in the Princeton University Library.

7. "Les Romans de La Rochefoucauld," *Nouvelles littéraires*, Aug. 11, 1934 (repr. in *L'Ecrivain public*, p. 46, and in *Tableau de la littérature française . . . de Corneille à Chénier*, Paris, Gallimard, 1939).

8. Unpublished manuscript previously mentioned in Chapter 3, note 11.

9. "Chronique de l'Œil de bœuf," *L'Œil de bœuf*, April 1921.

10. André Maurois: *"La Mort d'Hippolyte," Nouvelle Revue Française*, July 1923.

5. SILBERMANN

1. Frédéric Lefèvre: "Une Heure avec Jacques de Lacretelle," *Nouvelles littéraires*, June 16, 1925 (repr. in Lefèvre, *Une Heure avec ...*, 3d series, Paris, Nouvelle Revue Française, 1924–1927).

2. Unpublished letter from Rivière, dated June 19, 1922.

3. "Le Prix 'Vie heureuse.' Impressions de lauréat," *Nouvelles littéraires*, Dec. 16, 1922.

4. Note that Malo de Kerlon survives as Robin.

5. *"Silbermann," La Revue juive*, Jan. 15, 1925 (repr. in *Trébuchet* and in *Les Aveux étudiés*, p. 99).

6. Benjamin Crémieux: *"Silbermann," Nouvelles littéraires*, Nov. 4, 1922.

7. André Bellessort: *"Silbermann," Journal des débats*, July 9, 1930.

8. *"Silbermann," Les Annales Conférencia*, Oct. 1952.

9. Bellessort, *Journal des débats*, July 9, 1930.

10. Lacretelle read this story as it originally appeared in the *Nouvelle Revue Française*. The story is included in *Lévy: Premier livre de contes*. Lacretelle seems never to have read the short story, "Lévy," about the persecution of a Jewish merchant during the Dreyfus affair, found in the same volume.

11. See Lacretelle's preface to Pierre-Louis Lacretelle: *Plaidoyer pour deux juifs de Metz contre l'Hôtel de ville et le Corps des marchands de Thionville*, Paris, Lipschutz, 1928.

12. "Réponse," *Revue hebdomadaire*, Nov. 25, 1922 (repr. in *Trébuchet*, p. 26, and in Pierre Varillon and Henri Rambaud: *Enquête sur les maîtres de la jeune littérature*, Paris, Bloud and Gay, 1923).

13. Letter to D.W. Alden, Dec. 18, 1950. The missing manuscript belonged to Serge André, who, shortly before his death, reported having sold it to a bookseller. This bookseller disclaims all knowledge of the manuscript.

14. André Billy: *"Silbermann," L'Œuvre*, Dec. 19, 1922.

15. Abel Hermant: "La Vie à Paris," *Le Temps*, Dec. 22, 1922.

16. Anon.: *"Silbermann," Gazette de Lausanne*, Dec. 31, 1922.

17. André Chaumeix: *"Silbermann," Le Gaulois*, Dec. 2, 1922. Fernand Vandérem: "Les Lettres et la vie," *Revue de France*, Nov. 15, 1922. René Gillouin: "... *Silbermann," Semaine littéraire*, Jan. 6, 1923. Henri de Régnier: *"Silbermann," Le Figaro*, Nov. 21, 1922. François Le Grix: *"La Vie inquiète de Jean Hermelin; Silbermann," Revue hebdomadaire*, Dec. 9, 1922. Franc-Nohain: *"Silbermann," Echo de Paris*, Nov. 16, 1922. André Billy: *"Silbermann," L'Œuvre*, Dec. 19, 1922. André Thérive: "Avant le Prix Goncourt," *L'Opinion*, Nov. 24, 1922.

18. Jean de Pierrefeu: *"Silbermann," Journal des débats*, Nov. 15, 1922.

19. Anon.: *"Silbermann," Action française*, Dec. 17, 1922. Charles Bourdon: "Les Romans," *Revue des lectures*, Nov. 1922. Henri Massis: "Histoires de collégiens," *Revue universelle*, Jan. 1, 1923.

20. Alsaticus: "A propos de *Silbermann*," *Univers israélite*, Jan. 19, 1923.

23

21. Crémieux, *Nouvelles littéraires*, Nov. 4, 1922.
22. *Les Aveux étudiés*, p. 106.

6. THE BEARDED LADY

1. Henri Bardac: "Jacques de Lacretelle," *L'Eclair*, June 16, 1925.
2. André Maurois: "Jacques de Lacretelle de l'Académie française," *Nouvelles littéraires*, Nov. 14, 1936 (repr. in Lacretelle, *Morceaux choisis*, Paris, Gallimard, 1938).
3. While at Saint-Agrève, Lacretelle also received a visit from Jules Romains, the site of whose play *Cromedeyre-le-Vieil* was in the vicinity.
4. Vandérem, *Revue de France*, Nov. 15, 1922.
5. Henri Bidou: *"Silbermann," Revue de Paris*, Dec. 15, 1922.
6. Massis, *Revue universelle*, Jan. 1, 1923.
7. *Idées dans un chapeau*, p. 234. Actually this version of the text says "1922," but the original preface to the 1946 edition of *La Bonifas* says "1923," which is also the date given on p. 236 of *Idées dans un chapeau.*
8. "[Freud et la psychanalyse]: Jacques de Lacretelle," *Disque vert*, numéro spécial (1924), pp. 188–190.
9. Raymond Cogniat: "A propos de *La Bonifas* de M. Jacques de Lacretelle," *Comœdia*, July 7, 1925.
10. *"Mademoiselle de la Ralphie*, par Eugène Le Roy," *Nouvelle Revue Française*, Aug. 1921 (*Etudes*, p. 51).
11. *"Le Grand Ecart*, par Jean Cocteau," *Nouvelle Revue Française*, July 1, 1923.
12. Gaspar Lavater: *L'Art de connaître les hommes par la physionomie*. Paris, L. Prudhomme, 1806–1809. Vol. 9, p. 53.
13. Manuscript of unpublished radio dialogue dating probably from 1934.
14. Jean de Pierrefeu: *"La Bonifas," Journal des débats*, July 22, 1925.
15. Henri Bidou: "Parmi les Livres," *Revue de Paris*, July 1, 1925. Albert Thibaudet: "Une Vie: *La Bonifas*," *Europe nouvelle*, June 6, 1925. Pierre Lœwel: *"La Bonifas," L'Eclair*, June 3, 1925. Jacques Patin: *"La Bonifas," Le Figaro*, Aug. 15, 1925. Gérard d'Houville: *"La Bonifas," Candide*, June 11, 1925. H[enri] M[artineau]: *"La Bonifas," Le Divan*, Nov. 1925. Louis Martin-Chauffier: *"La Bonifas," Gazette du franc*, May 30, 1925. Albéric Cahuet: *"La Bonifas," L'Illustration*, July 11, 1925. Henri de Régnier: *"La Bonifas," Le Figaro*, June 2, 1925. André Chaumeix: *"La Bonifas," Le Gaulois*, June 20, 1925. Jean Le Meur: *"La Bonifas," Le Radical*, June 19, 1925. Franc-Nohain: *"La Bonifas," Echo de Paris*, June 4, 1925.
16. Fernand Vandérem: *"La Bonifas," Revue de France*, July 1, 1925. René Gillouin: "L'Evolution de M. Jacques de Lacretelle," *Semaine littéraire*, Dec. 5, 1925. André Thérive: "Hippolyte, cher cœur . . . ," *L'Opinion*, May 30, 1925. André Beaunier: "Un Romancier: M. Jacques de Lacretelle," *Revue des deux mondes*, Aug. 1, 1925. John Charpentier: *"La Bonifas," Mercure de France*, Sept. 15, 1925.

17. Edmond Jaloux: *"La Bonifas," Nouvelles littéraires*, July 25, 1925. André Billy: *"La Bonifas," L'Œuvre*, June 10, 1925.

18. Paul Souday: *"La Bonifas," Le Temps*, June 4, 1925. Alfred Colling: *"La Bonifas," Revue européenne*, Sept. 1925. Robert Kemp: *"La Bonifas," La Liberté*, May 28, 1925. Louis Laloy: *"La Bonifas," Comœdia*, June 23, 1925. Maurice Martin du Gard: "Jacques de Lacretelle," *Nouvelles littéraires*, May 30, 1925. Raymond Escholier: *"La Bonifas," Petit Journal*, June 30, 1925. René Lalou: *"La Bonifas," Journal littéraire*, June 13, 1925. Jean Remon: "Jacques de Lacretelle," *L'Humanité*, Aug. 16, 1925.

7. ERMENONVILLE

1. *Mort de la jalousie*, p. 21.
2. One cannot help thinking of the native boy in Gide's *L'Immoraliste* and in his *Si le Grain ne meurt*. However, the second Gide text appeared after *Dix Jours à Ermenonville*.
3. Lefèvre, *Nouvelles littéraires*, June 16, 1925.
4. Madame de Lafayette: *Romans et nouvelles*. Paris, Garnier, 1948. p. 113.

8. STENDHAL'S WAY

1. André Rousseaux: "Un Quart d'Heure avec Jacques de Lacretelle," *Candide*, April 7, 1927.
2. Fragments of the "Roman protestant" which survive in the short story are as follows (as republished in *Aparté*): p. 208, l. 25, to p. 209, l. 4; p. 211, l. 20, to p. 213, l. 9; p. 218, l. 16, to p. 224, l. 11.
3. "Mosaïque italienne," *Candide*, Feb. 16 and Feb. 23, 1928. "Un Chapitre retrouvé d'*Armance*," *Nouvelle Revue Française*, Mar. 1928. "Naissance de Sapho," *Revue européenne*, April 1928. "Addio," *Les Annales politiques et littéraires*, April 15, 1928.
4. Quoted in *Histoire de Paola Ferrani*, p. 86.

9. SILBERMANN COMES BACK

1. *Silbermann*, suivi de *Le Retour de Silbermann*. Paris, Gallimard, 1946. p. 109.
2. Unpublished and undated letter.
3. Benjamin Crémieux: *"Amour nuptial; Le Retour de Silbermann," Les Annales politiques et littéraires*, Jan. 1, 1930.
4. In the manuscript of the original *Retour de Silbermann*, Elise is called Jeanne and Mlle Mossé is called Mlle Roth.
5. From p. 223, l. 13, to p. 224, l. 22.
6. *Candide*, May 23, 1929.
7. *Candide*, Aug. 15, 1929.
8. See Lacretelle letter in D.W. Alden: "Jacques de Lacretelle for and against Proust," *Romanic Review*, April 1950.
9. *La Revue juive*, Jan. 15, 1925.
10. *Silbermann . . .*, 1946, p. 43.

11. André Thérive: *"Amour nuptial. Le Retour de Silbermann," Le Temps*, Jan. 3, 1930. Abel Hermant: *"Amour nuptial," Gringoire*, Dec. 27, 1929. Gabriel Marcel: "Postérité gidienne: à propos d'*Amour nuptial*," *Europe nouvelle*, Nov. 28, 1929. Albert Thibaudet: *"Amour nuptial," Candide*, Dec. 26, 1929. John Charpentier: *"Amour nuptial," Mercure de France*, Feb. 1, 1930. Gilbert Charles: "Jacques de Lacretelle et le Grand Prix du Roman," *Candide*, July 4, 1930.

12. Henri de Régnier: *"Amour nuptial. Le Retour de Silbermann," Le Figaro*, Dec. 31, 1929.

13. Robert Bourget-Pailleron: "En Lisant M. Jacques de Lacretelle," *L'Opinion*, Dec. 21, 1929. Ramon Fernandez: *"Amour nuptial. Le Retour de Silbermann," Nouvelle Revue Française*, Aug. 1, 1930. Jean Vignaud: *"Amour nuptial," Petit Parisien*, Jan. 21, 1930.

14. André Rousseaux: "Le Grand Prix de l'Académie," *Le Figaro*, June 20, 1930.

15. June 19, 1930.

16. André Rousseaux: *"L'Ame cachée," Revue universelle*, July 1, 1929.

17. Firmin Roz: "Encore un Roman du mariage," *Revue bleue*, Feb. 15, 1930, and "Le Déséquilibre contemporain et l'accord avec la vie," *Revue bleue*, Aug. 2, 1930. Charles, *Candide*, July 4, 1930. Thérive, *Le Temps*, Jan. 30, 1930. Philippe Amiguet: "Remarques sur Jacques de Lacretelle," *L'Ordre*, June 23, 1930.

18. Thibaudet, *Candide*, Dec. 26, 1929.

19. Paul Reboux: *"Amour nuptial," Chanteclerc*, Feb. 1, 1930. Charles, *Candide*, July 4, 1930.

20. André Rousseaux: "M. Jacques de Lacretelle, Grand Prix du Roman," *Candide*, June 26, 1930. In this 1929–1930 period there were also two full-length articles by two critics who had not hitherto been particularly favorable to Lacretelle: Paul Souday: "Un Jeune Psychologue: Jacques de Lacretelle," *Candide*, June 13, 1929. André Billy: "Des Pieds à la tête: Jacques de Lacretelle," *Les Annales politiques et littéraires*, June 15, 1929.

10. ATHENS

1. Letter from T.J. Guéritte to D.W. Alden, Aug. 16, 1950.

2. "Le Rêve de ma vie." Supplément aux *Annales* no. 2347, Dec. 1, 1929.

3. The following editions of *Sarn* have appeared since the first edition: 1948, published by Creuzevault, "pointes sèches de Hermine David"; 1950, published by Creuzevault, "compositions de Roland Oudot gravées sur bois par Théo Schmied"; 1950, published by Editions Terres Latines, "lithographies par Emilien Dufour." In collaboration with Marie Canavaggia, Lacretelle did another Mary Webb translation, *La Renarde*, published by Catalogne et Cie in 1933. This novel also has had two other editions: 1947, Club français du livre; 1951, Nouvelles Editions Latines.

4. Raymond Millet: "Jacques de Lacretelle et *Amour nuptial*," *Gringoire*, Dec. 20, 1929.

5. Letter to D.W. Alden, Oct. 20, 1953.

6. *Le Demi-Dieu*, p. 91.

7. Edmond Jaloux: *"Le Demi-Dieu, ou Le Voyage de Grèce," Excelsior*, May 27, 1931.

8. Albert Thibaudet: *"Le Demi-Dieu, ou Le Voyage de Grèce," Candide*, Mar. 26, 1931.

11. *LES HAUTS PONTS*—ELABORATION

1. Millet, *Gringoire*, Dec. 20, 1929.

2. "La Vendée," *Marianne*, Sept. 6, 1933 (*Les Aveux étudiés*, p. 110).

3. Unpublished letter dated Le Nid, Nov. 12. Quoted on page 11.

4. Henri de Régnier: *"Années d'espérance," Le Figaro*, May 30, 1935.

5. Robert de Saint-Jean: "Dialogue avec l'auteur d'*Amour nuptial," Revue hebdomadaire*, Feb. 22, 1930.

6. "La Vendée," *Marianne*, Sept. 6, 1933.

7. Letter to D.W. Alden, July 15, 1953.

8. Robert Bourget-Pailleron: "La Nouvelle Equipe: Jacques de Lacretelle," *Revue des deux mondes*, Nov. 15, 1933.

9. Unpublished letter to Yolande de Naurois, date unknown.

10. Letter to D.W. Alden, July 15, 1953.

11. *La Monnaie de plomb*, p. 128.

12. Natives seem to call this the Forest of "Mervent." However, Ardouin-Dumazet in his *Voyage en France* (16th series, Paris, Berger Levrault, 1898), has an entire chapter headed "La Forêt de Vouvant."

13. Louis Chaigne: *La Vendée*. Paris, F. Lanore, 1934, p. 195.

14. Benjamin Fillon and Octave de Rochebrune: *Poitou et Vendée*, Niort, Cruzot, 1887. Vol. 1, p. 97.

15. Saint-Jean, *Revue hebdomadaire*, Feb. 22, 1930.

16. Letter to D.W. Alden, Oct. 20, 1953.

17. Ardouin-Dumazet, *Voyage en France*, p. 115.

18. Unpublished manuscript.

19. Unpublished manuscript.

20. Marcel Augagneur: "Avec M. Jacques de Lacretelle," *Gringoire*, Mar. 11, 1932.

21. Unpublished letter of Roger Martin du Gard, dated July 5, 1927.

22. Unpublished letter of Roger Martin du Gard, July 3, 1930.

23. Preface to *Sarn*, p. 8 (repr. in *Les Aveux étudiés*, p. 152).

24. Ardouin-Dumazet, *Voyage en France*, p. 17.

25. Unpublished letter to Yolande de Naurois, date unknown.

26. Brasillach (cf. Robert Brasillach: *"Années d'espérance," Action française*, Mar. 21, 1935) thinks the map of the underground parts of the *lycée* is a reminiscence of the map of the castle in Alain-Fournier's *Le Grand Meaulnes*.

27. André Thérive:*"Les Fiançailles," Le Temps*, Mar. 30, 1933.

28. In 1933 Lacretelle published an interesting short story, "Emmeline ou l'autre Bovary." A pastiche of Flaubert, the story tells about Emmeline, the provincial woman who, after an amusing marriage related in a

Rabelaisian vein, falls in love with Charles Bovary. The story appeared in *Incarnations de Madame Bovary*, published by Dacosta in 1933, and also in the *Revue de France* for June 15, 1934.

12. *LES HAUTS PONTS*—ANALYSIS

1. "Mélisande ou Salammbô?" *Le Figaro*, Sept. 19, 1935 (*L'Ecrivain public*, p. 73).

2. Unpublished manuscript.

3. From introduction to *La Monnaie de plomb*, printed only in the *Revue des deux mondes*, July 1, 1935.

4. Unpublished letter of Roger Martin du Gard, dated Dec. 20, 1932.

5. Unpublished letter to Yolande de Naurois, date unknown.

6. *L'Ecrivain public*, p. 14 (original article not found).

7. *L'Ecrivain public*, p. 16.

8. "Le Réalisme de [*sic*] la littérature," *Marianne*, Jan. 15, 1936 (*L'Ecrivain public*, p. 78).

9. Unpublished letter of Gide, dated Sept. 6, 1931.

10. Robert Kemp: *"Sabine," La Liberté*, Mar. 15, 1932.

11. André Thérive: *"Les Hauts Ponts," Le Temps*, Mar. 10, 1932.

12. Henri de Régnier: *"Sabine," Le Figaro*, April 11, 1932. Marcel Prévost: *"Sabine," Gringoire*, April 15, 1932. H[enri] M[artineau]: *"Sabine," Le Divan*, May 1932. Ernest Seillière: *"Sabine," Nouvelle Revue critique*, May 1932. Eugène Marsan: *"Années d'espérance," Comœdia*, Mar. 19, 1935. Louis Gillet: *"Années d'espérance," Echo de Paris*, Jan. 23, 1935. Gabriel Marcel: *"Années d'espérance," Europe nouvelle*, April 6, 1935.

13. Pierre Lœwel: *"Sabine," L'Ordre*, Mar. 16, 1932, and *"Les Fiançailles," L'Ordre*, Mar. 22, 1933.

14. Edmond Jaloux: *"Sabine," Nouvelles littéraires*, Mar. 19, 1932. Benjamin Crémieux: "Le Carnet de Benjamin Crémieux," *Annales politiques et littéraires*, Mar. 15, 1932. Edmond Jaloux: *"Années d'espérance," Excelsior*, Mar. 24, 1935.

15. Robert Kemp: *"La Monnaie de plomb," La Liberté*, Oct. 14, 1935. Auguste Bailly: *"La Monnaie de plomb," Candide*, Dec. 26, 1935.

16. André Chaumeix: "Retour au roman de caractère: *Les Fiançailles*," *Revue des deux mondes*, April 5, 1933. Marcel Arland: *"Les Fiançailles," Nouvelle Revue Française*, April 1, 1933.

17. André Thérive: *"Les Fiançailles," Le Temps*, Mar. 30, 1933, and *"Années d'espérance," Le Temps*, April 25, 1935.

18. André Billy: "La Suite des *Hauts Ponts*," *Gringoire*, Mar. 29, 1935. André Rousseaux: *"Années d'espérance," Revue universelle*, April 1, 1935. Brasillach, *Action Française*, Mar. 21, 1935. Marcel Arland: *"Années d'espérance," Nouvelle Revue Française*, April 1, 1935.

19. John Charpentier: *"La Monnaie de plomb," Mercure de France*, Feb. 1, 1936.

20. Jean Baudry: *"Les Hauts Ponts," Revue hebdomadaire*, Nov. 9, 1935.

21. Gillet, *Echo de Paris*, Jan. 23, 1935.

13. THE PUBLIC LETTER-WRITER

1. Copied from the original card.

2. Jacques Hameline: "Elle et lui. Chez Madame de Lacretelle," *Nouvelles littéraires*, Mar. 8, 1951. Actually two pictures of Lacretelle, published in advertisements of *Le Demi-Dieu*, appeared at this time in the *Nouvelles littéraires*, one in No. 439 on March 14 and the other in No. 441 on March 28. One must assume that she saw the latter and that the number had appeared two days earlier since M. de Lacretelle claims to be certain of the date.

3. "Retour en Grèce," *Gringoire*, July 17, 1931 (*Les Aveux étudiés*, p. 215).

4. Unpublished letter to Yolande de Naurois, date unknown.

5. This information is from the wedding invitation.

6. "Une Semaine à Majorque," *Annales politiques et littéraires*, Sept. 1933 (*Les Aveux étudiés*, p. 217).

7. Post card dated Mar. 23, 1933.

8. Unpublished letter to Yolande de Naurois, date unknown.

9. Unpublished manuscript previously mentioned on page 200.

10. Gaëtan Sanvoisin: "Visite à un nouvel académicien," *Candide*, Nov. 19, 1936.

11. Marina Paul Bousquet: "Promenades d'automne à Montfort-l'Amaury (chez Jacques de Lacretelle)," *Nouvelles littéraires*, Oct. 30, 1937.

12. Maurice Romain: "Quel Livre écrivez-vous? . . . Jacques de Lacretelle," *Annales politiques et littéraires*, Dec. 25, 1937.

13. *Nouvelles littéraires*, Aug. 11, 1934 (*L'Ecrivain public*, p. 46).

14. Preface to Henry K. Marks: *La Fondrière* (*Quagmire*), Paris, Grasset, 1934 (*L'Ecrivain public*, p. 61).

15. *Le Figaro*, Sept. 19, 1935 (*L'Ecrivain public*, p. 73).

16. *Marianne*, Mar. 1, 1933 (*Les Aveux étudiés*, p. 177).

17. *Marianne*, June 19, 1935 (*L'Ecrivain public*, p. 40).

18. *Marianne*, Jan. 15, 1936 (*L'Ecrivain public*, p. 76).

19. *Le Figaro*, Nov. 13, 1936.

20. *Le Figaro*, Oct. 17, 1934 (*L'Ecrivain public*, p. 24).

21. *Marianne*, Jan. 15, 1936 (*L'Ecrivain public*, p. 83).

22. Preface to Marks, *La Fondrière* (*L'Ecrivain public*, p. 62).

23. *Le Figaro*, July 18, 1934 (*L'Ecrivain public*, p. 9).

24. Original article not identified (*L'Ecrivain public*, p. 13).

25. *Le Figaro*, July 28, 1934 (*L'Ecrivain public*, p. 113).

26. Originally "L'Aristocratie et la roture des écrivains," *Le Figaro*, July 20, 1935 (*L'Ecrivain public*, p. 17).

27. *Marianne*, Nov. 29, 1933 (*L'Ecrivain public*, p. 145).

28. *Marianne*, Feb. 21, 1934 (*L'Ecrivain public*, p. 17).

29. *Le Figaro*, July 15, 1935 (*L'Ecrivain public*, p. 154).

30. Original article not identified (*L'Ecrivain public*, p. 151).

31. Personal interview.

32. Alexander Werth: *Which Way France?* New York and London, Harper and Bros., 1937. p. 353.

33. Paul Chopine: *Six Ans chez les Croix de feu.* Paris, Gallimard, 1935. p. 69.

34. Sanvoisin, *Candide*, Nov. 19, 1936.

35. *Nouvelles littéraires*, May 20, 1933 (*Les Aveux étudiés*, p. 189).

36. *Le Figaro*, April 25, 1935 (*L'Ecrivain public*, p. 159).

37. Michel-P. Hamelet: "La Congestion des programmes III. Ce que pensent Jacques de Lacretelle et Jules Romains," *Le Figaro*, Oct. 5, 1935.

38. Original article not identified (*L'Ecrivain public*, p. 163).

39. *Candide*, May 27, 1937.

40. *Candide*, June 10, 1937 (*Croisières en eaux troubles*, p. 59).

41. *Candide*, June 16, 1938 (*Croisières* . . . , p. 94).

42. *Candide*, May 10, 1939 (*Croisières* . . . , p. 117).

43. Montgomery Belgion: *News of the French.* London, Faber and Faber, 1938. p. 334.

44. Alexander Werth: *France and Munich.* New York and London, Harper and Bros., 1939. pp. 230, 266.

45. *Petit Journal*, July 14, 1937.

46. *Petit Journal*, Aug. 22, 1938.

14. AMONG THE IMMORTALS

1. "The Legacy of Symbolism," *New Statesmen and Nation*, Sept. 19, 1936.

2. Nov. 14, 1936.

3. *Candide*, July 4, 1930.

4. Paul Brach: "Jacques de Lacretelle, académicien," *Marianne*, Nov. 18, 1936.

5. Parts of this same letter, dated Le Nid, November 12, 1936, were quoted on pages 11 and 12.

6. Anon.: "Trois Nouveaux Membres de l'Académie française. L'amiral Lacaze, Mgr Grente et M. J. de Lacretelle," *Le Matin*, Nov. 13, 1936.

7. Unpublished letter to Mme Jacques de Lacretelle, date unknown.

8. André Rousseaux: "La Réception de M. Jacques de Lacretelle," *Le Figaro*, Jan. 28, 1938.

9. *Discours de réception de M. Jacques de Lacretelle à l'Académie française*, p. 11.

10. Benjamin Crémieux: "Jacques de Lacretelle," *Marianne*, Jan. 26, 1938.

11. "De l'Art d'écrire à l'art de vivre," *Petit Journal*, Aug. 22, 1937 (*L'Heure qui change*, p. 150).

12. "*L'Eté 1914*, par Roger Martin du Gard," *Ami du peuple*, Dec. 26, 1936 (*L'Heure qui change*, pp. 34–41).

13. "*Retour de l'U.R.S.S.*, par André Gide," *Ami du peuple*, Jan. 10, 1937 (*L'Heure qui change*, p. 76).

14. "*Notre Ami Psichari*, par Henri Massis," *Ami du peuple*, Feb. 6, 1937 (*L'Heure qui change*, p. 66).

15. "*Le Réalisme*, par René Dumesnil," *Ami du peuple*, Mar. 7, 1937 (*L'Heure qui change*, p. 116).

16. *Candide*, June 16, 1938 (*Croisières en eaux troubles*, p. 67).

17. "Parmi les Sages. Impressions de Belgique," *Le Figaro*, Nov. 9, 1935. "En Belgique et en Hollande," *Le Figaro*, Nov. 16, 1935. "Impressions de Hollande. Le Secret du bonheur," *Le Figaro*, Nov. 30, 1935. All repr. in *L'Ecrivain public*, pp. 195–211.

18. "Alexandrie, balcon de l'Orient," *Excelsior*, Mar. 19, 1936. "Au Caire, point de révolution," *Excelsior*, May 2, 1936. Both repr. in *L'Ecrivain public*, pp. 180–184 and pp. 187–190.

19. June 10, 1937.

20. "La Fête du travail à Rome," *Candide*, May 27, 1937.

21. June 16, 1938 (repr. in *Croisières* . . . , pp. 65–114).

22. May 10, 1939 (repr. in *Croisières* . . . , pp. 117–168).

23. April 29, 1939 (repr. in *Croisières* . . . , pp. 171–189).

24. Letter to Maurice Coindreau, Oct. 21, 1938.

25. "Louis Hémon. Le Canada et la France," *Petit Journal*, Aug. 22, 1939 (*Idées dans un chapeau*, p. 280).

26. *Le Canada entre en guerre*, p. 12.

27. Unpublished letter dated Sept. 2, 1939.

28. "Une Nuit en Angleterre," *Le Figaro*, Oct. 11, 1939 (*Idées dans un chapeau*, p. 282).

29. Unpublished letter dated Feb. 24, 1940.

30. Unpublished letter dated May 15, 1940.

31. Unpublished manuscript.

32. Unpublished letter dated July 8, 1940.

33. Unpublished letter dated Aug. 7, 1940.

34. Unpublished manuscript.

35. "La Nuit longue," *Les Œuvres libres*, Vol. 230, 1945 (*Libérations*, p. 10).

36. "La Nuit longue" (*Libérations*, p. 12).

37. *Ibid.*

38. "Les Enfants et les nains"; original article unidentified (*L'Heure qui change*, p. 204).

39. "La Nuit longue" (*Libérations*, p. 10).

40. "La Nuit longue" (*Libérations*, p. 16).

41. "Na Nuit longue" (*Libérations*, p. 17).

42. *Le Figaro*, Jan. 16, 1941 (*L'Heure qui change*, p. 212).

43. "Les Racines du nouvel état français," *Petit Journal*, Mar. 24, 1941.

44. "Les Enfants et les nains" (*L'Heure qui change*, p. 203).

45. Text apparently not published during war; published, presumably for first time, in *France-Amérique*, Sept. 29, 1946 (*Idées dans un chapeau*, p. 199).

46. "La France à l'étranger"; original article unidentified (*L'Heure qui change*, p. 206).

47. *L'Heure qui change*, p. 207.

48. "Colette toujours nouvelle," *Candide*, Mar. 26, 1941 (*L'Heure qui change*, p. 144).
49. *Le Figaro*, April 9, 1941 (*L'Heure qui change*, p. 228).
50. Anon.: "Une Conférence de M. de Lacretelle à Genève, au Rialto," *Le Peuple*, April 8, 1941.
51. June 13 and 18, 1941.
52. April 26, 1942.
53. Jan. 24, 1942.
54. "Pour l'Unité de la langue. L'Enseignement des dialectes," *Le Figaro*, Mar. 3, 1942 (*Idées dans un chapeau*, p. 46).
55. *Ibid.*
56. "Revues d'hier et de demain"; original article unidentified (*L'Heure qui change*, p. 231).
57. "La Nuit longue" (*Libérations*, p. 24).
58. Nov. 28, 1938, and Mar. 31, 1939.
59. Feb. 13 and Feb. 15, 1941.
60. "Souvenirs de Crète," *Le Figaro*, May 30, 1941 (*Idées dans un chapeau*, pp. 288–289). "Alexandrie," *Le Figaro*, June 20, 1941 (*Idées dans un chapeau*, pp. 290–292). "Les Iles englouties," *Le Figaro*, Feb. 7, 1941 (*L'Heure qui change*, pp. 216–219).
61. *Journal de Genève*, Jan. 19, 1941 (*L'Heure qui change*, p. 238).
62. *Candide*, Feb. 4, 1942 (*Idées dans un chapeau*, p. 180).
63. July 6, 1941 (*Idées dans un chapeau*, p. 114).
64. "La Nuit longue" (*Libérations*, p. 24).
65. *Le Figaro*, Sept. 16, 1942 (*Idées dans un chapeau*, p. 79).
66. *Le Figaro*, Aug. 17, 1941.
67. Sept. 28, 1941.
68. Oct. 9, 1941.
69. Henri-F. Berchet: "Dans l'Intimité d'un vieux restaurant genevois Jacques de Lacretelle de l'Académie française nous parle de ses livres et de la France," *Courrier de Genève*, Mar. 14, 1942.
70. Letter to D.W. Alden, Nov. 13, 1954.
71. "Prix de vertu," *Présent*, Dec. 20, 1943.
72. "La Nuit longue" (*Libérations*, pp. 40–41).
73. "Ils arrivent," *Le Figaro*, Sept. 1, 1941 (*Libérations*, p. 46).

15. *LE POUR ET LE CONTRE*—DRAMATIS PERSONÆ

1. "La Vie à Londres," *Le Figaro*, Feb. 22, 1945 (*Idées dans un chapeau*, pp. 293–294).
2. Letter to Maurice Coindreau, Sept. 25, 1945.
3. Repr. in *Idées dans un chapeau*, pp. 181–184.
4. Feb. 4, 1942.
5. Letter to Maurice Coindreau, Feb. 2, 1947.
6. Unpublished manuscript.
7. Romain, *Les Annales*, Dec. 25, 1937.

8. From an unidentified clipping headed "M. Jacques de Lacretelle définit la position du romancier," and apparently published during the war (see page 248.

9. Thibaudet, *Candide*, Dec. 26, 1929.

10. "Le Réalisme dans la littérature" (*L'Ecrivain public*, p. 83).

11. André Régis: *"Le Pour et le Contre," Effort* (La Chaux-de-Fonds), June 7, 1946.

12. Edmond Jaloux: "Lacretelle et Edmond Bourdet," *Journal de Genève*, Sept. 1, 1946.

13. *Ibid.*

14. *Ibid.*

15. Pierre Lœwel: *"Le Pour et le Contre," L'Aurore*, April 25, 1947.

16. Marcel Thiébaut: "Parmi les Livres," *Revue de Paris*, June 1947.

17. Emile Henriot: *"Le Pour et le Contre," Le Monde*, May 28, 1947.

18. Thiébaut, *Revue de Paris*, June 1947.

19. "Va Paraître: *Le Pour et le Contre*," *Lumière de la ville*, Dec. 18, 1945.

20. André Gide: *Journal 1889–1939*. Paris, Gallimard, 1948. pp. 771–774.

21. Letter to D.W. Alden, Nov. 1, 1955.

22. Martin Turnell: *Jacques Rivière*. New Haven, Yale University Press, 1953. p. 21.

23. Lacretelle referred to such a letter in a conversation.

24. *Chantiers d'art*, no. 2, April 10, 1943.

25. *Chantiers d'art*, no. 1, Feb. 24, 1943.

26. Letter to Maurice Coindreau, Feb. 2, 1947.

16. *LE POUR ET LE CONTRE*—ANALYSIS

1. Personal interview with D.W. Alden.

2. Saint-Jean, *Revue hebdomadaire*, Feb. 22, 1930.

3. "La Lettre de Jacques de Lacretelle," *Candide*, Mar. 2, 1939 (*L'Heure qui change*, p. 101).

4. Letter to Maurice Coindreau, May 26, 1946.

5. Henriot, *Le Monde*, May 28, 1947. Lœwel, *L'Aurore*, April 25, 1947. André Rousseaux: "Les Romanciers chroniqueurs: Jacques de Lacretelle et Léon Bopp," *Le Littéraire*, May 10, 1947. Louis Barjon: *"Le Pour et le Contre," Etudes*, Dec. 1947.

6. Thiébaut, *Revue de Paris*, June 1947.

7. Jaloux, *Journal de Genève*, Sept. 1, 1946.

8. André Maurois: "Journal d'un tour en Suisse," *Nouvelles littéraires*, Mar. 20, 1947.

9. Armand Hoog: *"Le Pour et le Contre," Carrefour*, June 14, 1947.

17. FLAUBERT SEMPER FLAUBERT

1. Letter to Maurice Coindreau, April 29, 1946.

2. In Montreux, says another letter (to D.W. Alden, July 15, 1953).

3. Letter to Maurice Coindreau, Oct. 3, 1946.

4. Letter to D.W. Alden, Feb. 15, 1952.
5. Letter to D.W. Alden, July 15, 1953.
6. Anon.: *"Deux Cœurs simples," Libre Belgique*, April 1, 1953.
7. François Mauriac: "Bloc-notes," *Table ronde*, May 1953.
8. Pierre Lœwel: *"Deux Cœurs simples," L'Aurore*, April 21, 1953. Jean Nicollier: *"Deux Cœurs simples," Gazette de Lausanne*, May 5, 1953.
9. Robert Kemp: "La Vie des livres," *Nouvelles littéraires*, April 23, 1953. André Billy: *"Deux Cœurs simples," Le Figaro*, April 1, 1953. Emile Henriot: *"Deux Cœurs simples," Le Monde*, April 15, 1953. Jean Blanzat: *"Deux Cœurs simples," Le Figaro littéraire*, April 4, 1953.
10. Unpublished letter from Roger Martin du Gard, dated Bellême, Orne, May 21, 1953.
11. Letter to D.W. Alden, July 15, 1953.
12. *Le Pour et le Contre*, I, p. 223.
13. Letter from Roger Martin du Gard, May 21, 1953.

18. PIERRES D'ATTENTE

1. "La Rochefoucauld," *Hommes et mondes*, July 1948. "En Relisant Stendhal," *Nouvelle Nouvelle Revue Française*, March 1953. "Presenza di Valéry," *Convivium*, Aug. 1955. "D'Amsterdam à Lima," *Revue des deux mondes*, Jan. 1955.
2. The letters mentioned in this paragraph are all addressed to D.W. Alden.
3. "En Relisant Stendhal," *Nouvelle Nouvelle Revue Française*, Mar. 1953 (repr. as preface to Stendhal: *Le Rouge et le Noir*, Paris, Imprimerie nationale, 1953).
4. Jacqueline Cartier: "La Réception de M. de Lévis-Mirepoix sous la Coupole est marquée par de vifs incidents qui coupent le discours de M. de Lacretelle sévère pour Charles Maurras," *L'Aurore*, Mar. 19, 1954.
5. "La Réponse de M. Jacques de Lacretelle," *Le Monde*, Mar. 19, 1954.
6. Letter to D.W. Alden, Mar. 20, 1954.
7. Letter to D.W. Alden, Oct. 30, 1955.
8. Anon.: "Jacques de Lacretelle parle de Benjamin Constant," *Tribune de Genève*, Nov. 19, 1957. Henri Chevalley: "Romancier d'hier, personnage d'aujourd'hui: Benjamin Constant (vu par Jacques de Lacretelle)," *Gazette de Lausanne*, Nov. 11, 1957.
9. L'Auditeur: "M. Jacques de Lacretelle évoque l'actualité de Benjamin Constant," *Journal de Genève*, Nov. 19, 1957.

BIBLIOGRAPHY OF THE WORKS OF JACQUES DE LACRETELLE

I. Novels

1. *La Vie inquiète de Jean Hermelin.* Paris, Bernard Grasset, MCMXX. 238 pp. Ach. d'impr. le 13 avril 1920.

Fragment pub. in *L'Œil de bœuf,* May 1920. Other eds.: Paris, Emile-Paul, 1926; Paris, Arthème Fayard, 1928. Trans.: München, Dorn-Verlag G. Ullmann, 1930.

2. *Silbermann.* Paris, Editions de la Nouvelle Revue Française, 1922. 190 pp. Ach. d'impr. le 14 oct. 1922.

Pub. in *Nouvelle Revue Française,* Aug. and Sept. 1922. Others eds.: Paris, N.R.F., 1925 (gravures par J.-E. Laboureur); Paris, N.R.F., 1927 (Coll. "A la Gerbe"); London, Heinemann, 1954 (ed. by F. A. Shuffrey). Trans.: Wien, C.P. Tal & Co., 1924; Lwów-Warszawa, "Ateneum," 1925; Kjøbenhavn, H. Hagerups Forlag, 1926; Stockholm, P. A. Norstedt, 1929; Oslo, H. Aschehoug & Co., 1937; Wien, Pegasus-Verlag, n. d.; Pôrto Alegre, Edição da Livraria do Globo, n. d.; also in English (q.v.). Rumanian and Yiddish editions are listed on the jacket of the British edition but could not be found.

Combined with *Le Retour de Silbermann* (q.v.): Paris, Librairie Gallimard, 1932 (Coll. "Succès"); Montréal, Variétés, 1945; Paris, Gallimard, 1946; Paris, Gallimard, 1950 (Coll. "Pourpre"); Monte-Carlo, A. Sauret, 1951 (Grand Prix des meilleurs romans du demi-siècle).

3. *La Bonifas.* Paris, Librairie Gallimard, Editions de la Nouvelle Revue Française. 362 pp. Ach. d'impr. le 14 avril 1925.

Other eds.: Paris, Librairie Gallimard, 1929 (lithographies par Yvonne Préveraud); Paris, Librairie Gallimard, 1934 (Coll. "Succès"); Genève, Constant Bourquin, éditeur, 1946. Trans.: Stockholm, Albert Bonniers Förlag, 1926; Kjøbenhavn, H. Hagerups Forlag, 1927; Praha, Čin, n. d.; also in English (q.v.).

4. *Amour nuptial.* Paris, Librairie Gallimard, Editions de la Nouvelle Revue Française. 232 pp. Ach. d'impr. le 12 nov. 1929.

Originally part of "Le Retour de Silbermann," pub. in *Candide,* May 9 to Aug. 15, 1929. Another ed.: Paris, N.R.F., 1930 (Coll. "A la Gerbe").

Trans.: Madrid, Ediciones Literarias, 1930; Stuttgart-Berlin, Deutsche Verlags-Anstalt, 1931; Praha, Nakladatel F. Topič, 1931; also in English (q.v.).

5. *Le Retour de Silbermann.* Etude de Ramon Fernandez. Paris, Editions du Capitole. 206 pp. Ach. d'impr. le 20 nov. 1929.

Rewritten from part of "Le Retour de Silbermann," pub. in *Candide* from May 9 to Aug. 15, 1929. Another ed. (without study by Fernandez): Paris, Librairie Gallimard, Editions de la Nouvelle Revue Française, 1930. Combined with *Silbermann* (q.v.) after 1932.

6. *Les Hauts Ponts. I. Sabine.* [Paris], N.R.F., Gallimard. 272 pp. Ach. d'impr. en févr. 1932.

Pub. in *Revue des deux mondes,* June 15, 1931, to Aug. 1, 1931. Another ed.: Montréal, Editions Variétés, 1945. Trans.: Milano-Verona, Mondadori, 1933; Praha, Julius Albert, 1934.

7. *Les Hauts Ponts. II. Les Fiançailles.* [Paris], N.R.F., Gallimard. 272 pp. Ach. d'impr. en févr. 1933.

Pub. in *Revue des deux mondes,* Aug. 15, 1932, to Oct. 1, 1932. Another ed.: Montréal, Variétés, 1945. Trans.: Milano-Verona, Mondadori, 1934; Praha, Julius Albert, 1934.

8. *Les Hauts Ponts. III. Années d'espérance.* [Paris], N.R.F., Gallimard. 256 pp. Ach. d'impr. en févr. 1935.

Pub. in *Marianne,* June 6 to Aug. 22, 1934. Another ed.: Montréal, Editions Variétés, 1945. Trans.: Milano-Verona, Mondadori, 1937; Praha, Julius Albert, 1937.

9. *Les Hauts Ponts. IV. La Monnaie de plomb.* [Paris], N.R.F., Gallimard. 256 pp. Ach. d'impr. en sept. 1935.

Pub. in *Revue des deux mondes,* July 1 to Aug. 15, 1935. Another ed.: Montréal, Editions Variétés, 1945.

10. *Le Pour et le Contre.* Roman. Genève, Editions du Milieu du Monde. 2 vols., 318 and 346 pp. First vol.: bon à tirer le 15 févr. 1946. Second vol.: bon à tirer le 4 mars 1946.

Fragment pub. in *Les Œuvres libres,* vol. 230, 1945. Another ed.: Montréal, Editions de l'Arbre. 4 vols. (1. *La Belle Aurore,* 238 pp., ach. d'impr. le 15 nov. 1946. 2. *La N.E.J.,* 237 pp., ach. d'impr. le 30 avril 1947. 3. *Le Jubilé,* 263 pp., ach. d'impr. le 26 mai 1947. 4. *Le Jubilé,* 258 pp., ach. d'impr. le 28 mai 1947.)

11. *Deux Cœurs simples.* Lithographies originales de Valentine Hugo. Genève, G. Cramer, 1947. 195 pp. [Vol. not completed until 1951.]

Pub. in *Bataille politique et littéraire,* May 7 to July 30, 1947. Another ed.: Paris, Gallimard, 1953. 225 pp.

II. Theater

1. *Une Visite en été.* Pièce en quatre actes. [Paris], Gallimard. 197 pp. Ach. d'impr. en févr. 1953.

III. Short Stories

1. *L'Ame cachée.* Paris, Librairie Gallimard, Editions de la Nouvelle Revue Française. 242 pp. Ach. d'impr. le 7 sept. 1928.

Another ed.: Paris, Librairie Gallimard, 1932 (Coll. "Succès"). Reprints the following stories:

(a) *La Mort d'Hippolyte.* Pub. in *Revue hebdomadaire,* April 15 and 22, 1922. First ed.: Paris, Editions de la Nouvelle Revue Française, 1923. 86 pp. Ach. d'impr. le 20 avril 1923. Revised ed.: Paris, Editions Eos, 1926. Also in *Nouvelles littéraires,* May 16 and 23, 1925. Repr. in M. Coindreau and J. R. Loy, *Contes et nouvelles du temps présent,* New York, Reynal and Hitchcock, 1941.

(b) *La Belle Journée.* Pub. in *Les Œuvres libres,* Sept. 1923. First ed.: Paris, Au Sans Pareil, 1925. 56 pp. Ach. d'impr. le 27 févr. 1925.

(c) *Le Christ aux bras étroits.* Pub. in *Revue de Paris,* April 15, 1927. First ed.: Paris, Editions Eos, 1927. 108 pp. Ach. d'impr. le 12 juin 1927.

(d) *Le Cachemire écarlate.* Pub. in *Annales politiques et littéraires,* June 1 and 15, 1927. First ed.: Paris, Librairie M.-P. Trémois, 1927. 110 pp. Ach. d'impr. le 20 juin 1927.

2. *Histoire de Paola Ferrani.* [Paris], Ernest Flammarion, éditeur. 228 pp. Impr. en avril 1929.

Fragments pub. in *Candide,* Feb. 16 and 23, 1928; *Nouvelle Revue Française,* Mar. 1, 1928; *Revue européenne,* April 1928; *Annales politiques et littéraires,* Apr. 15, 1928. Nonfictional parts pub. as: *Album napolitain.* Paris, Emile Hazan, éditeur. 108 pp. Ach. d'impr. en avril 1928. Fictional parts pub. as: *Quatre Nouvelles italiennes: Naissance de Sapho—Histoire de Paola Ferrani—Un Chapitre retrouvé d'Armance—La Porte de Cipolin.* Paris, Editions Lemarget, MCMXXVIII. 114 pp. Ach. d'impr. le 21 mai 1928. See also *L'Enfance d'une courtisane.*

IV. Essays

1. *Lettres espagnoles.* Publiées par Jacques de Lacretelle. Paris, Emile Chamontin, 1926. 182 pp. Ach. d'impr. le 10 oct. 1926.

Pub. in *Revue de Paris*, May 15, 1926, and in *Nouvelle Revue Française*, June and Oct. 1926. Another ed.: Paris, Librairie Gallimard, 1927. 208 pp. Ach. d'impr. le 30 déc. 1927. Fragment "Histoire cynique" was repr. as: *Mort de la jalousie*. Liège, A la Lampe d'Aladin, 1926. 66 pp. Fac-similé photographique du manuscrit.

2. *Aparté: Colère—Journal de Colère—Dix Jours à Ermenonville*. Paris, Librairie Gallimard, Editions de la Nouvelle Revue Française. 224 pp. Ach. d'impr. le 10 janv. 1927.

(a) *Colère*. First pub. in Anon.: *Les Sept Péchés capitaux*, Paris, Simon Kra, 1926 (another ed.: Paris, Librairie Gallimard, 1929).

(b) *Journal de Colère*. Pub. in: *Colère suivi d'un journal*. La Haye, Le Bon Plaisir, MCMXXVI. 74 pp. Ach. d'impr. en sept. 1926. Fragment included from *Revue hebdomadaire*, Jan. 9, 1926.

(c) *Dix Jours à Ermenonville*. Paris, Le Livre, 1926. 64 pp. Ach. d'impr. le 15 févr. 1926. First pub. in *Nouvelle Revue Française*, May 1925. Also pub. as preface to: Rousseau, Jean-Jacques: *Les Rêveries du promeneur solitaire*, Paris, Le Livre, 1926. Repr. in: *Rêveries romantiques: Dix Jours à Ermenonville—Le Rêveur parisien*. Paris, Stendhal et Cie, 1927. 120 pp. Ach. d'impr. le 20 oct. 1927.

3. *Le Demi-Dieu, ou Le Voyage en Grèce*. Paris, A la Société d'édition "Le Livre," 1930. 203 pp. Ach. d'impr. le 30 oct. 1930.

Pub. in *Annales politiques et littéraires*, Mar. 15 to July 15, 1930. Other eds.: [Paris], Grasset [1931]; Paris, J. Ferenczi et fils, éditeurs, 1936; Paris, B. Grasset, 1944 (photographies de Bourdot-Lamotte); Paris, Editions de l'Odéon, 1954. Repub. with added material as *Le Voyage de Grèce*, Paris, Librairie Arthème Fayard, 1955.

Beginning with the 1931 edition, the title was changed to *Le Demi-Dieu, ou Le Voyage de Grèce.*

4. *Les Aveux étudiés*. [Paris], N.R.F., Gallimard. 230 pp. Ach. d'impr. le 18 avril 1934.

Articles from *Nouvelle Revue Française, Revue juive, Gringoire, Marianne, Nouvelles littéraires, Annales politiques et littéraires*. Also reprints the following:

(a) "L'Amour des livres." Originally: *Mélanges sur l'amour et les livres terminés par un envoi*, Paris, Librairie Gallimard, 1925, 8 pp. Another ed.: La Haye, 1925, 16 pp. Repr. in *Trébuchet* (q.v.).

(b) "Du Manuscrit." Originally: *Une Lettre authentique et quelques lettres apocryphes*, Paris, Marguerite Milhau, 1927, 26 pp. Also pub. as: Anon.: *Vente de très beaux manuscrits*. Préface de Jacques de Lacretelle. [Paris], Marguerite Milhau, libraire, n. d. Flaubert pastiche erroneously reproduced as authentic in vol. 8, *Correspondance* of Flaubert, Conard ed.

(c) "Le Rêveur parisien." Pub. in *Nouvelle Revue Française*, July 1927. Repr. in *Rêveries romantiques* (q.v. under *Aparté*).

(d) *D'Une Colline: Quatre Jours à Beyreuth*. Paris, Aux Editions des Cahiers libres. 64 pp. Ach. d'impr. le 15 mars 1928. Pub. in *L'Intransigeant*, Aug. 27, Aug. 30, and Sept. 1, 1927.

(e) "Vision d'Anatole France." Originally: *A la Rencontre de France*. Suivi de *Anatole France vu par un Américain*, par Edward Wassermann. Traduction de Jacques de Lacretelle. Paris, Editions M.-P. Trémois, 1930. 84 pp. Ach. d'impr. le 15 sept. 1930.

(f) Also various parts of *Trébuchet* (q.v.), preface to *Sarn* (q.v.), and preface to *La Renarde* (q.v.).

5. *L'Ecrivain public*. [Paris], N.R.F., Gallimard. 216 pp. Ach. d'impr. en oct. 1936.

Articles from *Marianne, Nouvelles littéraires, 1934 (le magazine d'aujourd'hui), Le Figaro, Vogue, Excelsior*. Prefaces from: Marks, Henry K.: *La Fondrière (Quagmire)*, Paris, Grasset, 1934 (preface also pub. in *Nouvelles littéraires*, May 5, 1934); Anon.: *Tableau de la littérature française (XVIIe et XVIIIe siècles) de Corneille à Chénier*, Paris, Gallimard, 1939 (also pub. in *Nouvelles littéraires*, Aug. 11, 1934).

6. *Croisières en eaux troubles*. Paris, Gallimard. 189 pp. Ach. d'impr. le 2 août 1939.

Articles from *Candide* and *Le Figaro*.

7. *L'Heure qui change*. Genève, Editions du Milieu du monde. 250 pp. Le bon à tirer a été donné le 24 mai 1941.

Articles from *L'Ami du peuple, Le Petit Journal, Gazette Dunlop, Candide, Le Figaro, Journal de Genève*. Also prefaces to: Kuncz, Aladar: *Le Monastère noir*, Paris, Gallimard, 1937; Nerval, Gérard de: *La Main enchantée*, Les Bibliophiles franco-suisses, 1938.

8. *Idées dans un chapeau*. Monaco, Editions du Rocher. 299 pp. Ach. d'impr. le 16 déc. 1946.

Articles from *Revue de la semaine, Europe, Petit Journal, Le Figaro, Journal de Genève, Milieu du monde, Candide, Présent, Gazette de Lausanne, Comœdia, La Victoire* (N.Y.), *Le Littéraire, France-Amérique* (N.Y.), *Carrefour*. Also prefaces from: 1946 ed. of *La Bonifas* (q.v.); Anon.: *Problèmes de la sexualité*, Paris, Plon, 1937 (another ed.: Montréal, L'Arbre, n. d.); Anon.: *Les Sports et leurs trophées de la Grèce antique aux temps modernes* [Paris], Galerie de l'Orfèvrerie Christofle, 1944; Anon.: *La Libération de Paris*, Paris, Fasquelle, 1945; Lods, Marcel: *L'Esthétique des constructions modernes*, Paris, 12, rue Brancion, 1945.

V. Minor Short Stories and Essays

(not in major volumes)

Short Stories

1. *Virginie ou les manies.* Les 49 Ronins du quai Malaquais. VII. Paris, Edouard Champion et ses amis, 1927. 28 pp. Ach. d'impr. le 20 déc. 1927.

Pub. in *Candide*, Dec. 29, 1927. Repr. in: Anon.: *D'Ariane à Zoé: Alphabet galant et sentimental . . .*, Paris, Librairie de France, 1930; *L'Enfance d'une courtisane* (q.v.).

2. *Luce, ou L'Enfance d'une courtisane.* Illustrations de Marie Laurencin. Paris, Editions M.-P. Trémois, 1931. 81 pp. Ach. d'impr. le 17 sept. 1930.

Pub. in *Revue de France*, Mar. 1, 1931. Repr. in: *L'Enfance d'une courtisane*. Paris, Editions de France. 217 pp. Copyright 1932. This volume also contained *Virginie ou les manies* (q.v.). and parts of *Histoire de Paola Ferrani* (q.v.): "Histoire de Paola Ferrani," "Porte de Cipolin," "Addio," "Naissance de Sapho," "Deux Images napolitaines."

Essays

1. *Quatre Etudes sur Gobineau.* Liège, A la Lampe d'Aladin, 1926. 56 pp.

Articles from *Revue hebdomadaire, Revue de la semaine, Europe, Nouvelle Revue Française.* Two of these articles repr. in *Idées dans un chapeau* (q.v.).

2. *Trébuchet.* Liège, A la Lampe d'Aladin, 1926. 96 pp. Ach. d'impr. le 15 févr. 1925.

Articles from *Nouvelle Revue Française, Revue hebdomadaire, Revue juive;* also *Mélanges sur l'amour et les livres.* All of *Trébuchet* repr. in *Les Aveux étudiés* (q.v.) except "Réponse" (also pub. in *Revue hebdomadaire,* Nov. 25, 1922, and in Varillon, Pierre, and Rambaud, Henri: *Enquête sur les maîtres de la jeune littérature,* Paris, Bloud & Gay, 1923).

3. *Aperçus.* [Paris], Chez Marcelle Lesage. 74 pp. Ach. d'impr. le 2 juin 1927.

Articles from *L'Opinion, Revue hebdomadaire, Nouvelle Revue Française.*

4. *Etudes.* Paris, Librairie Picart, 1928. 84 pp. Ach. d'impr. le 7 avril 1928.

Articles from *Nouvelle Revue Française.*

5. *Discours de réception de M. Jacques de Lacretelle à l'Académie Française et réponse de M. Abel Hermant.* Paris, Gallimard, 1938. 91 pp. Ach. d'impr. le 31 janv. 1938.

Pub. in *Le Figaro,* Jan. 28, 1938. Another ed.: Paris, Imprimerie de Firmin-Didot, 1938. 58 pp.

6. *Qui est La Rocque?* [Paris], Ernest Flammarion, éditeur. 48 pp. Imprimerie de Lagny, 1937.

7. *Le Canada entre en guerre: Choses vues.* [Paris], Flammarion, éditeur. 31 pp. [Ach. d'impr.] 3–1940.

Articles and speeches; one article previously pub. in *Le Petit Journal,* Jan. 13, 1940, and also repr. in *L'Heure qui change* (q.v.).

8. *Libérations.* [New York], Brentano's. 144 pp. Ach. d'impr. le 25 juillet 1945.

Articles from *Le Figaro, Les Œuvres libres.*

VI. Anthology

1. *Morceaux choisis.* Préface d'André Maurois. Paris, Gallimard. 332 pp. Ach. d'impr. en janv. MCMXXXVIII.

Preface pub. in *Nouvelles littéraires,* Nov. 14, 1936.

VII. Translations from English

1. Webb, Mary: *Sarn.* Roman traduit de l'anglais par Jacques de Lacretelle et Madeleine T. Guéritte. Introd. de Jacques de Lacretelle. Paris, Editions Bernard Grasset. 416 pp. Dépôt légal: 4e trimestre 1930.

Preface repr. in *Les Aveux étudiés* (q.v.). Other eds.: [Paris], Creuzevault, éditeur, 1948 (pointes sèches de Hermine David); Paris, Creuzevault, 1950 (compositions de Roland Oudot); [Paris], Aux Editions Terres Latines, 1950.

2. Webb, Mary: *La Renarde.* Roman. Traduit de l'anglais par Marie Canavaggia et Jacques de Lacretelle. Paris, Catalogne et Cie, 1933. 413 pp. Les Maîtres étrangers.

Preface pub. in *Nouvelles littéraires,* Oct. 14, 1933; repr. in *Les Aveux étudiés* (q.v.). Other eds.: [Paris], Le Club français du livre, 1947; Paris, Les Nouvelles Editions Latines, 1951.

3. Brontë, Emily: *Haute plainte*. Traduit de l'anglais par Jacques et Yolande de Lacretelle. Préface de Jacques de Lacretelle. [Paris], N.R.F., Gallimard. 336 pp. Ach. d'impr. le 16 juillet 1937.

Preface repr. in *L'Heure qui change* (q.v.).

4. Goodyear, Robert: *Mrs. Loveday*. Roman traduit de l'anglais par Jacques de Lacretelle de l'Académie française et Yolande de Lacretelle. Préface de Jacques de Lacretelle. Paris, Robert Laffont. 285 pp. Ach. d'impr. le 25 janv. 1949.

VIII. Contributions to Other Volumes

Most of Lacretelle's contributions to other volumes have been reprinted in his own works, as listed above. The following prefaces and other texts have not been so collected.

Prefaces

Lacretelle, Pierre Louis: *Plaidoyer pour deux juifs de Metz contre l'Hôtel de ville et le Corps des marchands de Thionville*. Paris, Librairie Lipschutz, 1928.

[Hompesch, Louise de]: *Journal d'amour d'une jeune Allemande, Louise de Hompesch (1797–1798)*. Avec une introd. et notes de Jacques de Lacretelle. Paris, Calmann-Lévy, 1936. (Preface pub. in *Revue de Paris*, Dec. 15, 1935.)

Bragard, René: *La Relève des vivants*. Lyon, IAC, 1940.

Rousseau, Jean-Jacques: *Les Confessions. Les Rêveries du promeneur solitaire*. Paris, Les Académies, 1947.

Les Pastorales de Longus ou Daphnis et Cloé. Les Bibliophiles franco-suisses, 1948.

Poe, Edgar: *Les Aventures de Gordon Pym*. Paris, Arthème Fayard, 1948.

La Rochefoucauld: *Maximes et autres œuvres morales*. [Paris], Bordas, 1949. (Preface pub. in *Hommes et mondes*, July 1948.)

Flaubert, Gustave: *Madame Bovary*. New York, Limited Editions Club, 1950.

Ogrizek, Doré: *Le Portugal*. Paris, Odé, 1950.

Mabille de Poncheville, André: *Lille-en-Flandre des origines à nos jours*. Paris, Editions SLEL, 1951.

Sandoz, Maurice: *Choix de poèmes*. Paris, Pierre Seghers, 1952.

Stendhal: *Le Rouge et le Noir*. Paris, Imprimerie Nationale, 1953. (Preface pub. in *Nouvelle Nouvelle Revue Française*, Mar. 1953.)

Sandoz, Maurice: *Le Beau Voyage*. Genève, Cailler, 1956.

Vilmorin, Roger de: *Plantes alpines dans les jardins*. Paris, Flammarion, 1956.

Sandoz, Maurice: *Choix de poèmes*. Monaco, Editions du Rocher, 1957.

Gaskell, Jane: *Une Etrange Aventure*. Paris, Julliard, 1957. (Trans. by Yolande de Lacretelle.)

Miscellaneous

Laurencin, Marie: *Pressentiments*. Suite de six lithographies originales en couleurs accompagnées d'un texte de Jacques de Lacretelle. Paris, Editions des Quatre Chemins, 1930. (Includes a text from *Le Divan*, June 1930.)

Anon.: *Incarnations de Madame Bovary*, d'après Odette Pannetier... Jacques de Lacretelle [etc.]. Paris, Dacosta, 1933. (Lacretelle contribution, "Emmeline ou l'autre Bovary," appeared in *Revue de Paris*, June 15, 1934.)

Anon.: *Parfums*. Rancour a édité cet album pour ses amis. Unnumbered pages. Ach. d'impr. en 1945. (Lacretelle: "Philosophie des parfums.")

Anon.: *Estampes*. Introd. de Robert Rey. Paris, L'Image littéraire, 1950. (Lacretelle article, "Brianchon," also pub. in *Fémina*, Noël 1950.)

Ogrizek, Doré: *La Grèce*. Préface de Jean Cocteau. Textes de Jacques de Lacretelle [etc.]. Paris, Odé, 1953.

IX. Speeches Published by the Institut de France

The following speeches by Lacretelle have been published in the official series of the Institut de France, printed by Firmin-Didot:

Rapport sur les prix de vertu, 1943; *Deuxième Centenaire de la mort de Vauvenargues à Aix-en-Provence*, 1947; *Discours prononcé aux cérémonies du centenaire de l'Ecole française d'Athènes*, 1947; *Bicentenaire de la fondation de Port-au-Prince*, 1950; *Centenaire de René Boylesve à La Haye-Descartes*, 1950; *Discours prononcées dans la séance publique tenue par l'Académie française pour la réception de Monsieur le Duc de Lévis Mirepoix*, 1954; *Inauguration du nouveau musée Barbey d'Aurevilly à Saint-Sauveur-le-Vicomte*, 1956.

X. Translations of Lacretelle's Works into English

Silbermann. Translated by Brian Lunn. New York, Boni and Liverwright, 1923. 191 pp. Another ed.: London, E. Benn, Ltd., 1923. 194 [1] pp.

Marie Bonifas. Translated by Winifred Stephens Whale. London and New York, G.P. Putnam's Sons, Ltd., 1927. 327 pp.

A Man's Life [*Amour nuptial*]. Translated by Edwin Granberry. New York, Henry Holt and Company, 1931. 200 pp.

"A Beautiful Day." In Eaton, Richard, ed.: *The Best French Short Stories of 1923–24 and the Yearbook of the French Short Story*. Boston, Small, Maynard and Company, 1923.

"The Lovely Day." Translated by Vyvyan Holland. In Maugham, W. Somerset, ed.: *Tellers of Tales*. New York, Doubleday, Doran and Co., Inc., 1939.

"Delos" [extract from *Le Demi-Dieu*]. In O'Hara, John Myers: *Hellas the Immortal*. Translations with an introduction. Portland, Maine, Smith and Sale, 1932.

A NOTE ON FURTHER BIBLIOGRAPHY

The working bibliography of this study is so extensive (550 books and articles by Lacretelle and 750 books and articles about him) as to preclude publication in this volume. Until this complete bibliography appears, the most inclusive bibliographical listings for Lacretelle will be found in Hector Talvart and Joseph Place, *Bibliographie des auteurs modernes de langue française*. A selective bibliography of books and articles about Lacretelle would be somewhat pointless, since no full-length scholarly work exists and since all the material consists of reviews or brief essays in the periodical press or in collections of essays.

INDEX

Date Due			